Teenage Hipster in the Modern World

Also by Mark Jacobson

Novels

Gojiro

Everyone and No One

Nonfiction

12,000 Miles in the Nick of Time: A Semi-Dysfunctional Family Circumnavigates the Globe

The KGB Bar Nonfiction Reader (edited)

American Monsters (edited, with Jack Newfield)

Teenage Hipster in the Modern World

From the Birth of Punk to the Land of Bush: Thirty Years of Millennial Journalism

Mark Jacobson

Foreword by Richard Price
Photographs by James Hamilton

Black Cat
New York

Published simultaneously in Canada
Printed in the United States of America

FIRST EDITION

Library of Congress Cataloging-in-Publication Data
Jacobson, Mark.
Teenage hipster in the modern world : from the birth of punk to the land of Bush : thirty years of millennial journalism / Mark Jacobson ; foreword by Richard Price ; photographs by James Hamilton.— 1st ed.
p. cm.
Collection of articles originally published in various periodicals.
ISBN 0-8021-7008-0
I. Title.
PN4874.J29A25 2005
814'.54—dc22 2004060859

Black Cat
a paperback original imprint of Grove/Atlantic, Inc.
841 Broadway
New York, NY 10003

05 06 07 08 09 10 9 8 7 6 5 4 3 2 1

For my mom, who kept the scrapbook

Also Michael Daly, a hardworking guy

And in the memory of Jack Newfield,
who knew where the bodies were buried

Contents

IN THE REALM OF THE SPIRIT

THE BIG CITY

THE HOME FRONT

Foreword

I've always felt that the only subjects worth writing about were those that intimidated me, and the only writers worth emulating were those who left me feeling the same way. I've felt intimidated by Mark Jacobson since 1977 when I first read "Ghost Shadows on Chinatown Streets," his portrait of gang leader Nicky Lui, in the *Village Voice*. I remember being overwhelmed by both Jacobson's reporting skill and intrepidness, empathizing with his attraction to the subject; could see myself attempting something like that if I had both the writing chops and the nerve. It was one of the most humbling and enticing reading experiences of my life, and in many ways set me on the path to at least three novels.

Jacobson belongs to that great bloodline of New York street writers from Stephen Crane to Hutchins Hapgood to Joseph Mitchell, John McNulty, and A. J. Liebling, through Jimmy Breslin and Pete Hamill, and now to himself and very few others (his friend and peer Michael Daly comes to mind). Jacobson is drawn to these streets and to those who rose from them: the outlaws, the visionaries, the hustlers, and the oddballs. His voice is often sardonic, bemused, and a little in awe of the man before him. Like a judo master, he knows how to step off and let the force of these personalities hoist their own banners or dig their own graves. But even in the case of the most heinous of men, Jacobson's ability to unearth some saving grace, some charm, or simply a shred of sympathetic humanity in the bastard is unfailing.

From heroin kingpin Frank Lucas to the Dalai Lama, Jacobson's fact-gathering is impeccable, his presentation of the Big Picture plain as day, the conversations (you can't really call them "interviews") often hilarious. Most important though, his love for this world, these people, is apparent in every nuance, every finely observed detail. His is the song of the workingman, the immigrant, the street cat, the cryptician with more crazy-eights than aces up his sleeve, and Jacobson knows that the bottom line for this kind of profiling is self-recognition; each character, each sharply etched detail in some way bringing home not only the subject, but the reader and author, too.

—Richard Price

Author's Introduction

Working in magazine journalism, which is most of the work I have done for the past three decades, can have its downside. You can make a living, but not a large one. You can get into shows and scenes for free and not have to pay for many CDs or books. This is a plus. But the truth is, most of the CDs and books they send you aren't anything you'd ever want to listen to or read. Plus, they clog up your house, and then you have to have a tag sale, during which some jerk's dog will inevitably pee on your merchandise. There is much to bitch about in the magazine-writing game: the onslaught of celebrity "journalism," which has taken a lot of the fun out of it; the increasingly crappy outlets to write for (which lends credence to the notion that the form is dead or dying); the humiliating process of attempting to get people to pay you the money they owe you; the chopping up of perfectly good articles, et cetera and so on.

The subhead of this book, "from the birth of punk to the land of Bush," lays out the chronological territory. The earliest pieces date back to the advent of punk rock and the most recent ones were written during the presidency of George W. Bush—a thirty year passage during which I have been transformed (evolved? devolved?) from the twenty-eight-year old wack-job party boy on the cover of this book (James Hamilton's photo was taken in the formerly funky downtown Las Vegas in 1977) into the gray-haired, lumbering thing I am today. Not that I'm complaining, lots of guys I know are dead. But there is also an unsettling full circle in this three-decade-long journey. The supposed punks of the middle 1970s, skulking about in a landscape of unprecedented urban decay, imagined themselves as leather-jacketed neoprimitives, cartoonish survivors in a post-apocalyptic world. Thirty years later, at the outset of Bush's second term, after the true terror of 9/11, the city, if not the entire country (downtown Vegas is now a covered mall) wears a shinier skin. The streets are fixed up, photoshopped, ready to rumble. Yet, there is undeniable suspicion this veneer covers a darker kind of soul.

Still, the reporter's job remains to write about whatever is put in front of him, to try to translate it into terms comprehensible to themselves and, hopefully, readers. It is a 24/7 job, the kind of hours I like. Besides, writing for magazines has gotten me around. Around town. Around the world. I've written about diamond miners in Angola, and then, two weeks later, found myself sitting in Yoko Ono's living room at the Dakota. This sort of cognitive dissonance and intellectual turnover has always been the true joy of my career path. It is an enduring rush, to be able to say to myself: "Look where I am."

In the end that is what it comes down to: The redemptive sense of mission I've had standing at the point of the Cape of Good Hope watching the Atlantic and Indian Oceans run together (they're different colors), or walking down the dark staircase of the Livonia Avenue stop on the New Lots Avenue train line (long the consensus choice for the scariest spot in New York City). No matter where I was, someone sent me. Someone was paying me to be there, to write down what I saw and what I felt. They did this because, mistakenly or not, they were under the impression that some reader somewhere might actually care what I thought, what I felt, who I talked to, what they said. For me, that is more than enough.

The kind of work I do often involves a collaborative process. During the past thirty years I've been thrown together with many editors, writers, and photographers who have helped me produce the body of work in this book. I'd like to mention a few of them. A good editor in a good mood will protect you from office cutthroats and, most important, yourself. I will always appreciate the efforts of Richard Goldstein, Clay Felker, Jack Nessel, Byron Dobell, my good friend Alan Weitz, Marianne Partridge, Terry McDonell, David Hirshey, Adam Moss, Will "Roy" Blythe, Jay Stowe, Bill

Shapiro, George Kalogerakis, Carolyn White, Caroline Miller, and the always discerning John Homans. On another front, I have often wanted to write an article called "Photographers I Have Worked With." These are an odd lot, possessed of many annoying habits and not always the most hygienic of roommates, but I've always gotten a kick out of their company, however maddening. James Hamilton, my longtime partner, whose pictures appear in this volume, remains an all-time favorite. Others who must be mentioned include Christopher Little, Scott Thode, Alex Webb, and the inimitable Antonin Kratochvil. In this business you meet plenty of writers, a good thing, since I like writers. Many—they know who they are—have become treasured friends over the years. But most of all, I'd like to thank my many, many subjects (in this I would include my loving family). Without all those quotes, I would be nowhere.

—Mark Jacobson, 2004

MEETINGS WITH SEMI-REMARKABLE MEN AND WOMEN

1
Sex Goddess of the Seventies

Pam Grier was a singular star of a singular time. No one has ever narrowed her eyes with quite this kind of menace, yet seemed capable of straight A's at the same time. The ending of this piece created some notoriety. From New York *magazine, 1975.*

Pam Grier peered around the corner of Seventh Avenue and Forty-second Street, squinted at the row of movie theaters, and quivered her upper lip. Across the street two small-fry superflies in rainbow shoes and felt felony hats had recognized her. They started to snake between the taxicabs, and Pam's panther body stiffened. She clutched her Gucci pocketbook and seemed to grow a few inches. As they got to the sidewalk, she wheeled on her boot heel, lowered her voice a couple of octaves, and asked what she could do for them.

It almost knocked those cats off their platforms; they hung there like vinyl Jell-O. Pam jabbed her aquiline nose into the air insistently. Finally the dude with the fake fox collar meekly asked her for her autograph. Pam loosened a little and signed. "OOOO-*eeee*," the other guy said, "you are dangerous. What would happen if I tried to get next to you?" Pam squinted again and sent a look that said, "You can *try* me." With that, the dudes got themselves lost under the marquees.

It was just like a Pam Grier movie, except nobody got shot in the groin. When people try to get next to Pam Grier, they usually wind up being very sorry. In a long series of films that will never be reviewed by John Simon, Pam has made a living out of beating up men. She gun-butted them in *Black Mama, White Mama*, cast voodoo spells over them in *Scream, Blacula, Scream*, ran them through with spears in *The Arena*. In *Coffy*, Pam was at her most outgoing: she blasted a pusher's head off, stabbed a kinky hit man in the eye with a bobby pin, ran a mafioso over in a Dodge, and blew away three different sets of genitals with a double-barreled shotgun.

Like the dude said, this lady is dangerous. She might even shake up a few preconceptions about blacks and women in today's movies. For one thing, those funky films she's been making have raked in prodigious amounts of money. *Coffy* has grossed more than $8.5 million (it cost about $700,000), and *Foxy Brown*, another nut-cruncher, has done almost as well. Pam Grier is now spoken of as a "bankable star," the only black woman around who fits that description.

The vast majority of the white audience doesn't know much about Pam. That's because, until now, she has been doing her "tough mama" number in what white reviewers generally call "blaxploitation movies." "Tough mamas" have been the thing in black movies for a few years now. There has been *Cleopatra Jones*, with Tamara Dobson; *Savage Sisters*, with Gloria Hendry; and also *TNT Jackson*, with Jeannie Bell. "Tough mamas" do much the same things as "mean street brothers": bust up slews of lowlife black hustlers, then stick it to the white baddies who really run things, getting laid a lot along the way. It's mostly comic-book stuff. But after the roles black women have traditionally played on the screen, it's got to be a step forward. No one would ever call Pam Grier a victim, not to her face, at least. At twenty-five, she's the toughest mama.

Since *Coffy*, in which she can be seen reading *Ms.* magazine (open to the Lost Women section), Pam Grier has become a heroine. More specifically, a black woman's heroine. She talks street self-sufficiency and attacks the macho's last refuge, his muscles. I saw one woman in a Forty-second Street theater smack her boyfriend's arm as Pam was icing half the Roman army in *The Arena*. The woman said, "See, fool, I'm going to get myself together like her, so next time you think you're Superman, watch out." Pam herself says, "It makes sense that strong women would come out of black films. The woman has always been the strength of our family. Because if one thing has always been true, it is that black boys are terrified of their mamas."

In her beige suite at the Regency on Park Avenue, physically a long way from Forty-second Street, Pam sits with her leather pant legs crossed, eating twelve dollars worth of fresh strawberries and talking about power. "Look," she says with a voice that seems to wrap around your windpipe, "I read a lot of scripts these days and most of them are terrible. Really bad. Or maybe the script isn't so bad and they mess it up in the production. Like *Sheba, Baby*. They get some guy to direct it who doesn't know what he's doing. I knew I could have done a better job, but they told me to sit down, you're only the actress, don't tell *us* what to do. So right now I'm setting up my own production company. I know I can do it. I read the trades, I know I'm big. I can get investors. And I'm going to make movies the way I see fit. No threatless, mindless women. No dumb situations. I know I have to go slow. But I'm going to sneak up on them little by little and then I'm going to create a monster. This girl isn't just another body for their cameras."

Her message comes hard and fast. She's learning everything she can about film by taking cinema courses at UCLA. She's been having long discussions with her friend and mentor Roman Polanski. She will pay her young screenwriters out of her own pocket so she won't owe anyone anything when the films are made (the first one being due "within a year"). She plans to become the first black woman to direct a major film.

Listening to Pam Grier is easy; trying to get next to her is harder. If you change your seat, she'll change hers. We've been jockeying around this hotel room for hours. Even though she isn't as overwhelming as she seems in the movies—about five feet eight and an almost skinny 121 pounds—she still looks dangerous. Her eyes are electric, dark, and smoldering, but she hides them behind bubble sunglasses; she won't let you get lost in them. Her skin is light caramel. It looks five inches deep, and you want to roll in it. But that might not be too smart. Her body, which looks so supple in her films, is all sharp angles and athletic steel from her daily martial arts practice. And her nose, easily her best feature, juts away from her face defiantly—a warning, or a dare.

Pam says she just likes to "have her own space," but you get the message that she isn't the trusting type. She grew up on U.S. Air Force bases in Europe, maybe five or six of them, with her mother and father, an NCO who said "positive" and "negative" instead of yes and no. Eventually the family settled in Denver, where the English accent Pam had acquired on a base in London made her appear like a snot to her classmates. She remembers being teased and beaten up regularly. Later her boyfriend, whom she hoped to marry, volunteered to fight in Vietnam; he died there. Still in mourning, she was spotted at a Colorado beauty contest (she was the only black) by an agent who invited her to Hollywood. She ran the American International switchboard for a while, listening in whenever producers called to talk about young actresses. "You should have heard what they said . . . it was like ordering meat in a butcher shop. Pretty disgusting, really."

In her first few months out West she depended on her cousin, Rosey Grier, the former football Giant turned actor, to show her around. But Rosey, she says, was too busy trying to project a slimmer image and wasn't much help. He did, however, introduce her to Kareem Abdul-Jabbar. Kareem and Pam lived together for a while, until his Muslim religion got in the way. Kareem expected Pam to leave the house when his friends came over because Muslim men cannot tolerate the presence of women when they are discussing the affairs of the world. One day Kareem came home in a rage and screamed at Pam for wearing a bikini on the beach. That was enough.

The roles she began to get didn't do much for her self-image, as a woman or as a human being. She mostly played "things." Her first part was an anonymous piece of flesh in Russ Meyer's *Beyond the Valley of the Dolls*. She played leopard women, Nubian princesses, and lesbian prison guards before she got a chance to be "a person" in *Coffy*. During this time, she was at the artistic mercy of men like Sam Arkoff, president of American International, whom Pam speaks of as "someone who can't see past the cash register, someone who has a peanut brain."

It sounds as if Pam plans to blast her way through the motion picture industry as easily as she brings a mafioso to his knees in her movies. But there are parts of her that don't seem to fit the quicksilver image. A hard-bopping feminist, she can't stop talking about all those beauty contests and who is pretty and who's really a dog. Also, the tough street mama doesn't want to go outside the Regency. Forty-second Street makes her nervous. She looks down the street and asks if it really is true that "down there" is where her films make their money. This morning Pam jogged up and down Park Avenue; her friends in L.A. told her Central Park was full of muggers.

Pam has other worries, too. Her image is about to be transformed. Now she's beginning to look on her "tough mama" movies as part of her "film adolescence." She's more interested in doing things like *Alice Doesn't Live Here Anymore* and *A Woman Under the Influence*. Starting with her next picture she is changing her name to *Pamela* Grier. "'Pam' was all right for those action pictures," she says, "but I can't spend my whole life wrestling." But breaking into "the general audience market" is touchy for a black performer, especially an independent woman. Everyone is telling Pam she's going to have to tone herself down. "They want me to be a noble slave or a doormat," she moans. "I can't end up like Sidney Poitier, he's pure Saran Wrap."

For a star, Pam's got a dumpy hotel room. You'd figure a big-money maker would at least have a view of the avenue. Pam sneers at the wall outside the window, blames it on American International, and says she's restless. But she's in town only for interviews, has never spent any time in New York, and doesn't know anybody. Finally we decide to go to the Hollywood, a discotheque on West Forty-fifth Street that some of Pam's L.A. friends talk about.

The Hollywood has seen better days. Its clientele has always been young and gay, but now the place has lost its glitter. The music is loud, so we dance—there's nothing else to do. Pam is the whole show. She's changed her clothes and is wearing a slinky knit dress that clings. Her hair rises in a great wave away from her unlined forehead. Her nose cuts through the cigarette smoke. Her dance style isn't flamboyant; it's close and clipped, more athletic than sensual. She's not interested in holding hands.

The floor is filled with gay white men. In her four-inch heels, Pam is one of the tallest people in the place. A towering, gorgeous black woman surrounded by a hundred men with skinny behinds. After a couple of tunes, she asks if we can leave. On the way out a squat man in a black leather jacket and a tiny fedora stops us. He looks like one of the Sicilian heavies Pam throttles in her films. He says he's got a piece of the Hollywood and wants to take Pam's picture and put it on the wall. His eyes are plastered to Pam's breasts the whole time he talks; she pretends not to notice.

In the limousine, Pam lets out a deep breath. She slouches and tells the chauffeur to drive up and down the avenues. She looks exhausted. She's been on tour to promote *Sheba, Baby* for about a month now. It was part of her contract and she's doing her best even though she hates the film. But now all the hotel rooms and limousine rides and acting tough to the superflies who want to steal a kiss are beginning to take their toll. Her backbone, which has been starched all day, is folding against the velvet of the limo seat and she feels like talking.

"You know," she says wearily, "I really only started to think about things about a year ago, I mean really think. Right now I'm just scratching the surface. I think I'd rather just make movies for black people. You know, just be satisfied with what I'm doing. But I can't. I'm too ambitious. I want all the acclaim. That bothers me. I think if I weren't an actress, I'd be a doctor by now. I'd have to, because I'm the first generation of moneymakers in my family, and I can't blow it now."

After nearly fifteen hours together, Pam and I are almost friends. We've played Pong in the arcades and had footraces in Central Park. She says I must be "from the Bronx or something" because my questions are "intellectual." She's sitting, almost curled into a ball, on one of the cream Regency couches, looking very tender. She takes off her sunglasses and invites further discussion. I tell her about the Brooklyn graffiti artist who has been writing, "That's good for her, what about the rest of us niggers?" on the glossy subway ads for *Sheba, Baby*. She doesn't want to hear that. She starts to tense again. "Everyone thinks I have an Eldorado. Well. I don't have an Eldorado. I have a Jeep. Eldorados are for fools; they waste too much gas." Then she says the guy ought to get an education so he won't spend time writing on walls. I ask her about a *Ms.* magazine piece that asserts that much of the violence in her films only serves to separate women by assuming that black women are athletically superior to white women. Now Pam is pissed off. "What do they know?" she rails. "They're just a bunch of rich bitches. What do they know about my problems?"

I can see it was a mistake—one hassle too many—and try to change the subject to her nose. I like it a lot, I tell her. "Yeah," she says tersely, "they used to call me hawk in school. You want to come over here and punch it?" I say I was only kidding, but it sounds like a dare, so I do it. I stand in front of her, legs spread, menacing her flared nostrils with a clenched hand. It is the closest we've been to each other since we met. Suddenly her mouth twists. Before I realize it, a fist is heading toward my groin. I try to block it, but it is too late. As I stumble across the thick Regency rug, Pam Grier says, "See, see what I have to do to defend myself?"

2
Teenage Hipster in the Modern World

The original subhead for this piece was "Cool in an Uncool World." Which is the crux of the matter, isn't it? So many brain cells down the drain trying to be cool—story of my life. The subject of this piece, Legs McNeil, actually managed to escape his widely predicted early demise. He lives even today, albeit still attired in black pointy shoes. He survived, like Ishmael, to tell (with Gillian McCain) the full story of New York punk, Please Kill Me. *From the* Village Voice, *1978.*

Two years ago, standing on a pier jutting into Delaware Bay, I told Legs McNeil, the "Resident Punk" of *Punk Magazoon*, the most moral thing I've yet said in my journalism career.

Legs and I were in Wilmington, Delaware, for the First Annual Sleaze Convention. Legs was the Con Special Guest Star. This owed to his then-inflating reputation for doing nothing much but drinking, eating in McDonald's, watching television, and reading comic books. Those days Legs's professed only goal in life was to sing the theme song from Eva Gabor's TV show *Green Acres* before a packed house at Madison Square Garden. He had also been known to take an elevator to the top of the Empire State Building, look out on a perfectly clear city night, and say, "Wow, you can see Nathan's from here."

This was very impressive to the organizers of "Sleaze Con," a group of Delaware weirdos who edited a magazine called the *Daily Plague*. Legs was the embodiment of sleaze, a true citizen of the Modern World. They treated Legs and me to an annotated tour of an all-night supermarket. All nine brands of pork rinds were identified and labeled. A boys' choir sang recipes for "mock apple pie" off a box of Ritz crackers. Later, Richard Nixon sugar packets were passed around. It was all "random American rot," the Sleaze Con people said.

Now Legs and I were waiting for Godzilla. There was some hope the great beast would raise his head above the electric green waters. After all, the entire state of Delaware is the personal playground of the Du Pont family, and the city of Wilmington puts up signs on Interstate 95 saying, WELCOME TO WILMINGTON, THE CHEMICAL CAPITAL OF THE WORLD. These factors seemed to produce a unique environment. Not long before Sleaze Con, the Wilmington city fathers paved over the decaying downtown streets where blacks hung out. Shiny malls full of potted oak trees and contemporary supergraphics were put in. The idea was to get white people to shop downtown, and that worked, but there was a problem. The development was overrun by Mall Monsters, a mutant strain of huge cockroaches. Supposedly swollen to an incredible girth by the concentration of test-tube runoff in the area, the giant bugs were the scourge of Wilmington's urban renewal plans. Baskin-Robbins employees reportedly got plenty of overtime sweeping the roaches away with push brooms.

Legs and I, both hypersensitive to the thickening rumble of the apocalypse, took the insects as a sign. Our sources had informed us that there was enough witch's brew in the Delaware River to make a comfy home for any Oriental radiation monster that no longer got high off the atomic surf in the Sea of Japan. Legs and I felt that if we watched the water long enough, things would begin to cook. The air would get dank and expectant. The water would begin to crash against the hulls of supertankers. Soon the trumpeting ring of raging foam would begin to form. And then, there he'd be—Godzilla, sardonic and magnificent, the soul of the Modern World, the patron saint of the postatomic age. Just sitting there, staring at the smelly water, made Legs and me feel like Wise Men, searching the skies for the right bright object.

But Legs, with an attention span as long as a manic-depressive's fingernail, got bored. He bought a twelve-pack of Rolling Rock and drank it all in about a half an hour, just the way he always did. Soon he was raving, screaming his usual shit about teenagers taking over the world.

"No one knows anything worth knowing," screamed the high school dropout, GED-less, nineteen-year-old Legs, adding that only teens, not "old fucks" like me, had the courage to admit their profound ignorance. "You think you know something because you went to college. But you're a sucker! A fool. You wasted your parents' money. You know that. Stupid hippie."

Shut up, I told him, yelling was spoiling the vigil. Fuck that, Legs said. Reptiles had cold blood. He knew that from when he had a pet snake back in Cheshire, Connecticut, not so far from the state mental hospital. If you were going to wait for a reptile to do anything, even an atomic reptile, you could wait all day, maybe into the night. He was a busy man. He had better things to do than sit on a scummy pier in Delaware. He was a seeker, and seekers had to be proactive. He was taking matters into his own hands. Seconds later he jumped off the pier and disappeared into the murk. Next time I saw him was a minute later. He had his spindle arms wrapped around a piling. Bright algae was smeared across his face so he looked like a messy kid eating a blue ice. After I helped him onto the dock, he looked at me with a desperate horror that had my socks going up and down. "I saw things down there," he said. "I saw things, but I didn't see him. I didn't see *Him*."

Then Legs collapsed. I had to carry the jerk back to the Lord Della-Warr Motel, the hooker-infested joint where we were staying, where he would be attacked by Debbie Harry and Chris Stein of Blondie. Debbie and Chris, feeling bored, dumped several plastic buckets filled with ice cubes on Legs's zitty back while he was in the middle of making it with a Sleaze Con groupie.

The whole scene had a desultory vibe, especially after the aforementioned groupie set the bedsheets on fire with an errant cigarette lighter, which is likely why I made this most moral comment I alluded to earlier.

"Legs, you asshole," I said. "I am not doing this story on you. I am not taking the responsibility for making you famous."

Teengenerate

Back then Legs was devoting most of his ferret energy to becoming "famous." He used to crawl around the beer-dripped floor of CBGB, biting people on the calf. When they looked down, Legs would be there with a shit-eating grin on his face. "Hi, I'm famous," he'd say, and scurry away. After the Godzilla incident, however, Legs and I weren't so tight. He'd see me on the Bowery and shout, "There goes the guy who didn't want to take the responsibility for making me famous."

Legs will never believe it, but I held off for love, because there's something about Legs McNeil I really love. I used to think that someday I'd write a novel with Legs as the leading character, and the book would contain everything I know about living in the Modern World. Legs's character would be similar to the one Ray Milland plays in the Roger Corman film *X—The Man with the X-Ray Eyes*. In that movie Milland is a doctor who discovers a special serum that enables him to see "what others cannot see." In the beginning Milland has fun. He cheats at cards and looks through blouses. But eventually he sees too much. He sees the center of the universe, the driving force of the galaxy. "No one," he says, "should see so much." The last scene in the film takes place at a revival meeting. The harrowed and half-crazed Milland tells his problem to the brimstone preacher, who says, "If thy eye offends you, pluck it out." Milland does.

Talking to Legs has always given me the ghostly feeling of being with someone who knows too much for his own good. In Legs's case, it is knowing too much about the true horror of his generation. That, as it turns out, is a road to madness.

Legs could have avoided this if he didn't have such a crazy desire to be cool. Legs has got to be cool, or Legs isn't anything at all. Once *Punk* ran a contest asking readers to write in why they were punks. The best reply came from somewheres in Queens. It said, "I'm a punk because I'm cool and I ain't got nothing to show for it."

That was Legs. He grew up in Cheshire, Connecticut, a suburban town that has MAXILLOFACIAL SURGEON written all over it. The streets in Cheshire are neat and Waspy. The kids go to college and have fathers like Ward Cleaver. Legs's life, however, did not coincide with this archetype. He lived across the tracks from the manicured lawns, on the edge of a swamp beside an irrigation canal. His father died of cancer when he was two months old. Before that, his grandfather blew his head off in the family chicken house, and his grandmother committed herself to a mental institution. Throughout his childhood Legs always asked his mother where his father was and why his grandmother's house had bars. His mother worked as a secretary to make sure the McNeils would always have a home in Cheshire. But they never really belonged there. Legs's face tells you that. It is a hollow-cheeked shanty-Irish face, the kind that rides a forklift in Fall River, Massachusetts. But Legs wasn't born for the treadmill. He felt a tiny artist's pitter-pat in his cholesterol-influxing heart and wanted desperately to have something to show for being cool.

To Legs, teenagers were the coolest. All the Archie comics he read and TV he watched in Cheshire told him that. He saw how the big kids drove cars and took chicks to the Fillmore blasted out of their gourd. He figured that must be what cool is. But by the time Legs got to be a teenager, in the early 1970s, everyone was telling him he was too late. All the cool stuff was over. The Summer of Love, acid, battling the government, splitting for the Coast, none of that was left.

Legs was stunned. Waiting all this time to be cool and getting *nothing*. There had to be something to break him out of Cheshire, something cool to call his own. The radio and everything else were still jammed up with the flotsam and jetsam of another generation. Crosby, Stills, and Nash, my asshole—Legs knew a burnt-out case when he heard one. He tried glitter rock, but that was, er, kind of embarassing. Everywhere they were talking about how this new batch of youth had the "new seriousness"; how kids today only wanted to get good grades and be corporation lawyers. No doubt, Legs thought, these have got to be the uncoolest times ever to come down the pike.

Desperate, Legs shacked up in his room overlooking the swamp and pondered his existential position. How could a cool person be cool in an uncool time? In the midst of familial despair, this was the real question, the true problem that had to be addressed. Legs schemed far and wide. Like Lord Buckley before him, his thought processes took him to the stratosphere, the gone-o-sphere, and the way-gone-o-sphere. Cool, Legs psyched out, is an arbitrary thing. Anything could be cool if you say it is. It wasn't so much the things you thought were cool that made you cool, it was the *feeling* of being cool—when you *know* you're cool—that *really* made you cool.

This head session gave the teenage McNeil a blueprint for action. Instead of apologizing for being born too late, Legs railed against his smug '60s-loving elders. "What do you love?" he demanded. "Pot, long guitar solos, battling the government, wearing bright colors, being mellow? . . . Well, I hate all that. All that sucks and is uncool."

"And what do you hate?" Legs went on. "Television, burgers, drinking, violent behavior? . . . Well, I love all of that. I declare these things to be mine. I appoint liking *Hogan's Heroes* and McDonald's to be cool. I love America, too. I love everything about Modern America, the long freeways, Republicans, marching off to foreign wars for no reason, the whole bit. Any country that produced Eddie Haskell has to be cool."

Legs's coolness cosmology was, of course, total reaction. But anyone without his brains buried on the Upper West Side has to realize the necessity and logic of it. I mean, the kids have to dance. But who would have figured Legs's coolness would turn out to be brave? By deciding the Modern World was his Godhead, Legs decreed that, in order to be cool, one had to be hip to how to live in such a contemporary landscape. It was a task an entire generation had called impossible, choosing instead to label the Modern World "plastic" and cuddle themselves in the fantasies of "going back to the land." Legs had picked a rough road to ride. But at least it was convenient. To be cool, Legs wouldn't have to go to Mexico and get the runs under a volcano. Nor would he have to give pennies to belly-swelled babies in Calcutta. Legs grew up in Cheshire, Connecticut. His muse was all around him, inside and out.

It didn't take Legs long to realize there were other disgruntled, would-be cool teenagers who shared his search for the hip. There was John Holmstrom and Ged Dunn, his buddies from Cheshire. They wanted to be cool, too, albeit without Legs's manic desperation. Better adjusted to the middle class, they dug Legs because he did reckless things like talk the local high school into giving him money to make a class film and then get expelled for spending all the bread drinking. One night, when the three friends were driving down the Wilbur Cross Parkway with nothing to do, Legs grabbed the wheel, swerved the car across three lanes of traffic, and drove it into a ditch. Then he jumped into the backseat, stuck his nose into the crease, and started whimpering about how he was having a "coolness freakout." He needed an outlet for his coolness or he'd commit suicide.

To save Legs's life, Holmstrom and Dunn decided to move to New York and start a magazine. At first Holmstrom wanted to call the mag *Teenage News* because they were only interested in teenage issues. But it was eventually changed to *Punk* because Legs was a big fan of a Dictators song, "Weekend." It goes: "Eddie is the local punk / throwing up and getting drunk / eating in McDonald's for lunch." ["Eddie" is Legs's real name, sort of—his actual name is Roderick Edwin McNeil. He took Legs because he loved the B-movie about Legs Diamond, or rather the forgotten Ray Danton's grade-B performance as the gangster.] Dunn, a budding capitalist who compared *Punk*'s mimeograph machine to a Carl Sandburg steel mill, became the publisher. Holmstrom, a genius cartoonist, and Harvey Kurtzman disciple, made himself editor. Legs, however, couldn't figure out what to call himself. He couldn't draw and had no head for business. Finally he decided on "Resident Punk," a combination "secret agent"/Alfred E. Newman title calculated to make him a legend by age nineteen.

At last, Legs was cool. It was the end of 1974, the beginning of the CBGB punk emergence that *Punk* would help turn into a national media phenomenon. Legs was key on the scene. Any night you could see him standing in front of CBGB, a loose cigarette hanging from his lower lip, two punkette groupies on either arm of his leather jacket—the one with the rips under both armpits—cutting a wicked figure.

Big deal if he read few to no books, that the entire reign of the Enlightenment seemed to be falling away in the Bowery soot, those days Legs's brain cooked like a burning idea factory. On the Bowery he met other suburban kids who had suffered the uncertainty of cool through their early teenage years. Kids who had also racked their brains for an answer to the question: How to be cool in an uncool time. Many of them, like the Ramones, the members of Blondie, and the Dictators, had come to the same conclusions as Legs and thrown themselves headlong into study of the Modern World. Legs spent those early CBGB nights discoursing on Bullwinkle Moose and TV commercials with Joey Ramone, and sometimes even Dee Dee when the bassist wasn't too stoned or scary with his male hustler act. To Legs, these conversations had the momentous freshness of Mao and Chou revealing their similar passions for ideas by the light of one candle in a cave.

One night Legs found out that he, Joey, and two members of Blondie had all had the same dream. They dreamed of Monty Hall saying, "Well, would you trade your life for what's behind that curtain?" After that, Legs knew that his generation, the first ever to grow up completely within the Modern Age, had acquired a huge collective subconscious. The power and vastness of this concept made Legs burst with creativity. Often he would sit in the back of CBGB, listening to the Talking Heads sing "Don't Worry about the Government" and make up his "Famous Persons" interviews for *Punk*. Legs did straight Q-and-As with "personalities" like Boris and Natasha and the cast of *Gilligan's Island*. Coming from his difficult home life, he poignantly (also insanely) wrote long letters seeking parental advice from father figures like Carl Betz of *The Donna Reed Show*.

I remember the day Milton Glaser came by my desk and picked up an issue of *Punk*. He thumbed through it, looking at the hand-printed features (it was Holmstrom's master stroke that made *Punk* the best magazine of neoliterate times—he made the whole thing look like a comic book; that way he could print the theory of relativity and kids would read it), the illustrated interviews with Lou Reed, Legs's craziness. Glaser sat down, visibly shaken. "These guys could put me out of business," he said. If *Punk* worried Milton Glaser, I knew here was something big.

This was the beginning of my appreciation of punk as a spectacularly American way of cool. How fabulous to have something new to dig after years of mealy-mouthed postmortems in Berkeley. A ton of punditry about what the seventies were really all about, and here it was: the real thing, stripped down like an arrow through the heart. I loved that the Ramones' first record was made in eighteen hours and cost only six thousand dollars. Figures like that cut away the flab of indecision. So did the music. The Ramones song "I Don't Wanna Walk Around with You," which asks the question, "so why you wanna walk around with me?" boiled away any other, superfluous ideas I had about high school cool. It was all anyone ever needed to know about high school and adolescence in general. It was as if the Ramones, none of whom were named Ramone, were saying to the dull sixties establishment: "See, we can express ourselves fast, cheap, and good. We'll tell you about our own experience as teenagers, and it will be real."

Like Legs said, "We don't care what no one says. Sure, things are supposed to be shit now. But, fuck it. We're here and we're gonna have our fun. We're gonna be cool." The audaciousness was super; Legs and his buddies were reinventing cool before my eyes. They were accepting the crap of the Modern World, all that mind rot, and they were *celebrating it*, not protesting against it. What a brilliantly existential decision! How modernistic a concept!

I thought back to all the philosophizing I'd once read about what was hip and what was not. And dredged up an old quote from Norman Mailer. Big Norm said, "For Hip is sophistication of the wise primitive in a giant jungle . . ." Who else was Legs? This described him and his fellow punks to a T.

It was early 1976, the Five Spot, where so much bop was played, had just closed for the last time. It was replaced by a clothing store called the Late Show, which catered mostly to the CBGB crowd and played Ramones records constantly over its booming speaker set. I made this a sign. It mattered little, then, that this whole new crew of cool read few to no books, that their surface anti-intellectualism seemed to consign the entire reign of the Enlightenment to the Lower East Side soot bin. It is still possible to envision the whole generation of newly configured hipsters lurking along the Bowery in their sub-Brando black leather jackets. A collection of wise primitives making incisive comments about a culture nobody even wanted to admit existed. To me, it was very moving.

Legs McNeil and the Obsolescence of the White Negro Theory

Legs became the spokesman, such as it was, for this new generation of hipsters, partially by default, since most of the band members were into catatonia, and partially due to his zeal for self-promotion. Legs would sit under the Fonz poster in the "*Punk* dump," the storefront "office" he, Holmstrom, and Dunn kept underneath the approach ramp to the Lincoln Tunnel, and pontificate to a near-unending stream of squarish pop-culture reporters, some of whom recognized that the joke was on them and some who didn't. Working on a generational icon stance, McNeil honed his lines into handy sound bytes.

About hippies he said, "A bunch of yin wimps. Woodstock was a hip capital pajama party."

About glitter rock, he said, "Homosexuality shouldn't be pushed on fifteen-year-old kids."

About the future of visual expression, he said, "I think movies should only be thirty minutes long and be in black and white. Kids don't have the concentration for more."

About himself, he said, "Every time I look in the mirror it's like watching a home movie."

One of the classic Legs McNeil interviews appeared as part of an August 1976 *Village Voice* article by Frank Rose. Rose was trying to decipher punk's effect on the supposedly large issue of "butch," a term Frank described as "self-conscious masculinity."

At the time, Legs was on a search-and-destroy mission against disco, which *Punk* had described in an editorial as the source of "everything wrong with Western civilization." Legs said disco was the creation of synthesizers, a fact he claimed left the limp shit devoid of human energy and turned listeners into "zombies." Disco, Legs asserted, was an uncool Communistic plot invented by jaded grown-ups to rob teenagers of their naïveté. But more interesting and inflammatory was Legs's conjecture that disco was the product of an unholy alliance between blacks and gays. Neither of these groups was currently in favor with Legs, and he routinely called them niggers and faggots. If Legs was the next big thing, as Lester Bangs and others suggested, then Rose was worried about this.

Rose's story had Legs saying all kinds of apparently reactionary and reckless things like, "Punks are normal people, that's what we are, normal. We're not a bunch of perverts" . . . "Punks are like—the guys know they're guys and the chicks know they're chicks" . . . "David Bowie is really sick. He's such a faggot" . . . Also, about blacks, he said, "We're not really racist. . . . We're just into our own thing. It's like saying to Italians [why don't you like] Polacks?"

Rose concluded, not incorrectly, or surprisingly, considering the evidence he was given, that Legs was a blue-collar poseur who saw life as "giant high school." Legs's racism and gay-baiting, portrayed as borrowed from Irish bars and idiotic right-wing pamphlets, were simply attitudes to fill in the image of a man's man. This seemed true enough on the surface, but I couldn't help feeling that in Rose's rush to tenderly put Legs and his punk crew down as still another potentially brutish terror a gay man in New York has to contend with, Frank had taken McNeil's quotes far too seriously.

I thought back to a night at the 82 Club. The Dictators were playing. *Punk* had run a "*Punk* of the month" contest. Readers were asked to send in pictures of themselves proving they were more punky than anyone else. One Ronald Binder won three months in a row. He sent in low-angle pictures of himself eating chains along with a number of telegrams threatening to blow up the *Punk* camp if he didn't win. Holmstrom said, "Wow, we got to give it to this guy. He'll kill us if we don't."

Still, no one had ever seen Ronald Binder in the flesh. Until that night at the 82. Binder came over to Holmstrom and said, "Hi, I'm the punk of the month." One look was enough. Binder was maybe five feet tall, he weighed plenty. He looked completely harmless. Holmstrom was beside himself. "My God," he said. "I thought you ate dead babies for breakfast. . . . This is terrible. Don't tell anyone who you are, you'll make us look bad."

Binder seemed hurt by Holmstrom's abuse. He went off in a corner and hung his head by the 82's Ukrainian wallpaper. He stayed there until Legs, who had seen the whole confrontation, came over and said, "Don't let it get you down. I'm a fake, too."

This was no surprise. Self-mockery has always been Legs's meat. He wore his leather jacket as a cocoon of fakery. He was to a real street punk as Domino's is to a pizza pie: a canny but not particularly faithful parody. Legs has never been tough at all. He weighs about 120 pounds. He couldn't break his own nose. As a macho aggressive, he's never been confused with a tiger fighting for his mate. That, of course, was the whole joke, the ironic core of the coolness.

But this didn't make Legs a clown. To me, his self-mockery recalled the way Thelonious Monk plays the piano or Earl Monroe dribbles the basketball. With those two there has always been a tension between the dead seriousness of technique and the ironical understanding that in the scope of the universe all those hours developing a style like no one else might mean nothing. They could drop a bomb on you. You could get hit by a truck. The only sane way to deal with this looming spectre of random destruction was to have a sense of humor about yourself.

This, I figured, was the key to Legs. No matter how ardently he argued his perceptions about the world, he didn't want to be held to them. For him, proselytizing was technique, but none of it was hard and fast. It was Legs's hipster nature, I thought.

But it also caused problems. If Legs was a hipster, and CBGB a hipster scene, where were the blacks? Not one of the first wave of punk-rock bands has featured a black musician. Outside of the Talking Heads' art version of Al Green's "Take Me To the River" and some ska stuff, CBGB music is basically free of traditional R&B or blues sources. In fact, outside of the Bowery fall-down guys who stumble over from the Men's Shelter, you almost never see a black person in and around CB's. This, coupled with Legs's remarks about how "blacks have their culture and we have ours," seemed to contradict everything I know about white hipsters.

Punk, a seemingly legitimate New York City bohemian hipster scene, appeared to fly in the face of most everything set down in the most famous manifesto that sought to separate the hip sensibility from what was square, Norman Mailer's epochal essay, "The White Negro: Superficial Reflections on the Hipster." I knew I'd have to go to the woodshed with Mailer if I wanted some enlightenment on this Legs puzzlement. Written in 1957, Norm's essay says the hipster was a man who realized that "our collective condition is to live with instant death by atomic war." This fact was particularly distressing to white men ticketed for two cars in the garage and a neat hedge around the lawn. With the threat of death haunting every moment, middle-class striving seemed a waste of time. According to Mailer, the only sane thing to do was "to encourage the psychopath in one's self, to explore that domain of experience where security is boredom and therefore sickness, and one exists in the present, in that enormous present which is without past or future, memory of planned intention, the life where a man must go until he is beat . . ."

This road, especially for the passel of Brooklyn-Queens Jews and Texas gays who felt compelled to take it, was totally uncharted. A guide was needed, and in the Negro these searching whites found one. Blacks had been living with the knowledge that they could be wiped out at any given moment for 350 years. Mailer called this "living on the margin between totalitarianism and democracy." He also said the blacks had produced an entire culture based upon living on the edge. They traveled light, spoke a secret and flexible language, gambled, and wore orange pants with green shirts. It was living on the brink, but their constant state of "psychopathy" had also produced the wondrous jazz, the perfect "orgasm" of brinksmanship.

Hipsters, or whites who recognized the descending sword for what it was, understood and dug the brilliance of the blacks' achievement. "So," wrote Mailer, "there was a new breed of adventurers, urban adventurers who drifted out at night, looking for action with a black man's code to fit their facts. The hipster had absorbed the existential synapses of the Negro and, for all practical purposes, could be considered a White Negro.

I was a White Negro for the better part of my consciously hip life. Probably still am. I worked as a porter at the Port Authority Bus Terminal so I could do a black man's job. I began smoking Pall Malls because the blacks did. Along with my other White Negro friends, I lived at the Brittany Hotel on Tenth Street. When Muddy Waters and Howlin' Wolf brought their blues band to stay at the Albert, we supplied them with smoke.

We hung around with as many jazzmen as would have us. Major Holley, who played bass with Roland Kirk occasionally back then, was our buddy. He knew we were just another bunch of hopeless Queens Mezz Mezzrows looking for a taste of the millennium, but he was sweet and let us play our game. In return we would sit ringside at the Five Spot and, when Holley soloed, we'd shout, "Major, you so fucking good, they ought to make you a general." Once, the Major must have been bugged because he put down his bass during a Jazz Interactions concert, went to the microphone, and said, "Damn, I am all tuckered out. So let's meet and greet Jake the Snake, who will provide us with some meal ticket in the meantime."

I didn't want to go onstage, I had never even held a bass before. But my buddies pushed me to it. I picked up the big momma and plucked it a couple of times. Then Roland Kirk turned to me. With the cigarette smoke around his beret like gauze, three fat horns stuck in his mouth, and wraparound sunglasses across his blind eyes, Kirk was a vision of boogie hell. But it was okay. He said, "Shit, sounds black to me."

This, I have always felt, was one of the crowning moments of my life. But Legs would not buy it. Explaining why African-Americans were cool and worth imitating was a pointless conversation to have with Legs. As pointless as trying to explain why Dylan going electric was important, as pointless as explaining why getting arrested at People's Park was both useless and consummate at the same time. Legs simply refused to comprehend why my generation of hipsters dug blacks. He would not even accept such seemingly irrefutable black-coolness raps as George Carlin's schoolyard scene. Carlin said put a bunch of white kids and a bunch of black kids together and after a week the whites will be talking like the blacks. But none of the blacks would be saying, "Golly, gee, we won the big game."

For Legs, blacks were mostly on the radio, making the rotten disco music he hated, or in the first three pages of the *Daily News* sticking 9mm guns into people's chests. He said he had "no guilt." The only other thing he'd say about blacks involved a bizarre theory about why listening to their music was so repugnant to him. He said that because of "racism, or whatever," most blacks didn't get on the radio until they were thirty or forty, so they always sang about thirty- and forty-year-old concerns. He said this was alien to him. If all blacks were teenagers, like the Jackson Five, singing "like A-B-C, One-Two-Three," that would be all right with him. Otherwise, blacks didn't interest him in the least.

This troubled me. Racism, or whatever, is understandable, even sickly poetic, in the mouth of a blue-collar worker or a Southern sheriff—it's an integral part of their worldview. But this attitude of racial indifference coming from a hipster hit a discord. If Legs McNeil were a hipster and he didn't think blacks were cool, my universe was about to go into a tilt.

Actually, I had been busting my brain with certain notions about the apparent deemphasis of blacks in the Hip and Square cultures respectively for some time.

Mailer's essay was better than a nice sum-up of fifties attitudes. He predicted the sixties, too. Big Norm drones on in "The White Negro" about hipsters relentlessly seeking their "orgasm," which I have always taken to mean the sexual-emotional act or state that would give meaning to their "psychopathic" position on the edge between oblivion and the security of the middle class. For me—and I assume this is true for most White Negroes of my generation—the entire sixties experience was an "orgasm." After all, what were hippies if not white kids acting like blacks? It horrified me when sign-wavers chanted about "student as nigger" and the rest of that. (It still seems sick, especially when Patti Smith tries it on.) Didn't these idiots know what they were saying? Smoking dope, being casual about sex, pretending poverty didn't quite come close to bridging that gap, any more than living in tepees made hippies into Sioux.

What exactly black people thought of this "white negro" stuff wasn't anything any of us (white people) thought of, much. Once, when I thought I was a dope dealer, I got ripped off in a Stanyan Street apartment by a black guy. I was supposed to pick up ten keys of Michoacan from the guy. But as soon as I got into the room, he stuck a gun in my ear and took the $750 my friends gave me. He tied me up so I wouldn't "even think" about following him and put a Jimi Hendrix record on the box. Then he looked at me, like this is just too easy, shook his head in sympathy, and said, "You know, I just don't understand you people. Don't you know this is dangerous?" Then he split. A few minutes later a paste-white chick with drugged eyes and matted hair came out from behind an Indian-print curtain. She squinted into the red light bulb, said it was cold, and lit the stove. After she untied me, she said, "Doug is really a dynamite guy, he just gets wild sometimes."

I don't know what I was expecting: to sit down with the ghetto guys, talk about the impending shadow of night, and have them say, "Hey, we're all in the same boat, welcome aboard"? It was never going to happen. Knowing handshakes and slick words didn't make you cool. Besides, the "psychopathy" in the blacks that we admired was not calculated to produce white-man-lovers or even very nice guys. You could dig their orgasm, feeling passionately about the plight that made them crazy men, but you had to be wise. Wise that getting next to them was like cutting your own throat.

Also, sometime in the early seventies, blacks began doing things that might be considered uncool. Their horrendous affectations of the worst parts of the hippie movement were embarrassing, no lie. Talk of astrology and wearing medallions didn't fit the image of the existential hero. What were the Temptations doing singing about "Psychedelic Shacks"? I felt like grabbing black kids with Robert Indiana Love pins stuck to their double knits and saying, "Don't do it. Don't go down that road. It's shit. I know." This was distressing. Blacks acting crazy, like psychopaths, made sense: being black drove you crazy. But blacks acting dumb was another thing; these were the people who were supposed to understand the secret of the twentieth century.

It didn't take long to figure out what was happening. When you have Diana Ross playing Billie Holiday in a movie made by blacks, when a WBLS destroys WWRL in the ratings, when macho singers get pushed out of the foreground by violin strings, it's pretty clear. The Nat King Cole element of black culture is overrunning the James Brown segment. Black culture is redefining itself in a middle-class mode. This, of course, is the blacks' right as Americans. In this country all immigrants—even ones who were brought here in chains—are allowed to become consumers.

But this produced a serious dilemma for White Negroes. If ghetto blacks were simply too dangerous to deal with, the middle-class ones, with their "crossover" concerns, were no longer compelling. George Jefferson wants the same things as my parents; his cleaning lady steals, too. This is not acceptable. It brings to mind the old hipster saw about blacks with seemingly white values: "What an Oreo. He's not a spade at all."

Doing a little cultural cross-referencing, I dug that so-called "Squares" had also made a shift on black people. During the civil rights time in the sixties, when the closet Commies and liberal types still had pull in showbiz, media blacks pretty much got the Eleanor Roosevelt treatment. Between them, Cicely Tyson and James Earl Jones produced more guilt through dignity than a million Jewish mothers could through nagging. But now, it's almost as if the guilt-exorcising Squares are saying, "Well, we gave these guys their chance. We highlighted their struggle. What did they do? Gave us Rap Brown, the ungrateful loudmouth, and mugged our grandmothers."

Therein, I think, is the basis for the elevation of the Italian-American in the mass media. With a self-propelled reputation for toughness and the supposed ability to call their Uncle Vinnie at the drop of a confrontation, Italians are perceived by black-fearing Squares (as well as black-fearing hipsters) as the only group of whites capable of fending off the onrush of "them." How many times have you heard the joke, "Well, I guess this is a safe neighborhood" while walking by Bella Ferrara? If you're dumb, that means Italians don't like "yoms" much and are willing to fight them on their own physical terms. Blacks know this, and they also know Italians are some cold-blooded motherfuckers (what they didn't know they saw in the *Godfather* movies, which were big in the black ghettos), so they stay away. This set of pseudo-facts is so ingrained in the public consciousness, it is no surprise that many of the TV cops—Baretta, Petrocelli, Delvecchio, and Columbo—are some have-been Italians. Who else can be depended on to keep the blacks in their place?

To facilitate this mythmaking, the media moguls have imbued Italians with much of the "soul" that used to be the exclusive property of blacks.

This is quite clear in the seminal work of revisionist racial theory, *Rocky*. You've got to figure Stallone knew what he was doing, I make him that cynical. He portrays Rocky as a guileless but lovable blue-collar plodder who has an indomitable spirit. The major black characters, the champ and the female TV reporter who interviews Rocky, are both seen as slick, hollow hustlers. Stallone's attitude toward blacks is similar to that of Americans toward Commies in the fifties: they're smarter and sneakier than us, so we have to stick together and be pure of heart.

A White Negro, even a disillusioned White Negro, watching the meatpacking scene in which noble-savage Stallone pleads to the middle-class black reporter, "Just don't take no cheap shot, please," is stunned by the manipulation of racial images since the sixties. It is almost as if whites have been given the message: You don't have to pretend to like "them" anymore. Now, to whites, blacks are either the faceless unmentionable or just another creep trying to take your job. Either way they are better off forgotten.

Eyeballing all this, Legs's indifference to black culture was more understandable. Legs is a hipster who takes his input from Square sources. If TV tells him Italians are cool, he may adopt their way of saying "fuck you"—a short, blunt blast as opposed to the sultry, many-syllabled "fuck you motherfucker" of the blacks—but he's not taking the whole thing. Catholics are far too earnest for a hipster like Legs; that's what he's trying to get away from.

But blacks have never even entered his mind as a role model. How could he dig jazz when the radio no longer plays jazz? Blacks had essentially been wiped out as a compelling cultural force before Legs ever got a chance to appreciate them.

But the more I dug, the more I realized blacks would have been irrelevant to a seventies hipster like Legs anyway. The old White Negro looked to the blacks to lead him through a landscape that was in the midst of total change, due to the introduction of the atomic bomb. That was twenty-five years ago, when the apocalypse was a new idea and truly existed as a meaningful force only in the minds of a few "urban adventurers." America still operated by pre-atomic rules. Buildings were still made out of bricks; people still read books, ate in real restaurants, and had families.

Now, of course, much of the above is gone. America has adjusted in profound ways to the spectre of the apocalypse. Now we have throwaway television, throwaway burgers, throwaway housing. None of it has the permanency of the pants your mother bought an inch too long so they'd fit next year. The society has caught up to Hiroshima. We are living, as Legs and I learned at the Sleaze Convention, in a fully fleshed-out post-atomic world. Everything we touch, eat, and see has the singe of doom on it. So Legs doesn't need anyone to tell him secrets; he knows the score in this world as well as anyone. He needs no guide; he's on his own.

Orgasm, Where Is the Orgasm?

Today, two years after we waited for Godzilla and I declined the responsibility for making him famous, Legs McNeil is in my kitchen, telling a tape recorder why the teenagers did not take over the world. 1977, Legs says, was a terrible year. *Punk* almost went broke. John Holmstrom and Ged Dunn battled. Holmstrom claimed Dunn's grandiose ambitions to make *Punk* another *Rolling Stone* within a year overextended the magazine's meager resources. Legs figured John was the talent and Ged was the business, and in that case you got to go with the talent, but it hurt him to have to make the choice.

Also, the CBGB rock scene had disintegrated before Legs's eyes. Many of the first-generation bands, the ones Legs thought spoke for him—Talking Heads, Ramones, Blondie, and the Dictators—got recording contracts and went away on tour. Legs was all for that. Hipster punks knew that the popular culture created them. And they were determined to do something—anything—to make their mark on it. The bands, Legs and Holmstrom figured, were the best bet to express "teenage" obsessions. Their missionaries, of a sort.

But once Joey Ramone and Chris Stein went out of town, Legs had no one to discuss Jerry Paris with. His fellow hipsters were disappearing. Everyone cool seemed to be. Who else but Handsome Dick Manitoba would go around blustering about how he could break Buddy (Nature Boy) Rogers's figure-four leg vine and then get himself flattened by a drag queen like Wayne County? What a punk. But now he wasn't around. The punk bands were diving into the nexus of the popular culture they worshiped like the sun, hardly ever to bubble up above the Hot Hundred again.

Those who came to replace them were a drag. Legs hated the British punks. They came humorless, snarling the same anti-establishment rant of the Animals a dozen years before. Don't things ever change in England, Legs wondered. The youth is always discontented. They always hate the government and punch each other about soccer. Rockers aren't supposed to care about sports, especially soccer. The Brits also brought bleached hair and a pile of punk paraphernalia. Idiot clothes, stupid T-shirts to buy if you wanted to be cool like Carnaby Street. It was like some reverse D-day beach storming of moron high school status freaks. Legs saw what was happening. Punk was being undermined as a moral, intellectual choice. Anyone who stuck a safety pin in his nose could be a punk.

This offended Legs's hipster nature. He never really quite decided whether he wanted punk to turn into a sixties-style movement or not. But now he'd be sitting with Joey Ramone, and some Westchester kid would come and say, "Hey, you're Joey Ramone. Hey, I'm a punk, too. I got a band. We cut up our cocks onstage." Then Joey would make with his Martian reflex and say, "Why do you do that?" The kid would say, "Because I'm a punk." And Legs would know that Hip cannot be a movement. Because if Hip is a movement and everyone's the same, that's not cool. Like Big Norman said so long ago, ". . . and, indeed, it is essential to dig the most, for if you do dig, you lose your superiority over the Square, and you are less likely to be cool . . ."

Legs understood coolness isn't something that comes easy. His cool had been achieved through spiritual agony, which led him to the basic precepts about how to be hip in post-atomic America. The Brits' egalitarianism was all wrong. First of all, they knew nothing about America. They didn't watch the same shows, or laugh at the same jokes. Rhyming slang, like how corny could you get? The knee-jerk rebellion of bands like the Clash and Jam, even if they were good, offered only some giant Nazi thing where a million kids got into some stadium and pumped their fists like in *Triumph of the Will*. The whole Brit deal didn't have the sense of struggle, the existential overcoming, or the sheer delicacy of kids trying to find their legitimate place in a really fucked-up world. What happened on the Bowery was higher order, not one more mass of jerks mudwrestling with Wavy Gravy. The Brits' popularity let too many assholes into the club.

Now Legs says, "I hate this punk thing these days. The kids at CBGB aren't cool. They don't have any opinions about anything. They just sit around saying, 'This place sucks,' 'This place is beat.' They all smoke pot and wear stupid clothes. It's just like the fucking hippies. Zombies. Just like them."

The anguish Legs McNeil suffered being the "Resident Punk" of a movement he had come to hate—no man knows. But he did the only thing he felt he could do: He threw himself headlong into the job as a protest. He drank more, offered more diatribes about the foul influence of faggots, and directed manifestos at the invading British. Weeks went by "out of control." The drinking ravaged his already beleaguered liver. He slept at a different frumpy "groupie's" house every night. Their names he did not remember. In his haggard look and dedication to the task at hand, Legs reminded one of the lead character in *Diary of a Country Priest*. One time, while a French reporter was asking him to compare the Three Stooges with Laurel and Hardy, Legs spewed forth a three-foot curtain of blood and phlegm.

From everywhere, uncool people who didn't get the joke besieged him. Once, a burly idiot from Ohio wielding a pearl-handled switchblade came into CBGB looking to dethrone Legs as "Resident Punk." Legs had to hide in Phebe's among the off-off Broadway failures. It appeared that Legs would soon fulfill John Holmstrom's blithe and oft-repeated prophecy: "Legs has to die young. Look at his eyes. Can't you see it? That's what makes him so romantic."

One week Legs's older brother, a hot-dog ski pro who Legs always thought was as cool as James Bond, came to town. The brother took one look at Legs and asked Holmstrom, "What's wrong with my brother?" John, who had been trying to get Legs to eat something for weeks, said, "I don't know, I think he's going crazy." The brother said something had to be done. According to Legs, "One minute I was upstairs, drinking. They called me down. An hour later I was on my way to the nuthouse. It happened just like that. They didn't commit me. I signed the papers myself. But they said it wouldn't be too good for me if I didn't. After all, I knew they could get everyone in this city as a character witness against me."

Legs was in the bughouse only for a month or so, but that was long enough for his roommate to kill himself. Every day the doctors dragged Legs to "creative" encounter sessions. He could hardly keep from cracking up every time one of the fright-wig ladies in the white smocks read their poems, usually about "the beauty of fucking nature or how they wanted to kill their mothers." Legs read no poems, but the doctors loved him. "They really thought I was an interesting case," Legs says. "They wanted to keep me there forever. They said I had a unique outlook on life. They kept poking me, wanting to know why I thought everything was so funny."

Legs signed himself out. Staying there wouldn't have done anybody any good, he says. The doctors didn't understand a word he was saying. Actually, the shrinks should have saved their breath. Big Norman said twenty years ago a "psychopath" hipster makes a bad mental patient because he is "ordinately ambitious—too ambitious ever to trade his warped brilliant conception of his possible victories in life for the grim if peaceful attrition of the analyst's couch." Big Norm, of course, knows what Legs's problem is: He ain't come.

Mailer says, "Orgasm is his [the hipster's] therapy." And it takes a hipster from the sixties, whose orgasm did come, over and over for three Tantric years, to dig the sadness of Legs's coital interruptus. Who knows why Legs's brand of punk failed to sustain itself as a meaningful hipster force? Probably the punk-hipster vision was too intellectual for most modern teenagers to relate to. Instead of offering the solid psychology of broadside rebellion against parents, Legs advocated the elusive psychopathy of dealing with the fearsome swell of Modern America by celebrating it. This is a difficult and ultimately unhappy way to think. Especially for someone as bright as Legs. For him, saying Modern America is great is just more of the joke. But it's hard to keep laughing when you walk into a supermarket and hear the clerk singing "You Deserve a Break Today" and you know that the McDonald's jingle is the only song in the whole world he knows the lyrics to.

That's why I guess I didn't want the responsibility for making Legs famous. I must have sensed defeat back on the dock waiting for Godzilla. But if Legs and his buddies are the direct descendants of me and my pre-hippie friends, we can sympathize with the bad hand the Bowery Boys drew. They really were born too late.

Now Legs is "Resident Punk" in name only. These days *Punk* comes out infrequently at best, and Legs is talking about moving on. So many things have changed in two years, Legs says with a beer-sodden nostalgia you expect from someone who carried the hippie coffin down Haight Street. "I don't even want to be famous anymore," Legs says. "I mean, being famous is neat and all, but I wasn't making no money. It's dumb to be famous without something to show for it. That's why I hate *People* magazine. Those people are famous for doing stupid things. Now I only want to be famous for doing cool things. That's what I want to do, cool things."

Legs's current cool thing is a band, Shrapnel. He manages them and is their "spiritual leader." The association began when Legs was in the bughouse. The Shrapnels, five teenage rock and rollers from Red Bank, New Jersey, then calling themselves the Hard Attacks, had read Legs's "famous persons" interviews and found them intense. They also liked the time they saw Legs pass out in CBGB's after making still another speech about teenagers taking over the world. They called Legs every day he was in the hospital, begging him to take them on. Legs thought about it for a while, asking the kids pertinent questions like, "If you had all the money in the world, what ten movies would you make?" They described ten war films full of fire, destruction, and Armageddon, all of it done in Frank Frazetta style with Venus Paradise color.

Legs recognized the modernistic values in such thinking. He decided that a "war band" was just what New York rock and roll needed. Living in New York was sort of a war zone anyway, he thought. Everywhere are contending platoons of ethnic groups, looking to aggrandize territory and goods. The fucking Bowery already looked like a B-52ed Nam village. Besides, war expressed Legs's frame of mind. His cool was under attack from Brits on one side, the dumb CBGB kids on another, and the snotty "punk as art" SoHo creeps on the other. The time had come for the true American teenager to stand up. Legs read that Dali said war was "a heightened state of awareness." If that's what the moribund punk hipster scene needed to fight miasma like disco, so be it.

Now, after a few months of woodshedding with Legs, Shrapnel may be the only rock and roll band outwardly advocating World War III. They appear onstage wearing army fatigues and carrying models of M-16s. They use sandbags, cardboard tanks, and mock incendiary bombs as props. They sing songs entitled "Get the World," "Girls and Guns," "Special Forces Boy," and "Cro-Magnum Man." Their lyrics include stuff like, "I'm fresh from a Vietnam hangover / I got nothing to do / So I'm going to a Texas tower / and rain bullets down on you / down on you." Daniel, their lead singer, who was ten years old during the Tet Offensive and looks like a suckling-pig version of Legs, yells "Hey, you, asshole creep, I bet you were against the war," and drinks out of a canteen.

Clearly, this is an idea with limited commercial possibilities. How do you hype this band? "Hey, kids, get with Sgt. Rock Rock!" or "Listen to the Curtis Le May Sound!" What do you say about a band whose most melodic song is called "Combat Love"? It is almost as if the Vietnam War is another of the sixties things Legs feels deprived of. But it's consistent with his hipster view. The group's best song, "After the Battle," which Legs wrote, tells the story of a soldier who gets lost from his platoon in the middle of a firestorm. "Guys," he screams. "Where are you? Are you out there? Littlejohn, Kinch, Kowalski, anybody?" Kinch and Littlejohn and Kowalski, of course, were members of the platoon on *Combat*, the television show. It's just like Legs to call out for pop-culture characters when he's lost in the Modern World.

Perhaps only the apocalypse itself can be Legs's orgasm. But Shrapnel makes him happy, that's good enough for me. We've always been kindred spirits, two white boys trying to be cool. And no matter how seemingly disgusting Legs gets, I prefer to see him poetically: the man who tried to be hip in an unhip time.

Besides, it's kind of funny to watch Legs and the Shrapnels in the band's one-room apartment on St. Mark's Place. The kids sit around in their dog tags, reading *Soldier of Fortune* magazine and singing "Hey, hey, we're the Shrapnels. . . . We like to Shrapnel around." Legs says, "I like these kids because they're real teenagers. The way teenagers should be. They're normal, they like to read comics, watch television, and get drunk. Being with them makes me feel cool. I kind of look out for them."

Legs McNeil as a daddy, the mind boggles. But there is a certain tenderness in the way Legs gives his kids advice on how to be cool. The other day he was telling his guitar player, "Don't go out with Catholic girls. They never fuck you until a year after they get out of Catholic school. I know." Legs also takes the Shrapnels up to Connecticut, where they play "army" together in the swamps around Legs's mother's house. They split into two squads and fight to take the bridge over the Farmington Canal. Legs says, "My guys are good. They are so fucking good. They'll wait in a bush for two hours. I'd put my guys up against an A-team Green Beret outfit any day."

Personally, I like this image of an aging Legs McNeil playing army with his teenage kids. I see him sneaking around the edge of a brick wall, lying low in the tall reeds fertilized by the bodies of so many other soldiers before him. Then he bursts out into the line of murderous enemy fire, his toy gun waving, his high-pitched voice screaming "budda-budda-budda" like some wild, degenerate manically cool Holden Caulfield.

3
"I, Myron"

The tech revolution is a useful thing, but it has done much to denude the landscape of outlandish characters. It is a safe bet that there will never be a blogger like Myron Fass*. Story of a mogul. From the* Village Voice, *1978.*

Beneath the five-foot-square self-portrait of himself as Christ on the cross, Myron Fass, the king of pulp magazine kings, reached across a few hundred pounds of belly, unholstered the Gold Cup Colt .45 automatic he always wears, and pointed the gun out the twelfth-story window.

"Life," Myron said with a heave: "What is it? I live another twenty-five years, who cares? Twenty-five more revolutions around the sun. So what?"

Then Myron pulled the clip out of the ivory handled pistol and fingered the top slug. "This is an exploding bullet," he said, "its like a little hand grenade. . . . You don't have to shoot it for it to go off. Just drop it. Bam! It's dangerous. Why make all those trips around the sun just to die of cancer? I'd rather die in a gunfight."

With that, Myron stalked around his office ranging his frame past a stack of UFO and horror movie titles mass-marketed by his company, Country-Wide Publications, relating a story about the time some fools made the mistake of accosting him in a supermarket.

"Let's just say some walked away alive, some did not," said Myron, who announced he was in his "George Patton mind-set." This was not unusual, since Myron often channeled the flamboyant World War II general, "even before the movie." A student of history, Myron claims to hear voices of great men. Great men of the present, Myron says in reference to himself, will always have a direct line to great men of the past.

"I always thought that I'd conquer the world. Like Henry VIII," says Myron, stroking the fifty or so strands of blackish hair on his head. "But I wouldn't be like him. I'm more the Claudius type, to tell you the truth . . . a philosopher king, I have personal affinity for such an individual. What is the use of being king without a philosophy?"

Myron stops talking and sneers. "But all this is above your head."

Moments later, in his Howard Roark/tycoon mood, Myron pointed to his office door. On it in plain view—just so the peons outside know exactly who they're dealing with—is a Dun & Bradstreet report saying Country-Wide Publications grossed $25 million last year. This year, Myron says, the gross will double. In fact, Myron is presently the single largest "multi-title" newsstand publisher in the country. In the past twenty years, along with brothers Irving and Leo, he has put out magazines on hundreds of subjects. That's because, Myron says, "my lifestyle is diversified, so my books are. The books reflect the different aspects of me."

This seems true. Myron publishes dog books, so he has prizewinning mastiffs. He does horse books, so he has a horse farm in New Jersey. He puts out car and hot rod books, so he has a forty-six-thousand-dollar 6.9 Mercedes, a customized Cadillac, and a Three Deuces mint-stock Corvette. Myron has also published dozens of titles like *Shooting Bible*, *Shotgun Journal*, and *Competitive Shooting*, so he is an "NRA master" who fires five hundred rounds a week.

Most of the gun magazines are filled with stories signed by Myron and testimonials by "retired detectives" declaring Fass to be a "great gun expert" and "public-minded individual." Without much prodding you can get Myron to tell you his "Theory of Deadly Physical Force," which, he claims, has been used by the FBI and CIA. It is mostly filled with arcane physiological chatter about "focal concentration points," but the final tenet is quite definite.

"Always be sure to empty your gun into the perpetrator," Myron says. "You can never be too sure."

Just to put his gun-loving into historical perspective, the fall issue of *.44 Mag and Magnums* contains a photo of Myron next to a drawing of Wild Bill Hickock. The caption reads: "Several nostalgia buffs have said Myron Fass bears a striking resemblance to Wild Bill Hickock." Myron, tipping at least 275 pounds in his severely stressed polyester shirt, looks about as much like Wild Bill as he does Jesus Christ.

Myron also publishes a slew of pulp pop rags, titles like *Rock, Hard Rock, Groupie Rock,* and *Punk Rock* as well as *14 Fever* and *15 Fever*. These last two appear in alternate months. To make sure his bulbous thumb remains on the teen pulse, Myron's son is a rock star. Or will soon. According to Myron, son David, often credited as editor of the rock publications, "can't miss. I got Carlo Menotti, Sinatra's teacher, to give the kid singing lessons. . . . I don't think about college. Either this kid becomes a rock star or he goes on unemployment." It's David's power over women that will make him big, Myron says. "He's got total sexual charisma. . . . I had to break him up with three married women already, and he's only sixteen."

Of the forty-nine or so titles Myron will publish this month, half of them probably won't be around next year. That's Myron's style of publishing. He doesn't care about subscriptions—"I'm not in the business to give anything away. Look at *Life*, they gave everything away." Nor is advertising much of a factor. Most of the mags have close to none, although the UFO books do pick up quarter-pagers from the Rosicrucian Order. He gets the things out as fast and cheap as he can, then four-walls candy stores everywhere. If enough truck drivers and teenage television watchers lay out $1.50, profits flow (the break-even point is usually 35 percent sold). If not, he kills the title and comes up with another one.

Myron leaves the daily operation of the "regular" books to his long-suffering brother Irving and various "editors," who write all the stories under assorted assumed names, using the same pictures over and over again. This way Myron is free to use his "beautiful brain" to conceive "one-shots"—mags rushed out to take advantage of flash audience reaction to a personality, trend, or event. Country-Wide can do one in twenty-four hours. They are Myron's bread and butter. Over the past few years, he has one-shotted Twiggy, *Led Zep vs. Kiss*, Son of Sam, a million television shows, and every rotten teen star to come down the pike.

To hear Myron tell it, "one-shots," ephemeral though they may be (usually on the stands for less than a couple of weeks) are his enduring art form, his great gift to the pulp mag universe. They give him the opportunity to use his Claudius-like "gift for mass psychology and bullshit." Death is Myron's biggest winner. Not any kind of death, he says. "It has to be a fun death." The pope is not a fun death. Neither is random pestilence, cancer from smoking, or swine flu.

"I stepped in shit on swine flu. . . . We had a great book, interviews with doctors, everything. The day the book comes out, six people die from the vaccination. I looked up and said, 'God loves me.' But the thing didn't sell. It did 6 percent, if that. People just don't want that kind of death."

Myron says death has to work on the fantasy level. Elvis's death did; Myron made millions on it. Myron hopes his current rock death book *Frampton Dead?* will do half as well. It contains an "editorial" denouncing "those rich, greedy, swine at the record companies trying to start the lousy, ugly rumor that Peter Frampton is dead." Before Myron's book no one even knew Peter Frampton was supposed to be dead.

Myron's greatest death score was the Kennedy assassination. He sold 4 million copies all told on his increasingly salacious coverage of the president's death and the conspiracy theories to follow. The Kennedy shooting was so big, Myron philosophizes, because "it made people feel good. When someone dies, no matter what you thought of him, no matter how much you might have loved him, there's part of you that's going to feel good. Maybe in life this guy was way better than you, a better father, a better son, a better fuck. Doesn't matter if he was better than you in life; now he's nothing. Just dirt. That's what Kennedy was about. It was a chance for everyone to feel superior to the president of the United States."

Myron has the classic background of the New York Jewish schlockmeister. His father was an Orthodox immigrant who spent the Depression working in the sewers for the WPA. Myron grew up in Brownsville, where he used to gain attention through his drawing. Most of his pictures, now spread around the Country-Wide office, are like Kafka doing Walter Keane: dark and sombre Jews hunched up but with really big, cute eyes. During World War II, his talent and "ideas" led to PR work, and Myron claims that Harry Truman personally gave him a commendation for devising the anti-VD slogan, "You may think she's your gal, but she's anybody's pal . . . use a pro . . . a prophylactic."

Later, in the early fifties, Myron, like almost all the illustrators trying to make it in the New York pulp-publishing world, was intensely affected by the wise-ass hack-inspired approach of William Gaines' *Mad*. Myron immediately tried to copy the Gaines model and succeeded in getting some backing for *Lunatickle*, a would-be satire that includes such ha-has as Westbrook van Pegler tied up in a truss with Eleanor Roosevelt. "Sold a million first issue, was dead by the third," Myron recalls. Later he did a book called *Fotorama*, which he describes as "full of panties and crotch shots." During this time Myron also met celebrities, people like Jayne Mansfield, who, Myron says, "was great. Her kids would be around, wondering why everyone was so interested in Mommy's tits. But Jayne would do anything for publicity. What drive. She was great."

Why did Myron make it so big while so many others failed? It's easy, he'll tell you, its the philosopher-king thing. His studious reading of Plato. This led him to decisions to do things like put Jackie O on the cover a crummy *Photoplay* knockoff, which was big, because "everyone thought they were making a movie where they'd see her with her clothes off." But more than likely, he owes his longevity to his remarkable consistency of sleaze. Never once did Myron ever try to move up in class. His paper has always remained the cheapest, his common denominator always the lowest. Of all his books, only *Official UFO Handbook*, which runs articles entitled "Polyester Fabrics Are Created by Space Visitors," shows any inspiration whatsoever.

It is almost as if Myron has a will to sleaze. In this he is like many of the people who work on the fringes of the "name" magazine business. Plenty of these people are talented, many eccentrically and brilliantly so. But for one reason or another they cannot bring themselves to work for "class" publications. "I don't think I'll ever see the day my stuff appears without pendulous breasts around it," says one hack friend of mine. Asked if he would trade places with the boss of Time-Life, Myron says, "No . . . I wouldn't want to be like that. Sitting in an office, smoking a pipe, that's not for me." Then he wiped the remains of an apple off his face with his sleeve.

But Myron is at least as shrewd as he is crude. He's like a good-copy machine. He can't resist saying certain things he knows he shouldn't say. But it's exhausting, too. A conversation with Myron is like a visit to a sadistic dentist who keeps probing with different kinds of abuse until he finds the one wound that's tender. Then he rams the high-speed drill in there and leans on it.

Aside from describing his looks, the only way to fight back is to call Myron's magazines schlock. "Not schlock! Masterpieces on cheap paper," Myron screams. "They called Van Gogh schlock. You'd call Van Gogh schlock if he wasn't in the museum" (Van Gogh is another of Myron's soulmates, and he says he'd rather be remembered as "an artist" than as a publisher). But no doubt Myron is defensive about his baser output. If he sees you looking at the cover of one of his detective books—the ones with the women covered with whip marks—he'll rip it out of your hands. "You only want to see bad stuff. You're looking to take a cheap shot." He gives you some other magazines, saying, "Here, why don't you look at some of the cute stuff?" Among the magazines he gives you is *Larry Flynt,* which came out soon after the *Hustler* publisher was shot. It features a comic strip in which Al Goldstein goes to visit Flynt in the hospital. He wants to see Flynt's prick, only to find that it has been blown off. There is also a story called "You Know You're a Vegetable . . ." One drawing shows Flynt in bed. The caption is: ". . . when you have to squeeze your shit bag to ejaculate." Myron says, "I just wanted to give Flynt a little bit of what he gives everyone else. I thought he'd appreciate it . . . But I guess he didn't think it was funny. Some people can't laugh at themselves."

Myron likes to ring his secretary and have her bring him grapes. Then he can say, "Like Caesar, they bring me grapes." But some of the plebeians of Myron's domain are not merry at all. They say Myron keeps the $25 million statement on his door just to taunt them, since he pays them squat.

They also say working for Myron isn't like working for anyone else, except maybe Emperor Bokassa. They recall incidents of Myron chasing editors down the hallway screaming, "You're yellow, you haven't got the balls to quit me." They also remember the time Myron walked around the office with a cassette recorder asking who sat at each empty desk. When told whose desks the empties were, Myron talked into the recorder: "Nine-thirty, and X is not at her desk." They also talk about the memos, one of which supposedly instructed people whose last names began with A to L what time they could go to the bathroom.

They also say they really can't talk about this now because they're certain the office operator listens in on phone calls and reports conversations to Myron. They even say, weeks after Myron's already fired them (Myron fires most people. He's got an itchy trigger finger when it comes to firing), that they're afraid to talk on their home phones. They think Myron is tapping them. They know they're paranoid, but say that is what working for Myron can do to you.

Some of this school of thought is corroborated by the testimony of one Stanley Harris. Stanley Harris used to be Myron's partner. A couple of years ago he sued Myron because, he said, Myron was "unilaterally dealing with distributors . . . and threatening employees if they communicate with the plaintiffs." Harris also said, "On August 19, Mr. Fass . . . threatened my life and made menacing gestures. On other occasions in recent weeks Mr. Fass has come into my office wearing a loaded gun in a holster. . . . It is a ploy of Mr. Fass to so display this gun when he is in an argument. I am informed that many of the employees are intimidated by his wearing a loaded gun about the office."

Myron's reply to the suit's gun-intimidation charge was: "We publish several gun magazines and are constantly receiving guns and ammo in our office, so no one should be intimidated by the presence of a gun."

Myron does remember that one young employee "saw my gun and threw up." But he says he'd never use his gun to intimidate anyone, and, to be sure, he's very careful with the thing. "The employees think I have a bad temper," says Myron, hurt by charges of his insensitivity. "I'm really just a good actor. But, like Patton said, 'Only I know when I'm acting.'"

Besides, Myron says, it's not the business of the philosopher-king, even a schlockmeister philosopher-king, to trouble himself with the pettiness of rabble. He is above that. He says he spends most of his time "pondering, reflecting on me and my place in the world." Then he says, "What they don't know is I'm a manic-depressive. I think it's the best way to be. You're either up or down. Its like being the Incredible Hulk. He's a manic-depressive. When he's the monster, he's manic; he's up. When he's human, he's down, depressed. I think about that a lot. My monster side and my human side. Humanity is basically a depressing thing."

Then Myron shakes his head. "Why am I telling you this for? My God, I hate to talk to inferiors. I can't communicate with someone who doesn't offer me a challenge. You have a puny mind. Just tell them one thing in your article. Tell them I never did anything to hurt anyone." With that Myron grabbed his little black bag, the one he keeps his vitamins and gun clips in, and motioned that he was leaving. On the way out he rammed the bag into the leg of an employee. He did not look back.

4

The Father of Rock and Roll Turns Seventy-five, Irascibly

After three or four trips to St. Louis over the period of a couple months, Chuck Berry finally stood me up. Everyone said he would, sooner or later. Still I was surprised. We were getting along so well. But this time he left me in the hotel. Reached at Berry Park, his former amusement park home, Chuck said he was just too busy to keep our appointment. "I'm setting up some cement on this walkway here. Been cracked for years and can't let it go anymore. I've just got to fix it, today," he said. "You can't expect me to drop that, can you? If you can, then you better stop writing about me now, because you haven't learned a thing." Legends remain true to themselves, always. Rolling Stone, *2002.*

The people at the Frederick Brown Jr. Amphitheater in Peachtree City, Georgia, wanted to pay tribute to the Great Chuck on the occasion of the rock and roll avatar's seventy-fifth birthday. The plan was fairly straightforward. After Berry got done playing his show, a cake baked especially for the occasion would be wheeled out and everyone would sing "Happy Birthday."

"Can't do that," Chuck said, looking up from under the brim of his commodore's hat.

"But it won't be any big deal," the manager said.

Chuck looked up again, as one would at a buzzing fly. His contract assured that he'd sing "Maybelline" for close to the 3,800th time (he keeps rough notes, and claims accuracy within twenty-five performances). But there was nothing about any "surprise" birthday party. Fact is, the inventor of rock and roll does not like surprises, not onstage anyway.

"But all you'll have to do is stand there and smile," the portly manager continued, cluelessly.

"Stand there and smile?" Chuck said tightly. "No, no. That would be out of character for me."

The venue manager shifted his weight. He was well aware of the Berry reputation, gained while playing one-nighters, from deep in the heart of Texas to the Frisco Bay, all over St. Louie, down in New Orleans and just about everywhere else. The manager knew Chuck was supposed to be hard-nosed, not mellowed and made cuddly by the passing years like Smokey Robinson, Tony Orlando, Dion, or any of the other oldies who regularly play Peachtree, a peachtree-less swampland turned Atlanta bedroom community best known for its long, winding "golf cart access only" trails.

The manager knew that the first man ever inducted into the Rock and Roll Hall of Fame—*numero uno, Jack!*—was famous for showing up five minutes before showtime, playing exactly fifty-five minutes, and never, ever, doing encores. He knew this was the man who had once, and not exactly by accident, dropped a lit cigarette down the shirt of Rolling Stone Keith Richards. Richards later called his all-time hero "a bitch sometimes . . . worse than Jagger."

"But Mr. Berry," said the manager, "we'd never ask you to do anything out of character."

"You're not going to try and tell me what my character is, now are you?" Chuck said.

"Shit. Just stand there and smile," Chuck mocked in falsetto imitation after the manager had left the room. Then he narrowed his famous brown-eyed handsome-man eyes and said, "I'm not going to *shine* for anyone."

This appeared to settle the matter. Except when Chuck finished his set, the house lights went up a bit to reveal everyone in the sold-out theater, twenty-five hundred fans strong, holding a lit candle. A large, double-decker cake was wheeled out onto the stage.

The singing began: "Happy birthday, Chuck, happy birthday to you . . ."

Except the birthday boy was nowhere in sight. Before the first "happy," Chuck had his guitar unplugged and was stomping offstage. As strains of "Happy Birthday" filled the air, Chuck was already in a golf cart, streaking through the backstage area toward his dressing room. Moments later, as Chuck peeled the red spangled shirt from his sweaty, still exceedingly fit body, the venue manager appeared at the door.

"Mr. Berry . . . ?"

Now what?

"You shouldn't have pulled that stuff with the cake—I told you that was a no, a definite no."

"But Mr. Berry . . ." It seemed the mayor of Peachtree City, the chief justice of the Georgia Supreme Court, and one of former president Jimmy Carter's sons, all huge fans, were outside. Might Chuck do a quick meet-and-greet with them?

"Meet and what?" Chuck seethed. There had been no discussion of meets or greets, not with the Mayor, not with the Judge, not even with any President's son, especially not the president who was in office when the feds stuck Chuck in Lompoc Prison and made him play a thousand hours of benefit shows due to a small accounting oversight.

From outside the dressing room door came the sound of Southern voices, loud, boisterous, full of privilege. Chuck sat there a moment, fanning himself, listening.

"No, sorry," he said. "No time now. Just tell them I am in the midst of justifying this elderly frame of mine. That ought to explain it."

Which means: When you're Chuck Berry, you're seventy-five years old, and you invented rock and roll, you can do—or not do—anything you want. Got that? And if you didn't know it, now you do, so tell Tchaikovsky the news.

* * *

In the oversized pantheon of personalities who came together in the 1950s to devise the miscegenist music Alan Freed named rock and roll, Elvis, the mythic white boy who could sing black, might have been the Zeus King, Little Richard the flaming Afro-dite, Jerry Lee Lewis the twice-born-again redneck Dionysus. But Charles Edward Anderson Berry, left-field Orphic/Yoruban poet-trickster, was and remains the key dropper of science, the Promethean intellectual of the bunch. Combining the common touch of an auto assembly line worker and a hairdresser's flair with pomade (and a diploma from St. Louis Poro School of Beauty to prove it), Chuck was the slick-pattered everyman, poet of the nine to five workaday humdrum, which Berry sought to undermine with his "drop the coin right into the slot, got to hear something that really rocks" subversive ethic.

With marginal help from people like James Dean and Marlon Brando, Chuck Berry conjured half the tropes of how pre-Beatle teenagers supposedly thought and acted—all that malt shop shit the creators of Archie comics whitened up—but the author of "School Days" was never a teen sensation. Twenty-six before he made his first dime playing music, Chuck was always a man, his own man. He doesn't care to be linked with his fellow old-time rockers.

"People think because we played shows together forty years ago I'm on the phone talking to Little Richard and Bo Diddley about the state of the world every day," says Chuck.

It is always that, Chuck says, "stupid assumptions just because I wrote 'Roll Over Beethoven.'" Even if he did drop out of St. Louis's Sumner High after the tenth grade, Chuck, ever the avid autodidact, has always been a reader. Fond of history and biography, he carried a copy of Albert Einstein's *The World as I See It* on the road with him for years, if for no other reason than to lord his fellow rock pioneers. Never one to suffer condescension lightly, Chuck rails about interviewers who misquote him, using words like "lawdy," exactly the sort of "rank Southernism" his schoolteacher mother taught him to rise above.

For Chuck, issues of race and class are never very far below the surface. "My mother never imagined we were white . . . because we were black, that was plain as day. But it was her plan that I be able to mix with whatever people I wished and do it in a correct way so as not to stereotype myself." From the beginning, Chuck, perhaps the most puissant "crossover" artist (outside of Elvis) in the history of twentieth-century pop music, has done his best to transcend typical race boundaries. Always a country fan, Chuck's blues was influenced by much time spent listening to Kitty Wells and Hank Williams and Little Jimmy Dickens. Once Roy Acuff described him as "that black hillbilly."

"Race matters, they can lay you low, or you can be savvy about them. Everything can be beaten, if one is smart and patient, and lucky," says Chuck, a black man who has spent most of his life playing almost exclusively for whites. For him, Chuck says, racial divides have always been a mysterious thing. On one hand he suffered from segregation like most everyone else growing up in the borderlands of Missouri. Early tours through the South included the usual soul-wrenching restrictions on what hotels he could stay in, which women he could date. Yet for much of his career, people encountering him for the first time were amazed to find out he was black.

"They hear the music, they take it into their heart, like it is their own, and they find out it was written by a black man, exactly the kind of person they would never allow to sit in their living room. That is a pretty unique feeling. In fact, as you can see, I am fairly dark-skinned. Yet many people tell me, in the right light, I even *look* white."

This is how it is with Chuck Berry, a big topic, who arrives with enough skittish race discourse and cool-breeze codes to keep whole American Studies departments knee-deep in subtext for semesters on end.

Case in deeply nuanced point is the story of how Chuck came to write "Sweet Little Sixteen." Number one on the R&B charts, number two on pop, the tune is one of the hallowed Great 28, the title of Chuck's most comprehensive greatest hits package, which includes such iconic fare as "Johnny B. Goode," "You Can't Catch Me," "Brown-eyed Handsome Man," "Memphis," "Rock and Roll Music," "Nadine," and "Havana Moon." Or, in other words, the near total fun side of rock's Rosetta Stone. Chuck talks about "Sweet Little Sixteen" in his endlessly entertaining, fabulously dirty, self-penned (among musician tell-alls, only Charlie Mingus's likewise sexed-up *Beneath the Underdog* comes close) autobiography, issued in 1987.

The song came out of an incident after a show in Ottawa, Canada, Chuck writes. "A small German doll . . . was in flight . . . mainly interested in getting autographs in her fat little Mickey Mouse wallet that she held like the torch on the Statue of Liberty." There were other autograph hounds, but it was this "pretty little tot" who was "actually around seven or eight" who "molded" in his memory, says Chuck, who was "one year past thirty at the time."

By the time he got around to writing the song's lyrics, Berry recalls now, "I was playing in Kansas City, staying in a four-story brick-faced hotel. It wasn't a high-class place, not at all. I was a star, but still this was the sort of place we had no choice but to stay in in those days. You had to strain to throw open the windows. I sat there on the bed and wrote out the verses: sweet little sixteen, just got to have about half a million framed autographs . . . sweet little sixteen, tight dresses and lipstick, sportin' high heel shoes . . . sweet little sixteen, with the grown-up blues . . ."

So there you have it, sweet little rock and rollers, a peek into the petri dish of the alchemical Dr. Berry. "Sweet Little Sixteen," and so many of the founding tropes of The Great (White) American Teenager, was synthesized in a Jim Crow hotel room by a thirty-one-year-old black man. A thirty-one-year old black ex-con, it might be added, a "downbound trainee in bandidoism." This owed to a "youthful spree" in which Chuck helped rob a bakery, barber shop, and clothing store, "a series of transgressions" that netted him a three-year term in Missouri's Algoa Reformatory. A singular ex-con he was, too, with a well-developed Nabokovian sex/race fantasy, in which a little Aryan doll, eight years old, was transmuted into a spike-heel *American Bandstand* rumpshaker whom "all the cats want to dance with."

It is kinky, but then again, any frat boy who ever saw that legendary home video of Chuck supposedly banging a groupie and then blasting a giant fart in her face knows of the rock and roll inventor's kinkiness. Chuck may not drink or do drugs, but he does, in his autobiography, admit, in apparent seriousness, to "have had a desire since childhood to be houseboy on a Southern plantation, preferably during the Civil War." More ominous are the tales about how he reputedly installed video cameras in the women's bathrooms of his Southern Air restaurant, in Wentzville, thirty miles west of St. Louis. Similar charges were lodged about the bathrooms at Berry Park, the hundred-acre erstwhile amusement park/campgrounds, also in Wentzville, where Chuck once hosted picnics for fifty thousand hippies at a time and imagined a potential rock and roll Disneyland. A class action suit citing invasion of privacy was filed by several women, which Berry eventually settled.

"I confess to schizophrenia," Chuck has said. "There is me, Charles Berry, and there is me, Chuck Berry. Sometimes you get the overlap, sometimes not. It is a controlled kind of schizophrenia, and I'm controlling it."

Well, kind of. For years Chuck swore straightfacedly, even defiantly, that he had never served a single day of time following his infamous 1959 arrest under the Mann Act for supposedly transporting Janet Escalante, a fourteen-year old Spanish-speaking Apache prostitute, across state lines for "immoral purposes."

"Nothing really came of it," Chuck told Patrick William Salvo in a 1972 issue of *Rolling Stone*. "You see, there were two or three different trials and one was thrown out of the courts because the judge was fairly biased, and finally I was acquitted, you see. That's the misconceptions that people have, that Chuck Berry went to jail."

But, of course, Chuck Berry did go to jail. It is true that Chuck's first conviction was overturned after it was found that United States District Judge George H. Moore "intended to disparage the defendant by repeated questions about race during the trial." But a year later, on October 28, 1961, the *St. Louis Post-Dispatch* reported the affirmation of "the conviction of Charles E. (Chuck) Berry, rock and roll singer and former night club owner" on the Mann Act. Escalante testified that Chuck "had been intimate" with her "in each of four states." U.S. District Judge Roy W. Harper sentenced him to three years in prison and a five-thousand-dollar fine.

The last paragraph of the *Dispatch* article said simply, "Berry is a negro."

It is a sordid tale, full of implications of racial, sexual railroading. The incident, which stopped the career of the man John Lennon called "the best songwriter, ever" right smack in its prime left Chuck Berry a bitter, suspicious man. Some say he has never recovered, never let himself relax again, that he will forever hold a grudge. In his autobiography, he recalls being transported to a federal medical facility near Springfield, Missouri, "somewhere near the Ozarks of Misery," where he would serve time. Waiting to be handed his prison clothes, he remembers thinking of a little poem. *"Down from stardom, then I fell, to this lowly prison cell / far from fortune, far from fame, where a number quotes my name."* He'd stay inside until October 18, 1963, his thirty-seventh birthday, when his wife Themetta picked him up from the prison in his Cadillac, which Chuck then drove home.

Part of Chuck's ground rules for interviews is that there be no "drawn-out questions about my so-called sexual peccadilloes," nothing about the videotapes or the stories Keith Richards tells about how Berry keeps two TV sets going in his living room, one with the Discovery Channel and the other showing loops of naked women throwing pies in each other's face. But none of this is really news. Everyone knows the rumors about Chuck.

Sure, he's kinky, yet somehow, after all these years, "Sweet Little Sixteen," which Chuck continues to sing, night after night, at age seventy-five, has never ceased to imbue a mystic sweet sock-hop innocence, a dreamworld of adolescent longing, both roused and doomed by "the grown-up blues." Which, of course, is the essence of Chuck Berry's unassailable achievement. The world may be big, full of strange trips, but there's hardly a sentient being alive, then or now, who doesn't get a little bit happy when a Chuck Berry song comes on the radio.

Today, Chuck, who continues to maintain his innocence (he says he had no idea how old Escalante was and that people were out to get him because his Club Bandstand catered to an interracial crowd) still doesn't want to discuss the case. Still, Chuck rubs his newly grown goatee in pleased surprise when he hears that others of the very few ever convicted of the Mann Act—formerly known as "the white slave act" and still on the books today—include the great black heavyweight champion Jack Johnson and Charlie Chaplin, whose failed prosecution was personally instigated by FBI chief J. Edgar Hoover himself.

"Jack Johnson, Chaplin, and me . . . I guess that's good company," he says.

But once you mention that perhaps America has a way of attacking its truly groundbreaking artists, Chuck gets testy. "This is the greatest country on earth, of that there is no doubt," he fires back, like some insulted Okie from Muskogee. "You know 'Back in the USA'? I was in Australia, and I found out they wouldn't even let a black man become a citizen there. That's why I wrote that song, 'Back in the USA.'

"You know 'Back in the USA,' *don't you?*"

This is how it is with Chuck Berry: put him up with Jack Johnson and Chaplin and he looks at you like you're some kind of commie, insufficiently loyal to the long freeways and those hamburgers sizzling on a red-hot griddle night and day.

Tell him his song "Promised Land," the mini-odyssey of a poor boy's journey from Norfolk to L.A., was praised in W. T. Lhamon's interesting tome *Deliberate Speed—The Origins of a Cultural Style* in the American 1950s as being "as apocalyptic as Martin Luther King Jr.'s last speech improvised in Memphis at the Mason Temple . . . the night before he was killed."

"People think up all kinds of things," Chuck says, rolling his eyes.

Mention that Russell Simmons, the hip-hop impresario, says there's an unbroken line between "Johnny B. Goode" and such crossover geniuses as Hendrix (who backed Berry while playing in the Curtis Knight band), P-funker George Clinton (also a hairdresser), and "the street talk of a hundred rappers," and Chuck becomes pissed.

"All those m-words and f-words, can't blame me for that," he says. "I'd rather hear Tommy Dorsey or Artie Shaw any day."

Inquire about his greatest moment in half a century of show business and he mentions a framed poster on the wall of his house. "Tonight, Chuck Berry," it says, and in little letters, "Extra Added Attraction, Ray Charles."

"Imagine," Chuck marvels, "the Genius opening for me, I'm still thrilled by that."

Tell Chuck he means as much to you as any of the people he's mentioned—and a fuck of a lot more than Harry Belafonte, Sammy Davis, or Bing Crosby—and he just looks at you with pity, poor benighted soul that you are.

"Look, I ain't no big shit, all right," he snorts.

"I wanted to play blues. But I wasn't blue enough. I wasn't like Muddy Waters, people who really had it hard. In our house, we had food on the table. We were doing well, compared to many. So I concentrated on this fun and frolic, these silly novelties. I wrote about cars because half the people had cars, or wanted them. I wrote about love, because everyone wants that. I wrote songs white people could buy, because that's nine pennies out of every dime . . . I've never had Nat King Cole's diction, Maya Angelou's poetic imagination, Duke Ellington's musical excellence. Nothing close to that. I had one goal, *my only goal:* to look at my bankbook and see a million dollars there . . . That satisfy you?"

The look on Chuck's face tells you that the discussion is closed. Think whatever you want about him. Just keep it to yourself.

So you take Chuck Berry as he comes. Which is: alone, a solitary traveling salesman/cowboy of the big beat, arriving in one city after another with nothing more than the well-used yet still glittery jewels of the Great 28. All that is in his contract, the same one he's used for years, a couple of pages of black and white, one of the shortest and most ironclad in the music business.

"I require two things," says Chuck. "A Lincoln Town Car at the airport and a Fender Bassman amp." If the promoter sends a stretch limo, or even a fifty-foot Mercedes with UFO running lights, Chuck sends it back. "They say, forget the Lincoln, this is better, I tell them I didn't say better, I said a Lincoln . . . I want what I want. If they do not provide the proper amp, there is a two-thousand-dollar fine, paid in advance." This penalty has been invoked "exactly twenty-four times," says Chuck, who has "a very good head for numbers."

One more item he asks for is "to be provided with able musicians, that is, musicians able to play Chuck Berry songs."

This is a point of much consternation amongst rock and roll lovers, since Chuck has long been famous for using whichever bar band happens to be in town to back him up. It has been said, most prominently by Keith Richards in *Hail, Hail Rock and Roll,* that this apparent total disregard of quality control on Chuck's part is something of a self-imposed kind of desecration. Pissing on the legacy, so to speak. On the other hand, however, there is a kind of egalitarian, typically garage rock spirit to Berry's seeming indifference. Because really: How can any band play *any* rock and roll song unless they can play Chuck Berry songs?

The night Chuck played Peachtree, Georgia, hanging out in the dressing room with a group of "able" musicians—able to play Chuck Berry songs—it was a half hour before showtime, but Chuck was nowhere to be seen. The concert promoter was starting to pace up and down, but the band, Freewheelin', out of New York, guys who had played with Chuck before, knew he'd be there.

"If the money's up, Chuck is always there," says Dick Alen, who's been Chuck's agent for going on fifty years. "He never blows a show," testifies Alen, comparing Chuck to his other immortal client, Little Richard. "With Richard things are always in flux. He calls at the last minute to tell you he needs twenty more tickets for his friends. Or that he can't go on because his hair isn't right, or that he's had some dream about not going out of the house that particular day. But Richard is really a sweetheart. Things go wrong, he's flexible. He can adjust. Chuck does not adjust. He doesn't have any give in him. He sticks to the plan, never changes."

To illustrate Chuck's adherence to his set script, Alen recalled an incident from several years ago. "I booked Chuck into a big hall in Philly. But there was this huge blizzard. The town was under ten feet of snow. The mayor closed the airport, they were about to call out the National Guard. So what does Chuck do? He flies to Pittsburgh, rents a car, drives three hundred miles on the turnpike. Somehow he gets there. He goes to the theater and the place is closed. The whole town is shut down. But Chuck demands to be paid. He's going to sue. And why not? He was there."

Nowadays, Chuck, a wealthy man, gets something like thirty-five thousand dollars for gigs like Peachtree, and sure enough, there he was, tearing into the parking lot in his rented Lincoln looking extra fine in his white slacks, blue blazer, and captain's hat. Yes, it was cutting it a bit close, but he'd changed his flight. His sister needed a tree removed from her yard back in St. Louis, so he'd spent the morning out at her property pulling the thing out with his backhoe.

But what was the big deal, the show wasn't due to start until 9:00 and it was hardly past 8:40.

Then, after smacking forearms with the band, his usual greeting, Chuck suddenly remembered something. Pivoting on the heel of his patent leather shoe, he went back out the door and walked across the parking lot. It was raining lightly now, with streaks of lightning high in the sky. Through the half-drawn blinds, the vision could take your breath away: watching Chuck Berry, six-foot-three brown-eyed handsome man, stride through the slanting rain, open up the Lincoln's trunk, and take out his big red guitar.

A couple weeks later, rolling through traffic on I-170, west of the downtown St. Louis neighborhood where he was born, at 2520 Goode Avenue, it figured Chuck would be in a brand-new Fleet De Ville, something low and sleek with "jet-fuel off-take" and "a Murphy bed in the backseat" like in "No Money Down." Or at least a V-8 Ford. Instead, Chuck was behind the wheel of a Toyota Avalon, tuned to NPR.

He had a fleet of vehicles out at Berry Park, Chuck acknowledged, right beside the twenty-six-thousand-dollar fallout shelter he built for himself back in the sixties just in case those trigger-happy Russians had a mind to take out Wentzville. There was also a Mercedes at his house in St. Louis's blueblood Ladue section, if he had a mind to burn a little rubber past the Bellerive Country Club as the log cabin Republicans lined up their putts on the sixteenth hole. But as for driving around town, the Toyota was best.

"In a Toyota, the cops don't think about stopping you so much," said America's leading poet of things automotive.

A few minutes later, Chuck is inside the Four Seasons recording studio. It is a momentous day. Chuck Berry, rock and roll godhead, has not been in a studio (excluding the one he built in his house) in seventeen years. He hasn't recorded an album of original material in more than twenty. His last widely distributed record was the underappreciated *Rockit*, made in 1979 and notable mostly for its guitar grooves. Not counting the stirring fugitive narrative "Tulane," released in 1970, and the fluke toiletry item called "My Ding-A-Ling" in 1972 (it is "an irony," Chuck admits, that after years of "artful disguising" of suggestive lyrics, he finally made number one with a nakedly blatant high school jackoff tune), Berry hasn't put out any sides of artistic or commercial significance since the middle 1960s. This underscores the usual theory about how Chuck's bitterness over the Mann Act imprisonment did much to take the heart out of what was one of America's greatest songwriting careers.

"For many years I've been reluctant to record songs," Chuck says. "There has been a great laziness in my soul. There were days I could write songs, but I could also take my four hundred dollars and play the slot machines at the casino. In a way I feel it might be ill-mannered to try and top myself. You see, I am not an oldies act. The music I play, it matters to people. People want to hear it a certain way. How they remember it. I honor that. I wouldn't want to interfere with that. I don't live in the past, but I am part of it for a lot of people. I have to respect that, especially now that it is so far into the future."

Now, however, Chuck, with uncharacteristic nervousness, has declared himself ready to augment the famous Berry canon, perhaps even add one or two numbers to the Great 28. Arriving with half a dozen cardboard boxes full of half-inch tapes containing various demos, Chuck says he has enough stuff for a whole new album, maybe even two. There are also piles of sheet music, stacks of looseleaf paper.

A page slips out and flutters to the floor. Dog-eared, it is the original lyric sheet of "Havana Moon," Berry's fabulously languorous, three-minute rock opera of tropical lost love. Chuck agrees that the tune is one of his best, but he doesn't care for it much since it hasn't generated much in royalties. Chuck attributes this lack of sales to "Fidel Castro, the whole communist Cuba association of Havana." In fact, he's seriously thinking of rerecording the tune on the new record, moving the locale to Kingston, and changing the title to "Jamaica Moon." For someone who has always loved "Havana Moon," this seems a bizarre notion, but Chuck, not the sentimental type, only shrugs as he picks up the fallen lyric sheet and shoves it back in the cardboard box.

A moment later, Chuck, the pearl buttons of his billowy white cowboy shirt and a stone inlay of his string-tie clasp shining in the vapor light, is behind the studio glass making a speech. "I don't know what you're thinking, but I am not going to be paranoid," he announces to Dave Torretta, a guitarist who once toured with Chuck and is now serving as his producer, and Joe Edwards, St. Louis's cultural patron/icon and owner of the Blueberry Hill Club over in the city's redeveloped University Loop, where Berry plays once a month.

"I am not going to be pushy or bossy or use the f-word," Chuck says. "I am an employee here just like anyone."

Chuck begins to work on the initial vocal track for "Dutchman," an expressionistic hip-hop/campfire-tale-cum-rap about "this huge, dark dude" who "cracks the barroom door" and tells a bunch of tired drunks the story of his amazing life and times. There's "Lady Be Goode," a feminized version of the old classic. Following this is "Loverman," a slow blues ballad, "The Big Boys," an up-tempo rocker with a signature Chuck guitar solo right out of "Maybelline," and "Loco Joe," a rewrite of "Jo Jo Gunne," a story set "*way back in evolution, 4000 BC / back in the jungle up a coconut tree.*"

Off a first listen, it doesn't sound like there are any late classics here. Still, it is a thrill, hearing Chuck make new (ish) music, to listen to his ever-inviting tenor, unthickened by age, tumble over you. Close your eyes and it would have been no great a leap to imagine yourself back in Leonard Chess's Chicago studio, with Chuck running through "Rocking and Reeling" one last time. But no one stays a sweet little sixteen forever (even if they never were). The highlight of the session is "Darling," a slow ballad about getting old, hair going gray, which is a long way from being a professional teenager.

"You know," Chuck shouts from the other side of the glass, "maybe it is true, what they say, that playing these Chuck Berry songs is easy. But try singing them. The words come out hard, like bullets."

Later on, back in the Toyota, Chuck is talking about how he imagines he'll be remembered. Even with the Hall of Fame election and his recent stint at the Kennedy Center, where he was honored (along with Clint Eastwood, Angela Lansbury, and Mikhail Baryshnikov) for his "contributions to American and world culture," Chuck is still suspicious. "There are always people around to toss dirt on what you've done," he says, sulkily.

Only last year, Johnnie Johnson, Chuck's famous piano player, filed suit against his old boss, contesting the authorship of many of Chuck's best-known songs, including "Roll Over Beethoven," "Rock and Roll Music," and "No Particular Place to Go." The suit alleges that Chuck "took advantage" of Johnson's chronic alcoholism and good nature to cheat the pianist out of his "rightful share" of royalties.

In ol' St. Looie, where the faces of both men adorn the University Loop Walk of Fame, the dispute has been a hot topic. Most people side with Chuck, pointing out that Johnson, while quite beloved, never wrote any hits prior to his association with Chuck and hasn't written any since. There's widespread feeling that Johnson, who has recently been touring under the outrageous billing "Father of Rock & Roll" (despite the fact that he does not even play on Chuck's supposed tribute to him, "Johnny B. Goode"), is quite possibly under the influence of greedy hangers-on.

"This is a shame," says Joe Edwards, who continues to book both men at his club. "I'm all for Johnnie getting whatever credit is due him, but he shouldn't do it at Chuck's expense. I think we know who created that sound, and it wasn't Johnnie Johnson."

"The lawyers are handling that," Chuck says with a shrug. "The judge already dismissed something like twenty-nine of the ones he claimed he wrote. People are upset about it, but personally, I don't care. I like Johnnie. He was a friend of mine. I hired him to come play on some things for this new record. He played, he got paid, never said a thing to my face. So I can't spend time thinking about that."

Certainly it's not on his mind tonight, at Edwards' Blueberry Hill. It has been a long day, with the morning spent at the former site of Berry Park, working alongside his good buddy James Williams (they were partners in crime before going to the Algoa Reform School fifty years ago), digging a drainage ditch. But Chuck says he's "feeling fine, ready to rock." Seventy-five might be nothing but a minor speed bump in Chuck's life, considering how longevity runs in his family. His maternal grandfather lived to be 104, "and he smoked," says Chuck, who quit years ago and now figures he's good for at least 105.

"And maybe more!" he shouts, pointing at the ceiling. "Hey, Elvis! Still here, man!"

Blueberry Hill is something of a Berry shrine, with old show posters, mounted guitars, and framed Alan Freed contracts. Chuck likes playing for the hometown crowd and the sprinkling of Euro tourists stopping in to see the American master at twilight. He even gets there half an hour early, to chow down on a couple of chicken wings. "Can't beat this," Chuck says, picking at the wings in the tiny dressing room beneath a black-and-white photo of him in his prime, duckwalking in a silk suit.

For Chuck, however, the best thing about the Hill gig is that he gets to play with his children, the fabulous Ingrid, a singer and schoolteacher, slinkily attired in the manner of Billie Holiday, and Chuck Jr., a systems analyst/guitar player in a George Clinton T-shirt. Chuck Jr., outgoing and regular, sports studious-looking horn-rim glasses, which prompts his father to say, "Who do you think you are, Malcolm X?"

"It's been wonderful, really," says Ingrid, herself a mother, about life as Chuck Berry's kid. "It's true, there were hard times, and a lot of traveling. But he was still Father. We still felt watched, we still felt loved, we still obeyed."

The show—as they always are at Blueberry Hill—is tremendous. Chuck even duckwalks across the stage during "Johnny B. Goode." The first time he duckwalked, which he calls "scooting," was under the dining room table of his youth. "I was about nine. I guess I did it to get attention." It wasn't until nearly twenty years later, while playing the Brooklyn Paramount with the Red Prysock Band, that he scooted in public. "I just did it," he says. "It wasn't planned. People liked it, so I kept it."

And so it goes, on and on, because at Blueberry Hill, the timer inside Chuck's head, the one that buzzes after exactly fifty-five minutes, has been turned off. "You don't know how good this makes me feel!" Chuck shouts to the crowd, unguarded at last.

After the show, Chuck gladly does a meet-and-greet for the line of fans snaking away from his dressing room door. One by one they enter for autographs, and to get their picture taken with the first man ever inducted into the Rock & Roll Hall of Fame.

"Saw you in '57 and again in '58, in Philly," says a retired plumber. "Saw you open for the Dead at the Fillmore," says a ponytailed pet store owner.

"Got every single you ever made," says someone who drove in from Kansas City, handing Chuck a 45 of "Nadine."

"When did I record this? 1844?" Chuck asks with a grin, affixing his flamboyant autograph to the disc to which he adorns with a happy face.

"You're the best," somebody says.

"Lies!" Chuck replies.

"The King!"

"More lies."

"You're the handsomest man in the world," a middle-aged woman in lime-colored polyester pants says, sitting on Chuck's lap.

"Ah, finally, a bit of truth," Chuck Berry says, bouncing her on his knee.

5

Yoko in the Dakota Twilight

On the legends tour. New York *magazine, 2003.*

Her hair is still black, her glasses still rectangular, except now she is seventy, born in 1933, the same year Adolf Hitler took over Germany, only weeks after FDR's first inauguration. This is late in the game to have a number one dance track, but Yoko Ono, who finished recording the original, unremixed version of "Walking on Thin Ice" in December 1980, hours before her husband, John Lennon, was shot dead in front of their Dakota apartment home, is a singular little old lady. Daughter of a wealthy Japanese banker (the emperor's sons were her classmates), survivor of the Tokyo firebombing, often deeply underappreciated visual and aural artist, nightmarish singer, real estate magnate (asked if she's bought up all the Dakota apartments, she says, "not yet"), Yoko has lived *a life*.

"My situation now . . . is . . . unique," she says in her softly accented voice as she sits, a tiny, oddly nervous woman in a forest green sweater, on a giant snow white couch in an art-filled, sunswept living room that overlooks Strawberry Fields, where the vendors hawk postcards of John wearing his famous New York City T-shirt.

It isn't anything "you get used to, this type of fame" says Yoko.

This is one of the reasons she is so gratified by the success of "Walking on Thin Ice," Yoko says. When they first laid down the track, John turned to her and said, "This is going to be your first number one hit." It was the day before he was shot. "It took twenty-three years to prove John right, but it has happened, and that pleases me as well as makes me sad. But there is much that makes me sad," Yoko says, with her Da Vinci half smile, adding that she plans on calling the *Guinness Book of Records* to make sure that she is the oldest artist ever to have a number one dance hit.

"I never thought of it as just screaming," Yoko says, gratified to hear that many think her musical work with John, especially in the Plastic Ono band, holds up better than a good deal of the late Beatles catalog, not to mention whole stretches of Paul McCartney's solo oeuvre.

Not that she plans on returning to the stage or recording. Rather, her days are often passed "working ten o'clock until five" on legal and commercial aspects of Lennon's never-ending career. Their son Sean sometimes stopping by, John remains central in her life. With the advent of the Iraq War, Yoko thought of restaging the couple's famous anti-Vietnam "bed-in." "But I thought, how can I do this without John? I considered using a cardboard John. But that would not be very nice, a cardboard John. Who wants to stay in bed for a week with cardboard?"

These days, when Yoko goes out, it is usually to eat with friends at local coffee shops, "with breakfast specials." She also enjoys long walks in Central Park. Asked if it bothers her, walking past the tourists who congregate every day around the entrance of the Dakota and across the street at Strawberry Fields in Central Park, Yoko, sitting in her parlor room surrounded by her three Magrittes (John's favorite painter because "he always saw himself as that man in the bowler hat"), sighs.

"Perhaps, people think it is morbid, me still living here . . . but this is my home. They look up to my window and think, oh, she's right up there. This is how I get around unnoticed. I wait for them to look up, then I scurry by."

Then Yoko brightens, wry and winningly. She supposes that this would be a grand time, if John had lived, the two of them together, celebrating Yoko's surprise number one. "We really were a perfect New York couple, you know," Yoko says. "Two immigrant artists, here in this place. It was the only city that made sense for us."

My half-hour audience now finished, standing by the door beside Yoko's sculpture of a dozen blue Siamese cats with yellow glowing eyes, I tell her:

"My wife was the biggest Beatles fan. From the beginning. She really loved them."

"Oh," Yoko says, almost with a wince. "Does she hate me too?"

It is an old saw: that Yoko, woman of color, used some avant art spell to steal John's rock and roll heart and break up the world's most beloved band. It was stupid then, stupid now, but for Yoko the spectre of bad feelings seems quite real.

"No," I say. "She said that anyone who made John Lennon happy must be a very good person."

Yoko looks relieved. She extends her hand, touches mine. "Thank her for that, please."

6
The Hippest Guy in the Room

Not everyone gets Humphrey Bogart to play them in the movies. The story of the ultimate been-everywhere, done-everything knock-around guy. A prince of a man, and a good friend. From Esquire, *1992.*

The last time I saw Harold Conrad, he was lying in a hospital bed wearing dark sunglasses. Leave it to Harold to stake out a small territory of cool amid the fluorescent lighting, salt-free food, and stolid nurses bearing bedpans. The results were in by then, a tale told in black shadows on X-ray transparencies: one in the lung, the other in the head. But Harold always had an angle, and even now, a step from death, the cancer throughout his eighty-year-old body, he sought a hedge.

He motioned me closer, rasped into my ear, "Did you bring a joint?"

A few weeks later, after Harold died, I told this story at a memorial service. It got a laugh. Several of Harold's old friends were there, telling Harold Conrad stories. Norman Mailer recalled the evening Harold once saved his life. Mailer was drunk that night, he didn't notice the television set falling off the shelf above him, hardly even saw Harold, stronger than he looked, snatch the machine out of midair.

"Harold Conrad preserved half my head," Mailer said.

Budd Schulberg (author of *What Makes Sammy Run?*) talked about a wild week in Dublin, where Harold found himself promoting a Muhammad Ali fight and how everyone lost money when the crowd stormed the gates because, people said, "It is an insult to ask an Irishman to pay to see a fight." Bill Murray recollected a particularly gelatinous massage and steam-bath procedure Harold once directed him to. "I was trapped. Melting away. Soon I would be a wet spot on the floor. And I said: I used to be somebody before I met this Harold Conrad." These stories got laughs, which was only right. Harold would never tolerate a wake that didn't turn into a celebration; that would go double for his own.

You could say this about Harold Conrad, newspaperman, superflack, friend to bard and bozo, custodian of a bygone age—he went out on his forever-bent shield. It was Harold's life mission: to be in his own particular vision of the right place at the right time.

Like just two months before he died, when we were in Vegas.

Harold had been to Vegas before, of course, about 9 million times. In fact, along with almost every other bit of semi-off-brand action worth a tumble in this hot-breathed century of ours, Harold Conrad was in Vegas at the beginning, before they even threw the switch on the first neon sign. Ground-floor kind of guy, Harold. It was Bugsy Siegel (Ben to you) who got him out to the desert back in '48, when the Strip was nothing but a dusty two-lane highway between here and L.A.

"I need you. Today," Siegel summoned. In the way of Aeneas, Bugs was possessed by a revelatory calling to found a great city. His Flamingo Hotel, all pink and heat-waved in the sun's blare, was ready to open, and he needed a mouthpiece, a PR sharpie to sling his ink, say how wholesome and all-American the slots and hookers were going to be. Harold had the bona fides. He'd handled the publicity for Meyer Lansky and the boys in Florida when they bought the Broward County sheriff and ran a Colonial Inn–cum–gambling joint down near Lauderdale in '47; he was wise as to what to put in the papers and what to keep out, how to smooth over the rough spots.

There was the time Harold helped the boys, fixing that dicey scene with Walter Winchell. Winchell was on a gangbusters kick, making noise in his column about blowing Lansky's whole operation. Winchell was big, you couldn't muscle him. No one knew what to do until Harold, just out of the Air Force's 101 Bomber Command, was riding in the car with Meyer, Frank Costello, and Joe Adonis. Never shy, Harold told the mobsters they had it wrong if they thought they could get tough with Winchell. The columnist was a royal prick, but he had this soft spot for Damon Runyon, who was dying at the time. A five-thousand-dollar check to the Damon Runyon Cancer Fund, of which Winchell was the chairman, would help, Harold suggested. It did, too, but a well-placed word that a cute little number from Kansas City—whom Winchell had been known to eyeball—was working in the Colonial chorus line didn't hurt either.

But the truth was, Harold didn't really care to work for gangsters, which is why he turned down Bugsy Siegel. "Can't help you," Harold said to Siegel as the gangster showed him around the Flamingo's best suite, the one with the escape chutes in the closets and steel shutters on the windows. "I'm a writer. This PR stuff's on the side."

"You can be a writer, too. I own Hollywood," Bugs said. "That's no problem."

Great, Harold thinks, that's all I need: to show up in Zanuck's office with my typewriter and say, "*Bugsy sent me*." Again he refuses. So Siegel shakes his head and says all right, if Harold doesn't want the job, that's good enough for him. That's Harold: He turns down Bugsy Siegel and lives.

Yeah, like Kathmandu and Monte Carlo, Maine and Monrovia, Harold had been to Vegas before. In '63, when he was hyping the Floyd Patterson-Sonny Liston fight there, he drove out from New York in his Ford woody, along with his wife, the fabulous Mara Lynn, his son, Casey, and the family cat, which ripped up all the upholstery. They stopped off along the way, took in a few sights: the Grand Canyon and Eisenhower's birthplace. Took six weeks. Flackery had a more unhurried aspect back then. Not now. This week they got Mike Tyson and Razor Ruddock over at the Mirage, where the fake volcano blows up every twenty minutes.

"Fucking town," Harold grumbles as he reconnoiters the tourist-dense casino. Forty-five years ago Runyon referred to Harold as "my good friend, the tall and stately columnist for the *New York Mirror*." Now, even as Harold remained seemingly eternally tall and stately in his dapper safari suit and pencil moustache, the *Mirror* was long gone, along with every other sheet he had ever worked for, including his beloved *Brooklyn Eagle*. Just the month before, after decades of smoking and drinking and staying out all night long, he turned eighty. He's not nuts about the idea. "You know what it's like to look in the mirror and see the big eight-oh looking back?" Conrad imagined if he got this far it'd be enough time to "get revenge." Instead, he opens his address book and "there's two dead guys on every page."

We went over to the Riviera coffee shop and talked with Gene Kilroy. Harold and Kilroy, a giant, raucous man who now works as an "executive casino host," go back a long way. Together they went around the world with Muhammad Ali, to Zaire, Manila, Kuala Lumpur. It was the most perfect party, a road show no one thought would end. Harold first ran into Ali at the Fifth Street Gym in Miami back in '61. He was working the third Patterson-Johansson fight, using every huckster's wile to propagate the notion that the shopworn Swede actually had a chance. Johansson needed a sparring partner, and a young, brash man, just a year out of the amateurs, volunteered. *Pop, pop, pop,* Ali—then Cassius Clay—surrounded the lumbering Scandinavian with zinging leather. "Sucker," the young man taunted, "I should be fighting Patterson, not you." Harold's eyes opened wide. He'd covered fights back to when they ran weekly cards in little dives like the Broadway Arena, where Murder Inc. had the first row on permanent reserve. Right off, Harold knew what he was looking at. "I saw the new champ today," he told anyone who'd listen. Later, after they took Ali's title because, as he said, war was against his religion and besides he didn't have "nothing against no Cong," Harold went around the country trying to get the Champ's license back; persistent guy, Harold—he was in twenty states before Georgia said yes and Ali got to knock out Jerry Quarry in Atlanta.

Being with The Greatest was always electric, the most vital place to be, like the time in the Philippines when Ali leaned across Imelda, over to Marcos, and asked, "You the president? President get a lot of pussy?" "Much pussy," Marcos nodded, with a curt smile. "You're not as dumb as you look," Ali returned.

Everyone figured Ali would be coming in for Tyson-Ruddock. He usually shows up for the big heavyweight fights and often picks up a few Gs from the promotion just for waving when they say his name. But the Champ's not here. The Parkinson's is getting worse, he's too sick to travel. "Last time I talked to him on the phone I couldn't understand a thing he was saying . . ." Harold says, softly. Kilroy nods glumly.

So it goes. In Conrad's neo-autobiography *Dear Muffo,* a wry and passionate chronicle of his near-lifelong interface with celebrity large and small, he talks about how, in the service of hawking the first Ali-Liston fight, he got the Louisville Lip together with the Beatles, who were then on their first American tour. Taking his accustomed long view, Harold noted: "The Beatles and Cassius Clay—the two hottest names in the news, worldwide. They are all about the same age. I wonder how posterity will treat them."

"I never expected to find out," mutters Harold, who for the last twenty-five years of his life lived in the Oliver Cromwell on West Seventy-second Street, his window overlooking the entrance of the Dakota, where John Lennon was shot dead. "At my fucking age you're supposed to be dead, or at least sitting on your ass in Florida getting stoned. I didn't know I'd still be out here hustling, trying to make a goddamned living."

For Harold, that was a big part of the disappointment at Ali not being in Vegas this week; he's supposed to be doing a piece on Muhammad for *Rolling Stone*, which probably made him the oldest freelance magazine writer in the world. A couple of years before, he had applied his special broth of piquant newspaperese to the pages of *Spin* magazine. *Seventy-eight years old! Working for a low-life rockrag like* Spin *magazine!* Getting cut for space between the Iron Maiden and Megadeath profiles. High blood pressure and arthritis—working for *Spin* magazine!

"What am I supposed to do?" Harold shouts in his ratchety voice. "I need the scratch." Then he smiles and his eyes come on like star sapphires. "Also the action."

Action. Harold's unquenchable desire, the *axis mundi* of his existence.

Action. Something genuine happening. People coming together, energy pouring into a room until your head's light and you can't breathe right. It doesn't happen every day, not the real stuff, Harold knew. He'd been in on more than his share of fakes and hustles. He was the point man in the promotion when Evel Knievel swore he'd soar across Snake River Canyon in a sawed-off rocket ship. He once put Casey Stengel on high-top skates to hype a roller derby in Oakland. He flacked for numerous wrestlers and six-day bicycle races. The smell of the unkosher come-on was not unknown to the less-than-petite Conrad honker. Legitimate action is a rare thing, eminently perishable. It can be a heavy jones.

Right now, here in Vegas, the tingle's beginning. The crowd torsos past the slots, a crush of velveteen, a sheen of sequins. Here comes Tyson's team, a dozen bodyguards, growly and hard, in black leather hats that say KICK ASS. Ruddock's people are wearing Day-Glo baseball jackets. They're singing Bob Marley songs, because Ruddock is from Jamaica. Harold has seen it before and better, way, way better. But shabby as it is, compared to the days of Sugar Ray and drinking coffee with George Balanchine (as Harold used to do), this doesn't get old. Not this—that time before the bell when the drumbeating and backbiting and cadging suddenly cease and, for an instant at least, there's a chance of witnessing something absolutely pure.

"Six forty-four, Pacific Time," Harold says, looking at his watch. "Six forty-four, and there's no place on earth where they have action like this. And we're here. This is what there is to live for."

Let me say, flat out, that Harold Conrad was the single most happening, been-everywhere/done-everything cat I ever met. For certain he had the best résumé. I mean, sure, there's that business about being Meyer Lansky's press agent, and all those days and nights hanging with his particular rouge's gallery of rats, badhats, and plutocrats, Runyon, Charley Lucky, Joe Kennedy, George Raft, Sonny Liston, Jackie Gleason, Milton Berle ("the biggest pecker in Hollywood"), Marilyn Monroe, John Huston, Howard Hughes (he tried to pick up Mara Lynn), and Mike Todd, not to mention Mailer, Murray, James Baldwin, and Hunter Thompson.

Besides, how many guys can say Humphrey Bogart played them in the movies? It happened back in '54, when Budd Schulberg wrote his novel about an even seamier side of boxing, *The Harder They Fall*, using his good friend Conrad as an exceedingly convenient model for the central figure of the somewhat dissolute, wholesomely cynical sports reporter Eddie Lewis. When they got around to making the movie, Bogart took the Lewis role.

"You can imagine how proud I am," Harold says. "Bogart, my favorite actor, playing me in the movies! So one night I'm in a Sunset Strip joint, and I see Bogart sitting at a table. He's got his head down over his glass, and I say, 'Mr. Bogart, my name is Harold Conrad. I just want to tell you how proud I am that you're playing me in *The Harder They Fall*.' Now he raises his head, and I can see how skulled he is. His eyes are barely open. I repeat my line about how proud I am.

'Why don't you go fuck yourself,' he says and drops his head back down over the glass. . . . I was never so crushed in my whole life."

The coda to the story is that Bogart later apologized, saying Harold caught him on an off night, that they both had a laugh about it. Good thing, too. Because, as Harold says, "If I hadn't got that squared away with Bogie, I don't think I would have ever been the same." And that makes you happy, because Harold was the sort of fellow for whom you want (after appropriate duress, of course) everything to turn out right.

Born in East New York, Brooklyn, in 1911, the only son of Romanian steerage travelers, graduate of Franklin K. Lane High School, Harold Conrad swaggered a broken field through the century with the consuming immigrant pluck that told him anything was possible as long he thought fast, talked faster, and kept his head down in the clinches. To me—one who has never been able to casually say, as Harold did so frequently, "So one night I walk into Lindy's," Harold Conrad was a conduit to another, more vibrant, infinitely more colorful age. In a sea of retro-gimmicked, James M. Cain fashion knockoffs in slouch hats, he was the legitimate article, a guy with a capital G, a gaudy-pattered, Basie-rhythmed remnant of a time when people made buildings with spires lurching to the sky because they believed their works were beautiful and assumed the heavens would concur.

Hanging out with Harold was never a sweat. You'd go up to his apartment, look at the photos on the wall—Harold with the young Joe Louis,

Harold with the old Joe Louis, Harold sitting at Sloppy Joe's bar in Havana with Hemingway, Harold sipping tea in Cairo with King Farouk—and light up. Harold, you see, was always what they used to call "a viper." He shared his first joint with Louis Armstrong and Dickie Wells backstage at Three Deuces on Fifty-second Street. Armstrong told Harold that reefer was "medicine for headaches, toothaches, and the blues," advice Conrad took to heart. He smoked marijuana every day of his life for the next fifty-five years. The haze lingered. In Vegas, Smokin' Joe Frazier greeted Harold with the shout, "Hey man, you still with them funny cigarettes?"

Once you're properly blasted, the stories can commence. Forever positioning himself as the bemused adjuster of bollixed-up situations, the sane everyman set down amid the messes of majesties and morons, saints and liars, Harold unveils his dense, textured oral history with snazzy syntax and much wingy body English. You hear of Harold's days on the newspapers, immerse yourself in the dense incense of the dripping lead type in Hildy Johnson's city room. Harold worked the Broadway beat and wrote sports. He covered the Dodgers for the *Brooklyn Eagle*, where they set the box score on the front page by hand.

It was frantic back when twelve dailies hit the New York streets with half a dozen editions each. Harold scored his own kind of scoops. Once he was sitting in a bar and everyone was talking about how tough Capone was, and someone said, "Yeah, but he ain't as tough as the guy who gave him the scar." Got to find that man, Harold vowed, and he did, locating an unassuming barber in South Brooklyn. The story was, the young Capone felt the barber hadn't given him the best cut. An argument ensued. Capone reached for his gun, but the barber was quicker with the razor. Slice. The fact that Capone never came back for revenge led Harold to conclude that Scarface didn't need a PR team to tell him the value of a good nickname ("*Nick*-name, Some pun, ha, ha").

The sagas go on from there, an eclectic, free-associated torrent owing nothing to chronology or rote, seamlessly stitched together by Harold's singular baritone scrape. Tales of Roy Cohn and Cardinal Spellman's strange liaison, days and nights with Ray Robinson, accounts of a month spent with Lucky Luciano in Naples, during the gangster's melancholy deportation. "You don't know what I'd give to go eating a hot dog behind third base at the Polo Grounds," Harold quotes Charley Lucky as mournfully saying over a double espresso.

Often the reverie rolled on deep into the night, an unflagging, unredundant product of the raconteurial mind. You could be walking down the street, and apropos of nothing Harold would say, "So I was screwing Jack Webb's girl. . . ." Then he'd be back to Ali, talking about the time he had to hide the Champ in his apartment before the Ken Norton fight at Yankee Stadium. Ali was running around "trying to give away all his money to every Boys' Club in town," looking peaked; he had to be taken out of circulation—after all, Norton was tough, he'd broken Ali's jaw back in San Diego. Harold tells how Dick Gregory came around with his health therapies and blenders. "You have to neutralize your poisons, Ali. You have to drink your own urine," Gregory said, demonstrating with a beaker of his own bodily fluids.

"Drink my own piss?" Ali boggled. "He poured out everything Gregory gave him after that, the vegetable juices, every elixir," Harold says. "Gregory never knew. But he kept raving, 'See! He looks better already.'"

Assessing the veracity quotient of Harold's stories, Norman Mailer, Conrad's friend for more than three decades, said, "I suspect they are more true than you might expect. They are true because we want them to be true, and it would break our hearts if they're not."

You wonder if it even matters anymore. Like Mailer says, we accept them because they're better than most other stories, tales handed down from a previous generation we here in the pygmy land of corporate spin can only regard as godlike. People like Harold hailed from a pre-TV day when it seemed as if American giants strode the earth, a time when wiseacres and sharpies, suddenly free of the *shtetl*, Sicilian village, and failed potato farm, were given free rein to self-invent a wholly new urban ethos ("action") in the hitherto-unexplored marginalia of the cityscape. In that way Harold, profoundly unsentimental with his faintly detached yet undeniably first-hand merge of style and substance, performed a patriotic service; he, alone, it seemed, survived for so long to tell thee of a time when the national spirit appeared to strike a bolder, more heroic chord. With the dekiltered surrealism Harold brought to that telling, he'd sometimes break through to what can only be called Art.

Like the time his first wife threw a lamp at him.

It goes, more or less, this way: "Yeah, I was living on Thirty-second Street at the time. Right near Sixth. Across from the Empire State Building. My first wife was a great babe. Great body. Eurasian. But sometimes she'd get crazy. So she picks up this lamp and throws it at me across the room. Did you ever have a lamp thrown at you? It takes a little bit of time to get there. So I'm looking at this lamp coming at me, and I'm thinking, *That plane outside the window is flying pretty low. Really low. Low and loud.* I'm thinking all this as the lamp is coming. Then it goes by my shoulder, smashes against the wall with this tremendous crash. *Bam!* A lot louder than I would have figured. I'm thinking, wow, she's really got a hell of an arm. The whole building shook. And know what? I didn't find out until later that it was right then that that plane smashed into the Empire State Building."

Ever offhand, relentlessly imperturbable, Harold was typically diffident about his appeal to the younger generation of would-be hepcats. He'd narrow his brown eyes (which so many women less than half his age found irresistible), puff on his cigarette (only adding to the aura of understated octogenarian sexuality), and unfurl his most compelling half-sneer. "I know about you guys, why you want to hang around with me, you fuckers. You see these pictures of me on the deck of the *Queen Mary* with a bottle of champagne, and you get all misty; you know there's nothing you can do about getting that. No amount of money buys it back."

But then, in the form of a disclaimer, he'd say, "Just stop me before I get to be one of those creaky fucks who sits around talking about how great the old days were. That's the worst. Of course the old days were better. In the old days, you didn't have arthritis. In the old days, you could get a hard-on. What scares me is when I can't help thinking: *It was better then*. I mean: look at it, on paper. Then against now. Forget about it. I don't want to let myself think like that. Instead I say, you just have to *look harder* to find the action now."

So that brings us back around to Vegas, where Mike Tyson is driving Razor Ruddock into the ropes, and the referee, Richard Steele, is stopping the fight. This denouement is not appreciated by the Ruddock camp, which all week long has been predicting that something exactly like this would happen, since Steele's got a track record for quick triggers, and besides he works as a pit boss for Steve Wynne, who owns the Mirage and happens to have a deal for Tyson's next fight with Iron Mike's paramour, the indefatigably skulduggerous Don King. Right now Murad Muhammad, Ruddock's smarmier-than-thou promoter, is in the ring kicking Tyson's trainer Richie Giachetti in his ample gut as a form of protest.

"Another black eye for boxing," Harold remarks with his seasoned sarcasm as he watches the ensuing riot, referring to the headlines he knows will appear in every paper tomorrow. "Boxing's like the night. It's got a thousand eyes, all of them black."

Harold gets up with a grunt. He's been feeling crappy since we got to Vegas, tired. It's a pulled muscle in his side, he keeps claiming, taking out another joint, playing craps until three in the morning. "It's all fucking downhill after eighty," he groans. It's not exactly like you'd notice, however, since Harold hasn't looked his age for years. As the decades wore on, Harold took increasing delight in telling people, especially women, his age. No squint-eyed carny could ever guess it; it's a shock to find out he's twenty years older than you always thought.

Mailer says, "I first met Harold in '61. I was thirty-eight and he was fifty. He looked fifty. Then he didn't age a day in the next two and a half decades. It's only since Mara died that you began to see a change. That was a blow. Mara was in every way Harold's equal."

About that there can be no argument. Mara Lynn was, by all accounts, a piece of work, a doll with a capital *D*. Twenty years of study with Balanchine, she made her mark dressed in funny costumes hoofing beside Bob Hope and Bing Crosby, playing a zany with Marilyn Monroe in *Let's Make Love*, and pouring a rum and coke over the head of an excessively raging Jake LaMotta. Budd Schulberg refers to her as "a one-girl riot." Mailer, who featured Mara in his movie *Wild 90*, says with a stab of reverence, "She was a blond witch and a blond angel, she could be both, often at the same time, depending on her mood. She could get a guy agitated. Like every man married to a beautiful woman, Harold, I think, was always a little in awe of her." Others, too. As one story goes, Bianca Jagger, impressed, once made a plaster cast of Mara's posterior.

Harold first met Mara back in '48, when he was doing a Broadway column for the *Mirror*. She was dancing at a place called the Hurricane Club. A deadly entry at any price, they got married in 1950, divorced in '56, got back together a couple of years later, and lived together for decades more. Life with Mara apparently could be quite stormy. Once, when he was doing the second Ali-Spinks fight in New Orleans, Harold and Mara had an all-time argument. He stomped out of the hotel room and found a French Quarter bar to get drunk in. Sometime during the night, he fell in with a shipload of sailors and found himself inside an all-night tattoo parlor getting a tricolor severed heart affixed to his bicep. MARA, it said. Mara was shocked—after all, sixty-seven-year-old Jewish men are not known for getting tattoos on their arms in the middle of the night. It'll keep you out of the cemetery when you die. But Mara was swayed. She said Harold's tattoo was the greatest tribute of love she'd ever seen.

The fun stopped when Mara got sick, and Harold spent all his money trying to save her, which is how at age eighty he wound up writing articles for *Spin* magazine. As horrific as the end must have been, it was in keeping with the romance of a certain romantic age. Harold and Mara remarried after nearly thirty years of living in sin, smoked a last joint together, and that was it.

"Been faking it since then," Harold would admit grudgingly. "I'm all front."

In Vegas, you could tell things weren't right. Even Don King—Harold's collaborator on several Ali fights, whose incessant effulgence of "wit, grit, and bullshit" Conrad approvingly recognizes as being in boxing's scalawag tradition—noticed. Nattily attired in a baggy red, white, and blue ONLY IN AMERICA sweatsuit, King was in the middle of swearing on a metaphorical stack of his dead mother's Bibles that the Tyson-Ruddock battle would "separate the pugilistic wheat from the chaff," quoting Frederick Douglass, George Bush, and Plato in the same sentence when he sees Harold. Losing no beat, the promoter abruptly launched into an apparently heartfelt, equally loud reverie about "Harold Conrad—*the legend!*—a man of much moxie, the nonpareil of sell!" But then King stops, tilts his multipronged coif, and says, "Hey, Harold, you all right, man?"

He's not. Maybe he shouldn't have had those couple of drinks with the Brit sportswriters, Harold says with the deep embarrassment of someone forever finicky about appearances, because when he got back to the hotel, he slipped in the lobby, fell down between the dollar slots, and his head's been spinning ever since. It's just his luck that there's a chiropractor convention at the hotel, because before he even hits the lobby floor, six guys are pushing cards at him.

The next morning, walking through the casino lobby, a woman in a stretchy orange dress comes over and asks Harold (who never ceases to look like *a somebody*), "Are you a movie star?" "Sure, I'm big," Harold replies. She takes out a piece of paper and asks for an autograph. Harold writes "Best wishes always, Ramon Navarro." She looks at the paper, back up at Harold, and asks, "Aren't you dead?" Harold only bugs his eyes, shrugs his shoulders, walks on.

A week after Harold's return to New York, however, with merciless diagnostic secession, the pulled muscle mutates to "a small stroke" and then inoperable cancer. Plenty of times Harold would talk about how he spent day after day at Damon Runyon's bedside, how one time Runyon, who couldn't speak near the end, once wrote him a crotchety note followed by three exclamation points. "You don't have to yell at me, Damon," Harold replied.

After that, Harold hated hospitals. Now, so soon after Mara's death, he was in Mount Sinai, the same place, "just about the same room," where a couple of years earlier he visited his longtime friend Buddy Rich, when the famous drummer was dying. It was terrible, Harold recalls, watching the great basher who only went one speed—fast—stare up at the ceiling. Then Harold raises his right arm, and real pain crosses his face. "That's what Buddy did," he says, "raised his arm and said, 'If I can't play I don't want to live.'"

This gets very sad because soon the tumor is pressing on Harold's brain, making it next to impossible for him to talk. Impossible to tell the stories, to rekindle the grander times. So you sit beside Harold's bed with his son, Casey, next to the flowers sent by the Friars Club ("Frank Sinatra—

Abbot"), watching him alternately doze and glance at the muted television, where the Mets are getting shut out, and the silence is awful, because three weeks ago Harold never would have tolerated such emptiness on the soundtrack.

A few days later Harold is on a plane to Mexico, going to a clinic seeking an alternative to the chemotherapy he was certain would kill him. It doesn't help. And a few days after that, the *New York Times* has a three-column-inch item headed by the phrase HAROLD CONRAD, BOXING PROMOTER. The obit indicates that Harold was "a colorful character." Likely, Harold would have accepted the short shrift with his usual cynic's grace. He knew they always screw you on space.

As a storyteller he would also know that you can't stop the tale there. So, allow me one more story about my old friend Harold Conrad. It was a night a few months ago when Harold and I went over to watch Sugar Ray Leonard fight an upstart named Terry Norris at the Garden. Harold, of course, has been to the Garden before, about 9 million times. Mostly he went to the old Garden, the one on Forty-ninth Street and Eighth that was torn down back in the late sixties. That was where the real action was, standing underneath the giant curve of the marquee, waiting for something to happen, sensing that this night—like so many before it—was magic. The new Garden, except for that one ecstatic evening when Ali fought Frazier twenty years ago, and a basketball game or two, has never had the same juice.

Tonight's event is typically desultory, overpriced, the half-filled building little more than a TV studio, the backdrop for the cable-TV broadcast. The canned music, heavy on the sampler machine, is blaring. Leonard has been a great fighter, no argument, and you can't knock a guy for getting rich, but with his viciously cute smile and bitchy demeanor, he's always been a tinny presence, especially now that he's a half dozen years past his prime. Harold's never been a fan. He wouldn't even have come to the fight if it wasn't for that outside chance, that possibility, that something, something memorable, might happen. It's the action, Harold's addiction.

The result is an upset. Leonard loses, but where's action in that? He was in there only due to his innate hubris and not knowing when enough's enough. As when Ali and Joe Louis had that one last, unnecessary fight, the whole thing is mostly depressing. Harold knew it in the first round. A minute in, he turns and says, "He's got nothing."

So the fight's over, and we're walking over to Broadway in the cold night air. We're at Herald Square, it's Saturday night, and the town's dead, no one moving except for some ragged figures over where the big welfare hotel used to be. "You could shoot a cannon off out here," Harold snorts. "Used to be, on a big fight night, by now everyone would be going up to Toots Shors: Winchell, Joe D if the Yanks were in town, the Fischetti Brothers, who ran Chicago, right next to J. Edgar Hoover. People would be all decked out, up and down Broadway from here to Fifty-seventh Street. . . ."

We walk on, freezing. Years ago Damon Runyon wrote a column about how Harold never wore a hat. Everyone else wore one then, why didn't he, Runyon asked Harold. "Because I do not look good in a hat," Runyon quoted Harold as replying. Tonight, however, Harold is wearing a hat, crammed down over his outsized ears. "Got to," he says, "my head gets cold." Then, reminded that when Runyon died he had his ashes thrown out of a plane so they sprinkled over Broadway, Harold says, "Not for me. Dust in people's eyes? No thanks. It's against my religion. Besides, you never know, maybe I'll live forever."

7

The Haint of Harlem:
The Nasty Life and Times of Frank Lucas

Face-to-face with the charming killer. If he weren't born black and poor, he could have been a really rich, corrupt politician. Instead, he became a really rich drug dealer. But he did call his mom every day. An epic tale of the vagaries of race in the U.S. of A. Basis for the long-planned movie American Gangster *with Denzel Washington in the Frank role. Originally called* Return of Superfly. *From* New York *Magazine, 2001.*

During the 1970s, when for a graffiti-splashed, early disco instant of urban time he was, according to then-U.S. District Attorney Rudolph Giuliani, "the biggest drug dealer" in Harlem, Frank Lucas would sit at the corner of 116th Street and Eighth Avenue in a beat-up Chevy he called Nellybelle. Then residing in a swank apartment in Riverdale down the hall from Yvonne De Carlo and running his heroin business out of a suite at the Regency Hotel on Park Avenue, Lucas owned several cars. He had a Rolls, a Mercedes, a Stingray, and a 427 four-on-the-floor muscle job he'd once topped out at 160 miles per hour near Exit 16E of the Jersey Turnpike, scaring himself so silly that he gave the car to his brother's wife just to get it out of his sight.

But for "spying," Nellybelle worked best.

"Who'd ever think I'd be in a shit three-hundred-dollar car like that?" asks Lucas, who claims that, on a good day, he would clear up to a million dollars selling dope on 116th Street. "I'd sit there, cap pulled down, with a fake beard, dark glasses, maybe some army fatigues and broken-down boots, longhair wig . . . I used to be right up beside the people dealing my stuff, watching the whole show, and no one knew who I was. . . ."

It was a matter of control, and trust. As the leader of the "Country Boys" dope ring, Frank, older brother to Ezell, Vernon Lee, John Paul, Larry, and Lee Lucas, was known for restricting his operation to blood relatives and others from the rural North Carolina backwoods area where he grew up. This was because, Lucas says in his downhome creak of a voice, "A country boy, he ain't hip . . . he's not used to big cars, fancy ladies, and diamond rings, so he'll be loyal to you. A country boy, you can give him a million dollars, 5 million, and tell him to hide it in his old shack. His wife and kids might be hungry, starving, and he'll never touch your money until he checks with you. City boy ain't like that. A city boy will take your last dime and look you straight in the face and swear he ain't got it. . . . A city boy'll steal from you in a New York minute and you've got to be able to deal with it in a New York second. . . . You don't want a city boy, the sonofabitch is just no good."

But trust has its limits, even among country boys, Frank says. "116th between Seventh and Eighth Avenue was mine. It belonged to me. . . . I bought it. I ran it. I owned it. And when something is yours, you've got to be Johnny on the Spot, ready to take it to the top. So I'd sit in front of the Roman Garden Restaurant, or around the corner by the Royal Flush Bar, just watching."

There wouldn't be much to see until four in the afternoon, which was when Frank's brand of heroin, Blue Magic, hit the street. During the early seventies there were many "brands" of dope in Harlem. Tru Blu, Mean Machine, Could Be Fatal, Dick Down, Boody, Cooley High, Capone, Ding Dong, Fuck Me, Fuck You, Nice, Nice to Be Nice, Oh—Can't Get Enough of that Funky Stuff, Tragic Magic, Gerber, The Judge, 32, 32-20, O.D., Correct, Official Correct, Past Due, Payback, Revenge, Green Tape, Red

Tape, Rush, Swear To God, PraisePraisePraise, KillKillKill, Killer 1, Killer 2, KKK, Good Pussy, Taster's Choice, Harlem Hijack, Joint, Insured for Life, and Insured for Death are only a few of the brand-names rubber-stamped onto the cellophane bags.

But none sold like Blue Magic.

"That's because with Blue Magic you could get 10 percent purity," Frank Lucas asserts. "With any other if you got 5 percent you were doing good. Mostly it was 3. We put it out there at four in the afternoon, when the cops changed shifts. That gave you a couple of hours to work, before those lazy bastards got down there. My buyers, though, you could set your watch by them. Those junkies crawling out. By four o'clock we had enough niggers in the street to make a Tarzan movie. They had to reroute the bus coming down Eighth Avenue to 116th, it couldn't get through. Call the Transit Department to see if it's not so. On a usual day we'd put out maybe twenty-five thousand quarters (quarter "spoons," fifty dollars' worth, enough to get high for the rest of the day). By nine o'clock I ain't got a fucking gram. Everything is gone. Sold . . . and I got myself a million dollars."

"I'd just sit there in Nellybelle and watch the money roll in," says Frank Lucas of those not-so-distant but near-forgotten days, when Abe Beame would lay his pint-sized head upon the pillow at Gracie Mansion and the cop cars were still green and black. "And no one even knew it was me. I was a shadow. A ghost . . . what we call downhome a haint . . . That was me, the *Haint of Harlem*."

Twenty-five years after the end of his uptown rule, Frank Lucas, now sixty-nine, has returned to Harlem for a whirlwind retrospective of his life and times. Sitting in a blue Toyota at the corner of 116th Street and what is now called Adam Clayton Boulevard ("What was wrong with just plain Eighth Avenue?" Lucas grouses), Frank, once by his own description "six-feet two-inches tall, a handsome fashion plate, rough and ready, slick and something to see" but now teetering around "like a fucking one-legged tripod" due to a cartilage-less, arthritic knee, is no more noticeable than he was all those years ago, when peered through Nellybelle's window.

Indeed, just from looking, few passersby might guess that Frank, according to his own exceedingly ad hoc records, once had "at least 56 million dollars," most of it kept in Cayman Island banks. Added to this is "maybe a thousand keys of dope" with an easily realized retail profit of no less than three hundred thousand dollars per kilo. His real estate holdings included "two twenty-plus-story buildings in Detroit, garden apartments in Los Angeles and Miami, another apartment house in Chicago, and a mess of Puerto Rico." This is not to mention "Frank Lucas's Paradise Valley," eight hundred acres back in North Carolina on which ranged three hundred head of Black Angus cows, "the blue ribbon kind," including several "big balled" breeding bulls worth twenty-five thousand dollars each.

Nor would most imagine that the old man in the fake Timberland jacket once held at least twenty forged passports and was a prime mover in what Federal Judge Sterling Johnson, who in the 1970s served as New York's special narcotics prosecutor, calls "one of the most outrageous international dope smugglers ever . . . an innovative guy who broke new ground by getting his own connection outside the U.S. and then selling the stuff himself in the street . . . a real womb to tomb operation."

Johnson's funerary image fits well, especially in light of Lucas's most audacious, culturally pungent claim to fame, the so-called "cadaver connection." Woodstockers may remember being urged by Country Joe and the Fish to sing along on the "Fixin' to Die Rag," about being the first one on your block to have your boy come home in a box. But even the most apocalyptic-minded sixties freak couldn't have guessed that the box also contained half a dozen keys of 98 percent pure heroin. Of all the dreadful iconography of Vietnam—the napalmed girl running down the road, Lieutenant Calley at My Lai, the helicopter on the embassy roof, and more—the memory of dope in the body bag, death begetting death, most hideously conveys Nam's still-spreading pestilence. The metaphor is almost too rich. In fact, to someone who got his 1-A in the mail the same day the NVA raised the Red Star over Hue, the story has always seemed a tad apocryphal.

But it is not. "We did it all right . . . ha, ha, ha . . ." Frank chortles in his mocking, dying crapshooter's scrape of a voice, recalling how he and fellow Country Boy Ike Atkinson arranged for the shipment. "Who the hell is gonna look in a dead soldier's coffin? Ha, ha, ha."

"I had so much fucking money, you have no idea," Lucas says now, his heavy-lidded light brown eyes turned to the sky in mock expectation that his vanished wealth will rain back down from the heavens. "The forfeits took it all," Frank says mournfully, referring to the forfeiture laws designed by the government under sundry RICO and "continuing criminal enterprise" acts to seize allegedly ill-gotten gains amassed by gangsters like Frank Lucas.

Some think Lucas still has a couple of million stashed somewhere, perhaps buried in the red dirt down in North Carolina. Hearing this only makes the old dealer grimace. "If they find it, I sure hope they send me some, a mil or two. Shit, I'd take a hundred, 'cause right now I'm on my ass," Frank says, driving downtown on Lenox Avenue behind the wheel of my decidedly un-Superfly powder blue Toyota station wagon, the one with Milky Way wrappers and basketball trading cards on the floor. We were going to go in Frank's car, a decade-old Sedan de Ville, but it was unavailable, the transmission having blown out a few days earlier. "Motherfucker won't pull, gonna cost twelve hundred bucks, that a bitch or what?" Lucas had moaned into his cell phone, calling from the rainy roadside where a tow truck was in the process of jacking up his bestilled Caddy.

An informative if wary guide, Lucas, who said he hadn't been to Harlem in "five, six years," found the place totally changed. Aside from the hulking, cavernous 1365th Infantry Armory, where Lucas and his Country Boys used to unload furs and foodstuffs from the trucks they'd hijack out on Route 9, nothing looked the same. Still, almost nearly every block, every corner, summoned a memory. Over on Eighth Avenue and 127th Street, up above the rim and tire place, used to be Spanish Raymond Marquez's number bank, one of the biggest in town. On one Lenox Avenue corner is where "Preacher got killed," on the next is where Black Joe bought it. Some deserved killing, some maybe not, but they were all dead just the same.

In front of a ramshackle blue frame house on West 123rd Street, right next to where the two-eight precinct used to be, Lucas stops and gets nostalgic. "I had my best cutters in there," he says, describing how his "table workers," ten to twelve women wearing surgical masks, would "whack up" the dope, cutting it with "60 percent mannite." The ruby-haired Red Top was in charge. "I'd bring in three, four keys, open it up on the table, let Red go do her thing. She'd mix up that dope like a rabbit in a hat, never drop a speck, get it out on the street in time. . . . Red . . . I wonder if she's still living. . . ."

At 135th Street and Seventh Avenue, Lucas stops again. Small's Paradise used to be there. Back in The Day, there were plenty of places, Mr. B's, Willie Abraham's Gold Lounge, the Shalimar if you were hungry, the Lenox Lounge, a nice place to take your girl. But Small's, then run by Frank's friend, Pete McDougal, was the coolest. "Everyone came by Small's . . . the jazz guys, politicians. Ray Robinson. Wilt Chamberlain when he bought a piece of the place and called it Big Wilt's Small's Paradise . . . At Small's, Frank often met up with his great friend, the heavyweight champ Joe Louis, who would later appear nearly every day at Lucas's various trials, expressing outrage that the State was harassing "this beautiful man." When Louis died, Lucas, who says he once paid off a fifty-thousand dollar tax lien for the champ, was heard weeping into a telephone, "My Daddy . . . he's dead." It was also at Small's, on a cold winter's night in the late 1950s, that Frank Lucas, haint of Harlem, would encounter Howard Hughes. "He was right there, at the bar, with Ava Gardner . . . Howard Hughes, richest mother fucker in the world, the original ghost—that impressed me."

In the end, the little tour comes back to 116th Street. When he "owned" this street, Frank says, "you'd see a hundred junkies, lined up, sitting there, sucking their own dicks. . . . That's what you called it, sucking their own dicks . . . their heads on their laps, down in the crotch, like they was dead. People saw that, then everyone knew that shit was good."

Now, like everywhere else, 116th Street is another place. Only a few days before, the *New York Times* had a piece saying that Frank's old turf was a key cog in the current real estate boom characterized as "a new Harlem renaissance." An Australian graphic designer just purchased a steal of a brownstone for $237,000, the *Times* reported, cheering that whole area "once destroyed by drugs, crime, and debilitation . . . [an area which is] on the way up." This news does not please Lucas. He and his Country Brother Shorty used to own property in the area, so that's just more money out the window.

"Uh oh, here come the gangstas," Lucas shouts in mock fright, as he regards a trio of youths, blue kerchiefs knotted around their heads, standing by a car, blaring rap music. Partial to James Brown, and "soulmen I knew like Chuck Jackson and Dennis Edwards," Frank says he is no fan of "any Wu-Tang this and Tu Pac that." One of his sons tried rapping, made a couple of records, but it was "that same ba-ba-ba . . . it don't do nothing for me." Once the possessor of a closetful of tailor-made Hong Kong suits, seventy-five pairs of shoes, and underwear from Sulka, Frank doesn't care much for the current O. G. styles, either. "Baggy pants prison bullshit," is his blanket comment on the Tommy Hilfiger thuglife knockoffs currently in homeboy favor.

"Well, I guess every idiot gets to be young once," Lucas snaps as he starts the car, driving half a block before slamming on the brakes.

"Here's something you ought to see," the old gangster says, pointing toward the curbside between the Canaan Baptist Church and the House of Fish. "There's where I killed that boy . . . Tango," Frank shouts, his large, squarish jaw lanterning forward, eyes slitting. "I told you about that, didn't I? . . ."

Of course he had, only days before, in distressing specific, hair-raising detail.

For Frank, the incident, which occurred "at four o'clock in the afternoon" sometime in "the summer of 1965 or '66," was strategy. Strictly business. Because, as Lucas recalls, "When you're in the kind of work I was in, you've got to be for real. When you say something, you've got to make sure people listen. You've got to show what exactly you're willing to do to get what you want.

"Everyone, Goldfinger Terrell, Hollywood Harold, Robert Paul, J.C., Willie Abraham, they was talking about this big guy, this Tango. About six-foot-five, 270 pounds, quick as a cat on his feet. . . . He killed two or three guys with his hands. Nasty, dangerous mother. Had this big bald head, like Mr. Clean. Wore those Mafia undershirts. Everyone was scared of him. So I figured, Tango, you're my man.

"I went up to him, just talking, I asked him if he wanted to do some business. He said yes. I gave him five thousand dollars, some shit money like that . . . Because I know he was gonna fuck up. I knew he wouldn't do what he said he would and he was never, ever, going to give me my money back. That's the kind of guy he was. Two weeks later I'm on the block, and I go talk to him. 'Look man,' I say, 'you didn't do that thing, so where's my money . . . ?'

"Then, like I knew he would, he started getting hot, going into one of his real gorilla acts. He was one of them silverback gorillas, strong, like in the jungle, or on TV. A silverback gorilla, that's what he was.

"He started cursing, saying he was going to make me his bitch, stick his whatever in my ass, and he'd do the same to my mama, too. Well, as of now, he's dead. No question, a dead man. But I let him talk. A dead man should be able to say anything he wants to. It is his right. Last will and whatever. Now there's a crowd, the whole fucking block is out there. They want to see what's gonna happen, if I'm going to pussy out, you know. He was still yelling. So I said to him, 'When you get through, let me know.'

"Then the motherfucker knows I'm going to kill him. So he broke for me. But he was too late. I shot him. Four times, right through here: bam, bam, bam, bam.

"Yeah, it was right there," says Frank Lucas thirty-five years after the shooting, pointing out the car window to the curbside to where a man in coveralls is sweeping up in front of the Canaan Baptist Church, Wyatt Tee Walker, senior pastor.

"Right there . . . the boy didn't have no head in the back. The whole shit blowed out. . . . That was my real initiation fee into taking over completely down here. Because I killed the baddest motherfucker. Not just in Harlem, but in the world."

Then Frank laughs.

Frank's laugh: It's a trickster's sound, a jeer that cuts deep. First he rolls up his slumped shoulders and cranes back his large, angular face, which despite all the wear and tear remains strikingly handsome, even empathetic in a way you'd like to trust, but know better. Then the smooth, tawny skin over his cheekbones creases, his ashy lips spread, and his tongue snakes out of his gatewide mouth. Frank has a very long, very red tongue, which he likes to dart about like a carny's come-on for real good loving. It is only then the aural segment kicks in, staccato stabs of mirth followed by a bevy of low rumbled cackles.

Ha, ha, ha, siss, siss, siss. For how many luckless fools like Tango was this the last sound they ever heard on this earth?

Frank's laugh translates well on tape. Listening to a recording of our conversations, my wife blinked twice and leaned back in her chair. "Oh," she said, "you're doing a story on Satan. . . . Funny, that's exactly how I always imagined he might sound." She said it was like hearing a copy of the real interview with a vampire.

"After I killed that boy," Frank Lucas goes on, gesturing toward the corner on the other side of 116th Street, "from that day on, I could take a million dollars in any kind of bag, set it on the corner, and put my name on it. *Frank Lucas*. And I guarantee you, nobody would touch it. No-body."

Then Frank laughs again. Ha . . . ha . . . ha. He puts a little extra menace into it just so you don't get too comfortable with the assumption that your traveling partner is simply a limping old guy with a gnarled left hand who is fond of telling colorful stories and wearing a five-dollar acetate shirt covered with faux-Nascar logos.

Just so you never forget exactly who you are dealing with.

When asked about the relative morality of killing people, selling millions of dollars of dope, and playing a significant role in the destruction of the social fabric of his times, Frank Lucas bristles. What choice did he have, he demands to know. "Kind of sonofabitch I saw myself being, kind of money I wanted to make, I'd have to be on Wall Street. From the giddy-up, on Wall Street. Making a damn fortune. But I couldn't have gotten a job even being a fucking janitor on Wall Street."

Be that as it may, there is little doubt that when, on a sweltering summer's afternoon in 1946, Frank Lucas first arrived in Harlem, which he'd always been told was "nigger heaven, the promised land," his prospects in the legitimate world were limited. Not yet sixteen years old, he was already on the run. Already a gangster.

It couldn't have been any other way, Lucas insists, not after the Ku Klux Klan came to his house and killed his cousin Obedai. "Must have been 1936, because I was born September 9, 1930, and I wasn't more than six. We were living in a little place they call La Grange, North Carolina. Not even La Grange. Way in the woods. Anywise, these five white guys come up to the house one morning, big rednecks. . . . And they're yelling, 'Obedai, Obedai . . . Obedai Jones . . . come out. Come out you nigger . . .'

"They said he was looking at a white girl walking down the street. 'Reckless eyeballing' they call it down there.

"Obedai was like twelve or thirteen, and he come out the door, all sleepy and stuff. 'You been looking at somebody's daughter. We're going to fix you,' they said. They took two ropes, a rope in each hand, they tied him down on the ground, facedown on the porch, and two guys took the rope and . . . pulled it tight in opposite directions. The other guy shoved a shotgun in Obedai's mouth and pulled the trigger simultaneous."

It was then, Lucas says, that he began his life of crime. "I was the oldest. Someone had to put food on the table. My mother was maxed out. I started stealing chickens. Knocking pigs on their head, dragging them home. . . . It wasn't too long that I started going over to La Grange, mugging drunks when they come out of the whorehouse. They'd spent their five or six bucks buying ass, getting head jobs, then they'd come out and I'd be waiting with a rock in my hand, a tobacco rack, anything. . . .

By the time he was twelve, "but big for my age," Lucas says, he was in Knoxville, Tennessee, on a chain gang, picked up by the police after breaking into a store. In Lexington, Kentucky, not yet fourteen, he lived with a lady bootlegger. In Wilson, North Carolina, he got a truck driver job at a pipe company, delivering all over the state, Greenville, Charlotte, and Raleigh. The company was owned by a white man, and Lucas started in sleeping with his daughter. This led to problems, especially after "Big Bill, a fat, 250-pound beerbelly bastard," caught them in the act. In the ensuing fight, Lucas, sure he was about to be killed, managed to hit Bill on the head with a piece of pipe, laying him out.

"They didn't owe me but a hundred dollars for the work I done, but I took four hundred and set the whole damned place on fire." After that, his mother told him he better get away and never come back. He bummed northward, stopping in Washington, which he didn't like, before coming to Harlem.

"I took the train to Thirty-fourth Street. Penn Station. I went out and asked the police how you get to Fourteenth Street, what bus you take. I had only a dollar something in my pocket. I took the bus to Fourteenth Street, got out, looked around. I went over to another policeman on the other side of the street. 'Hey,' I said, 'this ain't Fourteenth Street. I want to go where all the black people are at.' He said, 'You want to go to Harlem . . . one hundred and fourteenth street!'

"I got to 114th Street. I had never seen so many black people in one place in all my life. It was a world of black people. And I just shouted out: 'Hello, Harlem . . . hello Harlem, USA! . . .'"

If he wanted any money, everyone told him, he better go downtown, get a job as an elevator operator. But once Frank saw guys writing policy numbers, carrying big wads, his course was set. Within a few months he was a one-man, hell-bent crime wave. He stuck up the Hollywood Bar on Lenox and 116th Street, got himself six hundred dollars. He went up to Busch Jewelers on 125th Street, told them he needed an engagement ring for his girl, stole a tray of diamonds, and broke the guard's jaw with brass knuckles on the way out. Later he ripped off a high-roller crap game at the Big Track Club on 118th Street. "They was all gangsters in there. Wynton Morris, Red Dillard, Clarence Day, Cool Breeze, maybe two or three more. I just walked in, took their money. Now they was all looking for me."

The way he was going, Frank figures, it took Bumpy Johnson, the most mythic of all Harlem gangsters (Moses Gunn played Johnson in the original *Shaft*, Lawrence Fishburne did it twice, in *The Cotton Club* and the more recent *Hoodlum*) to save his life.

"I was hustling up at Lump's Pool Room, on 134th Street. I got pretty good with it. Eight-ball and that. So in comes Icepick Red. Now, Icepick

Red, he was a fierce killer, from the heart. Tall motherfucker, clean, with a hat. Freelanced Mafia hits. Had at least fifty kills. Anyway, he says he wants to play some pool, took out a roll of money that must have been that high. My eyes got big. I knew right then that wasn't none of his money. That was MY money . . . there's no way he's leaving the room with that money.

"'Who wants to shoot pool?' Icepick Red keeps saying. 'Who wants to fucking play?' I told him I'm playing but I only got a hundred dollars . . . and he's saying, what kind of sissy only got a hundred dollars? All sorts of shit. The way he was talking, I wanted to take out my gun and kill him right there, take his damn money. I just didn't care what happened.

"Except right then everything seemed to stop. The jukebox stopped, the poolballs stopped. Every fucking thing stopped. It got so quiet you could have heard a rat piss on a piece of cotton in China.

"I turned around and I saw this guy—he was like five-ten, five-eleven, dark complexion, neat, looked like he just stepped out of *Vogue* magazine. He had on a gray suit and a maroon tie, with a gray overcoat and a flower in the lapel. You never seen nothing that looked like him. He was another species altogether. You could tell that right away.

"'Can you beat him?' he said to me in a deep, smooth voice.

"I said, 'I can shoot pool with anybody, mister. I can beat anybody.'

"Icepick Red, suddenly he's nervous. Scared. 'Bumpy!' he shouts out, 'I don't got no bet with you!'

"But Bumpy ignores that. 'Rack 'em up, Lump!'

"We rolled for the break, and I got it. And I wasted him. Just wasted him. Icepick Red never got a goddamn shot. Bumpy sat there, watching. Didn't say a word. But when the game's over, he says to me, 'Come on, let's go.' And I'm thinking, who the fuck is this Bumpy? But something told me I better keep my damn mouth shut. So I got in the car. A long Caddy I think it was. First we stopped at a clothing store, he picked out a bunch of stuff for me. Suits, ties, slacks. Nice stuff. A full wardrobe. Bumpy never gave the store guy any money, just told them to send it up to the house. Then we drove to where he was living, on Mount Morris Park. He took me into his front room, said I should clean myself up, sleep there that night.

"I wound up sleeping there for about six months after that. . . . You see, Bumpy had been tracking me. He figured he could do something with me, I guess. After that night, things were different. All of a sudden the gangsters stopped fucking with me. The cops stopped fucking with me. I walk into the Busch Jewelers, look right at the man I robbed, and all he says is: 'Hello, can I help you, sir?' Because now I'm with Bumpy Johnson—a Bumpy Johnson man. I'm seventeen years old and I'm *Mister Lucas*.

"Bumpy was a gentleman among gentlemen, a king among kings, a killer among killers, a whole book and Bible by himself," notes the still-reverent Lucas. "He showed me the ropes—how to collect, how to figure the vig. Back then, everybody, every store, business, landlord above 110th Street, river to river, had to pay Bumpy. It was the Golden Rule: You either paid Bumpy or you died. Extortion, I guess you could call it. Everyone paid except the mom-and-pop stores, they got away for free. . . ."

After a while, Frank moved up. Three or four days a week he'd drive Johnson downtown, to the Fifty-seventh Street Diner across from Carnegie Hall, and wait outside while the boss ate breakfast with Mafia stalwart Frank Costello. On another occasion, around 1950, Bumpy told him to pack his bag, they were taking a trip. "We're on the plane, he says we're going to see Charley Lucky in Cuba. Imagine that! A Country Boy like me, going to visit Lucky Luciano!" reports Lucas, who spent his time guarding the door, "just one more guy with a bulge in his pocket."

"There was a lot about Bumpy I didn't understand, a lot I still don't understand," Frank reflects. "When he was older he'd be leaning over his chessboard up there at the Lenox Terrace, with these Shakespeare books around, listening to soft piano music, Beethoven—or that Henry Mancini record he played over and over, 'Elephant Walk.' Then he'd start talking about philosophy, read me a passage from Tom Paine, the *Rights of Man*. . . . What do you think of that, Frank, he'd ask . . . and I'd shrug, because I wouldn't know what to say. What could I say? What did I know? About the only book I remember reading was Harold Robbins' *The Carpetbaggers*."

In the end, as Frank tells it, Bumpy died in his arms. "We was eating at Wells Restaurant on Lenox Avenue, talking about day-to-day stuff. Chitchat. I think Billy Daniels, the singer, might have been there. Maybe Cockeye Johnny, JJ, or Chickenfoot. When Bumpy was around, there was always a crowd, people wanting to talk to him. All of a sudden Bumpy started shaking and he fell over, right up against me. Never said another word."

Two months after Martin Luther King's assassination, the headline of the front-page account of Bumpy Johnson's funeral in the *Amsterdam News* headline read, BUMPY'S DEATH MARKS END OF AN ERA. Bumpy had been the link back to the wild days of Harlem gangsterism, to people like Madame St. Clair, the French-speaking Queen of Policy, and the wizardly rackets magnate Casper Holstein, who reportedly aided the careers of Harlem Renaissance writers like Claude McKay. Also passing from the scene were characters like Helen Lawrenson, former managing editor of *Vanity Fair* (and mother of Joanna Lawrenson, who would marry Abbie Hoffman), whose tart, engrossing account of her concurrent affairs with Conde Nast, Bernard Baruch, and Ellsworth "Bumpy" Johnson can be found in the long-out-of-print *Stranger at the Party*.

Lucas says, "There wasn't gonna be no next Bumpy. You see, Bumpy, he believed in that 'share the fortune' thing. Spread the wealth. I was a different sonofabitch. I wanted all the money for myself. . . . Besides, I didn't want to stay in Harlem. That same routine. Numbers, protection, those little pieces of paper flying out of your pocket. I wanted adventure. I wanted to see the world."

A few days after our Harlem trip, watching a Japanese guy in a chef hat dice up some hibachi steak in a fake Benihana place beside an interstate off-ramp, Frank told me how he came upon what he refers to as his "bold new plan" to smuggle thousands of pounds of heroin from Southeast Asia to Harlem. It is a thought process Lucas says he often uses when on the verge of "a pattern change."

First he locks himself in a room, preferably a hotel room on the beach in Puerto Rico, shuts off the phone, pulls down the blinds, unplugs the TV, has his meals delivered outside the door at prearranged times, and does not speak to a soul for a couple of weeks. In this meditative isolation,

Lucas engages in what he calls "backward tracking . . . I think about everything that has happened in the past five years, every little thing, every nook and cranny, down to the smallest detail of what I put on my toast in the morning."

Having vetted the past, Lucas begins to "forward look . . . peering around every bend in the road ahead." It is only then, Frank says, "when you can see all the way back to Alaska and ahead as far as South America . . . and decide that nothing, not even the smallest hair on a cockroach's dick, can stand in your way"—that you are ready to make your next big move.

If he really wanted to become "white boy rich, Donald Trump rich," Lucas decided, "cut the guineas out from above 110th Street." He'd learned as much over the years, running errands for Bumpy over to Pleasant Avenue, the East Harlem mob enclave, where he'd pick up "packages" from Fat Tony Salerno's guys, men with names like Joey Farts and Kid Blast. "I needed my own supply. That's when I decided to go to Southeast Asia. Because the war was already on and people were talking about a lot of GIs getting strung out over there. So I knew if the shit is good enough to string out GIs, then I can make myself a killing."

Lucas had never been to Southeast Asia, but felt confident. "It didn't matter about it being foreign," Frank says, "because I knew it was a street thing over there. You see, maybe I went to school only three days in my life, but I got a Ph.D. in street. I am a doctorate of street. When it comes to a street atmosphere, I know what I'm doing. I know I'm going to make out."

Once in town, Frank checked into the swank Dusit Thani Hotel, where he often spent afternoons watching coverage of the war being waged a couple of hundred miles to the east. Lucas soon hailed a motorcycle taxi to take him to Jack's American Star Bar, on the edge of the then-notorious Patpong sex district. Offering hamhocks and collard greens on the first floor and a wide array of hookers and dope connections on the second, the Soul Bar, as Frank calls it, was run by the former U.S. Army master sergeant Leslie (Ike) Atkinson, a Country Boy from Goldsboro, North Carolina, which made him as good as family.

"Ike knew everyone over there, every black guy in the army, from the cooks on up," Frank says. "A lot of these guys, they weren't too happy to be over there, you know. That made them up for business. . . . " It was what Frank calls "this army inside the army, that was our distribution system." According to Lucas, most of the shipments came back on military planes routed to eastern seaboard bases like Fort Bragg, and Fort Gordon in Georgia, places within easy driving distance of his Carolina ranch. Most of Frank's "couriers" were enlisted men, often cooks or plane maintainance men. But "a lot of officers were in there, too. Big ones, generals and colonels, with eagles and chickens on their collars. These were some of the greediest motherfuckers I ever dealt with. They'd be getting people's asses shot up in battle, but they'd do anything if you gave them enough money."

But Lucas still needed a steady supply. Acting on information given him by a woman called "Nurse" whom he met in a Mott Street restaurant in New York Chinatown, Lucas located his main overseas connection—a youngish, English-speaking Chinese gentleman with a buzzcut who went by the sobriquet 007. "When he drove up in a Rolls and a white linen jacket, I knew he was my man. . . . 007, that was all I ever called him because he was a fucking Chinese James Bond." 007 took Lucas upcountry, to the Golden Triangle, the heavily jungled point where Thailand, Burma, and Laos come together, the richest poppy-growing area in the world. By Lucas's account, it was an epic journey.

"It wasn't too bad getting up there," says Lucas, who recalls being dressed in his uptown attire, with a brim hat and tailored pants. "Maybe a ten-day thing through the bush. We was in trucks, sometimes on boats. I might have been on every damn river in the Golden Triangle. When we got up there, you couldn't believe it. They've got fields the size of Newark with nothing but poppy seeds in them. There's caves in the mountains so big you could set this building in them, which is where they do the processing. . . . It was beautiful, mist hanging on the green hills. I'd sit there, smoking a cigarette, and watch these Chinese paramilitary guys come out of the fog carrying these rifles that looked like they hadn't been fired in twenty years. When they saw me, they stopped dead. They'd never seen a black man before."

More than likely dealing with soldiers who had fought with Chiang Kai-shek's defeated Kuomintang army in the Chinese civil war (Lucas recalls seeing Nationalist Chinese flags flying over several buildings), Frank purchased 132 kilos on that first trip. At $4,200 per unit, compared to the $50,000 that Mafia dealers were charging Harlem competitors like Nicky Barnes and Frank Moten, it would be an unbelievable bonanza. But the journey was not without problems.

"On the way back, that's when our troubles began," Lucas says. "Right off guys were stepping on these little green snakes. A second later they were dead. Then, guess what happened? Them banditos. Those motherfuckers, they came out of nowhere. Right out of the trees. Stealing our shit. Everyone was shooting. I was stuck under a log firing my piece. The guys I was with—007's guys—all of them was Bruce Lees. Those sonofbitches were good. They fought like hell. But the banditos, they had this way of sneaking up, stabbing you with these pungi sticks. All around me these guys were getting shot. You'd see a lot of dead shit in there, man. It was like a movie. A bad B-movie. A month and a half of nightmares. I think I ate a damn dog. It was the worst meat I ever tasted in my life. Very uncomfortable. I was in bad shape, lying on the ground, raggedy and stinking, crazy with fever, barfing. Then people were talking about tigers. Like there were tigers and lions up there. That's when I figured, that does it. I'm out of here. I'm gonna be ripped up by a tiger in this damn jungle. What a fucking epitaph. . . . But we got back alive. Lost half my dope, but I was still alive."

Embroidered at the edges or not, it is a fabulous cartoon, an image to take its place in the floridly romantic, easy-riding annals of the American dope pusher—Superfly in his Botany 500 sportswear, custom leather boots, and brim hat, clutching his hundred keys, Sierra Madre style, as he shivers in malarial muck, bullets whizzing overhead.

"It was the most physiological thing I ever done and hope not to do again," says Lucas, who would like it known that through all his wartime smuggling gambits, he never felt less than "100 percent true blue red, white, and blue, a patriotic American . . ." To this end, Lucas swears that details concerning the dope-in-the-body-bags caper have been wildly misrepresented. The story that he and Ike Atkinson actually stitched the dope inside the body cavities of dead soldiers is nothing but "sick cop propaganda" put out to discredit him, Lucas insists. "No way I'm touching a dead anything. Bet your life on that."

What really happened, Lucas recounts, was that he flew a Country Boy North Carolina carpenter over to Bangkok and had him "make up twenty-eight coffins identical to the ones the government was using. Except we fixed them up with false bottoms, compartments big enough to load up with six, maybe eight kilos. . . . It had to be tight, because you couldn't have shit sliding around. We was very smart in that respect because we only used mostly heavy guys' coffins. We didn't put them in no skinny guy's . . ."

Still, of all his various Asian capers, Frank still rates "the Henry Kissinger deal" as "the scariest and the best." To hear Frank tell it, he was desperate to get 125 keys out of town, but there weren't any "friendly" planes scheduled. "All we had was Kissinger. I don't know if he was secretary of state then. He was on a mercy mission on account of big cyclones in Bangladesh. We gave a hundred thousand dollars to some general to look the other way and we was in business; I mean, who the fuck is gonna search Henry Kissinger's plane? . . .

". . . Henry Kissinger! Wonder what he'd say if he knew he helped smuggle all that dope into the country? . . . *Hoo hahz poot zum dope in my aero-plan?* Ha, ha, ha. Good thing he didn't know or maybe he would have asked us for carrying charges. . . . Ha, ha, ha . . . fucking Henry Kissinger. . . ."

Asked how he invented these schemes, Lucas leans back in the dim light of the Japanese restaurant and, after a couple of Kirins, unleashes his most jocularly macabre smile. "When did I come up with these ideas? On September 9, 1930, at about four o'clock in the morning, that's when. The moment I was born . . . Instinct, man . . . Everyone's born to do something, and smuggling dope was it for me. To me that's the thrill, more than even the money. Beating the cops. Beating the feds. Beating everybody . . . ha, ha, ha . . ."

Back issues of the *Amsterdam News* from the late sixties and early seventies are full of accounts of what 116th Street was like during the reign of Frank Lucas. Lou Broders, who ran a small apparel shop at 253 West 116th, says, "We here are being destroyed by dope and crime every day . . . it's my own people doing it, too. That's the pity of it. This neighborhood is dying out. . . ." It was Fear City time, when the feds were estimating that out of all the heroin addicts in America, more than half were in New York, 75 percent of those in Harlem. In a city that would soon be on the brink of financial collapse, the plague was on.

In the face of such talk, Frank, who remembers the Harlem riots of the 1960s as being "no big deal . . . we waited it out, fenced some watches I guess," exhibits his typically willful obliviousness. "It's not my fault if your television got stolen," he says. "If everything is going to hell, how can I be responsible for all that? I'm only one guy. Besides, Harlem was great then. It wasn't until they put me and Nicky Barnes in jail that the city went into default. There was tons of money up in Harlem in 1971, 1972, if you knew how to get it. And I did. Shit, those were the heydays. That was the top."

To hear Frank (who never touched the stuff himself) tell it, life as a multimillionaire dope dealer was a whirl of flying to Paris for dinner at Maxim's, gambling in Vegas with Joe Louis and Sammy Davis Jr., spending $140,000 on a couple of Van Cleef bracelets, and squiring around his beautiful mistress—Billie Mays, stepdaughter of Willie, who, according to Lucas, he'd sneaked away from Walt "Clyde" Frazier. Back home there were community businessman's lunches and fund-raising activities for the then-young Charles Rangel. The gritty 116th Street operation was left in the hands of trusted lieutenants. If problems arose, Lucas says, "we'd have 250 guns in the street so fast your head would spin off your neck."

Frank was always the boss, handling all the cash, albeit idiosyncratically. His money-laundering routine often consisted of throwing a few duffel bags stuffed with tens and twenties into the backseat of his car and driving up to a Chemical Bank on East Tremont Avenue in the Bronx where he knew the branch officers. Most of the money was sent to accounts in the Cayman Islands, but if Frank needed a little extra cash, he sat in the bank lobby reading the newspaper while the bank managers filled one of the duffels with crisp new hundred-dollar bills. For their part in the laundering scheme, the Chemical Bank would eventually plead guilty to 445 violations of the Bank Secrecy Act.

As Bumpy had once had the Palmetto Chemical Company, a roach-exterminating concern, Frank opened a string of gas stations and dry cleaners, but this did not suit his temperament. "I had a dry cleaning place on Broadway, near Zabar's. I don't remember what happened, but there wasn't no one to watch the place. I had to go myself. Now, you know I ain't no nine-to-five guy. And these old ladies kept coming in, screaming, 'Look at this spot. . . . Why can't you get this out? . . . shoving the damn shirt in my face. I couldn't take it anymore. I ran out of the place, didn't lock up, didn't even take the money out of the cash register, just drove away."

Show business was more to Frank's taste, especially after he and fellow gangster Zack Robinson put "a bunch of money" into Lloyd Price's Turntable, a nightclub at Fifty-second Street and Broadway that soon became a must hangout for black celebrities. "There'd be Muhammad Ali, who was a friend of Lloyd's, members of the Temptations, James Brown, Berry Gordy, Diana Ross," says Frank, who calls the Turntable, "a good scene, the integration crowd was there, every night."

In 1969, Price, a Rock & Roll Hall of Famer who'd had huge hits with tunes like "Personality" and "Lawdy Miss Clawdy," got the idea to make a gangster movie set on the streets of New York. "There'd been lots of gangster movies before, and not too many black gangster movies, and none of them ever had real, practicing gangsters in them," says Price, always a sharp article when it came to cultural margins between white and black culture (now in his late sixties, he still looks good in a gold lamé suit). "We needed a guy to play the Superfly, the guy with the sable coat and the hat, so I thought, why not get Frank? He was real handsome in those days. A real presence. So he played the bad-guy romantic lead. He was a natural, really."

"It was like *Shaft* before *Shaft*—the first *Shaft*," reports Lucas, who sees a "young and dangerous" Morgan Freeman Jr. ("You know, in that movie *Street Smart*, when he terrorizes that reporter") in the prospective *Frank Lucas Story*. "We had this scene where I was chasing Lloyd down the street, shooting out the window of a Mercedes somewhere up in the Bronx. I put a bunch of money into the picture, seventy, eighty grand. It was real fun. Real fun."

Alas, never finished, the footage apparently disappeared. *The Ripoff* qualifies as the "great lost film" of the so-called blaxploitation genre. "A lot of strange things happened making that movie," says Lloyd, who recalls a trip to the film editor's office with Frank, whom the singer seems to regard with much affection and a touch of fear. "Frank didn't care for the way the cut was going," Lloyd says. "Some words were said, and then Frank is pulling out his knife. I had to tell him, Frank, man, I don't think this is the way it is done in the movie business."

A drug kingpin attracts a degree of attention from the police, but according to Frank, it wasn't the "straight-arrow types" who caused him undue problems. His trouble came from repeated shakedowns run by the infamously corrupt and rapacious Special Investigations Unit, NYPD's "elite" detective squad. Collectively known as the Princes of the City for their unlimited authority to make busts anywhere in New York, the SIU wrote its own mighty chapter in the wild street-money days of the early seventies heroin epidemic; by 1973, forty-three of the sixty officers who'd worked in the unit were either in jail or under indictment.

Lucas's relations with his fellow drug dealers were more congenial. "There wasn't one of those gang-war, fighting over territory things. There was plenty of customers to go around." Disputes did come up, such as the one that, according to Special Narcotics Prosecutor Sterling Johnson, once caused Lucas to take out a contract on his famous Harlem rival, Leroy (Nicky) Barnes. Frank denies this, but says he never liked the grandstanding Barnes, who Lucas thought brought unneeded heat by doing things like appearing on the cover of the *New York Times* magazine wearing his trademark goggle-like Gucci glasses, bragging that he was "Mr. Untouchable." The assertion soon had then-president Jimmy Carter on the telephone demanding that something be done about Barnes and the whole Harlem dope trade.

According to Lucas, it was Barnes's "delusions of grandeur" that led to a bizarre meeting between the two drug lords in the lingerie department of Henri Bendel. "Nicky wanted to make this Black Mafia thing called The Council. An uptown Cosa Nostra. The Five Families of Dope or some shit. I didn't want no part of it. Because if we're gonna be Genoveses, then before long, everyone's gonna think they're Carlo Gambino. Then your life ain't worth shit. Besides, I was making more money than anyone.

"Anyway, I was shopping with my wife at Henri Bendel's on Fifty-seventh Street, she's in the dressing room, and who comes up? Nicky fucking Barnes! 'Frank . . . Frank,' he's going . . . 'we got to talk . . . we got to get together on this council thing.' Talking that solidarity shit. I told him forget it, my wife is trying on underwear, can't we do this some other time? Then before he leaves, he says, 'Hey Frank, I'm short this week, can you front me a couple of keys?' That's Nicky."

Asked if he ever thought about quitting when he was ahead, Lucas says, "Sure, all the time." He says his wife Julie, whom he met on a "backtracking" trip in Puerto Rico, always begged him to get out, especially after Brooklyn dope king Frank Matthews jumped bail in 1973 and disappeared, never to be heard from again. ("Some say he's dead, but I know he's living in Africa, like a king, with all the fucking money in the world," Lucas sighs.) "Probably I should have stayed in Colombia. Always liked Colombia. But I had my heart set on getting a jet plane, learning how to fly it . . . there was always something. That was the way I was, addicted to action, addicted to the money . . ."

For Lucas, the end, or at least the beginning of the end, came on January 28, 1975, when a strike force of the DEA feds and NYPD operatives, acting on a tip from two low-level Pleasant Avenue guys, converged on the house where Frank was living at 933 Sheffield Street in leafy Teaneck, New Jersey. The raid was a surprise. In the ensuing panic, Lucas's wife Julie, screaming "Take it all, take it all," tossed several suitcases out the window. One of the suitcases hit a hiding DEA agent square on the head, knocking him out. The case was later found to contain $585,000, mostly in rumpled twenty dollar bills. At the time it was the second largest "cash retrieval" in DEA history, behind only the million dollars dug up in the Bronx backyard of Arthur Avenue wiseguy Louie Cirillo. Also found were several keys to Lucas's safe deposit boxes in the Cayman Islands, deeds to his North Carolina land, and a ticket to a United Nations ball, compliments of the ambassador of Honduras.

"Those motherfuckers just came in," Lucas says now, more than twenty-five years later, as he sits in a car across the street from the surprisingly modest split-level house where, prior to his arrest, he often played pickup games with members of the New York Knicks. For years Lucas has contended that the cops took a lot more than $585,000 from him when he was busted. "585 Gs . . . shit. I'd go to Vegas and lose 485 in a half hour." According to Frank, federal agents took something on the order of "9 to 10 million dollars" from him that fateful evening. To bolster his claim, he cites passing a federally administered polygraph test on the matter. A DEA agent on the scene that night, noting that "10 million dollars in crumpled twenty-dollar bills isn't something you just stick in your pocket," vigorously denies Lucas's charge.

Whatever, Frank doesn't expect to see his money again. "It's just too fucking old, old and gone."

Then, suddenly snickering, Lucas addresses my attention to the trunk of a tree in the front yard of the house. "See that little gouge there, where it goes in? Aretha Franklin's car made that dent. I think maybe King Curtis was driving. They had come over for a party and just backed up over the grass into it."

"Funny," Lucas says, looking around the innocent-seeming suburb, "that tree has grown a lot since then, but the scar's still there."

A few days later I brought Lucas a copy of his newspaper clip file, which almost exclusively details the Country Boy's long and tortuous interface with the criminal justice system following his Sheffield Street arrest, a period in which he would do time in joints like Otisville, Sandstone, Trenton, Rahway, Lewistown, Tucson, Elmira, the Manhattan Correctional Center, and Rikers. Squinting heavily, Lucas silently thumbed through yellowed, dog-eared articles that had heads like "Country Boys, Called No. 1 Heroin Gang, Is Busted," "30 Country Boys Indicted in $50 million Heroin Operation," "Charge Two Witnesses Bribed in Lucas Trial; Star Murder Trial Witness Vanishes." There was also an October 25, 1979, story in the *New York Post* entitled "Convict Lives It Up with

Sex and Drugs," which quotes a Manhattan Correctional Center prisoner named "Nick," convicted hit man killer of five, who whines that Lucas had ordered prostitutes up to his cell and was "so indiscreet about it I had to have my wife turn the other way . . . he didn't give one damn about anyone else's feelings."

In between bitching that the same mugshot of him looking "like I ain't slept in two weeks" accompanied almost every notice, Lucas, who likes to point out that "biography is history," said it figured that "the whiteboy press" only covered him in relation to his dealings with the cops. "Once they get you and think you're tame, then it's safe to say a bunch of shit about you."

One clip, however, did engage Lucas's attention. Entitled "Ex-Assistant Prosecutor for Hogan Shot To Death in Village Ambush," the November 5, 1977, *Times* clip tells how Gino E. Gallina, onetime Manhattan D.A. turned Pelham Manor mouthpiece for "top drug dealers and organized crime figures," was rubbed out "mob style . . . as many passers-by looked on in horror" one nippy fall evening at the corner of Carmine and Varick Streets.

Lucas reckons he must have spent "millions" on high-priced criminal lawyers through the seventies and early eighties, people like Ray Brown Sr., counselor for Rubin "Hurricane" Carter, and John H. Gross, a former Southern District D.A. under Rudolph Giuliani, who represented Frank in a series of cases. Gino Gallina, however, was the only lawyer Lucas ever physically assaulted, the incident occuring in the visiting room of the Rikers Island prison. According to later testimony, Lucas had given Gallina $400,000 to fix a case for him, and $200,000 became "lost." It was upon hearing this news that Frank, the *Daily News* wrote, "leaped across a table and began punching him [Gallina] savagely, knocking him to the floor before prison guards were able to subdue him . . . Gallina wore the scars from that assault for weeks" but "significantly . . . filed no charges against his client."

For his part, Frank acknowledges "beating the dogshit out" of Gallina. He also allows that the lawyer "stole my money," that "I told him he was a dead man if he didn't get it back to me," and that "the man did not deserve to live." However, Frank steadfastly maintains he has "no idea, no idea at all" about how and why Gallina was murdered, a crime that remains unsolved to this day.

Despite offering "little tidbits" like how he often talked boxing with Frankie Carbo and politics with Black Panther Joanne Chesimard while in prison, the Country Boy offers scant details about what he's been up to in the past twenty-five years of his life. Whole decades are dismissed with a shrug or wave of a hand.

What Lucas will absolutely not talk about is how he got out of jail, the stuff described in clips like the April 24, 1978, *Daily News* story, "Jailed Drug King Turns Canary to Cage 13 Old Pals," or a *Newark Star-Ledger* piece from 1983 entitled "'Helpful' Drug Kingpin Granted Reduced Term," in which Judge Leonard Ronco of Newark is reported as cutting in half Lucas's thirty-year New Jersey stretch "because of the unprecedented cooperation he has given authorities" in the making of cases against other drug offenders. This followed the previous decision by U.S. District Court Judge Irving Ben Cooper, who "granted the unusual request of Dominic Amorosa, chief of the Southern District Organized Crime Strike Force, to reduce Lucas's forty-year New York prison sentence to time already served."

"I am not talking about none of that Witness Protection shit," Frank declared in our first meeting. It was part of the oral contract between Lucas and myself. "I ask two things," the Country Boy said evenly: "One, if they are slamming bamboo rods 'neath your fingernails with ball peen hammers, you are not to reveal my location, and two, none of that buddy-buddy crap with the cops. That is out."

Staying to the bargain has been frustrating since, in law enforcement circles, Lucas's "unprecedented cooperation" is nearly as legendary as his stuffing bricks of heroin into dead soldiers' coffins. Dominic Amorosa, long in private practice, estimates Frank made "maybe a hundred cases all told . . . I don't know if anyone made more."

All Frank offers on the topic is "anything I said about anyone they would have said the same about me if they had the chance." As for anyone he gave evidence against, Lucas adds, "I've made my peace with them."

Well and good, but how was I, the journalist, supposed to explain how he, the drug kingpin, had come to serve less than nine years—barely double the time routinely handed out on shitty little possession charges under the loathsome Rockefeller drug laws, which were partially enacted in (over)reaction to big dealers like himself?

"You're the writer, you'll think of something," was Frank's response. Failing that, Frank suggested I could just "leave the whole fucking thing out . . . stop at 1975 and make everything else into a cliffhanger . . . if anyone asks what I been doing since then, just say I was in the oil business."

I'd been told this would be the most difficult part, that gangsters (or gangstas, for that matter) will go on forever about people they killed, how much dope they'd moved, but as for the inevitable "giving up"—Richard Roberts, former head of the Essex County Narcotics Task Force that would successfully prosecute Lucas, says, "In this business, everybody in this business cooperates, everybody, sooner or later"—no one wanted to talk about that.

"The betrayal, that's the thing you won't hear," said a writer well known for writing about criminals who inform on their fellows. And, soon enough, Frank Lucas, the Country Boy who insisted on blood loyalty, lost patience with my persistent attempts to get him to talk about flipping. Asked to tell "the worst thing he'd ever done," he said balefully, "You already know the answer to that so I won't dignify that with a reply." Later, hoping to get him to open up, I proposed a scenario in which Frank, ever the pragmatist, faced with the extreme "pattern change" of being in the joint for the rest of his life, entered into perhaps the most intense "backtracking" trance of his long career. Was it the simple arithmetic of being in his late forties and "forward-looking" into the black hole of a seventy-year sentence that made him decide to talk?

"Listen, I told you before," Lucas said, stone-faced, his voice halfway between a threat and plea, "I have hurt my mother and family before with this and I will not do it again. So don't go there, now or ever . . . don't cross me, because I am a busy man and I have no time, no time whatsoever, to go to your funeral."

Still, I couldn't give it up. Nicky Barnes, who'd also cooperated, making many cases, had only just been released after serving twenty-one years. How was it possible that when he was asked for a name in a repair shop, Frank said with appalling matter-of-factness, "Frank Lucas . . . my name is Frank Lucas." How could he just be *out there?* It was a mystery.

Finally, Frank said, "Look, you want to know what the bottom line is on a guy like me? It is that I am sitting here talking to you right now. Still walking and talking. That is all you need to know. That I am right here when I could have, maybe should have, been dead and buried a hundred times. And you know why that is?

"Because: people like me. People like the fuck out of me." This was his primary survival skill, said the former dope king and killer: his downright friendliness, his upbeat demeanor. "All the way back to when I was a boy, people have always liked me, wanted to do things for me. I've always counted on that."

That much had become apparent a few days earlier, when I went over to the Eastern District Federal Court to visit with Judge Sterling Johnson. During the plague year of 1976, when government alarmists claimed that junkies were stealing a billion dollars' worth of property a year, Johnson, a former NYPD beat cop and head of the Civilian Review Board, took several congressmen and local politicians on a walking tour of 116th Street, then still Frank Lucas territory. Events of the tour were noted during a hearing of the 94th Congress Select Committee of Narcotic Abuse and Control, a group that would make many key appropriations in the nascent War on Drugs. According to the testimony, at the corner of Eighth Avenue, some of Frank's "block workers," in addition to "flinging their heads into windows of passing cars hawking their wares," came over to outraged congressmen Charles Rangel, Fortney Stark, and Benjamin Gilman and told them, with all due respect, "If you're not buying, get out of here."

Frank had told me to look up Johnson, whom he refers to as "Idi Amin."

"Judge Johnson likes me a lot. You'll see," Lucas said. "I'm lucky for him, because if he didn't put me in jail, he wouldn't be a judge to begin with."

When I first called his office, Johnson answered the phone with a burnished dignity befitting a highly respected, distinguished public official. "This is Judge Johnson," he said. Yet when I mentioned the name Frank Lucas, Johnson's voice rose a couple of octaves and became notably more familiar. "Frank Lucas? Is that *mother* still living?!" A few days later, while talking in his stately chambers, the judge told me to call Lucas up.

"Get that damn old gangster on the phone," Johnson demanded, turning on the speakerphone.

Lucas answered with his usual growl. "This is Frank. Who's this?"

Johnson mentioned a name I didn't catch, someone apparently dead, likely due to some action involving a Country Boy or two. This got Lucas's attention. "What are you talking about? Who gave you this number?"

"Top!"

"Top who?"

"Red Top!" Johnson said, invoking the name of Lucas's beloved chief dope cutter.

"What the—Red Top don't got my number. . . ." It was at around this point that Frank figured it out.

"Judge Johnson! You dog! You still got that stick?"

Johnson reached under his desk and pulled out a beat cop's nightstick and slapped it into his open palm loud enough for Lucas to hear it. "Better believe it, Frank!"

"Stop that! You're making me nervous now, Judge Johnson!" Lucas exclaimed, before somewhat gingerly inquiring, "Hey Judge, they ever get anyone in that Gallina thing?"

Johnson laughed and said, "Frank. You know you did it."

Ignoring Lucas's effusive denials, Johnson said, "Well, come around and see me. I'm about the only fly in the buttermilk down here."

After he hung up, Johnson, who still has a rustic dope-weighing machine in his office, a souvenir bought on an investigation/field trip to the Golden Triangle, and says many of his recent cases can be "a snore," added "That damn Frank. He's a pisser. He always was a pisser."

"You know, when we were first investigating him, the feds, the FBI, DEA, they didn't think he could pull off that Southeast Asia stuff. They wouldn't let themselves believe a black man could come up with such a sophisticated smuggling operation. In his sick way, he really did something."

The memory clearly tickled Johnson, who quickly added: "Look, don't get me wrong, Frank was vicious, as bad as they come. But what are you going to do? The guy was a pisser, a pisser and a killer. Easy to like. A lot of those guys were like that. It is an old dilemma."

A couple of days later, Lucas and I stop for lunch at a local TGI Friday's. TGI Friday's isn't the Oak Bar, where he never tipped less than two hundred dollars, but at least it's better than Bennigan's, Lucas says, picking at his bowl of pasta and shrimp, which he pronounces "swimph." Scowling through the glare-proof glass to the suburban strip beyond, Frank deplores "this crummy shit" he finds himself surrounded by these days.

The giant Home Depot down the road especially bugs him. Bumpy Johnson himself couldn't have collected protection from a goddamned Home Depot, Frank says with disgust. "What would Bumpy do? Go in and ask to see the assistant manager? That place, it's so big, you're lost once you pass the bathroom sinks. That's the way it is. You can't find the heart of anything to stick the knife into. The independent man don't stand a chance. It is a sign of the times."

Then Frank turned to me and asked, "So what do you think? You gonna make me out to be the devil or what? Am I going to heaven or am I going to hell?"

As far as Frank was concerned, the issue of his place in the hereafter was a foregone conclusion, settled since he joined the Catholic Church while imprisoned at Elmira. "The priest there was recommending early parole if you confessed your sins, so I signed up," he says. If this didn't pan out, Frank had backup, since he was also a Baptist. "I have praised the Lord," Frank says. "I have praised Him in the street and I have praised Him in the joint. So I know I'm forgiven, that I'm going to the good place, not the bad."

But what did I think, Frank wanted to know, taking another swig of his Sam Adams. How did I see it going for the Country Boy after he left this world?

It was a vexing question, like Sterling Johnson said, an old dilemma. Who knew about these things? Catch him on a good day at the home and even the Führer might have seemed a charming old guy, with hilarious stories of the putsch times. Frank was a con man, one of the best. He'd been telling white people, cops, and everyone else pretty much what they'd wanted to hear for two and a half decades, so why should I be different? I liked him. Liked the fuck out of him. Especially when he called his church lady, wrestling fan ninety-one-year-old mother, which he did about five times a day.

But that wasn't the point. Cool copy was beyond Like and Dislike, beyond Good and Evil. Frank Lucas was, and is, cool copy. Braggart and trickster, he was nonetheless a living, breathing historical figure, tapped into a highly specialized font of secret knowledge, more exotic and certainly less picked over than any Don Corleone. Frank was a fucking gold mine, worth at least a couple of seasons of the Black Sopranos, Old School division. The idea that a backwoods Country Boy could somehow maneuver himself into a position to tell at least a plausible lie about stashing 125 kilos of *zum dope* on Henry Kissinger's plane—much less actually do it—mitigated a multitude of sins. Plague vector or not, Lucas filled an indispensable cultural niche. Who knows, if it weren't for vicious opportunistic crumbums like Frank, Lou Reed might never have written "Waiting for My Man," not to mention Marvin Gaye doing "Trouble Man." Somehow, morality didn't have anything to do with it.

In the end even Lucas's resounding unrepentance didn't matter. Former Essex County prosecutor-turned-lawyer Richie Roberts, who remains a great friend of Frank's despite the fact that the Country Boy once took a contract out on his life ("He busted my mom and dad, what else could I do?" Frank says), likes to tell how Lucas cried in his courtroom. "We had this woman testify. She was the mother of a drug addict. Her family had been destroyed by heroin, Frank's dope. It was really heartbreaking. A lot of people in the courtroom were crying, sobs all around. I was crying myself. . . . Then, I looked over at Frank. He was crying, too. Huge tears were rolling down his cheeks. There he was, Mr. Big, who had come into the courtroom like Al Capone, with Joe Louis and Johnny Sample from the

Jets, this whole entourage—and he was bawling louder than anyone. I never saw anything like it."

"There Richie goes again, telling that story about me crying," remarks Lucas, who says "but all I cared about was the mother. What she was going through, seeing her daughter suffer like that. It reminded me of my mom." As for the daughter herself, Frank has no sympathy at all. "Look, I gave strict orders to all my people, no selling to kids, no selling to pregnant women. She was old enough to know what she was doing. She did what junkies do. What happened was her problem."

Indeed, about the only flicker of remorse I'd ever seen Frank emit occurred one afternoon following a lunch we ate with one of his brothers, Vernon Lee, who is known as Shorty. Known as a particularly vicious Country Boy, Shorty, a squat, bespectacled man now in his early fifties and taking computer courses after a ten-year stretch, followed Frank to Harlem in 1965. "We came up from Carolina in a beat-up car, the brothers and sisters, Mom and Dad, with everything we owned shoved in, like the Beverly Hillbillies coming to the Land of Plenty," Shorty recalls. Frank was still working for Bumpy at the time, not the giant deal he would become, but Shorty knew what he wanted. "Diamond rings, cars, women, those things. But mostly it was the glory. Isn't that what most men really dream of? The glory."

Then Shorty reached across the table and touched his older brother's hand. "We did make a little bit of noise, didn't we?" Shorty said. To which Frank replied, "A little bit, all right."

A few minutes later we dropped Shorty off at the low-rise apartment development where he was living. It was early spring then and there was still ice on the ground. Frank watched his younger brother make his way across the frozen puddles in the late afternoon light and sighed. "You know, if I'd been a preacher, they would have all been preachers. If I'd been a cop, they'd have all been cops. But I was a dope dealer, so they all became dope dealers. . . . I don't know, I don't know if I'd done right or not."

Later on, driving around the funky suburban landscape, Frank says if he wanted to start up dealing again, "it would take me until about this afternoon." He says it is a rare week that someone doesn't come "looking for the connect . . . but that's not happening. I'm out . . . you know, people might see my shitty clothes, shitty car, and think, Hey, bigshot, you're nothing now. How's it feel to be down? Well, fuck them. I had my day."

Then Frank said he was late. He had to go pick up his three-year-old son. Frank has several other children, including a "stockbroker in Texas" and a daughter in Georgia who's already got her M.A. and soon will have her Ph.D. "They're all smart but she's the really smart one," says Frank, who says "if things had been different" he would have studied hard and gone to MIT like he always wanted to instead of getting his GED in a federal joint in Minnesota. Of all the kids though, Frank says his son, sharp-eyed and handsome, like a chip off the old Country Boy block, is "my heart . . . I really love that boy." The other day Frank said, "You know, he can read. He's just so little and he can read. He says to me, 'Look: C-A-R-T-O-O-N . . . cartoon network.'" Can you believe that? You know how long it took me to read?"

Not that parenting is a snap for the Country Boy. Frank's son, quick afoot, "gets into everything." For sure, he is not intimidated by his gangster dad. When Frank lurches for the top drawer of the bureau, blustering about "getting my belt," the boy just laughs. Luckily Frank doesn't have far to chase the kid. The former resident of the Regency Hotel currently resides in a two-room, haphazardly furnished apartment. The cleanup lady was due that day but didn't show, so Frank apologizes if the place is a little messy. If there is any suspicion that Lucas has held on to any of his millions, the busted chair in the corner dispels that. "Shit," Frank says, "my living room used to be bigger than this whole damn building."

"From the King of the Hill to changing diapers," Lucas says in the middle of his bedroom, which just about fits his bed and dresser.

We sat around for a few hours, waiting for the kid to go to sleep, watching *The Black Rose*, an old swordfight movie with Tyrone Power and Orson Welles. Lucas, a big fan of old movies, likes Welles a lot, "at least before he got too fat." Then, when it was time for me to go, Lucas insisted I call him on the cell phone when I got back to New York. It was late, rainy, and a long drive. Lucas said he was worried about me. So, back in the city, driving down the East River Drive, by the 116th Street exit, I called Lucas up, as arranged.

"You're back, that's good," the Country Boy croaks into the phone. "Watch out. I don't care what Giuliani says, New York is not as safe as they say. Not so safe at all. You never know what you might find out there." Then, Frank laughed, that same chilling haint of a laugh, spilling out the car windows and onto the city streets beyond.

8
Interview with Peter Tosh

In 1975, I was in Jamaica to talk to Bob Marley. But Bob, suddenly one of the richest men in the country, was being besieged. Everyone in Trenchtown seemed to have converged on his house looking for a handout. Instead, we went out Spanishtown Road to hang out with Peter Tosh, who had just split from Marley and the Wailers. Peter had a foot-high pyramid of marijuana in the middle of his living room. After a few spliffs, I interviewed him about his first solo record, Legalize It. *It was the best sort of Q and A: one Q, the rest A. From* High Times, *1975.*

Mark Jacobson: So, Peter, tell us about your new record, *Legalize It*. Do you think people will get the message?

Peter Tosh: Man of all description, man and men of all different category, you know? Just go in a studio, an' sit down, turn on a mike an' say, I am a lawyer an' I smoke herb, or anything you wanna call it—marijuana, or pot or anyt'ing. Every man would be wit herb irrespective of how big him t'ink him in society.

A man is not too big in society if herb is degradation of society, because according to de law of herb, only de small man get deprive, or go to prison, or bein' brutalize by police for herb. Only de small man.

Me come to de conclusion that de whole earth—well, let's say 99 percent of de earth—have some form affiliation wit' de herb, because dem call it ganja, an don't know ganja is a t'ing dat grow. Ganga is a bird in Australia, or ganja is a place in Russia, an' ganja is whole lotta different t'ing, but nothin' pertainin' to what him callin' it, legal t'ing. And the poor man who don' know him constitutional right, just get fucked.

Well, we like herb for free, man. Because herb is good for the earth. What fuck up de earth is the rahs-clot law! *Is* fuckin' up de small man, cause only de small man at all time go to blood-clot jail for herb, an' de beeg man just pass in him limousine. An' if he can have on him certain identification that society see man, o-so-well-it's-mister-Brown don'-touch-it/blood-clot-let-him-go-on. An' oh, *Yess man!* Just right! *Me smoke herb!* Me smoke herb, me pass my herb, me goin' free. You bigger, you smoke herb an' you pass it, an' you goin' free. But because you bigger an' you drive a bigger car dan me, an' you live up a Beverly Hill an' dem bum-clot, then you mus' come, you dominate de whole earth. An now dem rahs-clot Christopher Columbus, rahs-clot, Pirate Morgan, Francis Drake. All dem same, dem fuckers. Dem kinda work used to work, man, legal laws, dem sit around an' drink dem blood-clot whiskey and say, "Haw, haw, how, *Let us make law,*" callin em fucker an' t'ing, *yess mon!* Ya man, an' is just de small man *feel it at all times*. An' de small man, is not only domination of herb him feel . . . *incrimination* of herb; evryt'ing, every illegal law is put up to fight against the small man. An' is de small man who is buildin' up the resource of the earth.

Yess man! Slavery abolish! Dat was from about eighteenth or so sixteenth *blood-clot* century ago, dem say slavery abolish! Do right an' let every man be satisfied. Earth resource must be distribute right. Herb was made for the use of man, an' not for de use of some blood-clot drunkard. Herb was made for de use of man, an' not *men* in dem control de blood-clot *chamber!* An' man must get herb cause man keep de earth runnin' till today. Not *men* in him limousine, dem blood-clot luxurious fucker. An dem make de law. Rahs-clot mf'ing scum! Dem t'ing get me mad. Yeah, man. It's not me alone dat get mad. It's in some kinda madhouse de rahs-clot where some stay consciously mad and have to us just *abide* wit' de situation, until de situation changes. Y'know? But man, bum-clot, come to dat now, man.

Economical pressure, dem raise up everyting, an' herb will keep you from t'inkin' about what's going on now. Dem wanna come *dominate*. Dem put out, dem wanna bring out dem drugs. Come spring it up on us, fucker! Dem trip, dem fuck up your head. Wise man use herb. We can do dat. *We have to get out of hell man*, whadayamean, *or let hell get out of us*. What you t'ink man? Too heavy for dem? Well, I *know* it is right.

Dem say dat herb is a dangerous drug, and pie-zen, an' every day I pie-zen myself an' nevah die. So why? Fight against I? Pure Babylon. Fertilizer come from oil. An' rubbish. Oil an' herb don't mix. Yes, man. Herb must as plant a come by nature. Jus' grow, an' it *don't care* how it come. If it knot, or if it spread out. It nice same way. But as soon ya fertilize it, man, it pure fucker. Your belly hurt. Ah, ya feel bad like ya wanna vomit, man. Yes, man. But if you smoke some nice herb an' put your mind somewhere where inspiration flows, herb so nice.

9

The Passion of Doctor J

Michael Jordan is certainly the greatest basketball player of all time, but Julius Erving, the incomparable Doctor J, is my all-time favorite. No one ever gave me as much pleasure watching any kind of game. Since his retirement, Julius has been the subject of a number of distressing headlines, exactly the sort of stuff he sought to avoid during his career. He acknowledged the tennis player Alexandria Stevenson to be his out-of-wedlock daughter. Later, his son Cory drove his car into a lake in Florida and drowned. These are unfortunate, sad events, but even more so when connected to someone like Julius, who was once so effortlessly perfect. I've written numerous articles on sports figures, most of them basketball players, but Julius remains my number one. The fact that he used to pick me up at the Philadelphia train station in his Maserati, nearly unthinkable for a current-day player, is still one of highlights of my career. From Esquire, 1984*.*

I went for a ride through downtown Philadelphia with Julius Erving in his Maserati the other day, and with each passing block it became more apparent: Julius cannot drive very well. It wasn't a question of reckless speed or ignored signals. Rather, he seemed unsure, tentative. His huge, famous hands clutched the steering wheel a bit too tightly, his large head craned uncomfortably toward the slope of the windshield. He accelerated with a lurch; there was no smooth rush of power. Obvious openings in the flow of traffic went unseen or untried. All in all, it reflected a total absence of *feel.*

This struck me as amusing—Julius Erving, the fabulous Doctor of the court, driving a Maserati with an automatic transmission.

Just an hour before, I'd compared the act of seeing Julius play basketball to Saint Francis watching birds in flight. It was my Ultimate Compliment. When a reporter with pretensions meets an Official Legend, especially a Sports Legend, it is mandatory to concoct the Ultimate Compliment, something beyond a plebeian "gee whiz." Something along the lines of the august Mailer's referring to Ali as a Prince of Heaven, whose very gaze caused men to look down. Or, perhaps, Liebling's mentioning that Sugar Ray Robinson had "slumberland in either hand." Saint Francis was what I'd come up with.

Viewing Doctor J move to the hoop inspired what I imagined to be an awe similar to what Saint Francis felt sitting in a field with the sparrows buzzing overhead, I told Julius. It was as if a curtain had been parted, affording a peek into the Realm of the Extraordinary, a marvelous communication that ennobled both the watcher and the watched equally. What wonders there are in the Kingdom of God! How glorious they are to behold!

"What you do affirms the supremacy of all beings," I told Julius as we sat in the offices of the Erving Group, a holding company designed to spread around the wads of capital Julius has accumulated during his career as Doctor J. Large gold-leaf plaques calling Julius things like TASTEE CAKE PLAYER OF THE YEAR dot the walls. "Seeing you play basketball has enriched my life," I finished.

"Thanks, thanks a lot," Julius said politely. Then again, Julius is always polite. It was obvious, my Ultimate Compliment clearly did not knock his socks off. It was as if he were saying, "Funny thing, you're the third guy who's told me that today."

Every serious hoop fan remembers the first time he saw Julius Erving play basketball. My grandfather, a great New York Giants baseball fan, probably had the same feeling the first time he ever saw Willie Mays go back on a fly ball. There was Julius, mad-haired and scowl-faced, doing what everyone else did, rebounding, scoring, passing, but doing it with the accents shifted from the accepted but now totally humdrum position to a new, infinitely more thrilling somewhere else. Who was this man with two Jewish names who came from parts unknown with powers far greater than the mortal Trailblazer?

Flat out, there was nothing like him. No one had ever taken off from the foul line as if on a dare, cradled the ball above his head, and not come down until he crashed it through the hoop. Not like that, anyway. Julius acknowledges a debt to Elgin Baylor, whom he calls "the biggest gazelle, the first of the gliders," but, to the stunned observer, the Doctor seemed to arrive from outside the boundaries of the game itself. His body, streamlined like none before him, festooned by arms longer and hands bigger, soared with an athletic ferocity matched only by the mystical, unprecedented catapult of Bob Beamon down the Mexico City runway, or by the screaming flight of Bruce Lee.

Has any other individual in team sports radically altered the *idea* of how his particular game should be played to the degree Julius has? Jackie Robinson? Babe Ruth? Jim Brown? A more instructive comparison would be someone like Joe DiMaggio. DiMaggio was impeccable, the nonpareil. He was simply better. Yet there is something hermetic about Joe DiMaggio. He did what everyone else did, but with incomparable excellence. Joe's exemplariness is to be admired, but it doesn't offer a whole program of reform. His greatness is a dead end, specific to Joe and Joe alone. Julius, on the other hand, may not have invented the slam dunk, the finger roll, or the hanging rebound—the entire airborne game in general. But he certainly popularized it, and by doing so he announced that others could follow in his footsteps, even surpass him. Seeing Julius fly to the hoop spread the news: it can be done, so do it. Nine years ago Julius appeared alone in his ability to go pyrotechnic at any time. This past year, however, lined up against a gaggle of his poetic offspring, "human highlight film" youngbloods like Dominique Wilkins and Larry Nance, Julius was content to make his final attempt a running foul-line takeoff: the "classical" dunk, a bit of archaeology demonstrated by the father of the form.

Befitting the matter-of-factness of a legend discussing his craft, Julius is not falsely modest about his contributions to the game. In the clinical fashion he employs when delineating the *x*'s and *o*'s of his profession, he says, "I'd say I've had an effect in three main areas. First, I have taken a smaller man's game, ball-handling, passing, and the like, and brought it to the front court. Second, I've taken the big man's game, rebounding, shot-blocking, and been able to execute that even though I'm only six-foot-six. What I've tried to do is merge those two types of games, which were considered to be separate—for instance, Bill Russell does the rebounding, Cousy handles the ball—and combine them into the same player. This has more or less changed the definition of what's called the small forward position, and it creates a lot more flexibility for the individual player, and, of course, creates a lot more opportunities for the whole team. The third thing I've tried to do, and this is the most important thing, is to make this kind of basketball a winning kind of basketball, taking into account a degree of showmanship that gets people excited. My overall goal is to give people the feeling they are being entertained by an artist—and to win."

Then Julius laughs and says, "You know, the playground game . . . refined."

In Roosevelt, New York, the lower-middle-class, largely black Long Island community where he grew up, there is a playground with a sign that says THIS IS WHERE JULIUS ERVING LEARNED THE GAME OF BASKETBALL. Herein lies Julius's triumph. He successfully transmuted the black playground game and brought that cutthroat urban staple to its most sumptuous fruition. He, once and for all, no turning back, blackified pro basketball.

He did it by forcing the comparatively staid, grind-it-out, coach-dominated NBA to merge with the old ABA, a semi-outlaw league that played the run-till-you-drop "black" playground game with a garish red, white, and blue ball. Julius was in the ABA, and the older, more established NBA could not allow a phenomenon like Doctor J to exist outside its borders. Most observers feel the NBA absorbed the whole funky ABA, with its three-point shots and idiotic mascots, just to get Julius. Once they did, the entire product of pro basketball was refocused. Surprise! The ABA, comprising many performers from Podunk Junior College and some who never went to any college, had a lot more than Julius Erving. Many players long scorned by the NBA brass became stars, the incandescent "Ice," George Gervin, and Moses Malone among them. And there was a lot more running. Before the merger there was only one consistent fast-break team in the NBA, the Celtics. Now, with the ABA people around, it seemed as if the whole league was running, playing the playground game, Julius's game.

This is not to say Larry Bird isn't great, no matter where the game is, on the back lawn of Buckingham Palace or up in Harlem, but blackification was inevitable. No one will really deny that the majority of black players jump higher and run faster than the majority of white players, and that's what pro ball, as it's currently constituted, is all about—running and jumping with finesse.

Many people have wondered if all this running is such a good thing. Since the merger and the takeover by the "black" game, the pro sport has suffered reversals. Attendance is uneven and TV ratings are down; rumors of widespread social evils among the players abound. It is difficult to have any in-depth conversation about the status of the league without coming up against the Problem. A league official says, "It's race, pure and simple. No major sport comes up against it the way we do. It's just difficult to get a lot of people to watch huge, intelligent, millionaire black people on television."

When presented with the notion that by elevating his art he may have served to narrow its appeal, Julius says, "It's unfortunate, but what can be done about what is?" Well, at least the onset of the playground game has exploded several pernicious myths. If there is one thing Julius and his followers (Magic Johnson comes to mind) have proved without a doubt, it's that just because you play "flashy" doesn't mean you're not a team player. No longer is it assumed that the spectacular is really, at its root, just mindless showboating easily thwarted, in the crunch times, by the cunning of a small man chewing a cigar on the coaching lines. Julius's teams have always won.

For the hoop fan, though, likely the most treasured item concerning Julius Erving remains in that first cataclysmic moment of discovery, that first peek into the Realm of the Extraordinary. This has to do with the nature of the fan, the hoop fan in particular. All team sports have their cognoscenti, gamblers poring over the injury lists, nine-year-old boys with batting averages memorized, but somehow the variety of fan attracted to pro basketball is in a slightly more obsessive class, sweatier, seedier perhaps, but absolutely committed. This type of hoop fan I'm talking about isn't much different from the jazz buffs of the 1940s and 1950s, white people digging on an essentially black world.

How Julius, the Official Legend, comes into this is that he approached the beady consciousness as Rumor. He was a secret. He wasn't a well-publicized high school star like Kareem; he went to the University of Massachusetts (a school with no basketball reputation) and then played two years at one of the ABA's most remote outposts, the Virginia Squires. There was no hoopla surrounding him, no Brent Musburger hyping the size of his smile. The Doctor was something for the grapevine.

It cuts both ways. Probably, by somehow staying out of the limelight (that was easier in 1970) and by choosing not to go to a "big program" school where a crusty Adolph Rupp might have made it a principle to correct all that boy's strange habits, Julius was left alone to create his wholly new thing. And by virtue of this anonymity, the hoop fan was able to come upon Julius as a wondrous found object.

Magic Johnson, Sugar Ray Leonard—no one is knocking their talents, but they arrived on the scene tied in a bow, sold to anyone within eyeshot of a TV. They will always carry that stigma. Julius, however, remains eternally cool. You had to work to see Julius, seek him out. There wasn't any cable; maybe you could catch him on an independent station that had been hustled into picking up one of the numerous ABA All-Star games. Even after he came from the Squires to the Nets, then the ABA New York entry, the hoop fan had to ply the forlorn parkways to the Nassau Coliseum to sit with four thousand dour faces expressing regret that they weren't viewing a hockey game. You had to go out of your way to see Julius. But it was worth it. When you saw that Rumor was Fact, and a far more remarkable Fact than imagined, then you felt like you had your little bond with Julius, that he was in your heart.

That Julius has maintained the quality of play this long is gravy. How do you measure the benefit one gets from seeing beautiful things happen? Sometimes I find myself idly replaying some of Julius's more astounding moves inside my head. The one against the Lakers in the championship a few years back, the one where he goes behind the backboard and comes around for the reverse layup? Ones like that bring tears to my eyes. Really.

Of course, it can't last. Last season Julius's club, the Philadelphia 76ers, for whom he's played since the league merger in 1976, were mangled by the bedraggled New Jersey Nets, transplanted to the Garden State from Uniondale, New York. It was an upset. The year before the Sixers won the title in a near walkover. Of the thirteen games they played in the championship rounds, they won twelve. The Sixers didn't come close to repeating. Julius did not have a particularly good series. There were several reasons. For one, it had been a grueling season for the Doc. Numerous Sixer injuries forced him to play many more minutes than he might have wanted to at his age. He responded with perhaps his best year in the past three and had his backers for league MVP. By the playoffs, however, he was weary, worn out. In the last moments of the deciding game he made repeated turnovers and missed key shots. Had a b-ball cognoscenti arrived from Mars right then, dumb to the history of the past fifteen years, he could have watched Julius's play and pronounced it "ordinary."

So it goes. Athletes get old, and soon they're too old to play. In the variety of pro basketball Julius helped create, it happens even quicker. There is no DH in the NBA, and right now Julius, at thirty-four, is among the fifteen oldest guys in the league. If he stays another couple of seasons, as he hints he might, he could be the oldest. His Afro, once wild as a Rorschach blot and seemingly a foot high, is now demurely trimmed and flecked with gray. So it goes: a million dudes with the hot hand down in the schoolyard waiting for the Doctor to roll over so they can get their shot. No tears over that. But it's this driving that's upsetting, the way Julius is drivng this Maserati with the automatic transmission. It's all so ordinary, how Julius is driving.

"Don't ask me any questions or I'll miss my turn," Julius says, smiling, as if to comment on his competence.

Then he makes this flabby, too-wide turn off Broad Street. What a deal: soon enough Julius is going to retire from basketball, but likely he'll be driving that Maserati with the automatic transmission for years to come.

"As it came it can go, as it came it most definitely *will* go," he says cheerfully, unaffected by his companion's gloom. "It won't really be that big a change for me," Julius says. "I've always thought of myself as a very ordinary guy."

This is a little tough to swallow, the Doctor an ordinary guy. This is not to say Julius Erving is not a *regular* guy. Sports-page "class"—Julius is the embodiment of it. Probably no athlete still playing has signed more autographs. His marathon sessions are spoken of with awe. Talking about it, Julius gives a look that asks, "Weren't you ever a kid?" and says, "Sometimes I ask myself, 'Should I accommodate today, or go straight ahead?' and I usually find myself accommodating." There is a limit, however. Walking through the icebound streets of Milwaukee, a fat guy accosted Julius, screaming, "Doc! Doc! Where's the other shoe?" Julius frowned. "I gave that guy one of my sneakers three years ago," he says, "and now, every time we go there, he asks for the other one. Some people are never satisfied."

As far as hoop reporters are concerned, Julius is the best. "There is no second place," says a Philly writer. This means that when deadlines are approaching and sweat is popping out on foreheads, Julius can be counted on to produce the proper verbiage, a smooth rap that, without much time-consuming translation, can be plugged into hastily written stories as "game quotes." It is something Julius works on, like any part of what he calls "my basketball function." He knows what reporters need and tries to give it to them.

"A courtesy," Julius says. Ask the right questions (nothing controversial, if you please!) and Julius will, in a voice that makes Frankie Crocker sound shrill, calmly assess the team's mood for you. He'll also say that Denver's Calvin Natt is among the toughest for him to score against, and that it is difficult to play Dallas's Mark Aguirre because "his butt is so big you can't get close to him," and that George Gervin is his favorite player, and that the Knicks' Bernard King, considered by many the best forward in the league, "will never get up to the level of the real all-timers like, say, Kareem, or myself, because he looks like he's working too hard. When you reach a level of greatness, there's a certain added element that goes into making it look easy."

Mainly, Julius keeps a low profile. He will often make inquiries about jazz—more out of educational desire than passion, for he prefers fusion. You could call him elegantly laid-back, stylish, though certainly you'd never confuse him with Walt Frazier. He is always the clean-living family man and, while sharp, displays little outward flash. He leaves the five-pound jewelry to the Darryl Dawkinses of the world, although he appears to cop no attitude toward the more flamboyant displays, sartorial or otherwise, of his fellows. He has, after all, been around, and not much raises the Doctor's eyebrow.

In Milwaukee, however, one John Matuszak, late of the Oakland Raiders football team and the movie *North Dallas Forty*, came close. The Tooz, as he has been known to call himself, appeared unannounced in the Sixers' locker room, and he was calling some attention to himself. Even in a world of large men, the Tooz stands out. He goes six-foot-eight, about three hundred pounds. In addition, he sports a mug that resembles the sort of hood ornament Screamin' Jay Hawkins might have mounted on his '55 De Soto to ward off unfriendly spirits. This is not to mention his dress on this particular night, which included a black silk coat, tuxedo pants, patent leather shoes, and a white satin tie over a leopard skin print shirt. He was also affecting a manner that would put him right up there for the Bluto part, should a remake of *Animal House* be made anytime soon.

It was the Tooz's sworn purpose to have both Julius and Moses Malone, the Sixers' famously intimidating center, join him at one of Milwaukee's more stylish wateringholes.

First he invited Moses. "Gonna win this year, Moses?" was Tooz's opener. Moses, no midget himself, was sitting on a stool stark naked. "Yeah, we're gonna win, " said Moses, laying on his usual Sonny Liston–style bale.

Then, like a shot, the Tooz was down on one knee. He clasped his palms together and drove them like a hammer into Moses' thigh. "Don't say we're gonna win. Say we *gotta* win, Moses!!" the Tooz shouted, startling the few stragglers in the locker room. "Come on, Moses," the Tooz continued, "repeat after me: WE GOTTA WIN!" And, to the amazement of onlookers, Moses, who had not uttered a word in public since telling Philly reporters, "I'll be making no further comment for the rest of the season," repeated this after the Tooz. Moses, however, steadfastly refused to have a drink with the former lineman.

Thwarted, the Tooz went looking for Julius, who was in the midst of taking a shower. Unmindful of the water splashing everywhere, the Tooz confided to Julius how much he loved him. "I love you, Doctor!" the Tooz bellowed. Then he said, "Come on, Doctor. The Doctor and the Tooz must have a drink together. I got some friends, it'll be a party!"

Julius, never rude, thanked the Tooz for his offer but expressed his regrets, citing a 5:00 A.M. wake-up call the next morning.

"If you're worried about people hassling you, forget about it," the Tooz said with understanding. "No one will mess with you if you're with the Tooz!"

The football player had now stepped over the edge of the shower, his long hair dripping down over his drenched suit.

Backing into the stall, Julius, seemingly unrattled, said. "You're getting wet, you know that?"

"A drink, that's all I'm asking," Tooz repeated, reaching out to wrap his arms around the Doctor. "People love you, man," the Tooz said with sincerity, "people live to see you do your thing." Then, clearly disappointed, the Tooz left.

Several moments of silence ensued, during which Julius began to dress and Moses picked tape off his leg. Then Moses looked at Julius sleepily and said, "See those shoes?"

"What about the tie?" Julius said back.

Later Julius smiled and said, sure, it seemed like the Tooz was something of a boor, but you really had to get to know him better before you could say that unequivocally. After all, The Doc is not what you would call judgmental.

Teammates speak of him with healthy degrees of awe and camaraderie. Marc Iavaroni, a marginal forward cut by a couple of lesser NBA clubs before catching on as a "role player" in the Sixers' system, says, "Playing with the Doc? Don't pinch me, please. He looks for me. On and off the court. Can you imagine that! Doctor J looking to pass off to Marc Iavaroni? Know how that makes me feel?"

Nearly everyone close enough to Julius to have personal dealings speaks of some small kindness, a birthday remembered, an appreciated pep talk, a good laugh. League officials, always aware of the "image problem" of the sport, tell you how many young players Julius has done right by, how his example is primarily responsible for the "rehabilitation" of Chicago's troubled Quintin Dailey. Julius's community awards appear endless. Last year he got the Father Flanagan Award for Service to Youth at Boys Town; previous recipients include Mother Teresa, Danny Thomas, and Spencer Tracy's wife. The list of charities supported, youth groups spoken to (he read *Peter and the Wolf* at a special children's show of the Youth Orchestra of Greater Philadelphia), and hospital wards visited goes on and on.

"All part of my 'nice-guy image,'" Julius says with a wink. He is aware that all these good vibes add up under the economic heading of "Doctor J": is proud that the Q ratings of his numerous commercial endorsements show him rating higher in "believability" than in "popularity." "But really," he says, "I just try to be decent. I try to do the decent thing in the circumstances. Right now I happen to be a well-known professional athlete, so I attempt to be decent within that context. Being nice is pretty normal, I think. If someone was drowning in the river, you'd assume most people would throw them a life preserver. You'd figure most people would do that, under those circumstances. That would be the normal thing to do. That's what I like to believe I'd do, being a normal person."

This led to Julius's further insistence that, really, he was a very ordinary guy. An ordinary guy dealing with extraordinary circumstances, perhaps, but ordinary nevertheless.

"I've never felt particularly unique," Julius says. "Even within the context of basketball, I honestly never imagined myself as anything special. I remember, back home, when I first started playing. At nine, ten, I had a two-hand shot. Then by twelve and a half, thirteen, I got a one-hand shot. Always went to the basket, that pattern was set by then. Actually, I don't think I've changed much as a player since then. Back then, before I was physically able, I felt these different things within me, certain moves, ways to dunk. It sounds strange, being five feet tall, thinking about dunking in a clinical way, but that's how I was. I realized all I had to do was be patient and they would come. So I wasn't surprised when they did, they were part of me for so long. But I didn't find anything particularly special about it. I assumed everyone could do these things if they tried."

Julius claims the idea of being a professional basketball player didn't occur to him until he was among the country's leaders in both scoring and rebounding at UMass. He wanted to be a doctor. That's the source of his unbeatable nickname. In grammar school when the kids got up to say what they wanted to be when they grew up, Julius said, "A doctor." "Doctor!" the kids shouted, and it stuck. Later, when playing in the Rucker League, the deejay types "announcing" games were calling him the Claw, a moniker based on his large hands. Julius, always sharp to the distasteful, objected and, when asked for a substitute, said, "Oh, why don't you just call me Doctor." Doctors, after all, Julius felt, were white-haired men with soothing voices, who surrounded themselves with a great air of dignity. They also made a lot of money. These were Julius's two main concerns at the time. His father had left his mother and brother early on and wound up being run down by a car when Julius was eleven.

"I never really had a father," Julius says, "but then the possibility that I ever would was removed."

After that, security, financial and otherwise, became obsessional with Julius. Even today, with a contract that pays him more than a million each year and other lucrative interests (he refers to basketball as "my main business application"), Julius is notoriously parsimonious. Do not expect him to pick up the check. It was this desire for himself and his family (there are four children now, three boys and a girl, living in a mansion on 2.8 acres on the Main Line) that made Julius think of playing ball for money.

"That's when I started hearing all these people talking about how different I was supposed to be," Julius recounts. "When a hundred people, then a thousand people tell you you're different, you just say to yourself, 'Okay, I'm different. . . . Don't get me wrong, I liked it. I liked what it got me. I was a young player, I was doing what came easy to me, I was having a good time, so I accepted it as a fact of life." It was only during the stresses caused by his leaving the Nets (in a protracted contract battle), the subsequent league merger, and his arrival in Philadelphia to less than knockout notices when Julius began to ponder, "Why am I different? Why, with all these great players all around, guys who play as hard as I do, guys who want to win as badly as I do, why am I Doctor J?"

Quite a picture: the angst-ridden superstar, his piston legs rocketing from the pinewood floor into the glare of the houselights, his seemingly inexorable gaze transfixed on the orange ring, yet, in reality, his leap goes nowhere, for he is lost.

That's the way Julius paints it. During his first years in Philly it became commonplace to downrate the Doc. In the ABA he'd scored 28.7 points a game and nabbed nearly a thousand rebounds each season; now he was getting 21, 22, and his 'bounds were way down. Some nodded and said it was true what they said about the old league; it was a circus, after all. In 1978 an unnamed coach was quoted in *Sports Illustrated* as saying, "[Julius] has been on vacation for three years."

For his part, Julius complained that his knees were killing him (he has had a tendinitis condition for some time) and that he'd *purposely* hidden away much of the spectacular side of the Doctor, so as to better mesh with then-teammate George McGinnis, another ABA scorer not noted for his passing skills. Yet, it wasn't fun. None of it. He let it slip that more than likely he'd be retiring when his contract ran out in 1982. Now, though, Julius says his main problem was a spiritual, not a physical, one. "I felt totally hollow," he says. "It was eating at me. I started off asking, 'Who is Doctor J? How did I get to be him? What does being Doctor J mean?' . . . then it came down to asking, 'Who, really, am I?' I became very frightened when I began to sense that I really had no idea."

One can imagine the terror Julius felt. He seems a very methodical person, someone who likes everything in its place, not one to rush into things. Perhaps due to his longtime regimen as an athlete, where every day the practice is set for a certain amount of time and the bus leaves at such-and-such o'clock, he is given to compartmentalizing his life and talking of it in terms of small, constantly repeated activities. "I admit to liking the feel of things being in context," Julius says, "the sense of the familiar waters." This extends even to the court. Julius contends, "Out of one hundred moves I make in a game, I've made ninety-nine before, at one time or another. Sure, that one new one gives me a hit, but actually I get as much or more out of doing the other ninety-nine, because when I do something I've done before it means that I've compiled this information in my mind and selected the right action for the proper situation. That gives me a lot of pleasure.

"Back then, though," Julius adds, "I felt completely alone at times. Often, after a game and a late dinner, in one of those cities, I'd be sitting up, three o'clock, four o'clock, after eating a big steak, just watching that TV, with all the phones turned off. I never felt like that before.

"It was finding my faith that pulled me through," Julius says, leaning back from the desk in his Philadelphia office. In front of him is a rectangular paperweight you'd figure would be made of copper or brass and say, in embossed letters, something like JULIUS WINFIELD ERVING JR., PRESIDENT. But it is wooden and appears to have been made in a junior high school shop class. It says JESUS.

Julius's conversion occurred during the summer of 1978, at a family get-together in South Carolina. The previous season had been his worst yet. Julius had played poorly, and he was suffering from numerous injuries. The flak was getting intense. "I was feeling a little sorry for myself," Julius says, "but when I got down there and saw all those people, people I didn't know, some of whom I didn't even know existed, yet people who were connected to me in some way, it was really something. Because I was well known, everyone sort of used me as a lightning rod, a common denominator. They used me to get closer to each other. And I felt all that love passing through me. It was a very strange and wonderful feeling."

At the meeting Julius encountered an uncle of his, Alfonso, a preacher. He told Julius about a blessing that had been laid on the family that, Alfonso said, was now being manifested through Julius. "After that," Julius says, "things fell into place for me."

When the subject of Julius-as-Christian comes up, a good portion of the cognoscenti express surprise (it is not well known) and then shake their heads. However, to the reporter with pretensions, it seemed a great boon, a fabulous opportunity. This isn't to say Julius won't go Jaycee on you at any moment; no doubt his "Dare to Be Great" speech ranks with the best. He is also given to saying things like "Did I want to open the doors to essential knowledge or did I want to remain on the merry-go-round of nondiscovery?" Primarily, though, here was an intelligent, observant man, who by the vehicle of a mysterious "blessing" had been thrust into the Realm of the Extraordinary. The hope was that he would have the presence of mind to keep his eyes and ears open while in this marvelous land, and that hope was rewarded. I mean, you could enter into a metaphysical dialogue with this man!

On a Milwaukee street we mulled over the notion of the Divine Call. On a bus in Detroit we beat around the dichotomy of true Needs and venal Wants. In a Madison Square Garden locker room we pierced the outskirts of the Spirit of Giving. But it wasn't until our discussion in his office, during a laborious spiel of mine concerning the duty of the seeker to examine the varieties of religious experience, that Julius began to get pissed.

"I just can't agree," he said, "because even if you do manage to synthesize all these systems, what good is it going to do you? Even if you're the smartest man on earth, even if you're Albert Einstein, you'll still only have a thimbleful of all the knowledge in the world. Where does that lead you? Digging and grinding on this unbelievable quest? Is there happiness in that? So it comes down to making *concessions* . . . down to knowing you're not the wisest or the smartest, not the ultimate of anything, but knowing too that you have this powerful need to grasp something meaningful, something purposeful . . . you want a way, a way that makes sense for you, that you can embrace."

It was clear what Julius was getting at. After all, he is a black guy in America, the son of a very religious church lady mother. He reached out to what was available to him, and it worked. He found himself capable of faith. But really, was there any other solution for the intelligent, humble man with the nice-guy image? Doctor J has not simply been a great player, he has been *the epitome* of a player, God's own fantasy of a player. If Julius meant to "deal with logic, infused by faith," as he says is his bent, was there any other conclusion but to accept the notion of the involved, controlling presence of a Higher Power? There seemed a profound sanity in Julius's belief, and the reporter with pretension found it very satisfying.

Julius says he has no fear of life A.B. (After Basketball). "The thing that frightens me is what I heard about spiritual casualties. A spiritual casualty is someone . . . say a well-known athlete who takes a spiritual stand, and then the focus shifts from looking at that person as an athlete to something else. Suddenly there are all these people who want to put this athlete in the forefront because they assume he can be as significant spiritually as he was athletically. Then this famous athlete uses this forum to talk about what he feels about this new field he's entered . . . and he doesn't know what he's talking about . . . like, say, someone might say, 'Kareem, he's a superstar ballplayer, so he should be a superstar Muslim.' A spiritual casualty is someone who falls for that."

Julius shivers at the mention of Eldridge Cleaver, who did much to make a mockery of himself in his post-Panther days, showing up on *The Hour of Power* one minute and modeling codpiece trousers the next. Julius is well aware of what went into the creation and maintenance of Doctor J, and he will do almost anything to keep that image from being defiled. "The last thing I want to be perceived as is a flake," he says warily.

Some suggest that Julius might be a little less cautious. There have been intimations that by stressing his "Christian umbrella," Julius has demonstrated a degree of naïveté concerning day-to-day life in lower-rent districts. This talk became increasingly intense after Julius's no-profile stance in the recent Philly mayoral election, which pitted liberal black W. Wilson Goode against neo-Neanderthal Frank Rizzo. Hearing this, Julius gets as close as he does to bristling. "I'm very sensitive to this type of criticism," he says, "but I'm not going to be pressured by it. My track record in the black community speaks for itself. You know, I'm not blind, I understand how things are. I remember what it was like growing up, and when we go to Boston and Chicago, there's racism there. We hear what people shout, you know. I understand the danger of getting so far from a situation that you fool yourself and say it doesn't exist, or get the illusion that because you're a well-known ballplayer it doesn't apply to me. I'm not living in a dream world, but I'll tell you I'd be a fool not to use the advantages I've earned through playing in behalf of my family. But I'm not going to invite a potentially hostile situation into my life, into the lives of my wife and children, for just anyone's idea of solidarity. If I can afford an extra layer of protection, I will exercise it.

"I've never been a political person. I've never backed a political candidate in my life. When I was with the Nets, a picture came out of me in the newspaper with a local candidate. It was just some function for the team, but this guy was there and he was running for some office, and then all these people were asking me why I was supporting the Republican candidate. I don't want that to happen again. It would threaten my livelihood. If I backed the Democratic candidate, I'd run the risk of alienating half my public, and the other way around.

"But mostly it comes down to: I've played basketball for twenty-five years, almost every situation that can come up has come up. Therefore I'm qualified to sit here and talk to you about basketball. I don't have those sort of memory cells concerning other areas."

So, Julius says, he will enter the realm of the ordinary as a businessman. "An entrepreneur," he says, professing to have always had "a deep yearning" to be such a person. Typically enough, most of his investments have reflected a stolid, blue-chippy side. He is a large stockholder in the Coca-Cola Bottling Company of New York. He makes earnest use of the products he endorses, which have included Coke, Converse, Spalding, and Chap Stick.

Don't look for Julius dancing in the back row of a Bally's Park Place Hotel Casino commercial, or any Doc's Dunkshot Bar opening in the East Sixties. Julius does, however, keep some mad money around for what he calls "risk capital ventures." One of these ventures was the now-defunct Doctor's Shoe Salon, a chic fulfillment of one of Julius's long-cherished fantasies. Throughout his life, especially since he got rich, Julius found it galling that he could not find high-fashion shoes to wrap around his size fifteens. The Doctor's Shoe Salon assumed there were many others in the same boat and sought to fill that need by offering a wide selection for the hard-to-fit dog, mostly in the two-hundred-dollar range. The shop, poshly appointed and located on Philly's South Second Street, was slated to be the prototype for a far-flung chain that would eventually take in all the NBA cities. It was not a success. "It caused me untold duress and aggravation," Julius says sheepishly. "A lot of people expected, because my name was involved, that I'd be there all the time. When I wasn't, they got mad. And when I was, I couldn't concentrate on the business. I got bombarded with all kinds of questions, basketball stuff, A to Z. Plus we had a lot of trouble with kids who thought it was a sneaker store." Kind of humorous—the great Doctor as the harried shoe salesman. But never let anyone say Doc doesn't learn from experience. Currently his "risk" project is REACH, a camp for gifted and highly motivated children. Nowhere on the brochure will you find the name Julius Erving.

Basically, though, Julius says, his business goal is "to work four hours and rest twenty, as opposed to now, when I've got to work twenty hours to rest four." Until he gets there he has other things to think about. The end of all those hotel rooms and 5:00 A.M. flights to the next city will mean a lot more time at home, a *lot* more time.

"One hundred and thirty to 140 more nights," Julius relates, admitting some anxiety about this. Now, Julius, his wife Turquoise, and their four children (Cheo, Julius III, Jazmin, and Cory) are pretty much your all-American family, as was witnessed at last season's dunk contest, during which the kids told Dad which shots to make. But 130, 140 nights. "A lot of nights," Julius predicts, "they're gonna be saying, 'Him? Again?'" Then he laughs and says, "This is all first-generation problems for all of us, my wife and I, dealing with the circumstances we find ourselves in. There's going to be a lot of trial and error, that's for sure." Then he says he's thinking of calling up John Havlicek, Jerry West, "some old-timers, people on my level," to get some pointers on the life ahead. Somehow, you figure, he'll get over.

10
Dylan Archives

A historical drama concerning the writer's (one-way) relationship with his enduring hero, Bob Dylan. Here are two pieces written more than two decades apart, but very much connected. The first is a supposed "review" of Dylan's 1978 movie Renaldo & Clara. *Written quickly, it is a petulant review, (man, you try sitting through the movie), a negative review. It came out a little more negative than I might have liked. In fact, you could say the first line is on the harsh side. It got some feedback at the time, including a number of letters beginning with the same lines: "You wish Bob Dylan died, I wish you died." In the writing life, you will always write things you wish you didn't. This falls in that category. Still, I managed to forget (repress) the incident until a Dylan piece by Alex Ross appeared in the* New Yorker. *Right there in the first paragraph it was recalled how "Mark Jacobson wrote in the* Village Voice, *'I wish Bob Dylan died.'" Talk about the foot of pride coming down! I was, however, afforded a chance at Dylanesque redemption. To express my true feelings, so to speak. The second piece is not about Dylan per se, but about what is called "Dylanology," or "the study of Bob Dylan." In it I was able to address the previous incident, offer an apology of a sort. How Old Testament Bob is about forgiveness I can only guess. But I am not looking back. (A note to certain Dylan fans—please be forewarned that the widely reviled figure of A. J. Weberman not only appears in both Bob pieces, but also in the final article of this section, "The Strange Death of Bruce Lee." Just kind of worked out that way). From the* Village Voice, *1978;* Rolling Stone, *2001.*

Tangled Up in Gray: Renaldo & Clara

I wish Bob Dylan died. Then Channel 5 would piece together an instant documentary on his life and times, the way they did for Hubert Humphrey. The way they do for Chaplin, or Adolf Hitler. Just the immutable facts. Seeing all those immutable facts about Elvis made his dying worthwhile. The high points. What a sum-up. You don't get much gray, but like the reporter in *Citizen Kane* found out, gray doesn't necessarily amount to shit.

Of course, you couldn't expect facts from Dylan, and who wanted them? After the intermission of *Renaldo & Clara,* I was cruising along. The first half of the film ended with a nifty allusion to the beautifully incomprehensible *Belle de Jour,* a nice touch. *Renaldo & Clara* hadn't amounted to much, just a collage of charmingly old-fashioned Mailer–Rip Torn–type incantations of sixties obsessions. Still I defended it in the lobby, happy to be satisfied that nothing was revealed.

Unfortunately, *Renaldo & Clara* goes on for three or four more weeks, and although it doesn't get any more specific, the following are painfully revealed: All Indians and Hadassah ladies are fat, Allen Ginsberg can be completely insipid, Bob Dylan is the skinniest Jew living, Rubin Carter was a bore and probably killed those people, Dylan had a good reason to beat Sara (she being as whiny a hippie as any Gibran quoter), Dylan is totally bored of all his songs, or else he wouldn't uptempo that business about black being the color and none being the number, Dylan's concept of matched cuts wouldn't get him a B at NYU film school, and after twenty years I still hate Joan Baez.

As for anything new or revealing about Bob Dylan, it didn't come clear. Halfway through *Renaldo & Clara,* I was screaming for Westbrook Van Pegler. Or Jack Webb. I am sick and tired of vagueness in Bob Dylan. What is he afriad of? Four hours is a long time for nothing to be revealed. Just a succession of mystic-cryptic elusive ladies in the night and somber young men.

Maybe there is nothing to reveal. Where does this Malibu-dwelling record-industry master get off making a film three times as long as *Citizen*

Kane and then bleating in the production notes about Americans being too spoiled to sit still for art? A guy who only made one good record in eight years can't expect everything to be taken on faith forever. Goddamn, the only audible line Dylan speaks in the film is "Volkswagen bus."

I write off *Renaldo & Clara* as rich kid's vanity project. But of course I could be wrong. Missing the gray. So I called up A. J. Weberman to check it out. A. J., as any Dylanologist knows, was the Minister of Information of the Dylan Liberation Front. Reached at his Bleecker Street townhouse, A. J. said, "I can't talk about D. He just sued my ass for the second time. Folkways Records released the Weberman-Dylan phone tapes. D is suing me. The schmuck. Anyway, I haven't seen the picture. I couldn't comment yet. I've got to see it ten times on videocassette. Even then, I might not be able to talk. I'm sure it's all symbolism. D is the greatest symbolist of the modern age. To understand his movie would take ten years of serious study."

Tangled Up in Bob

Someday, no doubt, when the keepers of the tower officially allow that Bob was one of the two or three greatest American artists of the second half of the twentieth century, Dylanology will be boiled down to a standard three credits, a dry bonepile of jewels and binoculars to squeeze in between the Yeatsology and Whitmanology. You might even be able to major in Dylanology, hand in papers on the interplay between Deuteronomy and Dock Boggs in Bob's middle period. But for now, even as the Dylan economy grows each day (a mint copy of the rare stereo version of *Freewheelin'*, which contains four extra songs, goes for twenty thousand dollars), Dylanology, the semi–sub rosa info jungle of writers, fanzine publishers, collectors, Web page keepers, DAT tapers, song analyzers, old-girlfriend gossips, and more, retains a bracing hit of democratic autodidacticism, a deep-fried aroma of overheated neocortices.

"We are fanatical because we are fanatics," says the indefatigable Paul Williams, author of more than twenty-five books, whose *Bob Dylan: Performing Artist, 1960–1973*, *Bob Dylan: Performing Artist, 1974–1986*, and the ongoing *Bob Dylan: Performing Artist, 1987–2000* will likely approach an aggregate one thousand pages before he's done. Speaking of his Bob "compulsion," Williams, who is also the former literary executor of Philip K. Dick's estate, says, "If Shakespeare was in your midst, putting on shows at the Globe Theatre, wouldn't you feel the need to be there, to write down what happened in them?"

Williams, founding editor of *Crawdaddy* magazine, which featured Bob on its first cover in 1966, is a believer in what he calls "the process." For him, the more than forty conventional, nonbootleg recordings put out by the artist since 1962 are just the blueprint, the starting point, since Dylan, famous for a restless ambivalence toward his own creations, is constantly changing these songs in performance. This means Williams, who solicits donations from Dylan fans so he might continue his work, spends a lot of time comparing and contrasting tapes made at the thousands of shows Bob has given since 1961, which adds up to a lot of alt.versions of "All Along the Watchtower" (1,125 live performances as of January 1, 2001, according to Glen Dundas's *Tangled Up in Tapes*, as compared to 1,008 for "Like a Rolling Stone," 175 for "The Lonesome Death of Hattie Carroll," 53 for "Visions of Johanna," 22 for "Ring Them Bells," and one each for "Oxford Town" and "Bo Diddley").

"Writing a book about Bob Dylan is a twenty-four-hour-a-day, seven-day-a-week, 365-day-a-year project," Williams says.

This comprehensive approach is standard in D Studies. Bob is a big subject, getting bigger all the time, as he continues to flummox presumptions of reclusiveness by barnstorming a hundred dates a year, churning up ever more Dylanology in his wake. Clinton Heylin's recent update of *Bob Dylan: Behind the Shades Revisited* now tips in at 780 pages, a strain on the bookshelf that also includes Heylin's *Bob Dylan: A Life in Stolen Moments*—a day-by-day account of Dylan's doings from the years 1941 to 1995. Even more colossal is Michael Gray's ever-expanding revise of *Song and Dance Man III: The Art of Bob Dylan*, which now stretches to 918 pages, including a 111-page chapter titled "Even Post-Structuralists Oughta Have the Pre-War Blues." But even this seems curt compared with Oliver Trager's forthcoming (release is timed to Dylan's sixtieth birthday, on May

24th) *Back Pages: The Definitive Encyclopedia of Bob Dylan.* Talk about bringing it all back home (the UPS man who delivered the 1,179-page manuscript to my house was puffing hard): This deeply annotated sprawl of song analysis and cool gossip is enough to keep D fans occupied through a short nuclear winter.

It does not stop, as witnessed by the more-than-five-thousand-item sales list put out by Rolling Tomes Inc., the Bob megalopolis run by the charming Mick and Laurie McCuistion out in Grand Junction, Colorado. In addition to their quarterly *On the Tracks*, the McCuistions, who have four full-time employees engaged in what Laurie calls "Bob work," recently added a monthly newsletter titled *Series of Dreams*, because, as Laurie says, "There's just so much stuff happening all the time."

As everyone agrees, the current red-hot center of Dylanology is Bill Pagel's Boblinks Web site, based in Madison, Wisconsin, which, in addition to posting a set list (and several highly personalized reviews) within a half hour of Bob leaving the stage in any part of the world, also offers access to more than three hundred other Dylan Internet pages. Here, along with linkage to Sony's own "official" bobdylan.com and its mighty lyric-finder, one encounters the various personal Dylan shrines, cyber tours of Hibbing, Minnesota (where signs welcome the traveler to the "home of Kevin McHale"), hundreds of interviews with the Bobhead, and numerous pages such as "A Lily among Thorns: Exploring Bob Dylan's Christianity." "Lily" offers a compendium of Dylan's *Slow Train/Saved-Period* brimstone preaching: On one particular tempestuous evening in Tempe, Arizona, the Rev. Bob, in a sin-killing lather of overpersistent cries of "*Rock & roll!!!*" screams, "If you want rock & roll, you can go down with rock & roll! You can see Kiss! *You can rock & roll all the way down to the Pit!*"

Displaying ecumenicalism befitting its seeker hero, Boblinks also features a clickable connection to "Bob Dylan: Tangled Up in Jews." The site offers "highlights of Dylan's Judaic journeys" such as "changing his name from Zimmerman," "studying with Lubavitch Hasidim," and a description of the First Annual Bob Dylan Ceremonial New Year's Bread Toss, "in which Bob's rabbi shares where it's at and The Man himself blows the Jewish horn."

On Boblinks, one notes that a lot of the good Bob Web pages have already been claimed. Breadcrumbsins.com is taken. Foggyruinsoftime.com is taken. So is cowboyangelsings.com, powergreedandcorruptableseed.com, fantasticcollectionofstamps.com, and expectingrain.com. The latter is maintained by the genial Karl Erik Andersen, who works in the national library in a small Norwegian town astride the Arctic Circle and is happy to tell you how he rigged up a wireless system so he can listen to Bob while he shovels snow, which is most of the time. Still, with more than five hundred Bob song titles to choose from, many site names remain. As of this writing, such desirable addresses as huntedlikeacrocodile.com, bleachersoutinthesun.com, IstayedupallnightintheChelseaHotelwritingSad-EyedLadyoftheLowLandsforyou.com, Iputmyfingerstotheglassbowedmyhead andcried.com and hitthatdrummerwithapiethatsmells.com are all available.

So many quotations, so many conclusions written on the wall, I needed not remind myself as I went out walking through Greenwich Village a few days ago. Dylan can spend the rest of his life inside whatever gated Eden in Malibu, but the Village will always be the mystic Mississippi Delta of Dylanology—Bob Ground Zero. Over there, downstairs at 116 MacDougal, where a bar called The Wreck Room is now, that was the Gaslight. Dylan sang "Talkin' John Birch Paranoid Blues" there, opening for Dave Van Ronk. Upstairs was the Kettle of Fish, the bar where Dylan hung with the despondent Phil Ochs and once brought the Supremes, blowing blowsy folkie minds. Around the corner was the sainted Gerde's Folk City. Across Washington Square Park, now outfitted with surveillance cameras by Rudy Giuliani, was the Hotel Earle, currently renovated for tourists but then scruffy and bleak, nineteen dollars a week, home to Bob back in 1962.

That was a whole other Dylanological epoch, I thought, strolling, most positively, to the West Fourth Street subway station to take the ever-adventurous D train uptown to Fifty-ninth Street. I was on the way to talk to my old acquaintance A. J. Weberman, who is both the inventor of the term Dylanology and the discipline's most reviled figure.

As students of primeval D-ology know, A. J., who quit college in 1968 to create the first computer-generated Dylan Word Concordance, is most famous for going through Bob's garbage. This "garbology" action was part of a full-scale assault launched by the Dylan Liberation Front, a bunch of Yippie pot-smokers who thought Dylan, the most angel-headed head of the generation, had fallen prey to a *Manchurian Candidate*–style government plot to hook him to sensibility deadening hard dope. These findings were based on A. J.'s highly idiosyncratic interpretations of "Dylan's secret language," a code that, once cracked, revealed words like "rain" and "chicken" (as in "the sun is not yellow—it's chicken!") to actually mean "heroin." It was Dylan's addiction that led the poet to make sappy records like *Nashville Skyline* and *New Morning* when his great gift could have been better used speaking out against the Vietnam War, A. J. contended.

"Dylan's brain belongs to the People, not the Pigs!" was among the fervent cries back in 1970, as A. J. led the forty or so smelly hippies in his Dylanology class to Bob's home at 94 MacDougal Street, where they screamed for Bob to "crawl out yer window" and answer charges that he had been co-opted. After an unsolicited DLF-inspired block party for Dylan's thirtieth birthday, which resulted in the NYPD shutting down Bleecker Street, and a long series of hectoring phone calls (the tapes were compiled on a Folkways Records release entitled *Bob Dylan vs. A. J. Weberman*, now a major Bob collectible), Dylan struck back.

Three decades later, A. J., now fifty-five, his once-wild mane receded to silver fringe (but still talking very fast), recalls the incident, one of the more colorful in Dylanological chronicles: "I'd agreed not to hassle Dylan anymore, but I was a publicity-hungry motherfucker. . . . I went to MacDougal Street, and Dylan's wife comes out and starts screaming about me going through the garbage. Dylan said if I ever fucked with his wife, he'd beat the shit out of me. A couple of days later, I'm on Elizabeth Street and someone jumps me, starts punching me.

"I turn around and it's like—Dylan. I'm thinking, 'Can you believe this? I'm getting the crap beat out of me by Bob Dylan!'

"I said, 'Hey, man, how you doin'?' But he keeps knocking my head against the sidewalk. He's little, but he's strong. He works out. I wouldn't fight back, you know, because I knew I was wrong. I shouldn't have done what I did. After he's done hitting me, he gets up, rips off my 'Free Bob Dylan' button, and walks away. Never says a word.

"The Bowery bums were coming over, asking, 'How much he get?' Like I got rolled, or something. I told them, didn't you know who that was? It was Bob Dylan! They didn't know what the hell I was talking about . . . I guess you got to hand it to Dylan, coming over himself, not sending some fucking lawyer. That was the last time I ever saw him, except once with one of his kids, maybe Jakob, and he said, 'A. J. is so ashamed of his Jewishness, he got a nose job,' which was true—at least in the fact that I got a nose job. . . ."

It was all too bad, A. J. said now, remembering how Dylan had reportedly offered him a series of jobs if he would stop his "Free Bob" campaign. "He said I could be his chauffeur, but I told him I don't know how to drive. Then he said I could be his prompter, in case he forgot the words. But I said, 'Forget it! It's not going to work! I'm the one person you can't buy out.' In retrospect, that was a sad mistake. I could have had a career as a rock critic or something, and not as a pot dealer, and not, you know, ended up where I'm going to end up."

This was the news. Just the week before, A. J. had been in the Union County Correctional Facility, finally busted by the Feds for allegedly running a marijuana delivery service. He was out on one hundred thousand dollars bail, looking at a possible ten years in the joint.

When I called to ask if he was going to be home, he shouted, "Of course I'm going to be home, moron! I'm under fucking house arrest!" And there he was, the supposed Anton LaVey of Dylanology, with a plastic monitoring device snapped to his ankle, on the terrace of his apartment overlooking Central Park that had once been home to Antoine de Saint-Exupéry, author of *The Little Prince*. It was a far cry from the old days at the Bleecker Street bunker, where A. J.'s famous Dylan archives were zealously guarded by a trio of Doberman pinschers.

"As fate would have it," A. J. noted with bitter amusement, "the Feds watched my office and saw me throw away these big huge wrappers from the pot in the garbage, and they used that to get a search warrant. So the garbologist got caught with his own garbage."

This irony was not missed by the current generation of Dylanologists, the postings of whom can be found on the popular Usenet site rec.music.dylan. Under the thread "Weberman in jail!! I bet Bob is laughing," D fans rejoiced with comments like "not so instant karma but I'll take it" and the inevitable "don't need a Weberman to know which way the wind blows."

Dismissing this, A. J. stood by his recent highly controversial claims, notably that Dylan is suffering from AIDS, supposedly contracted from a dirty needle. As always, the proof was in the song interpretation, A.J. contended, especially in "Disease of Conceit," "Dignity," and the overall doomsday pall of the 1997 *Time Out of Mind* album. To show me what he meant, A. J. rang up his own Bob page, dylanology.com. But there was a problem. The site, written by A. J. himself almost exclusively in JavaScript, uses so much memory it often crashes computers. A. J. never noticed this until the Feds seized his high-powered system in their raid on his office. Now, forced to make do with a less zippy older machine, he found that dylanology.com kept getting blown off the screen.

"Fuck this!" A. J. screamed, smacking the computer; the whole thing was a disaster, especially since, along with everything else, the government had confiscated the Web site's backup discs.

"Yeah, Dylan's going to be glad I'm going to jail all right," A. J. began to spritz, getting that look in his eye. "This is going to revitalize his career! He's going to be so inspired by my downfall he'll write five great songs by next week! Dylan'll owe me for this!"

But then Weberman's wife and kid came into the room. The idea that he might not see them for a long time stopped the old Dylanologist in his tracks.

After a moment, he said. "You know, I come from a people that, they looked at every word in the Bible, and they commented on it, then they commented on the comments. In the Torah, the Gemara, the Mishna. They know it so well, they look at a word on a page and tell you what word is behind it on the opposite page. They studied genes and interiors of things like maps of the heart. So it doesn't matter what people think about me and Bob Dylan. Because he's from the same place I'm from. And that's the real Dylanology . . . and that never stops no matter what's gonna happen to me."

* * *

Rock is full of cults, but nothing—not collecting the Beatles, not documenting Elvis—rivals Dylanology. Back in his dark-sunglasses days, Dylan might have been the coolest, but Dylanology is not about cool. Neither is it a hobby, a fleeting affectation or indolent lord-it-over-you tastemaking to get girls, like in *High Fidelity*. Dylanology is a risk, a gamble, a spiritual declaration, a life choice, and if you don't believe it, ask those real Weathermen, erstwhile college students who took the drama of "Subterranean Homesick Blues" to heart, maybe too much. A year after Rubin Carter addressed the United Nations, several of those forgotten revolutionaries continue to rot in jail, so that's the way that wind blows. But this is how it is with Dylanology. To be a Bobcat is to acknowledge the presence of the extraordinary in your midst, to open yourself to its workings, to act upon it. In a world of postmod ephemera, this is a solemn bond.

In turns, a real folkie, a real rocker, a real lover, a real father, a real doper, a real shit, a real Christian, a real Jew, a real American from a real small town come to a real big town with real dreams and little false modesty, Dylan, big-tent preacher of millennial concerns both sacred and profane, has never offered less than authenticity to his variegated flock, no matter what peculiar axe they might grind. With Bob, you may feel betrayed, bitterly disappointed, but you never think it's a hustle. Because he has always been so willing to lay his heart on the line, so are we.

Nowadays it seems that without the Bible, McDonald's jingles, and Bob Dylan, there'd be gaping holes in half the world's conversations. Couple of months ago I went with my mother to Romania. We were supposed to find our roots, but all we found were the vanished graves of murdered relatives, and dart-eyed Gypsy boys looking for someone's pocket to pick in front of the hideous palaces built by the dead Commie leader Nicolae Ceausescu. "When you got nothing, you got nothing to lose," a Gypsy boy said, standing beside a pile of red peppers in the market.

I see that Michael Douglas and Catherine Zeta-Jones named their baby Dylan, which is very nice, but half the kids in my son's class are named Dylan. There are even girl Dylans. Buy whatever apocrypha you like about Bob taking the moniker from either Dylan Thomas or his gambling uncle

Mr. Dillon—now it's just one more name on the birth-announcement card, like Ashley or Justin.

Dylanology marches on; it's a continuity thing. Last week, I was eating breakfast at a formerly run-down East Village diner with Josh Nelson, who is twenty-four and aspires to be a psychology professor. In 1990, when Josh was thirteen, his father took him to see Bob for the first time at the Beacon Theater in New York. This was no surprise. As many fathers make a fetish out of taking their kid to their first ballgame, it is a Dylanological ritual responsibility to bring *der kinder* to Bob shows. Only a few weeks before, I'd accompanied my own seventeen-year-old daughter, Rae, to her first Dylan show, at Jones Beach, the same funky stretch of sand where, thirty-five years ago, I used to come with my friends, our bodies stark and white, stupid corduroy Bob hats on our heads.

But still, it was tense. Dads and teens, it's always tense, all the more because we were seeing Bob, and nothing about Bob is simply casual. It could have been didactic, another lesson, one more bit of proof of how my hallowed pop youth exceeded hers. But Dylan speaks to all, equally. The show worked out fine. Just for that ole-time Bob atmosphere, it rained apocalyptically, the speakers nearly blew up, and Dylan sang Rae's favorite apocalyptic comedy, "Ballad of Frankie Lee and Judas Priest."

"The rest is up to her, you've done your part," commented Josh Nelson, who, since his dad took him to the Beacon, has seen Bob Dylan perform "203 times and counting," at such far-flung locales as St. John's, Newfoundland; Regina, Saskatchewan; Cottbus, Germany; and Starkville, Mississippi. "In my mind, Dylan was just another of those older Jewish guys whom I had heard of only in name. It's scary, but, for some reason, I grouped him with Neil Diamond and Barry Manilow. Yes, in a word, I knew nothing . . ." Josh once wrote in a college essay discussing his immersion in Bobdom. Soon enough, however, he decided that "'Boots of Spanish Leather' is no longer about sailing and 'Mama You Been on My Mind' is a song about the hopelessly unforgettable . . . no longer all foreign and ungraspable but rather now somehow understood and real."

"That's the difference," Josh said. "For me, Bob Dylan isn't the man who played Folk City and Forest Hills. The Bob Dylan I know is the man on the stage at the Beacon Theater, older, sadder maybe, but still him." It was one thing to regret the long-missed past, and another to make the most of the present and future, said Josh, who, like most younger Dylanologists, leans heavily on usually neglected later work and his stage performances. "We're there, keeping the flame," Josh says, proud that he'd heard that Dylan made *Time Out of Mind* partially so his young fans would have some songs to hear for the first time, to call their own. Then, nervously pushing his kasha and eggs across his plate, Josh said that even if people called him "the walking Krogsgaard" (in reference to his encyclopedic recall of Michael Krogsgaard's authoritative listing of Dylan set lists), he didn't want to give the impression that "this" was his entire life. He'd graduated Phi Beta Kappa from Middlebury, after all. He didn't want to seem like some nut.

It was a theme, skirting the edges of lunacy in service to the Bob Muse; this much was apparent upon visiting Mitch Blank, an old-time Village guy. "Looking at this place, you'd think a normal person lives here," said Mitch, standing in the doorway of his remarkably neat (considering) walk-up apartment. Mitch's self-diagnosed mania is his Dylan collection, which includes: a magical set of sliding wall cabinets capable of handling more than twenty thousand tapes of Bob Dylan concerts, a collection of every Bob interview dating back to the 1960s, the cover of each magazine on which Bob Dylan has ever appeared, nearly every Bob Dylan poster or show announcement (a November 1961 playbill from Carnegie Chapter Hall reads "All Seats—$2.00"), a Xerox of the cover of Bob Dylan's copy of Woody Guthrie's *Bound for Glory*, a full collection of Bob Dylan postage stamps from Gambia and Tanzania (some of which Mitch arranged to have canceled by the Hibbing, Minnesota, post office on Dylan's fifty-second birthday, May 24, 1993), a Highway 61 sign from Minnesota DOT, a piece of the Big Pink piano, a Bob Dylan–signed baseball, a copy of a lease for an apartment Dylan moved into at 21336 Pacific Coast Highway that allows for "5" children and "1" dog. Also present is Mitch's typically complete database, which, along with much else, catalogs covers of Dylan songs ("I Shall Be Released" was done by Marjoe Gortner, Coven, Telly Savalas, and Big Mama Thornton; "Blowin' in the Wind" by Sebastian

Cabot, Marlene Dietrich, Brian "It-z-bit-z-teeny-weenie bikini" Hyland, and the U.S. Navy Steel Band).

"It's just the tip of the iceberg," announced Mitch, who works as a photo researcher by day and is on the advisory board of the Museum of Folk Music in Greenwich Village, as he graciously copied a documentary on collectors of eight-track tapes so I'd see what "the really sick are like." Yet there is a line even Mitch will not cross, such as when a good friend called up saying he had several Marlboro butts freshly smoked by Dylan.

"'What do I want Bob's cigarette butts for?' I asked this degenerate," Mitch recalled. "And he said, 'Don't you see? Dylan's DNA is on those butts. Sometime in the future we'll be able to clone a whole new Bob Dylan. The ultimate collectible.' I told him he was disgusting. You know, even for me, there's a limit."

The limit.

I was looking for the limit. I mean, it was fine thumbing through the hundreds of interviews Bob has given over the years, learning that on June 13, 1984, Dylan told Robert Hilburn of the *Los Angeles Times* that he didn't think he'd be "perceived properly till one hundred years after I'm gone." It was amusing to hear stories told by old Villagers about going shopping with Suze Rotolo, Bob's most mythic pre-Sara girlfriend (who was remembered as "quiet, pigeon-toed, and very fond of the color green"). Supposedly it was she who purchased those famous Boots of Spanish Leather. It was interesting also to read through many of the D-centric novels written over the years, from Diane Di Prima's Olympia Press porno scenes about fucking along with "Highway 61" to Don DeLillo's *Great Jones Street*, onward to *The Dylanist*, a recent, well-received novel of (lefty) upper-middle-class manners, which, outrageously, does not even mention Bob until page 83, and then, on page 139, manages to have the main character quote Dylan's line: "He's an artist, he don't look back." *He?*

There was even a satisfying touch of terror, walking by the Morgan Library on East Thirty-sixth Street in Manhattan, knowing the Red Notebook was likely behind those stone walls. The Red Notebook: the fifty-nine-cent spiral pad in which Bob wrote, in his crabbed handwriting, the lyrics for the *Blood on the Tracks* songs. The Red Notebook: a document of the poet's most consummate pain, legendarily stolen from Bob's house, passed along on the black market, every collector's forbidden grail, then, by dint of the Dylan Office's demand, donated to the Morgan. The Red Notebook: the Maltese Falcon of Dylanology, the stuff dreams and nightmares were made of. To hold even a Xerox in your hands was to risk any kind of karma.

I knew I was in too deep when I got a call from a friend in L.A. who said he knew the girlfriend of the chauffeur who drove Michael Bolton to Dylan's Malibu house the day the two pop stars coauthored "Steel Bars." Did I want her views on Bob's innermost thoughts?

I had a head full of Dylanology that was driving me insane, and I hadn't even called on the academics yet, people like Christopher Ricks, the Boston University poetry professor, to grok his axial analysis of Dylan's pentameters. I hadn't listened to the complete works of the Wilburys, avoiding the whole Tom Petty period like the plague. Nor had I rememorized the "11 Outlined Epitaphs," Bob's liner notes ("for I do not care to be made an oddball bouncin' past reporters' pens") on the back of my old vinyl of *The Times They Are A-Changin'*, which I retain, my high school girlfriend's phone number still visible in the upper-left-hand corner. I hadn't seen Mel Prussack's homemade "Dylclocks," each one marked with a Bob quote denoting the passage of "Dyltime." I hadn't even established if "Quinn the Eskimo" was really written as Dylan watched Nicholas Ray's 1959 picture *The Savage Innocents*, in which Anthony Quinn played an Eskimo.

Amid the glut, a million legitimate Dylanological mysteries remained. Issues. Questions. Legends to either puncture or leave alone. For instance, even after all these years, no one seems to have conclusively ascertained exactly how hurt Dylan was after the 1966 motorcycle accident; whether, as some suggest, he exaggerated his injuries to derail the hectic schedule the Machiavellian manager Albert Grossman had painted him into. Nor was it completely clear if Dylan is still a Christian. Clinton Heylin says yes—"Listen to the songs." Paul Williams says Dylan's current Christianity or Jewishness is secondary to his "overriding fundamentalism. . . . He is someone who believes in the literalness of the Word. He will be a fundamentalist in whatever he believes."

Whatever his current theology, I, for one, would like to know whatever happened to the Jewish jokes in Bob Dylan. Bob Dylan used to be at least as funny as Franz Kafka. "Motorpsycho Nightmare" (never performed live in concert) is full of yocks, a touchstone of surreal "dirt beneath my fingernails" *shtetl* humor. Maybe being born again beat the stand-up out of him, or maybe it was just the sheer weight of being Bob for so many years. But by the time Dylan got around to writing his "Lenny Bruce," the song was as turgid as the real Lenny, gone mad, reading his court transcripts from the stage. Somehow it slipped Bob's mind that Bruce used to make people laugh for a living.

Still, when you came down to it, the biggest conundrum in Dylanology was Dylan himself. The Living Bob. How to deal with the fact that the most inspiring artist of the times still walks among us, after all these years.

Written Dylanology breaks into three camps. Michael Gray's monumental, endlessly illuminating *Song and Dance Man III* most successfully places Dylan in his cultural context. (With resourceful scholarship, Gray finds the line "When you live outside the law you have to eliminate dishonesty" in the little-known 1958 Don Siegel noir film *The Lineup*, noting the obvious connection to the much better "to live outside the law you must be honest.") Gray ignores the Living Bob altogether. Referring almost exclusively to the fixed text of the "official" Columbia releases, he attempts no bridge to Bob the human, dealing only with the work, as if it were written by a poet in the thirteenth century.

Paul Williams, Clinton Heylin, and others take the middle path, acknowledging the Living Bob's presence while warily wishing not to unduly trespass on the artist's personal space. This half-measure is a difficult tack, as Williams notes, describing the publishing of his well-known *Dylan: What Happened?*—a book seeking to come to terms with Dylan's fan-boggling born-again shows at San Francisco's Warfield Theater in 1979. Dylan liked Williams's book, reportedly buying 114 copies (114 happening to be the exact number of sayings of Christ to appear in Gnostic Gospel of St. Thomas found at Nag Hammadi). Dylan invited Williams backstage and even performed the famously unperformed "Caribbean Wind" at the writer's request. However, Dylan was not much pleased with Williams's follow-up article, reportedly saying, "It happens every time—when I meet someone who's written something about me that I like, meeting me spoils them and the next thing they write doesn't work."

Williams, for his part, agrees with his subject. "After meeting him, I became very much aware that Bob Dylan would certainly read whatever I wrote. Maybe it took me away from what I usually do, which is only for fans. I think the idea that Bob Dylan might be looking over your shoulder damages a lot of writers."

Then, of course, there is the other approach to the Living Bob, which is to go forward, to stand naked before him, demanding his attention. Such was the methodology employed by Larry (Ratso) Sloman in his now out-of-print account of the Rolling Thunder Tour, *On the Road with Bob Dylan: Rolling with the Thunder*. Easily the most entertaining and strangely moving of Bob tomes, Sloman's book contains many good quotes. There is Dylan's mother, Beattie, saying, "He was born to us, but then he went away and did this on his own. . . . Bob Dylan is the writer, Dylan, not Zimmerman." And Bob himself, adding, "Well, I don't understand music, you know. I understand Lightnin' Hopkins. I understand Leadbelly, John Lee Hooker, Woody Guthrie, Kinky Friedman. I never claimed to understand music. . . . If you ever heard me play the guitar, you'd know that." To which Ratso, the fan, replies, "But I like the way you play the guitar."

A key moment in all of Dylanology occurs when Sloman, in the midst of a bookwide freak-out about his inability to "get" the story, confronts Dylan in a hotel lobby.

"C'mere, schmuck," Ratso reports himself as saying, demanding that Dylan listen to his plea.

Dylan addresses the distraught reporter: "Well, what is it that you want? Be specific. What do you need?"

Ratso searches for the word. His eyes suddenly light up. "I need access," he screams at the superstar. "I need access. . . ."

Dylan then reportedly "rolls his eyes in amazement" and says, "*Ex-Lax?* . . . Why do you need Ex-Lax? What you been eating?"

Not Ex-lax, Ratso shouted. *Access!*

This was it: access.

Access: What A. J. Weberman, in his dementia, demanded when he called for the return of "the Brain" of the Poet into the hands of "the People." Access: a backstage pass to that no-man's-land of Dylanological real estate between the artist and ourselves. Access: what we—the scholars, the fans, the lunatics—want.

What he, the Living Bob, will not give.

Access. Proximity to the Bobhead. It is a Dylanological obsession. Whole books, like *Encounters with Bob Dylan: If You See Him Say Hello*, offer chronicles of chance meetings and near-meetings between Dylan and cabdrivers, secretaries, salesclerks. To see him is something not to be forgotten, a memory handled with care. For instance, considering how many bands Bob has had, Dylanology is surprisingly free of sideman stories. Possibly this owes to the scuttlebutt that Bob has very little to do with his fellow players—for years, supposedly, it was *verboten* to even make eye contact with Bob even while playing with him onstage. There is also a notion of sacred time, that for a musician, playing with Bob Dylan is nothing to speak about idly. Guitarist Steve Ripley, who toured with Dylan in the eighties, did, however, tell me this story: Apparently, Ripley arrived at the venue at the wrong time for a sound check and found no one around. He was about to go back to his hotel when he saw Dylan, sitting near the stage all by himself. Up to this point, Ripley, on the tour for months, had exchanged few words with his enigmatic boss. But there was no way to avoid talking now: It was just the two of them.

"I really didn't know what to say to the guy," Ripley recounted. "I mean: He's Bob Dylan. What do you say to Bob Dylan?"

After a long pause, the guitarist finally blurted, "Hi, Bob, hey, how's the family?" whereupon Dylan literally bounded toward the sideman and gave him a big hug.

"Great!" Dylan exclaimed, a giant smile spreading across his craggy face. "Thanks for asking!"

Access.

I suppose it was selfish of me, a typical invasion of hallowed Dylanological space, but I felt I had no choice. At least this is what I'd decided, from a

Chevy Blazer, on the road again. I'd been on Bob's tracks for a couple of weeks, trailing him through the Northeast, through Hartford, Connecticut; Mansfield, Massachusetts; Saratoga, New York; Scranton, Pennsylvania; Camden, New Jersey; Columbia, Maryland—everywhere Bob went, I was there, watching The Man in his short black coat and the pants with the honky-tonk stripe up the leg (known for wearing the same clothes for weeks on end, this was the same outfit Dylan wore while singing for the pope, a bit gamey but still way better than the outpatient's hooded sweatshirt he wore throughout the late eighties). I was studying the strange half smile, the playful Chaplin-cum-Elvis-impersonator guitar moves, the sawed-off duckwalks, diffident roll of the rheumy eye, the drop of silver sweat poised at the end of his hooked nose, waiting for my chance.

The time had come to apologize, I thought—to apologize to Dylan for wishing he was dead.

I thought it was a memory buried forever in a trunk, but not deep enough, it seems, for there it was, in the 1999 *New Yorker* article about Bob, in the first paragraph, for chrissakes: "In 1978, after the fiasco of *Renaldo & Clara*, Dylan's four-hour art film, Mark Jacobson wrote in the *Village Voice*, 'I wish Bob Dylan died.'"

It was true. There, in the very newspaper where I'd first read of this skinny Jew, son of an appliance salesman, who'd blown in from the North Country to turn my little Flushing, Queens, world upside down, I had written, "I wish Bob Dylan died. Then Channel 5 would piece together an instant documentary on his life and times, the way they did for Hubert (Humphrey). The way they do for Chaplin, or Adolf Hitler. Just the immutable facts. Seeing all those immutable facts about Elvis made his dying worthwhile. . . ."

Geez, couldn't I at least have left out Hitler? The idea, I guess, was that even Bob dying would have been better than sitting through *Renaldo & Clara* twice. Maybe in 1978, I thought this was some kind of joke.

The incident is well documented. In *No Direction Home: The Life and Music of Bob Dylan*, former *New York Times* folk-music critic Robert Shelton says, "Dylan was most hurt by the reaction from his old neighborhood paper, the *Village Voice*." Bob himself is quoted as saying, "Did you see the firing squad of critics they sent?" Worse yet is the notation in Clinton Heylin's biography, *Bob Dylan: Behind the Shades*. In a chapter titled, "Someone's Got It in for Me," Faridi McFree, one of Dylan's post-Sara girlfriends, reads the *Renaldo & Clara* reviews to Bob over the phone. "It was horrible, absolutely horrible what they said about him, especially in the *Village Voice*."

"Bob," McFree tells Dylan, "they actually really wish you were dead."

But it took the *New Yorker* piece to identify me by name. To point the finger, as Dylan used to say about his early protest songs, at the man in the lonely crowd who was to blame.

I had become Dylanology. I was the man who wished Bob Dylan was dead. What a nightmare. I mean: Bob Dylan was, and remains, my hero. For decades I held on to a letter, signed by Albert Grossman, thanking me for my interest, but no, Bob would not be available to be interviewed for the Francis Lewis High School *Patriot*. Once, sometime in the late sixties, I saw Bob coming out of Manny's Music on Forty-eighth Street carrying a white paper bag. Half an hour later, I saw Muhammad Ali, my other lodestone, standing at the same exact spot where I'd seen Dylan. Ali shook my hand. Bob only nodded, but it was enough.

I was there, too, at Forest Hills in 1965, booing Dylan for going electric. Nowadays there are 20 million ponytailed ex-hipsters claiming to have been at the old fifteen-thousand-seat tennis stadium cheering the zeitgeist as "Tombstone Blues" serrated the late-summer air. But really, it was better to have booed. All the real Dylan fans booed. Booing was part of the Dylanological continuum—having expectations shattered, feeling rejected, and then realizing how better, way better, it was to live in this new, bigger world he'd thrust you into.

In retrospect, it seems the ultimate noncompliance that Dylan didn't die taking his Triumph too quick around that curve on Zena Road in Woodstock back in '66. If anyone ever fit the live fast/die young/beautiful corpse trope, it was Bob Dylan. Then, like Rimbaud and James Dean, Dylan could have been one more over-romanticized Jim Morrison to sit around acting like a smart alec in *Don't Look Back*, ranking on poor Donovan and claiming he could hold his breath three times as long as Caruso. Indeed, it makes a good scene, like a *Behind the Music* tale from the crypt: the Bobster, in a steam room, playing rummy with the twin poles of his cross-race pollination-inspiration: Hank Williams (dead at twenty-nine) and Robert Johnson (dead at twenty-seven). Charlie Parker (dead at thirty-four) could sit in, too, if he were in town.

Except Bob Dylan wasn't going for it; this was not his Fate. By whatever confluence of DNA and destiny, he has persisted far beyond the days of his own infallibility. Fifty-nine now, he's had plenty of time to make a nutty movie like *Renaldo & Clara*, be charged with hitting his wife, get born again, make a bunch of intermittently inspired records, etc., etc., and have dickheads like me wish he were dead.

He has lasted long enough for that old-time religion to return. Only yesterday I was able to sit on the subway, listening to the 1994 version of Dylan creaking through the old folk song "Delia," tears in my eyes at the harsh, ravaged beauty of it all. When he was twenty, he wanted to sound like an old whore singing "House of the Rising Sun," one foot on the platform, the other on the train. Now he'd gotten there. In the end, this was Dylan's true greatness, his spectacular humanity, the keep-on-keeping-on of it all, the adherence to the life cycle. At least this was the rap—my rap until that *New Yorker* came through the door.

I mention all this because everyone—everyone I know, anyway—has their own Dylanology. Their own little *chazerei* about how it is between Bob and them. And, like me, they want to tell you all about it.

Could be now or never. Since the 1997 histoplasmosis scare (noted by *New York Post* headline writers as "Bob Dylan Heart Mystery"), mortality issues have dominated Dylanological dialogue. How does Bob look, people ask; what's his physical state, his mental state, think he's been drinking? Now, for sure, was the time to be with the Bobster, to follow him around from show to show, to get unashamedly paternal about the guy, not to let the little fucker out of your sight.

It was also very convenient, now that Bob has become an opening act. In the beginning this was a shock, watching Dylan blast out "Down in the

Flood" before sixty thousand empty seats at Giants Stadium in 1995, roundly ignored by stray early-bird Grateful Dead fans. But now this seven o'clock starting time is one more Dylanological boon. This way the D fan can easily commandeer a spot in the still-empty first few rows, see Bob's seventeen-song set, be back on the highway (or tucked in bed at the Marriott) by nine, and never hear note one of headliner Phil Lesh.

Bob is like Ali now, lighting the Olympic torch, a (usually) silent Buddha, acknowledging the sweet autumnalness of it all. In current Dylanology the set list is everything, and these days the poet was offering mostly a greatest-hits, pre-motorcycle-accident package. You can sit behind where Pablo, the sound man, burns the sticks of Nag Chompa incense, "a Bob Dylan tradition for the past twenty years," and wonder about the oldies menu. Wonder if Dylan, the rebel morphed to Sunshine Boy/National Treasure/Beloved Entertainer, has decided to close his show with "Blowin' in the Wind," his corniest signature song, because he really thinks this is what we want: this show biz victory lap, this "Forever Young" schmaltz. Or maybe, after much thought, he's come to the (painful? joyous?) conclusion that these older tunes, the famous ones of his youth, like "Mr. Tambourine Man," "Don't Think Twice," and "Stuck Inside of Memphis"—not the gospel, not "Ring Them Bells," not *Time Out of Mind*—are really his best, the things he really wants to play so we'll remember him right.

Like in Revelation, in seven shows, Bob played seven "Tangled Up in Blue"s, seven "Highway 61"s, seven "Like a Rolling Stone"s, seven "Blowin' in the Wind"s. The Dylanologist, understanding that some around him have been waiting twenty years to hear "It Ain't Me Babe" live, sits patiently, anticipating the "variable" slots, the ones reserved for the special items, the one-offs, the deep rarities. As always, they come: a speed-metal revise of "Drifter's Escape." A version of "Long Black Veil," the ultimate murder ballad, never more high and lonesome. A two-night revival of "Tears of Rage." "Maggie's Farm" (played at Scranton, exactly thirty-five years to the day from the first electric version at Newport, a fact duly noted by attendant tapeheads). An old Stanley Brothers tune. And finally, "Every Grain of Sand."

The "Every Grain of Sand" was especially excellent because that was what the seventy-eight-year-old blue-haired lady in Columbia, Maryland, said she wanted Dylan to play. Leaning on her cane, she said she'd gotten into Bob "about twenty years ago" when her son, who'd been living in the basement, "finally" moved out. Cleaning the place, she found dozens of scratched vinyls under the cigarette-scarred couch. "I always was afraid about what he was doing down there. When I heard this Bob Dylan, I felt a lot better about my son." Then, looking around at the gathering tribes, the old lady smiled and said, "It's so nice that he can draw such a crowd at his age."

"Rainy Day Women #12 and 35" was her favorite Dylan song, the woman said, somewhat surprising for a "churchgoer." But this being the anniversary of her husband's death, she was really hoping Bob would do his great post-Christian spiritual "Every Grain of Sand," which is described by Michael Gray, in his twenty-five-page chapter on the tune (complete with copious footnotes mentioning Edith Piaf, Frankie Laine, Cain, Abel, Saint Matthew, Saint Paul, Tony Bennett, William Blake, Allen Ginsberg, Bruno Bettelheim, and the Reverend Dr. John Polkinghorne, canon theologian of Liverpool), as a work that is "really about faith vs. doubt."

And, of course, even though Dylan hadn't yet played "Every Grain of Sand" on the then-thirty-two-date-long tour, he did it that very night at the Merriweather Post Pavilion in Columbia, Maryland. Did it great, too—ethereal, elusive, and pure, and not even that far off from the record.

This is how it is with Bob in these latter days, as he makes his fitful rounds of summertime music sheds and second-banana fall apple festivals. He is the gift that keeps on giving, a wish-fulfilling jukebox of high modernism, speaking, as always, in new ways beyond our knowing. Then again, Dylanology has always been a synchronicitous thing: the meaningful coincidence expressed via the mysterium of Bob.

How else to explain the message on the radio driving down the Jersey Turnpike, on the way to the Camden show? The announcer was talking about how then-governor Christie Whitman was finally going to close Greystone Hospital due to "a series of patient suicides, assaults, unsanitary conditions and understaffing at the hundred-year-old facility."

Now, any cub of a Bobcat knows the story of how the first place Dylan went when he came east from Hibbing in February of '61 was Greystone Hospital in Jersey, to see Woody Guthrie. It says so right in the liner notes of the first album, the only one with the cherub-faced Bob in his corduroy hat. So how do you figure that after one hundred years of understaffing, patient suicides, and who-knows-whatever botched operations, the governor of New Jersey picked that exact day to close Greystone?

And how do you figure that Dylan picked that night to play "Song To Woody," the 1961 tune in which D foretells to Guthrie "funny ol' world," sick, hungry, and torn, that looks like it's dying "before it's been born," which is a heck of a bleak bouquet to lay at the hospital bed of a victim of Huntington's chorea, even a canny hard traveler like Woody Guthrie. Quite a vision indeed to behold now, forty years and three generations on the other side of all that, especially when you're stuck in traffic, and it's Jersey, too.

Access. If I was going to apologize to Dylan, to somehow erase my insignificant notation in Dylanological history, "the formation" was my best chance. It was something new this tour, with Bob and the boys—Charlie Sexton, Larry Campbell, and good ol' Tony Garnier, in his purple suit, twelve years on the bass. When the set's over, the band stands there for a minute or so and stares back at the audience. They don't say anything, only peer off into the cold distance, like a spaghetti western. Bob keeps his hand on his hip, Bette Davis style.

"Bob!" I shouted from the edge of the stage. "I'm sorry! I'm sorry I said I wished you died!"

But unlike the cry of the legendary "Judas!" screamer at the Manchester Free Trade Hall in July of '66, my words did not pierce the din. Dylan did not turn and call me "a liar," scream "I don't believe you!" In Hartford, Scranton, Saratoga, Camden, and Columbia, not once did Bob look my way. Eventually a friend of mine told me to stop. My friend, a Dylan hand who knows these things, said if I kept insisting on apologizing, I'd be on the verge of becoming "a profile," which is what the "Dylan Office," in its well-documented paranoia (paranoia being a hardy perennial in all things Dylanological), calls those who try to get too close, those who too aggressively attempt to break the plane between Him and us, who want more access than they deserve.

"If Bob wants to forgive you, he probably already has," said my friend.

And I thought of this a couple nights later, driving back toward New York with my wife. We'd thought we would be able to see Bob again that night, which would have made eight straight shows, but the holiday was over. So we headed home, reaching the Holland Tunnel a little after 7 P.M., about the time Dylan would have gone onstage.

"Get a Bob Dylan song on the radio," I said to my wife. This was no doubt a fruitless gesture because maybe thirty-four years ago Murray the K, stone mellow and on FM by then, but with the grease of pastrami still seeping through his veins (but really hip pastrami), said that "Like a Rolling Stone," seven minutes long, was Top Ten. But now there is almost never a Bob Dylan song on New York radio, if you don't count movie tie-ins like "Hurricane" (unplayed live by Bob since 1976).

But then there it was, as we approached the toll plaza, dim at the edges of reception but unmistakable: "Desolation Row."

Dylan had revived the song on the current tour, performing it several nights in a row, third in the set list. There was a good chance he was playing the epic tune at that exact moment, on the muddy field of Waterloo Village in north Jersey. When Sinatra got old, he did "My Way"; when Elvis was near the end, he did "My Way," too. Bob Dylan does "Desolation Row."

The first time I heard the song was the first time he performed it, the night I booed him at Forest Hills. The *New York Times*, in a review I clipped, called it "a major new composition." Now the "*Titanic* sails at dawn" verse was fading out as we entered the tunnel. Was there absolution in this Cocteau-like visitation? Was this Bob's way of taking the curse off me? Who knew? In my time of Dylanology, it has always been like this. You forget about him for a decade or more, then he's back in your head, suddenly a matter of life and death, again.

11
Chilling with ODB

For sheer stylistic street hegemony, there's never been anything like hip hop. Ol' Dirty Bastard, a founding member of occultist Wu Tang Clan (ardent kung fu movie fans, they regarded their communal home, a Staten Island split-level, as a Shaolin Temple) was a singular practitioner of the form. When O.D.B. passed away about a year after this piece appeared I was asked to write an obit for the rapper. I said I already had. From New York *magazine, 2003.*

Amid the variegated chambers of Wu, home to RZA, GZA, Method Man, Ghostface Killah, and Raekwon, the Ol' Dirty Bastard—a.k.a Big Baby Jesus, Joe Bannanas, Dirt McGirt, Osirus, and the Unique Ason—has always been the major off-angle, The Clan's most arresting and arrested member, the Ringo of the group.

"Sometimes I was the clown, sometimes I was the thug, that was what I was," says ODB, yawning, his diamond-encrusted gold teeth glinting in the dim room light of a Rockland County "luxury rental condominium." The condo setting was a departure for ODB, as almost always these days he can be found under the watchful eye of his mom at her house across from John Jay High School in the Park Slope section of Brooklyn. Dirt loves his mom, but he doesn't have much choice as to the location of his domicile, not since he was ordered into his mother's custody after his most recent release from prison. Dirt was okay with that, saying, "My mom is the only one who can check me, I have no choice but to mind her."

Things were going well, too, but a couple of weeks ago, Dirt's mother, now remarried, went on a long-delayed honeymoon. Dirty promised to stay home, but he somehow "fucked up" and went AWOL. In the midst of finishing a new comeback disc for Jay Z's Roc-A-Fella label, the Dirt's disappearance caused widespread panic amid the rapper's far-flung community of record execs, PR people, and sundry hangers-on. He wasn't answering his cell. No one knew where he was. Streets were combed, as far away as Staten Island, where the Clan once lived in phantasmagoric semicommunal splendor. Eventually Dirt was found, "shacked up" at an undisclosed locale. Which is how he got to this unlikely Nanuet condo in the middle of the Westchester suburban nowhere. The consensus was that Dirt needed to be "removed from the element" to someplace where he might be more comfortably watched, night and day, until his mother returned. This was basically okay with Dirty, who said he regarded this condo stay as a much-needed "vacation." Soon to turn thirty-five, about two hundred in rap years, he felt the rest would do him good. He was very, very tired, he said.

It has, after all, been a hectic decade for the erstwhile Russell Jones. Father of thirteen, ODB's police record is equally fecund. It is part of the script for rappers to have run-ins with the cops, but Dirty's docket got to be a joke after a while, what with the rapidfire busts for assault, crack, missing child support, threatening his wife Icelene, and wearing "body armor" (ex-felons can't wear bulletproof vests, even if they've been shot several times, like Dirty). Few can take it to the outlaw mattress like ODB, who recorded the scabrously entertaining *Nigga Please* on the lam and, several months later, while still the subject of a nationwide manhunt, turned up onstage with his Wu brothers at Hammerstein Ballroom to perform a few numbers off the new disc. Somehow Dirt gave the cops the slip at Hammerstein, only to be caught a few nights later in a Philadelphia McDonald's signing autographs for fans. With the hip-hop mags fearing for his well-documented tenuous mental condition, jail did not agree with the rapper. Placed on a suicide watch, his leg was broken by another inmate.

Asked how he's feeling, ODB, sitting on the condo couch fingering his Five Percenter pendant as he watches *Mrs. Doubtfire* on TV, does not look up.

"Haldol" is all he says.

Once a more manically profane Redd Foxx, the still handsome ODB's responses rarely exceed a sentence these days. As for his tightly synclined career, Dirty says, "Some ups, some downs, but I feel good about being a legend." Still "a name," someone who sells records, Dirty is, improbably, in the midst of an upswing. In addition to the almost completed Roc-A-Fella record, there is a VH1 "reality show" pilot called "On Parole with ODB." The idea is that the new show will make a nice bookend with the infamous MTV spot in which the rapper arrived at the welfare office in a limo and proceeded to get his check. There is also a new line of Dirt McGirt Wear, jeans and athletic shirts, "you know, the usual stuff," says ODB, who is modeling an oversized football jersey with the name DIRT stenciled on the back.

"The wear is gonna sell, big-time," says Jared Weisfeld, ODB's most recent comanager. A twenty-something man in a baseball hat, it has fallen to Jared, who is the producer of the would-be VH1 series (which he calls "an urban *Osbournes*") to keep an eye on Dirty up here in the condo. "Dirty's feeling really great, totally together," Jared says, regarding his motionless client. Then, as if to prove that Dirty is outrageous as ever, Weisfeld shouts, "Hey, drop some Dirtyisms on us . . . come on."

After getting no response, Weisfeld tries again. "Come on, Dirty . . . what's your favorite part of a woman?" Weisfeld cajoles the notoriously lascivious rapper. "What is it, Dirt?"

ODB looks up and squints. Seemingly on tape delay, he finally smiles broadly and shouts, "*The vagina!* The vagina is the best."

"Right!" Weisfeld shouts, cracking up loudly. "You're still funny D . . . still fucking funny, Dirty!"

ODB smiles wanly and returns to watching *Mrs. Doubtfire*. Then, after several awkward moments, Dirty screams, "*Jared!! . . . Sushi!! Sushi now!*" This means he wants Weisfeld to drive to the local Japanese restaurant.

After the manager leaves, Dirty turns somewhat elegiac. When he is old and "sitting on his porch," Dirt says he'll tell his grandchildren "I was a rapper. That's what I did for a living." Not that they'll know what that is "because rap will be gone with the wind like everything else." Then ODB excuses himself and walks stiff-leggedly into the condo bedroom, where he sits down and slowly lights a cigarette. He takes a puff, coughs a while, then sighs.

12
Paranoid Notes On the Strange Death of Bruce Lee

A.k.a.: war of the termite wackos. Ossified post-1960s fringe operatives take on emerging issues of post-modern street culture, find themselves stumped, battle on nonetheless. From the Village Voice, *1978.*

The gray-haired judge presiding in Arraignment Room No. 2A had spent the better part of the morning listening to the same old story about how this defendant put a voodoo spell on that plaintiff's gypsy cab, thereby causing the vehicle's steering column to come loose while making a forty-mile-an-hour U-turn on the FDR Drive. You know, the usual stuff.

Now, however, the judge was up against something really tough. The plaintiff, Alan J. Weberman—a.k.a. A. J., garbologist, assassinationologist, and semileader of the Youth International Party (YIP)—was charging that defendant William H. Depperman—former YIP fellow traveler, now leader and close-to-only member of the Assassination Information Committee (AIC)—had menaced him with a six-inch blade on Bleecker Street.

The pulling of a shiv was well within the gray-haired judge's frame of reference. The reasons for the alleged crime, however, were somewhat baffling. According to Weberman's statement, Depperman is in the midst of waging "a one-man counterinsurgency campaign against the Yippies because he claims we're not Communistic enough." Depperman, a hairy hulk of frazzled nerves, loudly dismissed these allegations as impossible since Weberman is "no legitimate leftist" but rather "a CIA agent." Depperman countercharged that it is actually Weberman who plans violent action. As proof, Depperman waved a WANTED-DEAD OR ALIVE, WILLIAM H. DEPPERMAN, A.K.A. THE DIAPERMAN poster in front of the judge, claiming the placard had been distributed by Weberman and his Yippie cohorts. The text of the WANTED poster depicts Depperman as a "rat-faced, asshole, scum-faced NAZI pig Nark." It goes on to charge that Depperman is nothing more or less than an "FBI informer."

With each new assertion by Depperman that it was really Weberman, not he, who worked for the intelligence arm of the United States government, the gray-haired judge rolled his eyes. He had been cast as arbitrator in a maniac war between conspiracy-addled paranoiacs, and he wasn't happy about it, which was too bad for him, because it is hard to come by material quite this rich.

Paranoia and/or Conspiracy Texts are required 101 classes for anyone seeking to study the present-day national mood. It is important to understand conspiracy, especially the post-Dallas variety, as basically theologic, since all conspiratists know that nothing happens by chance in this world. The Trilateral Commission, Rockefeller, Satan, CIA, Reverend Moon—name your gnarly little man behind the curtain—*some one, or thing,* is always pulling the switch. If there's one thing the 1970s have taught us, it is that absolute paranoia is absolutely corrupting, or deranging, as witnessed by Michael Corleone's stolid testimony about not wanting to wipe out "everyone, just my enemies." Or, as A. J. Weberman put it, "Just because you don't think they're out to get you doesn't mean they're not."

But it was not my appreciation of Weberman's talent for the coining of the conspiratorial koan that attracted me to his war against Depperman. It was my consuming interest in the strange death of Bruce Lee.

I first became aware of the awesome cross-cultural power of Bruce E. Lee while watching *Enter the Dragon* at the Lyric Theatre on Forty-second Street. The vengeful Bruce was on the verge of killing a bad white guy who earlier in the film had tried to rape a Lee sister, causing the woman to commit suicide. Now, however, the hoodlum was staggering on one edge of the CinemaScope screen, while on the other Bruce was winding himself into a corkscrew of death. Then Lee flung himself, feet first, toward the bad guy. Bruce slow-motioned through the air for what seemed an eternity. Just before Lee planted his dynamite feet into the white guy's soon-to-be-demolished rib cage, a cry came from a black wino sitting behind me.

"Don't hurt him so bad, Bruce. *Kill the motherfucker*. But don't hurt him so bad." All movie long the wino had been rooting for all the whiteys to get dead, so his show of mercy for the chief bad white guy puzzled me. The only conclusion was that somewhere down deep the wino had connected with the notion that Bruce Lee possessed within his seemingly slight body a cosmic force far more terrible than a battery of M-16s. Even a Forty-second Street wino doesn't want to be eyeball to eyeball with that kind of power.

This incident occurred soon before the fall of Nam. I coupled the calendar reference with the fact that audiences for Bruce Lee movies have always been almost exclusively black and Puerto Rican—even when the films were playing only down in Chinatown—and came up with the Third World Alliance Theory. The theory postulates that blacks and Puerto Ricans in New York were giant Bruce Lee fans because the United States lost the Vietnam War. Sense could be made of it: For years blacks and Puerto Ricans hadn't been getting squat in the city due to a heavy white bootheel. Now they were checking the *Daily News* and seeing little guys, a bunch of eggroll makers, laundry ticket cats, kicking whitey's butt in Nam. Kicking whitey's technological butt! But how were they managing it? What secret weapon did they have? The answer was clear to anyone watching *The Chinese Connection* or *Fists of Fury*.

To any student of paranoia (those with some instinct for pop culture, that is) the Third World Alliance Theory had to seem tenable. After all, times were changing. The Nam war exposed the folly of blindly relying on a computerized military. Balances were turned upside down. No longer could the Cleaver Family sleep sound snuggled beneath the thick metal sheets of vaunted American industry. Jimmy Stewart and the SAC were not up there ready to ward off real and imagined cascades of plague. If they were, they were cooping. It was every man for himself—I mean, how capable are you with your hands and feet, buddy?

To the student of cross-cultural paranoia, this situation was fascinating. Kung fu could be the ultimate weapon of these new times, and Bruce Lee its Messiah. And before Lee was finished preaching in the drive-in and sleaze Temples of the Inner City, Western Civilization could go down the tube in a flurry of sidekicks and numchakas. Would the CIA allow a menace to exist? Obviously, something had to be done.

Perhaps that something was done back in 1973 when Bruce Lee died in Hong Kong under distinctly mysterious circumstances. The first report of Lee's death said he succumbed to "marijuana poisoning." This had to be the most laughable cover story ever invented. Later the cause of death shifted to "water on the brain," whatever that is.

I decided to do some checking. I went to Aaron Banks' New York Karate Academy, then and now located above a male burlesque house and Spanish-language theater on Seventh Avenue near Forty-ninth Street. Banks, who looks like Dracula and once claimed to have held the record for the most boards broken within a given space of time, turned out to be a valuable source. He said, "quite confidentially," that Lee had died of the Iron Fist.

"An ancient martial arts ritual," Banks intoned as he shoved several monthly student fees into his pocket.

Banks's story went as follows: Several of the elder Manchu dynasty martial arts teachers were worried about Bruce Lee. Having watched several of his films, they decreed that Lee—who was no fake, but rather a kung fu genius who developed his own style of Jeet Kune Do—was giving away too many of the ancient Oriental secrets. The Masters acquired some box-office figures from *Variety* and saw that Lee's movies were cleaning up in America. This was terrible, the Masters decided, since Americans are inferior, potentially mindlessly violent people and thus not to be trusted with these secrets to ultimate power. Then, according to Banks, the Masters dispatched an emissary to reason with Lee. Bruce, however, was already as big as Valentino in Hong Kong and arrogant to boot. He would not agree to stop making films. So the emissary, a Great Master, simply laid his hand on Bruce's shoulder for a moment. This, Banks said, was the Iron Fist, a martial arts technique only the Great Masters, with their consummate knowledge of brain- and body-waves, can apply.

"It works slowly, like a poison cancer spreading through the body via vibration which eventually breaks down cells, leading to total exhaustion of various organs. It is like a snake inside you, constricting and squeezing, until you're nothing but a bag of physiological dust," Banks said in a low, guarded voice. That was why, Banks said, the doctors could never successfully determine the cause of Lee's death. To do so would be like admitting the Hippocratic Oath wasn't worth the rationalism it was printed on. This sounded a little odd to me, but a quick check of dojo around the city indicated that, almost to a man, martial arts students believed in the Great Masters Theory. Surprising too was the fact that most students, almost all of them American, accepted the Great Masters' assessment. Black belts to the fifth degree, down deep they knew that people like them were unworthy of the great knowledge.

The Great Masters' theory sounded morally logical on the surface. But natural paranoia told me not to accept it wholesale. Someone, I suspected—probably Rockefeller—had to savvy the significance of the Third World Alliance Lee was forging through his films. The fact that Lee died while making *Game of Death*, in which he costarred with Kareem Abdul Jabbar—a pairing that would have cemented the black-Asian sector of the Alliance—added to my suspicions. I figured the Great Masters were paid to off Bruce Lee, assuming that Great Masters can be bought.

So, you can dig my surprise and all-consuming interest when I first came upon the slew of wall posters currently plastered around downtown claiming Bruce Lee was Murdered by Hong Kong and Worldwide Film King, Multi*National Capitalist*Banker Run Run Shaw.

The poster goes on at great length, in copious detail and minute type, to outline how Bruce, once a low-wage contract employee for the Shaw Brothers' Hong Kong cinema combine, broke away and formed his own production corporation. This new company, spearheaded by Lee's own fabulous box-office appeal, soon was on the verge of eclipsing Shaw's empire. Shaw, according to the wall poster, "a monopoly capitalist like the Rockefellers, Mellons, Du Ponts, and Rothschilds," had no choice but to destroy Lee. Shaw had no compunction about murder, the poster says, once being responsible for blowing up "a planeload of Cathay Productions executives over Taiwan." Shaw contacted one Betty Ting Pei, a girlfriend of Lee, and a Dr. Chu-Pro-hywe (described as a "contract killer"). Together, these two cooked up an elaborate poisoning scheme that succeeded in killing Lee on July 20, 1973.

As outlandish as these charges appear to be, I made it an interesting graffiti, at least as interesting as anything by Keith Haring, and the equal of the WORSHIP GOD scrawl on every pay phone from here to Sheepshead Bay, SAMO, and the BECOME A CATHOLIC legend spray-painted onto the majority of abandoned buildings in Harlem. The poster's assertions flew directly in the face of the "Great Masters Theory" accepted in almost every dojo around the city.

A small sidebar on the poster said it was the work of a group called the Assassination Information Committee.

The AIC described itself as "originally a government counterinsurgency group that 'formed' after a Mark Lane talk at NYU in the spring of 1975. The AIC was taken over democratically on October 23, 1975, when members voted by secret ballot to present the Dealey Plaza 'tramp' photographs and Watergate 'burglars' photo overlays [positive transparencies that line up the ear cartilages on Frank Fiorini Sturgis and E. Howard Hunt] at a talk again to be given by Mark Lane, but sponsored by the NY AIC. Lane refused. Government people . . . ran off with the keys, mailing list, and the checkbook of this supposed 'grassroots' organization, but by doing so they lost control, and discredited themselves and their methods. Consequently, the AIC of NY is probably the only legitimate assassination research group in this country."

Telltale post-acid paranoia phrases like "counterinsurgency," to say nothing of the description of E. Howard Hunt's ear cartilage, informed me that I was most likely dealing with a termite left group pushing the old trope about how *Rush To Judgement* author Mark Lane is nothing more than a government plant attempting to divert "real" investigations into the John F. Kennedy assassination. This is pretty much yesterday's papers when it comes to assassinationological research. However, after glancing at other wall posters under the AIC banner, including LARRY FLYNT SHOOTING IS LATEST CIA PUBLICITY STUNT, I understood that the mania at work ran far deeper than the usual. This assessment was borne out by subsequent postings on the wall of Whelan's Drug at the corner of Eighth Street and Sixth Avenue. This said: Total Media Blackout . . . with trumped-up charges, Capitalist State harassing William H. Depperman, coordinator of the Assassination Information Committee of New York. . . . First Assassination Researcher Arrested." Then I dug that if I was to get information on the Great Masters and Third World Alliance Theories, I would have to deal with this Depperman.

At the outset I knew nothing of Depperman other than he sometimes gave out leaflets in Washington Square and was rumored to have once broken Bob Fass's (late of WBAI) nose with a short right. But, being an auteurist, I was determined to ferret out the possible role of Raymond Chow, director of *Enter the Dragon*, in Lee's death.

I went to 10 East Sixteenth Street, the address given on the AIC posters. The place, a gray apartment house nestled amongst warehouses, turned out to be Depperman's home. I rang the bell under his mailbox and was buzzed in. After an unpleasant ride in a cattlecar elevator, I knocked on Depperman's door. Nobody answered. But considering who I was dealing with, there was no reason to believe he would open the door for someone he didn't know. I slipped a note under the door describing who I was and my interest in the wall posters.

The next day I got a call from Depperman. Before he even let me say word one about the Third World Alliance Theory, Depperman commandeered the conversation. "Don't tell me you're interested in Bruce Lee," he began screaming in a voice that moved quickly from a low rumble to a falsetto. "I know who you are. I've checked you out. You work with Weberman. You are straight from Central Intelligence. That's a fact. If you want to talk to me, you'll have to put up money, big money. Five thousand. Maybe ten. You might not have the money, but your boss does. So listen, you agent, pay. Cash. No checks." He hung up.

This was the first time I had ever been accused of being a CIA agent. It was no fun. Sure, I knew that calling other people government agents is common among assassination researchers. Once Mae Brussell, who calls everyone an agent, said I. F. Stone was a ClA operative at the Elgin Theatre. That just about killed her credibility amongst the old-line leftists, and Brussell's career suffered afterward.

Moreover, I was certainly not "with Weberman." Yes, I'd once marched in an A. J.–organized Yippie smoke-in parade up Fifth Avenue during which a straggle-haired protester reached over the picket fence surrounding the sidewalk café of the St. Moritz Hotel, thrust his greasy hand into a lady's spinach salad, gobbled a fistful of leaves, and then stuck his green-specked tongue out, saying, "Your lifestyle stinks."

But I wouldn't exactly call this being "with Weberman." Who was this idiot Depperman to call me a CIA agent?

I decided to find out. Discounting talking to Depperman directly, inasmuch as I doubted Rupert Murdoch's people would look too kindly on an expense report that listed, "talking to wacko paranoid nut, $10,000," I called Joel Meyers. I got Meyers's name from a Depperman wall poster entitled TAKEOVER FROM WITHIN OF ASSASSINATION INFORMATION COMMITTEE BY COMMUNIST CADRE 'MARXIST' IS DEFEATED. In this poster, Depperman accuses Meyers, an old-line Trot whose group was one of the few to support so-called anti–Red Guard Lin Piao at the recent City Center Mao rally, of being the leader of a "government group designed to pace, contain, manipulate, sabotage, and neutralize the Assassination Information Committee of New York."

In a counterposter also affixed to the wall of Whelan's Drug, Meyers responded by painting Depperman as a right-wing son of a "rock-ribbed Republican family" who had gone to medical school in Kentucky but was alledgedly thrown out for smoking pot. Meyers said Depperman's left-wing activity was new, and that he "voted for Barry Goldwater in 1964 and Nixon twice, in 1968 and 1972." Depperman previously had worked in a "united front" with Meyers's group, but split after a tactical dispute over an incident with police in Washington Square Park, the poster related, adding that the Assassination Information Committee "consists of only

Depperman and one dogged follower," the teenaged Brian Huber, "whom Depperman calls Brainless."

On the phone, Meyers presented a somewhat more charitable view of Depperman. "Well," he said, "I have no evidence that he is hopelessly psychotic at this time. Trouble is, Depperman has a conspiratorial theory of history. He thinks everyone is an agent until proven otherwise. But we still maintain hopes of making a Bolshevik out of him yet. Small groups tend to be desperate for members. We will spend huge amounts of time trying to win over a very few people."

About the Bruce Lee material, Meyers thought, "It's something out of the ordinary for Depperman. He probably read some Kung Fu magazines and made the rest up."

This was not encouraging news. Besides, Depperman's subsequent wall posters began to take on a woolier tone, claiming that he had been "the target of a coordinated attack by many arms of the state," as well as "24-hour telephone harassment and a mail cover." Part of this harassment, Depperman says, was his recent arrest on criminal mischief charges for allegedly stenciling the Washington Square arch with slogans to the effect that Moonies and Yippies are government agents. In subsequent wall posters, Depperman claimed that the "endless series of pre-trial hearings (10 to 15) are . . . one of its prime ways of neutralizing legitimate leftists." He further charges that he has been sabotaged in much more elaborate and nefarious ways, asserting that "on *every* court date a demonstration was planned to protest this unlawful harassment . . . *and on every court date it rained!*" As an addenda, Depperman adds, in parentheses, "USA admitted to increasing the monsoon rainfall on the Ho Chi Minh trail during the Vietnam War."

Recently the plot has thickened, with several unfamiliar names beginning to appear on Depperman's missives, many of which now could be found as far uptown as Thirty-fourth Street. One of these names was that of John Zirinsky, a legal aid lawyer and member of the Lawyer's Guild who has often been identified with left causes, who had been assigned to represent Depperman in his criminal mischief case. Reached at his office, Zirinsky said he did his best to help Depperman, but all sorts of arguments arose with his client.

"Here I am trying to defend the guy," Zirinsky said, "and he's plastering the entire courthouse area with posters attacking me as a government plant. All during that time he was pleading with me to continue with his defense. Everyone was asking me what was going on." Zirinsky, a sober type, did not see the humor in this situation. He says, "Besides, it was clear to me that Depperman, this supposed revolutionary, didn't have even the rudiments of leftist thought." Eventually Zirinsky withdrew from the case, prompting a triumphant Depperman wall poster saying, "Zirinsky's withdrawal reflects the failure of the state and the Rockefeller Family strategy against Depperman . . ."

Woe is the Dep. A few months ago he was fired from his job as a cardiopulmonary technician at the Hospital for Joint Disease. Depperman says it was for his "political activities," primarily his drive to organize RNs at the institution. The management claims Depperman "falsified records" to avoid getting caught for coming in late. Depperman has described the case in two lengthy wall posters, one entitled DEPPERMAN CASE GOES TO ARBITRATION, MANAGEMENT LOSES AT 1ST HEARING, and another explained WHY THE CIA IS LIKELY TO BE BEHIND MANAGEMENT'S NEW STRATEGY. Both of these posters were signed by the "Save the Jobs Unity Coalition," not the AIC.

As of now, Depperman has yet to be rehired. David White, of the medical services union No. 1199, represented Depperman at his arbitration hearing. In the wall posters, Depperman implies that White was working in collusion with management. White says, "He thinks I was working with management? Oh boy. I don't know. I'll tell you, there was no reason we should have lost that case. Management really didn't have a thing on Depperman. He said he filled in the wrong time because his watch was slow. Anyone's watch can be slow. That's not grounds for firing someone. But during the hearing, Depperman just wouldn't shut up. I had to stop the proceedings a dozen times to tell him to quiet down. He kept jumping up and calling the arbitrator a tool of the oppressors."

White agrees that most likely management was "just trying to get rid of Depperman." But not because Dep was union-organizing. "Are you kidding?" White says, "he almost killed our drive. He was going around talking about general strikes and preparing the workers for revolution. You can't talk to workers like that."

With each new piece of info I picked up on Depperman, I became more convinced that a freshly slivered section of the Dep medulla sold to an independent laboratory might fetch a handsome price. For sure the cat was going into the Paranoia Hall of Fame on the first ballot. I was beginning to give up on ever getting any intelligence out of this guy in either the Great Masters or the Third World Alliance Theory.

But the most damaging anti-Depperman testimony was yet to come. It was provided by Depperman's archenemies, the Yippies. In his wall poster campaign, Depperman regularly derides the Yips as a government-funded group attempting to "sidetrack people on drugs and counterculture," thereby leading the masses "back into the fold of the Republican Party." The most recurring and bizarre Depperman charge, however, is that A. J. Weberman, the Yippie theoretician, is "suppressing his own book."

The book, *Coup d'etat in America,* written by Weberman and Michael Canfield, details how the CIA allegedly seized control of the United States government on November 22, 1963. Depperman claims *Coup d'etat,* which contains the famous "tramp" pictures and photo overlays that supposedly prove Frank Sturgis and Howard Hunt were on the scene that day in Dallas, is an example of "controlled release" of assassination material. He says A. J. "must be" a CIA agent to gain access to the overlays in the first place, and that since "exposing" the evidence, Weberman has done much "to make the information contradictory," thereby confusing real assassination researchers.

Now, in the interests of full disclosure, I must admit that I have known A. J. Weberman for some time, most often in his self-declared role as the world's greatest Bob Dylanologist. A. J. is keeper of the archives of the Dylan Liberation Front, mostly devoted to "liberating Dylan's mind" of the famous singer, which the DLF claims has been subverted by a government plot to addict him to heroin, thereby minimizing the singer as a force for revolutionary change. And, knowing A. J. as I do, I could see that Depperman's conjectures regarding *Coup d'etat in America* were really getting under his skin.

Going into one of his hour-long stare rages, Weberman barked, "What a Daffyman the Deppermonster is! Why would I fucking suppress my own book? I worked months on that book. It's the hardest thing I ever did. Harder than the garbology project. Supress my own book? Only a moron with a low-rate of metabolism like the Daffymonster would think that."

Then A. J. discussed Depperman from the historical perspective, saying "He first came around in 1974, around there. He said he wanted to help put out the *Yipster Times*. You know, he'd do any shit work. Dana [Beale] was suspicious of him, but I was taken in. I went by his pad and he had all the Dylan records and the Dylan bootlegs, I thought he was cool. It was a moment of weakness. But after the book came out he started acting suspicious. He put out stickers for people to buy the book everywhere. He was overzealous. He put stickers all over the bookstores and they started calling me saying they wouldn't stock the book anymore. I didn't know what was happening, then I find out its Depperman. We told him to stop, but then he gets his own stickers printed up. Then we realized he was waging some kind of campaign against us. He was spreading all kinds of disinformation. Then he started beating up Yippies. He broke Fass's nose. He gave Aaron [Kay, the Yippie piethrower] a black eye. He's tough, he's a fucking powerful guy. We knew he couldn't be a Yippie, he's too crazy to be a Yippie. We had to investigate him."

Then A. J. pulled out part of his FBI file. A. J. had obtained the file under the Freedom of Information Act, a statute he makes use of quite often. FBI files supposedly contain most of what the government has on you, but the names of the "informants" and anything you really want to know is blacked out with magic marker. The Yippies have spent many evenings over a piece of hash the size of a deflated football attempting to remember if it was really Sally from Madison or Jim from California who was present on the nights described in the file. On this particular page, however, A. J. claims, the "informer's" name was insufficiently disguised.

"Look," Weberman said, pointing to a Xeroxed smudge, "you can see the D and the top of an E, also, look, there's the two Ls. It's Depperman, no doubt about it. He's an informer sent to infiltrate us. Probably got into it after he got kicked out of medical school. The reason the FBI sent us this file with the name not completely blacked out is even they couldn't stand the Deppermouth anymore. The Deppermonster is too obnoxious even for the feds!"

Try as I might, however, I could only distinguish half an L, no D or E. I smoked two more joints, after which I did spot another L, which was not enough to convince me, beyond a shadow of a doubt, that it was actually Depperman's name beneath the blur. I did, however, agree with Weberman that Depperman's Yippie-beating activities were to be scorned. And I also promised to show up a few days later when A. J. said Depperman would have to be in court to answer charges of knife-wielding.

I left the Yipster Mansion thinking it was kind of ironic that Depperman, in his unwavering bleat that A. J. had "surpressed" his own book, had, more or less, taken over the role in Weberman's life that A. J. himself had once played in Bob Dylan's. Back in the days when the Dylan Liberation Front assembled on MacDougal Street screaming, "Hey Bob, crawl out your window," A. J. stole the singer's garbage as a "people's act." Dylan always yelled at Weberman to "stop hassling me, man," and eventually beat A. J. to a Greenwich Village sidewalk with karate blows.

Thinking about this left one question unanswered: If Depperman is Weberman's Weberman, who is Depperman's Weberman? Someone, I figured, always has to be around to keep you honest.

In spite of it all, I felt a little sorry for Depperman. My heart goes out to anyone who sincerely feels the government is manipulating the weather just to harass *him*. After all, Depperman really was being "persecuted" for his politics, whatever they may be. I decided to attempt to open the dialogue with Depperman again, affording him a chance to tell his side of the story and possibly giving me a shot at obtaining his Bruce Lee information. After learning from a reliable source that Depperman had once been approached as a potential mensa member, I wrote him a closely reasoned letter asking him to give free press a chance. I was, however, still smarting from Depperman's accusations about me, so, just to be a bastard, I crossed out several passages in the letter and did a cut-paste job. I figured Depperman would spend a few anxious minutes holding the letter to a naked light bulb, attempting to see what was missing. I taped the letter to Depperman's mailbox.

This was Sunday. Monday I stayed by my phone hoping Depperman would call. He did not. Tuesday was the hearing date, so I trudged over to the Tombs at 9:30 A.M. Near the second floor D.A. intake room I ran into Aaron Kay. Aaron pointed out two people standing below, leaning on the circular first-floor information desk.

"It's Daffyman and Brainless," Aaron said. Depperman looked pretty much as I expected, except that he was wearing a paisley tie and seemed to have not slept in a month. Brian Huber, or "Brainless," could have passed for a Tex Watson double.

I went downstairs to engage the pair in conversation. Depperman was in the midst of abusing Huber. Soon as I identified myself, however, he recoiled and clutched his tan attaché case as if it were a doll stuffed with money. "Get away from me, you government . . . government pig," he said as he edged around the circumference of the information desk. Huber followed Depperman. "I just want to ask you a couple of questions," I said, trailing both of them. We must have gone around that desk three times, with Depperman shouting "Stop harassing me. Beat it. Stop harassing me," before I gave up the ghost.

Soon, the courtroom drama, which I gave you the gist of at the top of this tome, ensued. Depperman, demanding to defend himself and using some legal terms lifted out of Perry Mason, did most of the talking. A. J. was content to play the injured citizen. And, sure enough, Depperman talked himself into trouble, getting close to a contempt citation on more than one occasion. The judge told Depperman, "Look, the court is not your adversary." To which Depperman raised his eyes, as if to say, "You expect me to fall for that?"

The judge held the case over until the next month, prompting Depperman to quote loudly and extensively from a book called *The Iron Fist and the Velvet Glove*. These quotes threw the West Indian court officers into giggling fits.

There will, however, be quite a bit more court in Depperman's immediate future. After this case was adjourned, the Yippies, who were afraid to stare at Depperman during the proceedings, unfurled their sneak attack in the person of one Detective Guariello of the Sixth Precinct. Guariello was waiting in the hallway outside AR 2A to arrest Depperman on charges that he assaulted Yippie electrician Robert Druskin. Upon having the cuffs snapped on his wrists and told he was "under arrest," Depperman screamed, "By whom, by whom?"

Then he yelled, "It's more harassment, it's more harassment of legitimate leftists," as Guariello hauled him into the D.A.T. intake room. Just before disappearing, Depperman shouted in panic to Huber, "Brian, Brian, my briefcase." Huber, who seemed stunned by this turn of events, was slow to react, prompting Depperman to a more frenzied plea. Finally Huber picked up the case. As he did, one of the court officers pointed to Depperman's head and then to the briefcase, intoning, "Tick, tick, tick."

Moments later Depperman was gone, except for a few muffled protests emanating from the other side of the door. He would spend that night in the can. Huber waited a few moments, then split aimlessly with Depperman's briefcase, Renfield lost a master. The Yippies left, too, celebrating their victory.

And I figured, what a drag it all was. Dealing with paranoids is a thankless task. Depperman saw me talking to Guariello before the pinch and probably, knowing his mania, thinks I was in on the arrest. Plus, who knows, we may never find out who killed Bruce Lee.

IN THE REALM OF THE SPIRIT

13

B Is for Buddhist, *D* Is for Death

Interview with a Theocrat

You don't always get to travel seventy-five hundred miles for a one-hour appointment. But time and space become relative in the presence of the Ocean of Wisdom, the fourteenth Dalai Lama. An added benefit occurred one year later, when I encountered His Holiness once again in Chicago. "Jackupson!" he shouted and rushed across the room to shake my hand. Those bodhisattvas, they sure know how to make a guy feel good. Esquire, *1993.*

For the determined pilgrim, keeping an appointment with the Dalai Lama ("for one hour only" says the paper faxed from the Office of Tibet) is a matter of conveyance. The twenty-hour flight from New York to New Delhi on Air India is a cramped pro forma. More difficult is the final three hundred miles from Delhi to Dharmsala, the Himalayan foothill town where the former Tenzin Gyatso, the fourteenth reincarnation of the Dalai Lama, has lived since his exile from Chinese-held Tibet in 1959. There are flights, notably on Viadoot Airways, a local concern that is pronounced "why-a-doot" as in "why-no-a-chicken?" However, even on the rare occasions that the weather is good, the airline runs into problems. After sitting for three hours, the prospective passenger will be told his scheduled flight has been canceled due to "snakes in the engine."

"Snakes?"

No, the Viadoot employee replies with a crane of the neck. Not snakes. "S-*nags* . . . some snags in the engine."

The obvious alternative, the railway up to Himchal Pradesh, is not available. A bridge in the vicinity of Chandigarh has been washed out. This leaves the hiring of a car, two days of ear-splitting horn-honking and dense exhaust-breathing. But no matter, when the pilgrim finally arrives in Dharmsala and treks up the hill from the lower Indian town to the Tibetan settlement of McLeod Ganj, His Holiness, the Wish-Fulfilling Gem and Nobel Prize–winning Dalai Lama, is standing on his cement slab porch in his maroon and saffron robes waiting to greet you.

"Jockupson!" he shouts, with a wave as if you just happened to be in the neighborhood and were thoughtful enough to stop by during this particularly severe monsoon season to see how he was doing. A bear hug and a solid slap on the back follow. His arm is fleshy and he's bigger than you'd imagine, nearly six feet tall, probably close to two hundred pounds. How nice of you, he says, with a widening smile, to have been so kind as to have brought him a gift from faraway America.

It is the thing to do, after all, to bring the Dalai Lama a present. But what? What do you bring the Ocean of Wisdom, what does a bodhisattva really need? It was a vexing question, one that preoccupied me in the last days before beginning my journey to Dharmsala. Then, the afternoon before I left, while strolling by a sporting goods store on Seventh Avenue near my Brooklyn home, it came to me. There, in the window beside the Phat Farm sweatshirts and Roc-A-Fella jeans, was a replica of the cap once worn by the Dodgers, the beloved baseball team that broke the heart of the long-suffering boro when they moved from the sooty confines of Flatbush to the Los Angeles money fields. Seen through the streaked plate glass of the store window, sky blue with a snow white B embossed on the crown, this hat suddenly seemed the only possible present to carry eight thousand miles, on trains, planes, and stuttering Ambassador sedans, to give to the Dalai Lama.

As to why this was the perfect gift, I did not find out until I put the hat in his Holiness's large and pillowy hand. He stood there a moment, regarding the mysterious object as I explained the item's origin and function in the context of the game of baseball, which was much like cricket, of course. I also touched on the deeper symbolic meaning of this particular hat, as opposed to one that might be worn by relatively faceless ballplayers from Kansas City, Seattle, and any number of less-storied franchises. This was the iconic cap worn by Reese, Snider, and the grand avatar of nonviolence, Jackie Robinson. It was the lid of a team that had moved away, a relic of the bygone recent past, yet whose memory, both real and deeply sentimentalized, was still very much alive in many souls in their former homeland.

"Hmmm," the Dalai Lama emitted with a stern and serious look, perhaps contemplating the arrangement of white bases on a field of green and their correlation to the diamond-cutter sutra, one of the Buddha's most beloved teachings. Then, his large, tawny head exploding into a vast smile, he slapped the cap onto his close-cropped monk's head.

"*B!* . . . B is for Buddhist!" he rollicked, pointing to the letter on the hat, seemingly enchanted to have it covering his head. "These Dodgers—they are exiles from their native country . . . *like Tibetans!*"

Well . . . *yes!* Exactly right!

Through whatever capacity of mind and study, His Holiness had cut through the morass of endless commentary and useless nostalgia to bring the snow white B on the sky blue cap into the realm of the here and now, forging the connection between two apparently wholly unrelated existential situations and, perhaps more important for the purposes of our "one hour only" interview, cementing the bond between him and me.

This was why he was the Dalai Lama and everyone else was not.

"Very amusing, this hat," his Holiness said, chortling, something he does a lot. He is widely celebrated for being an easy laugh. It doesn't take much to get him to access his ample jollity, unfurl a syncopated jumble of giggled snorts, twitters, bellyroars, and mega-crack-ups. His intermittently askew English will octave from basso overtone to pinched Eddie Kendricks–like falsetto within the stretch of a single sentence fragment. It is as Tibetans say: When confronted with the ever-ensnaring minutia of everyday (surface) life, one often has no choice but to break out laughing.

Once upon a fabled time, prior to the Chinese invasion of Tibet in 1951 and his famously narrow, copiously documented escape into exile following the national uprising eight years later, Tenzin Gyatso lived in the Potala, the 350-year-old, thousand-chambered "penthouse of the gods." According to the scholars of the day, he never left the palace unless "ensconced in a yellow palanquin pulled by twenty men" preceded by "horsemen, all nicely turned out, caparisoned and led by grooms" and dozens of porters carrying his personal songbirds inside gilded cages.

Now, after more than thirty years in exile, the leader of what can only be called a virtual state, he lives in this single-story building with cement floors and wears scuffed rubbersoled brown oxfords on his feet. Not that these material things are supposed to matter to him. "The world is a place of change—this is a condition we can only ignore with danger," His Holiness says, settling into his leather chair in his thinly carpeted "office." One's surroundings can be "important or not so important, it is a choice left to the individual." While it is "nice to be rich," not being so "is a condition in which someone can be upset or not upset." As far as he is concerned, he is "not upset," echoing his standard, possibly disingenuous, line. "Because I am nothing but a simple Buddhist monk."

But there is little time for small talk when visiting His Holiness. With only one hour scheduled, his numerous "special assistants" warn against wasting "precious seconds." However, the DL, as he is sometimes called, does not share this hurry-up attitude. When you are with him, temporality suspends, you're in another zone, one where clocks stop. Flanked by his two translators, one for religious matters, the other for political concerns, His Holiness is unfailingly patient with clueless westerners. Dumb as you get, he never makes you feel like you just sneezed and scattered the sand mandala around the room. He regards your every question, however inane, with thoughtful concern, pushing his strangely froglike visage closer in rapt attention.

Care to engage in a twenty-minute exegesis on the Doctrine of Impermanence as it pertains to the coffee table, attempting to equate the boundaries of the said table to the political borders of nation-states? No problem. Cognizant of (but too polite to mention) the Tibetan bromide asserting that a mind that finds logic "too interesting" only sows the seeds of its own confusion, His Holiness will oblige by dutifully delineating the various tenets of the Impermanence Doctrine, eventually concluding that "from the Buddhist point of view," even though the table/space boundaries and the borders of nation-states may both be examples of phenomenological thinking, most likely the two constructs have nothing to do with each other.

"That, of course, is my opinion only," he remarks, grinning. "You, perhaps, do not agree."

You recognize that he's inviting argument, urging you to challenge the Dalai Lama, peerless Master of Metaphysics, on matters such as *prajnaparamita* (the Wisdom Path) and *pramana* (epistemology).

Like, sure, dude. But beyond a gracious overture to a dunce, His Holiness's solicitation resides well within the scope of Mahayana practice. For Tibetan Buddhists, no education, however rigorous, or scrupulously nonviolent, is complete without dharma combat.

Even now, outside His Holiness's window, the Namgyal monks are going through their debates, as they do twenty days a month, six hours a day. Once monks debated at Ganden, Sera, and Drepung, the three great monasteries of Old Tibet, prior to the defilement of these massive institutions by rampaging Red Guards during the Cultural Revolution (according to the claims of the Washington-based Tibet lobby, 6,254 monasteries have been damaged during the Chinese invasion and occupation, during which 1.2 million Tibetans have reportedly lost their lives.)

These days the monks attend McLeod Ganj's cramped Institute of Buddhist Dialectics, conducting their disputations in the concrete courtyard of what was once a primary school. It is a sensational thing to see. Moving with the sultry deliberateness of ritual inside a circle of his fellows, one palm held out in front of him to symbolize the Buddha's helping outreach, a monk frames a question of dharmic import. Then, fast, like elocutionary kung fu, he slaps the open palm with his other hand, thrusting it toward one of the sitting monks.

"What is it? *What is the answer?*" he shouts, like a third-degree-wielding policeman in a padded room.

The designated monk does not respond hastily, but rather sits passively, quietly contemplating his reply, and then—this is the real goal—attempts to stump the questioner with an inquiry of his own. Should this comeback include a modicum of denigrating wit toward the questioner (such as "Are you such a fool, so ignorant of Buddhathought, as to pose such a meaningless query in the thin air for all to see?"), so much the better, for then the original interrogator is roundly heckled and everyone falls down in hysterical laughter. In Old Tibet, dialectics were considered great psychic sport. Illiterate nomads would travel days on yaks and camels to Lhasa just to watch.

Now, outside the Dalai Lama's window, it sounds as if there's been a serious rhetorical chumping. Monks' voices ring like boys who've just thrown the weird kid's sneakers over the telephone pole wire. His Holiness grins when he hears this, because, as he says, "It reminds him of times gone by . . . now, since I am the Dalai Lama, no one engages me in such combat and I miss it."

Then, for the first time in the conversation, he seems very far away. I'd been told about this, the sudden detachment, how it's not that you're boring him but rather that the Dalai Lama, for all his impeccable civility, sometimes "goes off, to another place." You wonder: Have those young voices transported Tenzin Gyatso back to his lonely childhood in the dank and forbidding Potala, when, separated from his parents, kept apart from other children his age, he passed his days being drilled by the most learned and venerable rinpoches and scholars in the disciplines deemed necessary to the instruction of a God-king?

Or maybe even further back, to that spring day in 1938 when a search party arrived in Takster, a small village in Amdo, in what was once northeast Tibet. Advised by the fact that the thirteenth Dalai Lama, the squat, politically skillful Thubten Gyatso, had, while lying in state, turned his head from the south to the east, the searchers came upon a house with an oddly shaped gable similar to one cited in the dream of Reting Rinpoche, the government regent. There, Lhamo Thondup, not yet three and the ninth child of peasant farmers, born amid a series of auspicious signs, pointed to a box containing Thubten Gyatso's dentition and exclaimed, "My teeth are in there."

You're daydreaming how this incident correlates to the segment of the American mythscape depicted in *Citizen Kane*, the scene in which banker Walter Thatcher comes to fetch the young Kane, when His Holiness's guffaw truncates this reverie. It's as if he's been following your rendition of the inevitable Hollywood movie of his life and, confronted by the (equally inevitable) sentimentalized gnarling of biographical particulars, he had no choice but to break out laughing.

Then we were talking about Death.

Tibetans, after all, are something of authorities on death, wrote the book on it, so to speak. The *Bardo Thodol*, otherwise known as the *Tibetan Book of the Dead*, meant to be read aloud as a preparatory tonic to the "soon-to-die," describes the symbolic forty-one days following physical death during which the Mind (soul is the wrong term), borne by "karmic winds" like a "feather riding a horse's breath," arrives at the succeeding "womb door."

The *Bardo Thodol* can make arresting airplane reading, especially when those electrical storms start zinging thirty thousand feet above Turkmenistan, telling as it does of "The Judgment," the moment when the deceased's good and bad deeds are laid out in the form of white and black pebbles. "Lying will be of no avail," the text imparts, for "The Lord of Death will say, 'I will consult the Mirror of Karma'" . . . and then "place round thy neck a rope and drag thee along; he will cut off thy head, extract thy heart, pull out thy intestines, lick up thy brain, eat thy flesh, and gnaw thy bones . . ." This will cause "intense pain and torture," the Book of the Dead says.

Yet it urges the "soon-to-die" to not be frightened or terrified. "The Lords of Death are thine own hallucinations . . . and have no existence apart from one's own hallucinations." In other words, the horror's all in your severed head, another piece of grasping, illusionary carry-on baggage to addle the distracted Mind.

Hearing how westerners visiting India say it's better to get a Sikh cabbie since they're the only ones around (outside of the Muslims) who don't believe in reincarnation and consequently take more care on the roadways, the Dalai Lama giggles. Jokes about comparative religions, especially eating habits, "always" make him laugh, he says. "About this I am not fundamental, more ecumenical," he notes.

Nonetheless, he says, "Death should not make one afraid, or cause worry. Why worry about what cannot be escaped? Death is no predicament, it is sad sometimes, and can come without warning. But it is to be welcomed as well. Death is to be treasured as life is treasured since the two are really one."

His Holiness, of course, is familiar with the process. He has died and been reborn many times and had numerous encounters with The Clear Light of the *Book of the Dead*, described as "like the cloudless sky . . . a naked, spotless intellect." As a *tulku* (someone so highly evolved as to be able to dictate the circumstances of subsequent rebirths), he is the fourteenth reincarnation of a line that goes back to Gedum Truppa, the first Dalai Lama, who was born in 1391 and, following a deal struck between the Mongols and Galupa sect (to which all Dalai Lamas belong) was put on the throne by a great-grandson of Genghis Khan. The DL is also considered to be the seventy-fourth manifestation of Chenrezig, the Bodhisattva of Infinite Compassion (twenty centuries of rebirths right there). Indeed, His Holiness has no idea how many times he has lived previously, nor does he recall many events of his antecedent incarnations. ("This way I can read the history books with suspense.") But he maintains no doubt of the absolute factual certainty of cyclical existence.

"None at all," he says evenly.

It's about here that the head of the religiously disgruntled seeker/cynic begins to ache. After all, Buddhism, at least in its Stateside version, is remarkably free of these hard-to-swallow assertions. The Buddha left eighty-four thousand separate teachings, and nowhere is there a blustering "Let there be light" tale of Genesis for evolutionists to choke on, or a single truncheon of Armageddon to be wielded by the wild-eyed. Rationalism takes precedence over faith—a gestalt that quite possibly accounts for Buddhism's remarkable growth amongst alienated westerners. If Protestantism's credo of individualism was essential to the rise of capitalism, Buddhism creates a comfort zone for present-day yuppies to practice late-capital's obsession with self-improvement. They don't even ask you to believe in God, for Christ sakes!

It might be twenty-five hundred years since the former Prince Gautama sat beneath the Bo Tree near Bodh Gaya, but His Holiness appears a thoroughgoing modernist. As a child he delighted in fixing up the Aston Martins (the first internal combustion engines to appear in Tibet) his Britophile predecessor, the thirteenth Dalai Lama, had imported from India. In his obsession to "find out how things work," movie projectors were taken apart, watches scrupulously dismantled and reassembled. Now the Dalai Lama is a regular participant in roundtable discussions on topics like the cognitive sciences conducted by MIT and Harvard. An ardent BBC World Service listener, he likes to "keep up," never letting a day go by without watching "some" television, a routine enhanced by McLeod Ganj's recent twenty-four hour (fuzzy) reception of MTV.

This is "important . . . not to become lost in the past, to accept the present, to look forward to the future . . . a mixture of these is very important," the Dalai Lama says, a sandalwood rosary wrapped around his wrist right beside the Rolex (a watch he can't fix, just as he can't fix the fuel injectors in the Mercedes he rides around in). It is one thing to laugh about death, to see the lighter side of dying and rebirth, to mix, as he says, "the modern world with the mystery world," but there is also a time when "a degree of seriousness is necessary."

It is about then you notice he's staring at you, his brown eyes suddenly adamantine behind the bifocal shades, and there's a chill in the room. It's a moment (further) out of time, a place where the twinkly mirth has vanished. He's peering deep inside you, possibly for no other reason beyond that he can, and it's not that the transcendent kindness has disappeared but rather that he's showing you more of Tenzin Gyatso, another side of the Dalai Lama: a hard, hard trader, a man whose gaze reportedly shrinks monks and nuns because they know, deep in their hearts, they haven't practiced enough, haven't done enough prostrations, not truly lived up to his unapproachable example.

Then it clicks in, the mindfulness of exactly who you've been chatting up, laughing with, venerating. You understand he's not simply another roadside attraction on the guru path, not the "simple Buddhist monk." The smiling man seated across from you is the current repository of the compassion and experience of ten thousand reborn saints, the conduit of the lineages from time past and here forward. It doesn't matter if you believe it or not. You know: *he believes it*. You know too that here is a man who was forced to take over the leadership of his country at age fifteen, who played a (losing) game of high stakes politics with Mao and Chou, who has presided over the heartbreaking dissolution of his nation. He is the head of state, as much of a theocrat as any supposed fanatical Iranian mullah. Every decision he makes, every thing he says, has a double function. His solutions, he says, "can never truly be political, or purely religious. We must think of both at the same time." It is a duality that only the most mushyheaded of his admirers can blissfully ignore.

This said, it was no real surprise that the Dalai Lama was currently confronting what he agreed was a personal existential dilemma concerning Death, most specifically his own.

He often likes to joke about his health. Asked if he ever gets nervous, the Ocean of Wisdom said, "*nervous?* Yes! . . . my last medical checkup . . . after the first check the doctor want another. To take some blood. The nurse try to take some blood from here. It failed. No blood come. Another visit was arranged. Second try. Failed. Then he tried to take from here. Third time, no blood. Then I am *nervous!*" But jokes aside, there have been many tests recently, a number of personal appearances and tours have been canceled.

The inevitability of demise created a singular problem, the DL allowed. Succinctly as possible, the dilemma could be interpreted this way: On one hand, acceptance of death is at the very core of Buddhist teaching and His Holiness's own psychic and historical being. Yet in his unique niche as the spiritual and temporal leader of Tibet—the popular face of a nation that few current maps acknowledge as existing—his death would be, in the words of Lodi Gyari, the politically savvy Tibetan representative in Washington, "an absolute disaster."

"A crisis, certainly," His Holiness allows. "Owing to particular situation we find ourselves in, a definite crisis."

So now modernism and mysterium play dissonantly. Once, insulated by harsh geography and its own xenophobia, Tibet, populated by people who have a genius for religion, could be a closed mountaintop land led by a man in a crested yellow hat. It could be the unreached mythworld, object of any number of fairy stories made up by the likes of Madame Blavatsky. It could be Shangri-la. But the planet's rhythm has thrummed faster than that for some time now, synchronized to what was once called the barbarous clangor of a gong. Holy mountains are no longer unassailable. The way it is now, there's no time, no time at all to find a two-year-old boy in a rural village and wait for him to grow up to be one more Dalai Lama.

The lamaist state has fallen, victim of its own flamboyant idiosyncrasy. China has claimed the Tibetan plateau for centuries, calling Tibetans one of the "five races" of the "indivisible Motherland." What has happened since 1959, says the DL, whom the Chinese refer to as "a splitist" and "a wolf in monk's clothing," amounts to "cultural genocide." Sparked by rumored forced population transfer policies, an estimated 7.5 million Han Chinese have migrated to the Land of Snows (the Chinese call it Xizang, or "western treasure house") enough to make the 6 million Tibetans a minority in their own country. Lhasa is on the verge of becoming, says His Holiness, "just another Chinese town."

Western support, while full of keening sympathy, is difficult to count on when newspapers report the Beijing economy is growing at a burgeoning 13 percent a year. With the so-called "government" in McLeod Ganj hopelessly rinky-dink (a sign in the "Planning Office" announces "rules for motorcycle" and you think they just forgot the "s" until the pleasant woman behind the counter tells you there's only one motorcycle), the Dalai Lama, icon of nonviolence, Nobel Prize winner, is considered to be the best, and perhaps only, weapon in the dharma combat/PR war with the dour, implacable People's Republic.

This is no news to Tenzin Gyatso, who could have long ago ascended toward nirvana, but as a bodhisattva, or Buddha-to-be, he chooses to remain here on the grinding wheel of samsara as "a helping spirit." Mostly, the DL sees his mission as "helping the Tibetans . . . to keep our nation alive." In this cause he has trundled his current, decaying body around the world, making speeches, raising money, simply showing his face. Often he looks sick, disinterested, or simply jet-lagged, yet he soldiers on. The Tibetan PR machine has made him synonymous with the country he represents, and he knows that without him, there is little chance history will be reversed. But even bodhisattvas can't live forever. The Dalai Lama is sixty now, and, modern medicine aside (he prefers the Tibetan kind anyway), is already the longest-lived of his incarnations outside of the Great Fifth, who, in a similar time of crisis, was "kept alive" ten years after his death (at sixty-seven) through the use of doubles and other subterfuge, lest the populace become aware of his passing.

"Time," says His Holiness, "the Chinese play for time, they know our situation."

The Dalai Lama says Tibetans find themselves in "a transitory state" not unlike "a Bardo" of the sort described in the *Book of the Dead*. Certainly the general feeling you get in McLeod Ganj—previously a favored, if rainy, "hill station" of the British Raj—is one of limbo. Long a staple destination of the "traveler" circuit throughout India, much of the money here comes from visiting hippies in town to soak up the DL's vibe and stay in the Tibetan-run hotels. This has caused tension with the Indian population in "lower" Dharmsala, leading to several violent incidents over the years. At one point the DL even threatened to move his residence south, to the Tibetan community around Bangalore.

In 1993, no one would confuse McLeod Ganj with Shangri-la. Slog through the muddy street, past the open sewers and legless beggars, over the Tibetan Children's Village, and the teachers will show you the paintings the kids do. The drawings fall into two categories. One depicts majestic sunrises, verdant landscapes teeming with wildlife. The others are terrible scenes of death and destruction.

"That's my mother," one child reported, pointing to a stick figure she'd drawn. The figure was lying on the ground, red crayoned "blood" pouring from its head. Several men, whom the kid identified as "Chinese," were hitting the woman with sticks.

"You look at these drawings and see only heaven, the Tibet of our dreams. And hell, the Tibet of our worst memories. Dreams and nightmares. Nothing in between. No daily life, no normal reality . . ." says a former teacher. "The outside world invented its own Tibet—*Lost Horizon*. Sam Jaffe sitting on a throne. Fantasies. Now we invent it for ourselves."

There are about five thousand Tibetans in McLeod Ganj, refugees recent and not so recent, all of them here because this is where the Dalai Lama lives. As with so much in the current Tibetan condition, the entire settlement revolves around the physical person of the DL, and the town functions as a benign cult of personality.

That said, His Holiness does draw an interesting crowd. The word is, you can't tell who's who in McLeod Ganj, not by looking anyway. You meet an old monk, toothless and wizened, who bows and shuffles on, limping as he goes. "He meditated in a cave for seventeen years," says your informant deferentially. Then you meet a twelve-year-boy, a monk, and he's really knocked out that you're from the States because he's heard a lot about Elvis. Not until he regretfully returns the water gun you've given him (because it's "not allowed") do you find out he's a "really, really high tulku," recognized by His Holiness himself as a reincarnation of a "big lama," that he lives in special quarters bedecked by antique *thankas* and is attended to by three full-time servants.

His Holiness says that one thing you learn about in exile is the practice of "waiting." Therefore, much of what happens in McLeod Ganj, a less romantic kind of Casablanca, is about passing time. Waiting and talking about waiting. Much of this talk is done in teahouses: the Om, the Snowland, the

Trans-Himalaya. You sit there with the Euro backpacker/hippies (whose gone-native wardrobe leads one longtime nun from Brooklyn to remark, "They're the reincarnated souls of everyone who OD'ed at Woodstock"), watching the hideous new Indian hotels slowly slide down the mountainside and listening to the town gossip, about how maybe the monks are not all that celibate and how "leg fucking," in which one devotee's member is massaged between the legs of another, is considered okay as long as "the plane of orifice" is not broken. There are plenty of rumors about randy "ricochet rinpoches" and willing Western "dharmasluts."

Then, of course, there's the usual celebrity watch, the bevy of H-wood Buddhists, above the title and not, staying at the Kashmiri Cottage awaiting their obligatory private audience with His Holiness. Aside from testy debate about what kind of *mallah* (Buddhist rosary) he uses—is it sandalwood? crystal?—Richard Gere is kind of taken for granted in McLeod Ganj. There are more arcane sightings. The other day Marvin Hamlisch was reportedly seen dodging cow-dung on the main street. "Yes, Marvin Hamlisch," says a wizened Tibetan prayer wheel salesman, reciting the Broadway composer's name several times as if the mere sound of it amounted to some merit-accruing karmic practice.

One afternoon a Dutch tourist sat in the Om screaming about what the Chinese are doing to Tibetan culture. "In Lhasa they've opened discos, with waitresses in *chupas* dancing to Madonna records," the outraged Dutchman, who only two weeks earlier had climbed the steps of the Potala and circumambulated the Jokang Temple, explained to a wide-eyed Tibetan boy, who was born in McLeod Ganj to refugee parents and would likely never see the Potala anywhere but on a calendar photo.

"It's a ridiculous consequence we find ourselves in now, isn't it?" remarked my dinner companion Lhasang Tsering, the Tibetan-born owner of the Bookworm, McLeod Ganj's leading English-language bookstore. We were in the midst of a typical McLeod Ganj conversation: a lamentation over the pathetic state of the Tibetan army prior to the Chinese invasion. According to Lhasang, a fabulously well-read, bearded "failed Eurotrash" of about forty, it was the forgiving Buddhist attitude toward Death, that no macho advantage was to be received from "staring down" the Reaper, that accounted for the pathetic stunting of the Tibetan martial urge.

Told that His Holiness had suggested that insight into the current fate of "this generation of Tibetans" might be gleaned from an investigation of the "possibly bad collective karma" of previous generations, Lhasang rolled his eyes. "I hope he includes himself in that assessment."

This is one of the interesting things you learn in the McLeod Ganj teahouses—something you'll never hear in the West—that the Dalai Lama is not universally adulated by all Tibetans. While it is impossible to find anyone to defend China's moral position in Tibet, there are plenty of people, and they don't have to be Marxists, who will echo Party pronouncements to the effect that the DL is a relic of feudal times, a product of an elitist, oligarchical, sometimes corrupt system bent on the maintenance of a status quo that doomed a large portion of the Tibetan people to poverty and backwardness.

"We're not against the Dalai Lama exactly, or the Dalai Lama institution," says Jamyang Norbu, an urbane Tibetan playwright who has both participated in short-lived, CIA-funded Mustangi resistance against the Chinese and spent several years living abroad reading, among other things, many science fiction books. "We're saying only that we need to change, or we'll die."

Jamyang, along with Lhasang and others, has founded the Amnye Machen Institute, which they describe as an independent center for the dissemination of Tibetan "culture, literature, history, and society" with "emphasis on the neglected, contemporary, and lay aspects of these subjects." Lhasang, who for years headed the radical Tibetan Youth Congress, says the most important thing the institute can hope to do is "create a new foundation for the remaking of what we call Tibet. My father was an ascetic, a traveling mendicant, a religious man. I'm Buddhist. We're all Buddhist. But Buddhism cannot solve political problems, the Buddha never said it could. We need another direction."

Then he takes you into a cramped room where half a dozen men are sitting at computers translating Tom Paine's *Common Sense* into Tibetan.

After recounting the difficulty in finding Tibetan fonts for obsolete Apple computers, Lhasang, standing below the giant panorama of Lhasa showing exactly how much of the city remains Tibetan-owned (not much), launches into his series of charges against the Dalai Lama. He says His Holiness's nonviolence is fine for international consumption but not so uplifting to the people living under the Sino yoke. He says that the Dalai Lama has acquiesced on his demand for complete independence, and that his government-in-exile is so riddled with contradictions as to be incapable of a coherent stand, going so far as to say that the DL might just be satisfied to keep things as they are, as long as all the Hollywood stars keep lamping to his feet. Even if it's unlikely that China will self-destruct in the Soviet manner, Lhasang says, "freedom is something you may never get, but you have to *want* it."

That's when Lhasang and Jamyang began acting out part of *King Gesar*, the great Tibetan epic poem in which the sword of the hero is left amongst the Amnye Machen, the great mountain range that traditionally defines the northeast border of the nation.

"The great sword will stay there, waiting to be retrieved by the next great, *true* Tibetan hero!" Lhasang exclaims joyously.

As I left, the two of them were arguing over whether to translate Nabokov's *Lolita* or *Ada* into Tibetan. (Jamyang was a *Lolita* supporter, with Lhasang in favor of *Ada*.) These volumes would be added to *One Day in the Life of Ivan Denisovich*, *Bury My Heart At Wounded Knee*, *The Time Machine*, and a hundred others. It was a potential elitist guilty pleasure, fighting over a mythic canon, they admitted. But it was something of which to be envious too, reconstructing an alternative moral life for your country like that.

Tell some of this to the Dalai Lama, who has joked about imagining himself a reincarnation of Thomas Jefferson, and he nods accommodatingly. While frowning at the notion (expressed by Lhasang) that his brand of Mahayana might serve as "an anti-intellectual force," His Holiness says he "appreciates" the thoughts of all Tibetans seeking to make "a contribution." Yet, in the spirit of dharma combat, he asserts that while the "universal Buddha nature in all sentient beings" has been proved compatible with liberal democracy, now may not be the time to fully separate the

Tibetan church and state. This is because "Buddha teaching aside, for our people, it is better to have a firm idea of something than for them to have a firm idea of nothing."

To wit: the case of Chine Rinzen, who, along with a group of fifty-eight refugees from Lithang, in eastern Tibet, had arrived in MacLeod Ganj just a few days before. Sitting inside the dark, thick-aired Refugee Center surrounded by his fellow exiles, Rinzen, a thirty-five-year old carpenter fingering a crystal *mallah*, told how his "root teacher" advised him to lead the people from his village away from the Chinese. The refugees heard that Solocombe, an eighteen-thousand-foot-high pass, was the best place to cross the mountains into Nepal. This turned out to be incorrect. Caught in the snows, they began to starve. Several children were frostbitten. They succeeded in crossing over, but were soon set upon by the Nepalese police, who shot at them, killing at least two. The Nepalis captured Rinzen, torturing him until he handed over the money he'd collected to pay for the group's safe passage. Finally they made it to Kathmandu, and eventually McLeod Ganj. In retelling these events, Rinzen was soon beside himself with rage. He got up from the cot on which he sat and started stamping his feet, slamming his fists together. A moment later, asked "What kept you going?" during all the travails, he quickly calmed down.

"We meditated on His Holiness. To see His Holiness, that's what kept us going," Chine Rinzen said.

Hearing this story, the Dalai Lama, who personally greets every refugee arriving in McLeod Ganj, grimaces. "This is a serious matter. . . . Something I am aware of," he said in low register. For, just as Chine Rinzen meditates on His Holiness, the Dalai Lama spends a good deal of time thinking about Chine Rinzen.

Agreeing with Lhasang Tsering, His Holiness says it irks him, the manner in which many Tibetans continue to rely on him personally, as "a child does a Father . . . something which is not healthy." Often referring to himself as both the "strength and the weakness" of the nation, he says he understands the "historical and religious" tendency of Tibetans to revere the Dalai Lama but insists the people will eventually come to accept the "necessary and modernizing" changes he proposes, including his "final decision" to abdicate his position as the temporal head of the government in favor of an elected Kashag, or congress. Then, His Holiness muses, he might become a "Buddhist pope like the Catholic pope," a bodhisattva responsible to followers of the dharma worldwide.

Then we were talking about death again. A weariness in his voice, His Holiness said he was giving serious consideration to not reincarnating as the Dalai Lama again, as if he's decided that, after 602 years, enough is enough.

Somehow it's shocking, hearing that, somehow awful. "So you'll break the lineage?"

"The institution will remain," His Holiness replies.

"But not as it's been."

"The search for a reincarnation will be through some kind of election," the religious translator puts in.

"Is that okay with you?" I ask His Holiness.

"Of course!"

"Is that okay with your next incarnation?"

"Absolutely! I personally sometimes feel even more healthier." Then he smiles and says something only he, or some other equally highly realized bodhisattva could. Considering the urgency of the Tibetan situation, a radical move was necessary. Consequently, the Dalai Lama said he was contemplating reincarnating himself into the body of another before his death, or, as the translator said, "the reincarnation of one who is not dead."

"That means that," His Holiness imparts, "the fourteenth Dalai Lama is still alive and if I find someone who has really good potential, I will be able to . . . call that person my reincarnation."

"While you're still alive?" What matter of theocratic hocus-pocus might this be?

"Yes."

"But that's not how it's been done."

That's when, seeing my obvious distress, the Dalai Lama broke out laughing once more. There were precedents for the "reincarnation of someone who is not dead." Names of great rinpoches who "gave up their life" were well known.

"*Don't worry, Jakupson!* It is not good to worry so much! You will see. It will be all right! If not right away, soon. In a few years. Or maybe a hundred years. But better. You will see."

"But . . ."

It was about then, according to His Holiness's secretary, that my "precious seconds" with the fourteenth Dalai Lama, were up. A Japanese TV crew was waiting to set up. A tour bus full of well-heeled Germans was up from Delhi, and a public audience was being arranged.

They say talking to bodhisattvas is like a drug, and I felt a little blitzed walking out of His Holiness's office into the courtyard beyond. The monks were still out there, engaged in their dialectical dharma combat. I hadn't noticed it before, but they were not all so young. Some were quite elderly, sixty or more. Watching them together, it was easy to imagine them as one single being, all born and reborn so many times as to fuzz the boundaries of their individuality. There was an awesomeness to it, being around all that continuity.

Did it matter if it was true—any of it?

I was weighing this further plunge into the mysterium as I wandered across the courtyard and went into the temple dedicated to the Kalachakra initiation, a long and exceedingly complex ritual meant to be performed in "degenerate times." His Holiness has given more of these initiations than any of his predecessors. In the temple is a likeness of Chenrezig, embodiment of Infinite Compassion and protector deity to all Dalai Lamas.

Supposedly, back in primordial times, Chenrezig was so engaged in the contemplation of how to best extend happiness to every sentient being that his head split into a thousand pieces. The Buddha's luminosity restored him to his former state, but to this day Chenrezig is depicted with numerous helping heads and hands. In Old Tibet there are many ornate and spectacular icons of Chenrezig, so seeing the one here in McLeod Ganj, all puny and shut up behind a gray steel security gate, at first appeared to be just another jail image, one more limbo thing to be depressed about. Except now, peering through the gate and noting the faint, Mona Lisa–like smile on the effigy's face, there seemed no choice but to break out laughing.

14
Birth of an Optimist

In the late 1980s, I wrote the Ethics Column for Esquire *magazine. This lasted about a year until they decided I was really writing a religion column, and kind of an idiosyncratic religion column at that. It was a great job for a lot of reasons, not the least of which was being able to work through some metaphysical issues. This saved a lot on therapy. From* Esquire, *1987.*

In our crowd, I have often been considered a cynical kind of guy, overbearingly streetwise, hawking the harshness of humanity. Consequently, it's been a shock for my friends to listen to several of the arguments I've been pushing recently.

Like the other day, when I unveiled my "happy ending" spiel.

"The responsibility of art in this day and age is to find the happy ending," I declared. "The job is no longer to make sense of the way things are. People don't need art to tell them about alienation, depression, and hopelessness. Anyone can deconstruct the modern world just by looking around. Art must grope in the labyrinth, find the way out."

The recipient of this rap, a friend who is well known in our scene for his "dark vision," was on me in a flash. What exactly did I mean by a happy ending, he demanded to know. Was this TV-movie talk?

"No," I said. "Nothing is more depressing than a fake happy ending. That shit where you know the next frame after the movie ends the main characters are going to kill each other or themselves. The transparently bogus happy ending is what undermines the cause of truth in middle-class art, leading to school shootings and the rest. I'm talking about *legitimate* happy endings that are as inexorable as unhappy endings."

He defied me to think of one legitimate happy ending. I mentioned *Moby-Dick*, citing one of my happy ending criteria, which is "to inveigh against chaos." My friend scoffed. He said Ahab's failure only proved the triumph of chaos.

"Depends on your idea of the natural order of things," I shot back. We went around on this for a few hours, dusting off metaphysics I hadn't touched since I'd dropped out of college. Eventually we arrived at a tentative agreement that for a happy ending to work, it had to suggest plausible hope for the future. With the loom of apocalypse around every corner these days, that seemed good enough.

After our chat, my friend slipped me a sly smile, asking, "Since when did you become such a sentimentalist?"

"Not sentimentalist. Optimist!" I returned testily. "Reagan is a sentimentalist disguised as an optimist. I am a true optimist."

My friend smirked the smirk of the natural born scoffer. "Okay, optimist. When did you become such an optimist?"

Good question! Cynicism, what is sometimes referred to by the readers of *Spy* magazine as "irony," had been a major building block of my worldview. Cynicism made sense. Didn't cynicism (and/or pessimism) equal a hardbought variety of realism? Didn't the cynic spring from the embers of rumpled ideals? Cynicism is the perfect distancing vehicle; it protects against embarrassment like Gardol's shield. Besides, cynicism just plays better. Suppose Sam Spade comes back today as the host of a revival of *Who Do You Trust?* Who does he trust? No one. Right answer! No, cynicism is the survivalist's tool, the prickly heat of every boy's heroes. The cynic's always been the cool guy, and the entire twentieth century, repository of shattered scruples, is his argument. I have never seen myself as anything but a creature of my times.

My shift occurred soon after the space shuttle blew up. I had a terrible fight with my wife over the incident. My wife, an unrepentant Robert Heinlein fan, who has been known to start sniffling every time she sees

Neil Armstrong sidearming a stone through the airless gloom of eternal night, finds the notion of men and machines venturing forth into the blackness of uncharted space very compelling. If NASA sold stocks, she would buy them, even if I keep telling her those spaceheads are really nothing but shills for Reagan's Star Wars missile plan to blow up the world. For my wife, who has twice journeyed to Cape Canaveral to see rockets blast off, the shuttle explosion was overwhelming.

I was not nearly as moved. My basic reaction was: big deal. The first thing I said was, "Oh, how are the Republicans going to make hay out of this?" Then I chipped in some bromides concerning what I considered the specious moral justification for spending "all that money on a project that's basically for the ruling class and military, when the earth's a mess." Sure, I was sad the astronauts died; Judith Resnick, the first (and probably only, now) Jewish woman astronaut got killed. Still, I said, but their deaths bothered me no more than the expiration of seven Cambodians in a godforsaken refugee camp on the Thai border.

That was when my wife stopped talking to me.

A couple of days later, I apologized. It was predictable. If there's a battle, I'd much rather be in the wrong. Then I can get all contrite, prostrate myself, say I'm sorry, and hope that will be that. If I think I'm right, I feel I've got to hold out longer before folding. It is the principle of the thing.

"I'm sorry," I told my wife. "I shouldn't have laid my line on you when you were upset like that. I was insensitive."

My wife did not accept my apology. "What good is that?" she said. "You still think it, right?"

This was the hard part. "Yeah, I do," I said, swallowing. "I haven't changed my position."

"How can you take a 'position' on this? There is no 'position'. This is about the future. The idea of our species, the same species to which our children belong, going on. How stupid can you be?"

I sat there, groaning. Women are always handing men this "future" line, as if being secondary in the procreative process somehow makes us remote to the true generational emotion. As if we are so self-centered as to be blind to the actual forge of progress beyond that which makes money and feeds our voracious little egos. This was how my wife viewed the shuttle's explosion. It wasn't about some frozen O-ring, or maybe they forgot to put enough gas in the tank. Tech items were men's things, and since I couldn't even drive a nail straight into a three-quarter-inch board of plywood, I couldn't even hide behind a thicket of toolbox detail. She was daring me to think cosmically. It was a test I couldn't get out of.

It was the Image that made me see. Not the one of the actual explosion of the ship, but that of the booster rockets lurching off into the sky, forming a crazy angled *Y* with their contrails. It was one of those Images, those Ruby-shoots-Oswald, burning-Vietnamese-girl-runs-down-road icons that, by dint of their accessibility, bully themselves into the mind with an archetypal force. It was terrifying, seeing that *Y*, that appalling wedge, and knowing it would be emblazoned not only onto the consciousness of Christa McAuliffe's children, who got to see their mother blown to bits on TV, but into the minds of everyone else in America as well. It seemed a grotesque invasion of the McAuliffe children's privacy.

That was, at least on the surface, much of what my wife was trying to tell me. We have kids, and as hideous as it might be for them to see us die on television, worse yet would be for our demise to leave an Image, a primordial scratching in the sky, to make them think, on some soon-to-be wholly subconscious level, that *Y* = Death. That was the unspeakable part.

There's something about seeing such an Image that knocks the swagger right out of you. I made a video recording of it and kept running it back and forth. It was a wild experience. It made me wonder about the nature of these images and how the modern world changes things. The image of Christ's passion must live in the heart of every Christian who believes he makes conscious contact with it through his faith. But here I could manifest this Image, play it as many times as I wished, make a visual mantra of it, with the push of a button on a machine that I'd bought at Crazy Eddie's. The technology itself was the instrument of my faith.

I watched those booster rockets fly aimlessly across the Florida sky over and over. When I was done, I decided that what I'd seen was not, after all, some devalued corporate twist of the old Icarus riff. It wasn't that Heaven had peered down and swatted away Morton Thiokol's flawed petition for entry to the Realm. Rather, I thought, a direction was pointed in the strange Y-shaped divining rod and, with the right moral outlook and frost-resistant booster seals, success might yet be reached.

That's what I got out of it: try, try again. It was as if to recognize that Y = Death was to gain the power to reject it as such. For me, that Image wasn't just about the space shuttle anymore. Now it was about hope, hope for the future. It was hope, pure and simple. Y = Hope.

It was only then that I came to understand my wife's grief. It was the kids thing, of course, but it was more than that. She feared all Hope was under siege in the too-cold January sky. She was afraid for the future itself.

Truthfully, I feel a little sheepish, sitting here telling you "that's when I stopped being a cynic." Nevertheless, I believe it. Personality shift is probably like any kind of change. Events go in one direction for a while, without apparent significance, and then, in one moment, *wham*, in a spiritual version of Thomas Kuhn' s notion of scientific revolution, speed is reached, critical mass achieved, and things start happening. This isn't to say my "position" has turned the full 180. I'm not contemplating embroidering a sampler that says LIFE IS TOO SHORT TO LIVE IT AS A CYNIC. In my dream of myself, I'm still striking all the noir poses. I've seen *Double Indemnity* too many times to lose that altogether. I've got plenty of skepticism left over to trust a light too easily seen. Perhaps some people transform themselves via inspiration, but most change through necessity. Don't tell the ole lady, but that's really why I'm trying to shed my cynicism. It doesn't quite fit into the context of my current configuration as husband and father.

That's the core of it. Having children is like saying you believe in happy endings, that you hold out hope for a world after your own last page is written. There is no other way to think. Kids make cynicism unaffordable. You've got to get rid of it. If you've got to con yourself, substitute the word *hope* for *death* in a made-up equation, you do it.

Still, there are tremendous problems in this. Like the other day. I was with my four-year-old daughter in the waiting room of a doctor's office. The secretary was black, a fact that my daughter called attention to. She went right up to the woman and in a too-loud voice, said, "We don't know many black people." The woman took this as well as could be expected, but I, of course, was mortified. It's been on my mind a lot recently, how few black people we know. This bothers me. I worry I may be tacitly railroading myself into accepting the general segregation of the races that is so ingrained and powerful. I often talk about the situation with white friends who feel similarly. Between us we've more or less come to the conclusion that the racial condition in this country is, on a very real level, fundamentally hopeless.

"Acceding to the hopelessness of it is the only liberating way to feel about it," one friend says.

Now, you can take a comment like that any way you want. You can keep caring in the face of that hopelessness, or you can turn cynical. You can read about the deadly incident in Howard Beach and deplore it, or you can shrug and say, of course, there's always been racial tension in New York City, this just got out of hand.

I was hoping my daughter would drop her inquiry into American race relations and go back to talking about Barbie or her *My Little Pony*. But she didn't. After we left the doctor's office, she started asking questions about the differences between blacks and whites; somehow she'd picked up the news that the two races occasionally did not get along. She was trying to understand the whole thing in her mind, looking to me to give her some word on the topic.

As it was, just the night before, I'd been watching *Eyes on the Prize*, the PBS documentary on the civil rights movement. It had a segment on Mississippi's Freedom Summer, the student-powered voter registration drive of 1964. It was during that summer that civil rights workers Chaney, Goodman, and Schwerner were murdered. A fresh-faced, very earnest white student was on the screen. Indicating some blacks beside him, he made a statement to the effect that, "If they're not free, then I'm not." Hearing this, almost twenty-five years after it came from that so righteous face, jolted me into a typical response: I wondered which brokerage house this guy now worked for. However, within a moment I found myself weeping. It just seemed so brave to say that then, as if I were seeing the absolute best that person had to offer. Thinking of it caused me to give my daughter the most stirring invocation of the moral imperative of brotherhood I could muster.

Was it a lie? Did the scenario I painted for her fall within the parameters of a "plausible hope for the future"? Is the world any less empty and heartless than I used to think it was? I can't tell. I just know I couldn't face my kid and say, "It's hopeless."

15
Merchants of the Future

Who are those strange ladies in the ubiquitous storefronts with the signs claiming they are "psychics"? They call themselves Readers and Advisers, but what to they read and what advice do they dispense? Blues songs begin with stories of what the gypsy woman told my mother, before I was born, but what does the gypsy woman really know? What will she tell? An account of urban belief and disbelief. From New York *magazine, 2003.*

The reader was reading me, the ancient tarot cards spread across the table in the same way they have been for hundreds of years. But to call this a simple fortune-telling parlor would be to ignore the Fortunoff-plus ambience of the surroundings, the marble steps leading to a second story, and the decorative glass embossed with the medium's name: Zena. Few of New York's ubiquitous storefront reader-and-adviser establishments can match Ms. Zena's hep Greenwich Village location (she owns the building and is thinking of expanding next door), her frosted blonde coif, or her elegant manner (according to her business card, when not reading palms on lower Seventh Avenue, she can be found in Cannes or Palm Beach). Nonetheless, there was a familiarity in Ms. Zena's assessment of my prospects, both imminent and long range.

Noting the placement of my death card, Ms. Zena said my life would be long, into my eighties. I was an honest person, a loving person, looking to do good things for others. But there was a problem. Something was standing in the way of my total happiness. No matter how much I tried to move toward my goal, I was held back, thwarted. I had heard similar things before, from a dozen other readers and advisers: news of a darkness in my aura, a blockage in my soul, the influx of negativity sullying potential success and contentment. None of this was my fault, or God's. It came from other human beings, people out to get me. This was the critical point in my various palm, face, vibration, tarot, aura, and chakra consultations, when the reader stared into my eyes and offered to intercede on my behalf, to root out the mendacity directed toward me.

Various remedies were prescribed. Ms. Carol of Madison Avenue recommended that I carry a pair of protective crystals she would provide for the nominal fee of $100. Ms. Selena of Brooklyn also suggested crystals, but better ones, for $160. Ms. Ann of Midtown said I should write my name and date of birth on a piece of paper, which she would meditate upon with the help of burning candles. These were not just any candles but "special" ones, capable of divination, $50 a pop.

Ms. Zena put forth a more nuanced analysis. She posited that the dissatisfaction that stalked me might not be a product of this life but a karmic echo of a previous existence. Like Orpheus's guide, she proposed to lead me through a regimen of past-life-regression therapy. It might take three sessions, it might take as many as five or six, but the problem would be found out. It would be dealt with. As for the price of this action, we could discuss that later.

Hearing that I needed to think it over, Ms. Zena shrugged. My fate was my responsibility, she said. But I shouldn't tarry too long, because the cards were sending another alarm. There was someone who meant me no good, someone trying to impede my progress.

"I see two initials," the psychic said. "I see an M . . . I see a *J*. Do you know anyone with these initials?" "Er . . . Michael Jordan?" I joked weakly. I hadn't told her my name, not my real one anyway.

"No. Someone close. Very close. This person is always looking to take advantage of you. He is not your friend. . . . Think about it. The letters M and *J*. Watch out . . ."

Back out in the bitter winter evening cold, taxis honking down the Avenue, bums shouting at the sky, the mind reeled. No doubt the psychic game, a carny grift older than the hills, was rigged—even if you didn't know exactly how. Still, even armored by layers of everyday rationalism and thicker cordons of cynicism, it was taking a chance: entering the storefronts of these women, with their bogus candles, crystals, and cheesy maps of the palm, the line of lust leading to the mound of Saturn, beside the index finger of Jupiter. Because you never really did *know*, did you? Just because the overturned rock might be fake didn't mean that real revelations—or real nightmares—might not be found beneath it.

Watch out for the M and *J* . . . I always suspected I was my own worst enemy.

Among the neon-lit ephemera of storefront and second-story businesses in this ratty city—the nail parlors, ambulance-chasing lawyers, gold buyers, walk-in podiatrists—none covers as much real estate as the reader and adviser. This is due in part to the fact that the vast majority of these establishments (perhaps three hundred in the metro area) are owned and operated by Romani—a.k.a. Roma or Rom, people better known, pejoratively from their point of view, as Gypsies.

Self-imagined to be descended from the stars, fiercely unassimilated into the *gadjé* world through which they perpetually travel, few groups have inspired such ire, awe, misconception, and mystery as the Rom. Called Gypsies because they were erroneously thought to have come from Egypt, the Romani (the preferred p.c. spelling is Rroma, the double r scuttling confusion with Romania and Rome, two notable Rom oppressors) claim to trace their origin to the Rajput princes of India. Resident throughout the globe, there are a roughly estimated 1 million *Rom Ameriko*—about 100,000 of whom can be found in New York.

There are Rom lawyers, Rom doctors, Rom musicians (Django Reinhardt, the three-fingered guitar wizard, was one), a whole Rom middle class of sorts, but for the most part, the Romani remain apart, with their own rules and moral structure, in which disputes are still adjudicated by a *kris romani* (a Gypsy court) presided over by a *rom baro*, whom some refer to as the king, as in King of the Gypsies. It is a hidden world of people who have names like Harry the Nose, Sissy Steve, Pizza Yonko, Sammy Cheese, Black Charlie, and Big Pete Costello. What we *gadjé* see, at the street level, at least, are the psychics. When you enter those doors and the lady *pen dukkerin* or *drabardi* (Rom for "fortune-teller") asks you to put a twenty-dollar bill in your hand and make two wishes—"Tell me one and keep the other to yourself"—you've entered an outcropping of twenty centuries of otherness.

Racist lore about Gypsies kidnapping children aside (there is no record of this occurring, ever—likewise accounts of Rom involved in violent crime are exceedingly rare), this doesn't mean that the typical Reader and Adviser is not looking to relieve the credulous tarot inquirer of considerable cash. People wonder about storefront psychics, how they survive, since no one ever seems to be inside having their fortune told. The answer is, it doesn't take very many customers, provided they are the right ones. Listen up in various Rom hangouts, mostly clam bars on the edge of Little Italy and Bayard Street Chinese restaurants after midnight, and you might pick up tales of the *hokkani boro*—the big con. Notable among these rumored scores are the respective quarter-of-a-million dollar fleecings of a lovesick Brooklyn rabbi and (deliciously) an Upper East Side shrink. Supposedly John DeLorean, he of the gull-wing car and coke busts, was taken for hundreds of thousands by a local card reader.

Key to the big hustle is the idea of curse removal—i.e., someone has put a curse on you, and this is causing all your problems. The severity of the curse is established in a number of "tests." Once the reader has decided you are a live one (as a result of your snapping up the prayer candles or crystals), she may ask you to carry around an egg for three days, then return it to her. The psychic holds the egg against your forehead or chest, substituting another egg for the one you've brought. When the egg is cracked open, it will be full of rotten meat wrapped in rat hair, or some such disgusting item, graphically demonstrating the impurities the curse has transmuted into your body. A similar trick involves a jar of water, which suddenly turns blood red after a sleight-of-hand infusion of cherry Kool-Aid. The reader, your personal spiritual warrior queen, will then pledge the use of her time-honored esoteric talents to exorcise the evil, a tortuous process that has been known to run up some serious expense.

All this is against the law, of course. Fortune-telling for money (rather than purely for "entertainment") runs contrary to Section 165.35 of the New York State Penal Code. But except in truly spectacular "curse" cases (and other alleged Rom specialties such as slip-and-fall insurance fakery, odometer rejiggering, and the emptying of lonely elderly men's bank accounts—known as a "sweetheart swindle" or "cruising for willies"), few arrests are made.

Since most readers also live where they tell fortunes, it can be an instructive voyeurism to walk into their storefront and second-story apartments. Some are ornate, such as Ms. Grace's sprawling digs on West Forty-eighth Street, with her catering-hall-style chandelier and big-screen TV, in front of which, when I visited, sat half a dozen portly Rom ladies watching (so help me) *Wheel of Fortune*. Ms. Sylvia's parlor, up a flight of rickety stairs in downtown Brooklyn, is more modest. The front room, bathed in a sickly pink from the giant neon outline of a palm hung in the window, featured a Naugahyde loveseat on which slept two children. A pile of laundry occupied one corner. Sylvia said she would have cleaned up, but she was suffering from a bad cold.

"I will tell you what I see—it might be good and it might be bad, but it is what I see, so don't be offended," began Sylvia, a thirtyish-looking woman with striking dark eyes, in the detached yet staccato cadence common to most readers. "You are good man. You don't want to hurt no one. You are generous. But people are trying to stop you from success. You take one step forward, and then you go two back. You are at a standstill . . . being kept from happiness . . ."

It was the same spiel I'd heard around town, nearly word-for-word, somehow even more desultory in Sylvia's presentation. Maybe it was because she was sick, or perhaps it was the presence of the man in the next room waiting to continue the argument I'd heard as I walked up the stairs (the women make the money, but often it is the men, the "managers," who wind up with it). Whatever, Sylvia's extreme beauty, the suppleness of her high-boned cheeks, only accentuated an awful weariness. She could barely summon the energy to pitch me the crystals that she dolefully declared came straight from "the holy mountains of Jerusalem." With those piercing eyes, orbs that could—and no doubt had—convinced *gadjé* and Rom alike of many things, she seemed to say: *Help!* Get me out of here.

Not that this was an option, at least not from me. First off, Romani women do not have anything to do with *gadjé* men. To do so would be to risk being declared *marimé*, in a state of spiritual pollution, which can lead to excommunication from the community. Living within the Rom code, with marriages often still arranged among the various extended families, is not easy. But to be cut off is the ultimate calamity. Belonging has always been the great strength of the Rom community, the way they have maintained their uniqueness all these years since coming out of India, in a thousand ports of call, through myriad pogroms including Hitler's policy against "the Gypsy nuisance," a horror called *O Porrajmos*, or "the devouring," in which more than million Romani were killed, including four thousand in one day, August 1, 1944, at Auschwitz.

No, it was not likely Sylvia would be taking a swell job as a legal secretary anytime soon. She would remain a psychic, no matter how rotten she appeared to be at it.

Still, I was becoming a sucker, a Gypsy's fool. While not quite curse material, I began to look forward to forking over $20 for a palm reading, $45 for a full tarot deck. It was fun sitting with Dee, on Rivington Street. Since her spot is located a couple of doors down from the feminist sex emporium, Toys in Babeland, Dee's customers often arrive with shopping bags full of double-pronged dildos and glow-in-the-dark condoms, which may add a rakish touch to her readings as she cajoles you to purchase the "spiritual work" you so desperately need.

Linda, a younger, rapid-fire tarot reader who cheerfully admits to making her own "holy crystals" and keeps a large-print King James Bible along with much Christian iconography in her second-story place near the Port Authority Bus Terminal, operates with a different business plan. For $240 for the first month and $8 a day subsequently, if she is not busy praying for one of her clients, Linda will answer your call at any time of the day or night to advise you about a troubling matter. To me, this seemed an excellent offer, way better than those of most shrinks, maybe even better than Prozac. There was only one catch. During this process, Linda cautions you to not see other readers. This will "conflict with the energy" emitted by the angels she has summoned on your behalf and result in her being forced to "pull the rug out from underneath you" without warning.

A strange thing happened soon after I visited Linda. On the F train, I saw a woman, an older black lady, whom I'd seen earlier that day in a psychic's office. Recognizing each other, we smiled and held up our open palms. Like: *You never know*.

That was the core of it. On one hand, I justified giving money to these fakers as a form of grifter tax, a perverse appreciation of the long-running, ritualized con. But there was more to it than that. Hunted by the Nazis just like the Jews, the Rom might weight the wheel for the *gadjé*, but that didn't mean they didn't believe, totally, in the all-encompassing vagaries of chance and fate, or what they call *baxt*. "*Baxt* is everything," one fortuneteller told me. It is a gambler universe out there, where fate, if it exists, plays a cat and mouse game with expectations. This is how the Gypsies see it. If you want to shake people up, sign on to a Romani Internet chat room (they exist) as *prekaza*, which means "bad luck." Faster than cyber lightning, you will be told to get lost.

As with a Coney Island ring toss, knowledge that a game is fixed doesn't stop the urge to play anyway. It didn't make sense, but there it was, beckoning me in. That's what these ladies offer with their specious regimens and far-off looks: an escape to a world of old-style irrationality, where *baxt* is everything.

I was thinking of this as I drove out to see El Indio Amazonico, a storefront psychic who sports a full Amerindian headdress and a large white feather through his nose, and who refers to himself as "*el mejor . . . guía espiritual*," no small claim on Roosevelt Avenue in Queens, where the

7 train clatters overhead and the *parasicología y metafísica* parlors are thicker than spinning spits of *pollos a la brasa*. Gabriel García Márquez's *One Hundred Years of Solitude* tells of gifts Gypsies would bring to the Colombian countryside, but El Indio Amazonico, late of Bogotá, drew a blank when asked if he was Rom. Then again, he could have been fibbing, since the walls of his waiting room (along with the large-screen projection TV playing Mexican soap operas and the piles of supposedly discarded crutches) were plastered with promises to cure problems of love, luck, and business through testing by *huevo*, *agua*, and other Romani staples. Either way, El Indio, who charges sixty dollars for a reading, is doing such land office business that he recently opened a second outlet across Roosevelt where supplicants can purchase his branded varieties of holy water and ticking clocks bearing his weathered face.

El Indio, who looked to be any age over 150, spread my tarot across a table covered with the green felt cloth usually found on a roulette table. Even in Spanish, the findings were not unfamiliar. I would live a long time, ninety-eight years exactly. I was a good person, an honest person, I wanted to do good things for others. But there was a problem. I wasn't totally happy. Things could be better. Here, El Indio added a Latin macho spin to the proceedings: My sexual activities had led to a dropping-off of potency. Placing a sandy substance that appeared to be cornmeal on the table, El Indio said he could arrest this decline. But it wouldn't be easy. First I would need a major overhaul, a "spiritual vaccination." Asked how much this inoculation would cost, El Indio wrote "$1,000."

"A thousand dollars? *Es muy alto!*" I replied.

El Indio smiled sheepishly. He'd been around forever. He knew a live one when he saw him. Likewise, he knew the tourists, the dabblers, the ringers. I was one tree not worth barking up. He reached into his pocket and pulled out a foot-long piece of rope with seven knots tied in it. He told me to untie one knot on successive Fridays and make a wish. These wishes would come true.

But what about my sexual potency? I asked.

"Oh, don't worry, you look fine to me. See a doctor if you're worried," El Indio Amazonico said, waving in the next client.

16

Al Out of Town

The Rev. Al, Man of God, Runs for President

A chronicle of the Reverend Al Sharpton's semi-quixotic run for the presidency in 2004. As with most things Al, much was promised, little delivered. He talked about winning the South Carolina primary but only got 7 percent, his best showing in the entire election cycle. But he did get a lot of face time. As he said, "Ever think you'd see me on network so much? Not cable. Network." So all was not lost. Asked if being a minister might give him a leg up in the election, the Rev. raised his eyes toward heaven and said, "I'm close enough to God to know it is a waste of time trying to figure out what He wants from this little world of ours." From New York *magazine, 2003.*

The Candidate's car lurched past the White House and turned left, and now the Capitol dome, huge and even whiter, like Moby-Dick in the late-afternoon sun, loomed ahead. Did the proximity of these icons of the American Republic, the leadership of which he presently sought, prompt a pitter-pat in his heart?

"*Pitter-pat?*" the Candidate replied, squinting, his brown brow furrowing, as it does when he's confronted with a question he hasn't applied his gravelly baritone to five thousand times before. "I have serious regard for the seats of power. But my pulse is not quickened by the goings on beneath that Dome. What matters to me happens outside, in the shadows of those buildings. . . . Here. Look at this guy."

Traffic was jammed up in the 95-degree heat. A scruffy-looking Hispanic man in a snap-back cap was hawking bottles of Poland Spring.

"Here, in the shadows of the ultimate power, is a man selling water. *Selling water!* Trying to make a living, salvage dignity. Yet most people inside the Capitol probably think he's a beggar while Ken Lay is a responsible businessman. Exposing that lie from the shadows—that's what puts the pitter-pat in my heart."

It was a good answer. A characteristically florid yet properly populist answer. Unscripted as it was, some might even consider it a presidential answer.

The Candidate is full of such answers. In the thrall of his rhetorical fire, it is not impossible to imagine the impossible: that we weren't cramped into a small foreign car going to the Florida Grill on the chocolate-city side of town for one more plate of smothered chicken, but rather in a steel-plated limo, surrounded by pomp, sharpshooters, and the Secret Service, curly cords coming from their ears, wired for sound.

To say it couldn't be so is a denial of the American Dream. Compared with the dossier of unearned privilege often peddled to the electorate, current frat-boy CEO not excepted, the Candidate's life story is downright Lincolnesque, in a New York urban-contemporary way.

Here is the bootstrap saga of the "boy preacher," seized by the Spirit at the tender age of four, when on July 9, 1959, he first whooped the Gospel (John, chapter 14) to a church of the faithful at 1372 Bedford Avenue, Brooklyn. Then, disaster. His father, whom he calls "a slumlord" and "an exploiter," left his mother to take up with his half-sister. Cast from the relative middle-class comfort of P.S. 134 on 109th Avenue in Hollis, Queens, he found himself living in the toughest of Brooklyn projects, on the New Lots line to the hellish Livonia Avenue station. A fat kid who couldn't fight or play ball, a proto-Beat reader of Allen Ginsberg's *Howl*, he could have folded. But he did not feature himself one more ghetto casualty, cannon fodder for the rigged system. Powered by an unwavering sense of personal destiny—and the untamped wanting of more (and more) —he rose by scratch and claw, thinking fast, talking faster.

Mobility via mouth—the time-honored street triptych of wit, grit, and bullshit, hustle born and bred—what could be more all-American than that? The Candidate also saw the USA, although not from a Chevrolet, but riding shotgun in James Brown's bus. It was while traveling with Mr. Dynamite that he met his wife, then a backup-singing Famous Flame. Indeed, the Godfather of Soul is already booked to sing "The Star-Spangled Banner" at the inauguration—long as the money's right, of course.

Wouldn't that be *A Day?* A wondrous, uplifting Day—a triumph over the brutal, tawdry history that has undermined the utopian presumptions of this New World land since 1619, when the European settlers first brought Africans here in chains. Painting the White House black, like the def jam comics say.

Yes, a truly great, liberating Day. Except for one thing. It's Al. The Candidate is Al.

You see, in New York, we know Al. We know the hair, the jumpsuit, the medallion, the stomach. We know his no justice, his no peace. We know he once called the Jewish owner of a 125th Street furniture store a "white interloper," and several weeks later the place was burned down in an arson fire that killed seven people. We know he knows he didn't pay his taxes, or his rent. (Just last month his travel agent sued him for $193,000, which is a lot of airplane tickets.) We know, too, about Tawana Brawley, how Al believed the story but the grand jury did not, how in the ensuing defamation case, Sharpton claimed he didn't own his silk suits but rather only had "access" to them. And we know how, no matter what, this is something for which Al, like Pete Rose, will never apologize.

We also know the so-called New Sharpton, the more statesmanlike, skinnier model. Redemption took more than faith. It took Giuliani. In the face of *Der* Rudy ("a worthy adversary," Al says), Sharpton emerged as legitimate, necessary, even strangely heroic. Someone had to show some leadership after Abner Louima, Amadou Diallo, and Patrick Dorismond, and there was Al, his hacked-off bouffant flecked with gray, solemnly leading thousands, including a hundred rabbis and Susan Sarandon (she arranged to be arrested first due to scheduling conflicts) in protest. It was Al, the erstwhile rabble-rouser, who kept the lid on. Not a single stone was thrown. This was the post-Damascus Road Rev., the Al who would spend ninety days in a Sunset Park jail after his arrest in the Vieques bombing protests, deprived of his cell phone, deep in meditation on Gandhi, Mandela (twenty-six years for him, also no cell phone), MLK, all the avatars of resistance and nonviolence.

We know Al like we know Bensonhurst and Howard Beach, like we know Bernard Goetz, Michael Griffith, Joey Fama, Yusef Hawkins, Yankel Rosenbaum, and Justin Volpe—to name only a few on the long, grim roster of racial strife in this town. Always, Sharpton was there, tossing in his ample two cents, pounding podiums and pulpits alike. Could it be only a coincidence that the acronym used to identify him in the memos of his National Action Network, RAS, for the *R*everend *A*l *S*harpton (not Ras Tafari) would be identical to Ras, the Exhorter, the hoodoo shouter from Ralph Ellison's 1952 novel, *Invisible Man*, the fictional character many suggest Al most resembles?

Yes, we know Al. We know that despite his surprising totals in various primaries for senator and mayor, Sharpton has not been elected to anything, not even city council.

Still, there he is: Al, a.k.a. Al Charlatan, bigmouth race man, on *Face the Nation*, like any other supposedly serious national candidate, reasonably calling for a "multinational agreement" on both Iraq and Liberia. There he is, deploying his mad Tilden High/pulpit-pounding debating *skillz*, talking rings around his thick-tongued opponents—more confident than the Lurchlike Kerry, more passionate than the sleepy Lieberman, more generously spirited than the school-marmish Dean, and not as wild-eyed as the vegan, Marianne Williamson–advised Kucinich, about whom the Rev. sometimes worries, wondering if the former Cleveland mayor is "out on a weekend pass."

It is strange, knowing everything we know about Sharpton, to watch him being smarter and funnier than the rest, and feel, well, *proud* of him. To know that, hate him or not, he's our native son, the real New Yorker in the race. Our candidate, *our Al*.

* * *

The ladies drinking sweet iced tea under the cypress trees beside Lake Marion at the Edisto Fork United Methodist Church picnic in Orangeburg, South Carolina, say they don't think all that much about Tawana Brawley. "The man believed a young girl, what is wrong with that?" says sister Ruth, from down the road in Bamberg. Didn't Ted Kennedy drown a woman in a car? What about Carter, who said he had "lust in his heart," or Bush—he was a drunk, that's what you hear. Clinton? Ha. No, this wasn't New York, said brother L. D. Williams, smiling beneath a wide-brimmed trooper hat identifying him as the duly elected Sheriff of Orangeburg County. This was South Carolina, "2003 A.D." Down here, there were plenty of things to worry about besides Tawana Brawley.

As everyone, white and black, tells you, South Carolina was and is the "heart of the Confederacy." It was off the coast on Sullivan's Island—the black Ellis Island—that an estimated 50 percent of African slaves first arrived in America. The 1740 South Carolina Slave Code, a key founding document of the Confederacy, declared "all Negroes, Indians, and their offspring . . . remain forever slaves and shall be deemed to be chattel in the hands of their owners." The Civil War's first shot was fired in Charleston harbor, at Fort Sumter. With many streets still named for Confederate generals, this state sent Strom Thurmond to the Senate for forty-eight years and would have sent him another forty-eight if he'd lived that long.

It was here, too, that George W. Bush shored up his Neanderthal right-wing bona fides in 2000 by smearing John McCain with rumors that he had fathered a black child, here that W. made his infamous speech at Bob Jones University, noted for its prohibition of interracial dating.

"It's all race politics in South Carolina—all race, all the time," says Kevin Gray, Sharpton's thorny S.C. campaign coordinator. In the late sixties, Gray and his sister were the first blacks to attend his formerly all-white local elementary school. Decades later, when his own children entered elementary school in South Carolina, it was all black, or, as he says, "segregated again." This was the sort of "progress" being made down here, says Gray, who once ran as a Green Party candidate for governor, burning a Confederate flag on the statehouse steps while wearing a bulletproof vest, an act he refers to as "my major policy statement."

But race politics cuts both ways. South Carolina, where as much as 45 percent of the primary electorate will be black, is the Rev.'s best shot in next year's primaries. A big Sharpton showing could land him on the cover of *Time* (the grail when you're Al). Then, so goes the scenario, the eventual Democratic nominee, mindful of the conventional wisdom that he has no chance without a clean sweep of the black vote (even Gore, the stiff, got 92 percent), will have no choice but to talk to the Rev.

Speculation on what Al wants in return for his support falls into two general camps. The cynical, anti-Rev. position says he'll demand plenty of cash and a private campaign jet. The nice-Al version, as promoted by Sharpton himself, entails inclusion of his progressive issues in the Dem platform and a primetime slot at the convention to deliver his big-tent message of uplift.

Either way, the Rev. is going for it. He's already passed a dozen weekends amongst Carolina's verdant fields, plans many more. Time is spent at picnics and attending fund-raisers held by leading local black businessmen, owners of car dealerships and directors of funeral homes. But the real campaigning is done on Sunday morning, in church.

So it is this steamy summer morning in Orangeburg, inside the Reverend Hayes Gainey's clapboard United Methodist Church. Sharpton sits beside the pulpit as Gainey, stout and genial, rises to announce the guest speaker. "Welcome this titan of right, this truth-*seeker*, this Gospel *preacher*, this world *teacher*, this grassroots man," Gainey extols, offering an introduction Dick Gephardt will never hear.

"Raise up this man! *This man of God, sent by God!*"

Al begins slowly, humbly. But with forty-four years of practice (his fourth-grade teachers forbade him from writing "Rev. Al Sharpton" on his papers), he is soon rolling, delivering what has become, more or less, his stump sermon, easily the most effective, even stirring, political oratory of the current season.

A couple of days earlier, asked by the lefty editors of *The Nation* how he felt about faith-based government programs, Al declared the separation of church and state inviolate, saying, "Let the church into it, you know there's going to be proselytizing." But this is a different crowd.

"Once we had the KKK," Al declares as the church ladies jump to their feet in praise. "Now we got the RRR, the Rich, Right-wing Republicans! Well, let me tell you something. It is time for the Christian right to meet the right Christians!"

"*Question!*" Al shouts, employing one of his favorite rhetorical devices, the Socratic self-cross-examination, a one-man call-and-response. "They ask me, *Sharpton!* Why you running? You can't win! . . . I say: Nine fools running, eight gonna lose . . . But you get a lot more out of losing with me than winning with anyone else. No one else is gonna say what has to be said, for *us*."

As a case in point, Sharpton is now into the 2000-election fiasco, one more issue all the other Democratic candidates seem to have punted on. "They say get over it," he booms. "How can I get over it when it wasn't so long ago people right here in this room weren't even allowed to vote! . . . Our grandmothers and -fathers had to fight for the vote! So don't tell me to take something that is soaked in the blood of the innocents *and get over it!*"

Hallelujahs erupt. Of all his issues of Republican inequity, this is the one that gets the most response. The election: stolen from all Americans but felt more acutely by blacks, who have always loved this country more than it has loved them. Finishing with a flourish, Al melds the story of David to his own. "If God could take a shepherd boy and make him the king of Israel," he yells, before the piano starts up and he hurls his stumpy body into an obligatory 360-degree spin, "then God could take a boy from the housing project—*from the Brooklyn ghetto!*—and have him beat George Bush in 2004!"

It is hard to figure how well Sharpton's doing. Most recent polls have him second in South Carolina, behind the fast-fading Joseph Lieberman. Nationally, he fluctuates between 3 and 6 percent, decidedly a "second tier" candidate for sure, but ahead of supposed pros like John Edwards and Bob Graham. Not that polls matter when it comes to his chances, says Sharpton. When he got 32 percent in the mayoral primary, the morning papers had him at 14 percent. "My voters are not plugged into the Internet like Dean's. You call them on the phone and start asking a lot of questions, they hang up," the Rev. explains. But this could be moot, because, as many claim, Sharpton is not really running for president of America but rather for president of Black America—i.e., against Jesse Jackson.

It may take Sharpton's run to fully appreciate what Jackson was able to accomplish in his 1980s campaigns. Jesse got a combined 10 million primary votes in his '84 and '88 campaigns, trouncing Michael Dukakis in several states, including Michigan, carrying New York City. Matching that seems way out of reach for Sharpton, who went to work for Jackson's Operation Breadbasket at age twelve and has long maintained a complicated relationship with the man he once called "Big Rev," as opposed to his own "Li'l Rev."

"Jesse's family and mine would have Christmas together," Al recalls. "The two of us would sit in the front room moaning about all the stuff that was happening. Our wives would laugh, 'there they go again, two fatherless preachers feeling sorry for themselves on the birthday of the Son of God.'"

More recently, however, Li'l Rev. Al, always on the short end of the substantialness stick, began hinting, none too discreetly, that Jackson's time was done, likening his mentor to Muhammad Ali—"still the champ, except he can't fight no more." However, even if Al carries around a printout of the 2004 primary calendar with Jackson's '88 totals handwritten in the margin, he rejects the idea that his main goal is to "beat Jesse."

"How come if it's two black guys, they've got to always be against each other, trying to beat on each other? I'm *building* on what Jesse did."

This generational angle is seconded by Bill Lynch, the semilegendary political operative who worked for Jackson and now calls Sharpton "my present oar in the water." Asked if Sharpton's ability to make you laugh but not cry—as Jesse made people cry in his eighties convention speeches—constitutes a significant difference between the two men, Lynch agrees, offering the surprising conclusion that "this ends up in Al's favor." Sixties civil rights movement language retains moral power, Lynch says (and resonates with "Kumbaya"-singing white liberals), but young people "don't want to hear that old stuff." It doesn't matter which Rev will get a bigger welcome in heaven, Lynch says. His job is to get votes. Al, at forty-eight, shockingly the youngest candidate in the race, makes the best connection to the "hip-hop generation." The 19 to 35 voter is the "wild card" in this election, Lynch says. No reason they won't be for Al.

This said, Al finds himself in a unique Oedipal sandwich between two generations of Jacksons, since much of his platform can be traced to the ideas of Jesse Jackson Jr., the congressman from Illinois. Jackson Jr., who is without a doubt the only member of the House of Representatives to recommend eighteen books either by or about Hegel on his Web site, is the author of *A More Perfect Union: Advancing New American Rights*. Five hundred pages of very tiny type, Jackson Jr.'s book, written with Frank Watkins, proposes to be nothing less than a political history of race in America and actually comes close. It was a book he *had* to read, says Brooklyn College dropout Al, speaking quite literally.

"That was the deal if Al wanted me to work for him," says Watkins, a soft-spoken former seminary student who held high-ranking jobs on the elder Jackson's eighties campaigns and now manages Sharpton's. Al had to agree to take Jesse Sr.'s path: running, and staying, in the Democratic Party. He also had to read *A More Perfect Union*—Al claims to have done so three times—and to consider championing three of the amendments to the Constitution proposed by Jesse Jr. These are House Joint Resolutions 28 to 30, which, respectively, seek to federalize "the fundamental right of citizens to vote," "the right to equal, high quality public education," and "health care of equal high quality." This was fine, said Al, since he is in favor of large outlays for public ed (even if his two daughters attend Brooklyn's private Poly Prep) as well as single-payer health care.

The voting amendment causes the most stir, since, as Al points out, "most people think they've already got the right to vote." But voting remains a state's right, a right under the authority of the states, a situation that *A More Perfect Union* argues, is just one more bit of unfinished business from the Civil War. Sure as John C. Calhoun, Confederate ideologue, lies moldering in his grave, this is the reason, Sharpton says, the Supreme Court could, under the law, decide that Katherine Harris had the power to cut off the Florida vote, thereby making George W. Bush president.

Walking through the Capitol, Jesse Jackson Jr., a very young-looking thirty-eight, is talking about "the strong rationale" for Al Sharpton's run. Stopping in the old House of Representatives, now the National Statuary Hall, Jackson pauses in front of a likeness of Alexander Hamilton Stephens, a vice president of the Confederacy most famous for "the Cornerstone Speech," which proudly declared the new Southern nation to be founded on "the great physical, philosophical and moral truth that the Negro is not equal to the white man, that slavery . . . is his natural and normal condition." The fact that Stephens's statue (along with those of Jefferson Davis, Robert E. Lee, and Brigham Young, who helped found a religion which decreed that black people could not get into heaven) stands in this hall reserved for heroes of the Union is reason enough for Al Sharpton to run for president, says Jackson.

Yeah, but . . . does Jackson think Sharpton, loudmouth of Harlem and Brooklyn, with more baggage than a Samsonite showroom, is capable of articulating these constitutional and moral arguments? Is Al up to it?

Jackson, who has spoken harshly of his father's reported adultery, smiles and, paraphrasing II Corinthians, says, "Humans are all created imperfect vessels . . . all we can hope to do, with God's help, is to become more perfect."

Life on the road suits him, says the Rev., God's own imperfect vessel. It has ever since his advance-man days with James Brown. He says he misses his family and the nice corner house in Ditmas Park. But wherever he opens his suitcase, that's his home. Today, silk suit in the closet, a white undershirt loose across his still-ample chest, the Rev. lies on a couch in the Presidential Suite of the Sheraton in Shreveport, Louisiana, remembering when he met Martin Luther King Jr.

"I was nine or ten, still the Boy Preacher," says the Rev. "The Vietnam War was on, Dr. King had just begun to speak out against it. 'You're too young to get drafted,' he told me. 'But you're old enough to join the fight.'"

Growth has become a watchword in this current Sharptonian episode.

After the Rev.'s recent boffo performance at a forum on gay marriage, the moderator, erstwhile ABC kingpin Sam Donaldson, grabbed him. "You've grown so much," Donaldson said giddily, mirroring the banter of Bob Schieffer and Dan Balz after a recent Al appearance on *Face the Nation*. The pair couldn't get over how "clever" the Candidate had become.

"That's how it is," Sharpton says. "They say I've got *talent*, like I'm a talking seal. Wow: it is amazing what he can do! They never say I also have a brain . . . happens all the time, being patronized."

But growth, real growth, is a subjective thing. Could Al get past race? Could he truly cross over? In South Carolina, the Rev spoke almost exclusively to blacks. His positions on Nader-like "white" issues are perfunctory at best. In true New Yorker style, he hasn't driven a car in years, yet dimly congratulated himself for bringing up ethanol at a recent debate on the environment, even if it was clear he knew next to nothing about fuel economy, fossil or otherwise.

Al says politics as usual will not unseat Bush, that it will take a "movement." But could Al organize such a movement? According to the most recent Federal Election Commission filings, Al reported having raised $137,415 (only $14,010 of which was gathered in New York), compared with the $10 million–plus in Dean's bankbook and Bush's $35,148,847. Even bizarro Lyndon LaRouche has raised more dough than Al.

But this is how Sharpton does it, under the radar. Apprised that his supposed press officer never returned a call, he says, "Just ring me." Told that it felt a little, er, ad hoc to call a presidential candidate on his cell phone to find out what was going on in his campaign, Sharpton seems hurt. "Don't you like to talk to me?"

Perhaps someday Sharpton's vision will transcend race and class, but it remains to be seen if Al will ever move beyond Al.

"He is an extreme micromanager, used to deciding everything himself, making it up as he goes along," says a close campaign watcher. Suffice it to say that very few decisions are not funneled through the two-inch-square cell the Rev. keeps plastered to his ear. "He doesn't even have a media consultant," marveled one well-groomed Dean person, a media man himself.

But then, after watching Al buttonhole DNC leader Terry McAuliffe, the Dean guy said, "Well, what could someone like me do for someone like him anyway? He knows what he's selling."

His seat-of-the-pants method has led to some awkward moments, such as the recent Democratic National Committee fund-raiser at the Mayflower Hotel in Washington. The obligatory red, white, and blue balloons looked festive, the booze was flowing, but there was an unmistakable tension in the air. The Dems, widely seen as too impotent to exploit Bush's post-Iraq weakness or stop the Republicans from dismantling the last remnants of the New Deal, are in desperation mode.

Al planned to use the dinner to take one more swat at the ruling Democratic Leadership Council, the Clintonite faction the Rev. charges has brought the party so far to the right that its members are nothing but a bunch of "elephants in donkey coats." The fact that the Republicans will stage their convention in New York, a mile from ground zero, "right in our house," while the Dems will be trundling off to "good ol' boy" Boston was one more sign of the DLC's "loser mentality," Al says. If the DLC wasn't so asleep at the switch, it would have gone south, to Miami, or even Jacksonville, which, after all, was "the scene of the crime."

"We have to slap that donkey," Al likes to shout. "*Slap that donkey* until it wakes up and kicks George Bush out of the White House!"

But Al never said those things, not on that night. He had to be back in New York, and with the last shuttle leaving at 8:30 and the DNC dinner not beginning until seven, it was going to be tight. As party chairman Terry McAuliffe introduced fat-cat donors, Al nibbled at his salad, looked at his watch. Then, carrying his own bags, he left. No big deal, he said, waving as he went out the hotel door to the loud cheers of bellhops and cabdrivers. "My vote's out here anyhow."

Unfortunately, the podium didn't get the message. After the emcee announced *"From the great state of New York: the Reverend Al Sharpton!"* there was a strained pause before Al's "unavoidable" departure was announced. Groans filled the room. Sen. Ted Kennedy, looking rumpled, said, "That was too bad. I'd been looking forward to hearing him all night long."

* * *

With Rev., you take the downside with the up. Ronald Reagan once said, "Facts are stubborn things." Not for Al. It isn't that Sharpton is *all* that much more careless with the truth than most politicians. Rather, as one observer says, "It's that preacher thing. If it sounds good, he keeps on going." This proclivity has come up in the campaign, as Al, eager to push his progressive credentials, has claimed he is "the only candidate who is against the death penalty" and that Howard Dean "has a 100 percent rating from the NRA."

Informed that Dennis Kucinich is against the death penalty and that Howard Dean doesn't actually have an NRA rating (the organization doesn't rank governors), Al squints. "Hmmm . . ." he says. "It is good to be accurate. Kucinich is only recently against capital punishment, so I'll say I'm the only candidate who is *historically* against the death penalty." Al did, however, continue to claim that Dean had "a 100 percent NRA rating." Must have just sounded better that way.

Say he's a trickster, repeat the claim that some think of him as a back-channel Republican supporter (he egregiously endorsed Al D'Amato in 1986, and many reports claim he's taken large sums of money from Republican party fixer Roger Stone), berate him for all the stupid things he's either said or tolerated his cohorts saying about Jews, ask him anything about money, like where he gets it and where it goes, and Al just widens his eyes and licks his lips. Thick-skinned as a stegosaur—you can't call him anything he hasn't been called before. For him, mixing it up, warding off accusations, and generally talking his way out of anything is sport, like speed chess in the park.

It is a grand spectacle watching Sharpton run around a hotel room in his underwear, denouncing Mark Green, the one man he seems to truly despise, and going through the details of Steve Pagones' case against him in the Brawley affair yet again, saying, "I don't know, the man is obsessed with me." Almost always totally easy about race on a personal, one-to-one level (*Wow*, the white reporter thinks, *Al really likes me*), he's your best friend if there's ink on the table.

As long as nobody takes his campaign seriously, Sharpton can basically say almost anything. "They need me for the ratings," he says, noting how deadly the debates would be without him. But if he actually begins to pile up some real numbers, sharks like Dick Morris and Karl Rove will drag those skeletons out of the closet, start flipping the race cards. "Bring them on," Sharpton trash-talks, quoting the leader of the free world. "Rove pulls a Willie Horton on me, he'll see—I shoot back."

Meanwhile, Al keeps the laughs coming. Hearing that Freddy Ferrer was joking about "staying up at night" trying to decide whether to be secretary of state or defense in the new Al administration, Sharpton frowns, "Well, I got a nice ambassadorship for him. *Antarctica!*"

This is the way it is with Rev.: He rides along in the back of a car with two other ministers, one of whom says, "That guy, he's not white; he's Cajun." The other minister says, "Ain't Cajuns white?" To which Al, engrossed in a conversation on his cell, pipes up, exactly on cue, "He's kind of half-white. A *Cau*-Cajun." In an airport, the new Robert Dallek book about John Kennedy on his lap, Al looks pensive, seemingly pondering the great responsibilities that might lie ahead. Finally he says, "One thing has really been on my mind . . ." You wait for the revelation or confession. "If you win the *American Idol,* what do you win?"

That's the trap, not to let yourself like him too much. Not to forget he's Al.

Sharpton was in Shreveport, a gone-bust oil-and-gas burg turned thriving casino town, on a familiar errand. Last March, not far from downtown, where the Stars and Bars still fly on a memorial maintained by the Daughters of the Confederacy, Marquise Hudspeth, a twenty-five-year-old black man who reportedly had been driving erratically, was shot dead in the parking lot of a Circle K convenience store. It was one of several recent police shootings in the area, but the Hudspeth case was different: There were videos. The tapes showed Hudspeth getting out of his car holding what turned out to be a cell phone and being shot in the back several times.

"He fell right about here, then they shot him two more times," says Dr. Artis Cash, a Pentecostal pastor, pointing to a spot of concrete near the Circle K self-serve pumps. "They called it justifiable force." That was why Cash called Al.

With something like this, who else was there to call? "I've heard some negative things," Cash admits. "I heard he miscalculated on the Tawana Brawley thing. I heard that he was an informer for the FBI." But Al had spine, and besides, Cash says with a sudden smile, "he showed up."

"People said I was an ambulance chaser. I said, 'Fool, *I am the ambulance*.' Now I'm the *national* ambulance," says Sharpton. Once he went to Howard Beach, now it was Louisiana. "It is the same," Al says. "Except for the frequent-flier miles."

The first time he went down to Shreveport on the Hudspeth shooting, twenty-five hundred people came out to see him. Now, mindful that Jesse Jackson won the 1988 Louisiana primary with almost 36 percent (another number Al will never come close to), Sharpton was back, meeting with Marquise Hudspeth's bereaved mother and wife. Sneaking a glimpse through the window of the small office, you could see the Hudspeths sitting with Al, holding hands, soundlessly praying. Hudspeth's wife, mother of his two children, a tall, strikingly beautiful woman with a blonde rinse, had tears rolling down her face.

"*Reverend Sharpton is with the family*." It is one of those charged phrases of recent race matters, a typical Al conundrum, intractably tangled with our perceptions of the man. It usually means someone of color has been shot, likely by a police officer, and that Al is there, offering comfort to the relatives and the assurance that their grievance will not go unheeded. On the other hand, there are dark thoughts, rumors. One of the nastiest whispers about Al is that he arrives at these scenes, sets up the shattered family with his legal buddies, then takes a cut of whatever settlement is made. It is a repellent, ghoulish notion for which there is not a shred of proof, and Sharpton vehemently denies it. But there it is, that shadow you can't cast out of your consciousness. With Al, there is always a shadow, another side.

Dr. Cash promised a full house for a fund-raiser, but the room is only a third filled. Al is not surprised. You can always get a crowd for a rally, but writing checks is a whole other deal. After the usual honorifics ("Welcome this pilgrim from the courts of glory, a pilgrim from the flaming hills of

Calvary . . . this twenty-first-century prophet"), Al is back onstage, working the stump sermon, lambasting Clarence Thomas, who voted against the recent affirmative action measure, saying that just because a man is "your color doesn't make him your kind."

It isn't anything Al hasn't said fifty times this week. But then, quieter, unexpectedly, he leans forward: "You know . . . people ask me: Why don't I cut my hair? Because this is me. This is *who I am.*"

Suddenly something registers, the feeling that he really means it—as if Sharpton, imperfect vessel, after listening to a ceaseless soundtrack of himself since that first four-year-old preaching gig, has actually heard what he says and come to some sort of personal epiphany. It is as if the various warring Als—the hustler Al, the good-in-spite-of-himself Al, the helping Al—have merged to reach across the divide of race and his own contradictions in a real attempt to make himself more perfect, and us along with him.

Or maybe that's just what he wants us to believe. With Al, you go round and round.

The stump sermon is over now, the money-gathering segment of the program has begun. In New York, Al yells, "I need ten people to come up here and give me one hundred dollars! Right now!" But this was Shreveport, where people's minimum wages are often sucked up into the slot machines, and a lower key was demanded. The pickings are slim. No wonder Al's FEC filings are a joke; even with the biblical exhortations about how "the Lord loves a cheerful giver," most of his envelopes are filled with cookie-jar money.

Hearing that Bush asks twenty thousand dollars from supporters who want to pose with him, Al tries the same thing, albeit on a less pricey level.

"Ten bucks?" the candidate is heard yelling. "Twenty grand for Bush, and I'm only ten bucks? I'm *way* better-looking than him!"

A few days later, Sharpton is back in the city. He has just spoken at the weekly National Action Network rally, denouncing Bush's Liberian policy, saying it was "an insult" that the president would go to Africa but not meet with African-American leaders. Describing his own journey to "the door of no return" on Goree Island in Senegal, where so many were shipped out as slaves, Al said, "You can hear the voices of your ancestors, those who went to the bottom of the ocean, those who came here to live in bondage." Now, to turn on the TV and "see that little Texas cowboy" in the same place, describing slavery as "a crime" as if this were a new revelation, was "sickening," Al said.

That done, Sharpton is walking across Seventh Avenue, renamed Adam Clayton Powell Jr. Boulevard after his greatest hero, the flamboyant preacher of the Abyssinian Baptist Church and defrocked congressman. The Rev. talks a lot about Adam Powell these days, saying he once thought the minister's famous catchphrase "Keep the faith, baby" was shallow, but now he realizes the power of it, even compared with Jesse's "Keep hope alive." This is because, Al says, when it comes down to it, "Hope can only take you so far." Faith never ends.

Naming thoroughfares for great and beloved figures is a Harlem tradition. There are street signs honoring Malcolm X, Frederick Douglass, Duke Ellington, and, of course, Martin Luther King Jr. Might there someday be a Reverend Al Sharpton Boulevard?

"If I get elected, they'll have to," Al says, warming to the idea. But right now he is pretty hungry and on his way to Amy Ruth's Restaurant on 116th Street, which is owned by his former chief of staff Carl Redding. In the old knock-around style, the food at Amy's is named after various uptown political and showbiz personalities. They've got dishes called "The Rev. Calvin O. Butts III," "The Rev. Dr. Wyatt Tee Walker," "The Percy Sutton," "The Roberto Ramirez." But "The Rev. Al Sharpton" is at the top, the first item on the menu.

"Chicken and waffles—that's me," Al says.

17
Fear of Giving

The heart-felt handout. Searching for the saintly in yourself. Esquire, *1986.*

The flyer stuck to the wall of a stupa in Durbar Square in Kathmandu read MEET-GREET MOTHER TERESA. BLESSINGS-AUTOGRAPHS. I was kind of taking it easy that afternoon, eating pieces of chocolate cake and listening to Jimi Hendrix records with the rest of the hippies, so that sounded all right: meeting and greeting a living saint and getting her blessing-autograph. It would fit nicely into my collection, alongside the signatures of Leo Durocher and Johnny Otis.

She must have sensed my skepticism because when I got to the front of the meet-greet line, she looked up from her blue-and-white habit and asked, "Can you help?"

Her gaze was arresting. It felt penetrating. "How," I stammered.

She didn't answer, only returned a thin smile that said: that is for you to find out.

I have no way of knowing if Mother Teresa dispenses this sort of conundrum to all luggish Americans out for self-motivated adventure in South Asia. It is within the scope of my natural distrust to suppose even living saints have some kind of an angle. Do-gooders make me nervous because it is hard to believe anyone does anything for nothing. Official charity smacked of blue-haired Park Avenue ladies, polite paternalism, and tea parties in the parlor. Telethons and their offspring could be scoffed at. Does wishing Jerry's kids well include a blessing on Jerry?

It was more than that, I didn't see what could be accomplished. Confronted with the extreme poverty in places like Bangladesh, I had become progressively inured to human suffering. There was so much of it. Everywhere you looked people were starving, maimed. Shot up, fucked in the head. The legless beggars in Benares, the shoeless mountain people in Muktinath: Sometimes you'd just have to stop in your tracks, sit down, and let your head spin. The chances of helping these people, eight thousand miles from home, people who spoke languages I would never learn, seemed so remote I ceased to feel any responsibility, or love, for them.

But saints are saints; if they set you a task, it is difficult to ignore it altogether. Over the years there have been patches of time when I couldn't get through a day without swinging 180 degrees on Mother Teresa's question, "Can you help?" One moment I'd assert starving people in Somalia are just none of my business, that my job in life is to wait by the telephone night and day for a return call from that Hollywood guy who said, yes, my notion for the next sci-fi blockbuster was absolutely "er . . . very interesting." After all, I had a family to provide for, to insulate in the upcoming age of scarcity. Sure, money couldn't buy happiness, but it did buy off unhappiness. I didn't need John Huston to tell me that.

Then, an hour later, I am telling my wife that we should just give away all the furniture and book ourselves on a flight to East Timor. The Indonesian government was bleeding the people there, the land is a tropical moonscape, and no one is making any speeches about it. We can help in East Timor, I tell my wife. What's the cheap fare to Jakarta? For tomorrow.

But it all comes to nothing. My two impulses collide and I am paralyzed. I slump down in my chair, defeated. Playing at the notion of becoming a do-gooder, I couldn't even decide whether such a thing could exist. I mean, I had whole philosophy classes where the professor doubted if anything known as The Good was truly knowable. A concrete kind of guy, I needed the knowable. You couldn't go off to East Timor, or Ethiopia, or Mindanao, or the Sahel on faith alone. Could you?

For me, it gets only thornier when I hear stories about people like Stan Mooneyham. Once an air force flyer in Vietnam, Mooneyham is the former head of World Vision, an evangelical group based in Southern California. He was a prime mover in the construction of a children's hospital in Phnom Penh, Cambodia, prior to the catastrophic takeover of that country by Pol Pot's Khmer Rouge. A nominally communist millennialist cult determined to turn the clock back to "The Year Zero" during four years of power, Pol Pot's group murdered as much as 25 percent of the Cambodian population. Finally, in an act of nationalistically motivated benevolence, the Vietnamese army, acting when the Western powers would not, overthrew the Khmer Rouge, vanquishing Pol Pot to the hinterlands where he continues to fight on to this day.

Hearing of this new development, Mooneyham, anxious to find out the fate of the children's hospital, petitioned the Vietnamese government to be allowed to enter Cambodia. Receiving no reply through bureaucratic channels, Mooneyham decided to take matters into his own hands. Traveling alone in a small plane, he flew over the Cambodian countryside and landed right in the middle of ravaged Phnom Penh. Surrounded by startled Vietnamese soldiers, Mooneyham declared, "I am here to find out what happened to our hospital. Kill me if you have to, but I'm not leaving until I see what I came to see."

Taken prisoner, Mooneyham was delighted to find that the local commander spoke some English. He explained his case, how his was the Lord's work and he meant no harm to anyone. The commander refused to let Mooneyham see the hospital. At this point, so the story goes, Mooneyham reached into his boot and pulled out a four-inch Bowie knife and plunged the blade into his wrist. With blood spurting, Mooneyham looked the commander in the eye and said, "I ask you not to look at my face. For if you do you will see only your enemy. I ask you to look at my blood, and then you will know that we are truly brothers under the skin. When you do that, you know that love talked about can easily be turned aside, but love demonstrated is irresistible."

Rattled, the commander made the necessary calls, and soon enough World Vision was allowed to rebuild the shattered hospital. Even now, nearly ten years later, their hospital is only one of the few modern medical facilities in Phnom Penh, the only children's hospital in the whole depleted country. This story, partially related in William Shawcross's book about international aid, *The Quality of Mercy*, is both inspiring and troubling. Shawcross's point is that while many of the secular agencies failed Cambodia, especially in the horrendous famine that followed the Vietnamese takeover, someone like World Vision's Mooneyham, a noted "soul-winner for Christ" and author of several over-the-top tracts decrying the power of Satan in the universe, was able to succeed.

It is that lack of that kind of assurance—the feeling that there is no choice but to do your particular version of God's work—that defeats me. It is an old problem for the rationalist do-gooder: envy of sacred certitude. You don't want to think about The Good, you just want to *do it*, like some Nike sneaker ad reflex. What else was Mother Teresa supposed to do but serve after receiving God's command to go to Calcutta? Exorcism of doubt, it must truly be bliss. Sometimes I suppose that people like Mother Teresa, or the holy roller preacher down on First Avenue, are a different species than myself, as if acceptance of faith has had a galvanizing, neo-evolutionary effect on their morphological structure.

How to get past the check-writing stage? (Yeah, but how much? How much can we afford? What's the tax thing?) Mahayana Buddhism says true charity springs from emptiness (absence of self), which engenders compassion. Ultimate compassion does away with the distinction between yourself and everyone else, rendering the thought of not helping unthinkable. Maybe the Buddha could pull off that trick. Maybe Mother Teresa can. Myself, I'm not so sure. No saint, I live in the shabby world of the everyday. I watch TV, I know I only go around once in this life and I've got to reach for all the gusto I can get. Look out for number one.

I'm not crazy about being this way, but what can I do? It is my life, forty years of working out the DNA. When I start whining about this, the only question is why I don't act on what I know to be my best intentions? To this my best answer is that I am afraid, that I fear whittling away at the tiny sliver of identity I've eked out.

Robert Hayes, head of a group called the Coalition for the Homeless, which seeks to aid the nation's burgeoning street population, understands these feelings. Hayes, who left a high-paying job as a Wall Street lawyer to become an advocate for people who dwell in tunnels beneath the tracks in Grand Central Station, says, "You don't need to be a saint to help. We operate on the theory of 'tolerable hypocrisy.' We try to help these people, but we' re not going to live in the streets with them. The fact is, some of them are always going to live in the streets. For whatever reason they're street people. Deny that and you will fail."

In the old philosophical argument that wonders if altruism can or should be separated from egoism, Hayes comes down on the side of self-interest. Buddhist tracts, karmic implications: these esoterics do not complicate matters for Hayes. "Even dilettantes can do good," he says. "Go to East Timor if that's what you need to do to convince yourself you are more good than bad. That's your romance. We've all got our romance, which is nothing to be ashamed of. But I've got a lot of convenient trouble right outside my door."

Certainly there are enough opportunities out there. Indeed, I live a block from the Bowery, just four streets over from the city-run men's shelter on Third Street, dismal in its way as anything in a Calcutta railway station. When I first moved in, about fifteen years ago, I'd get panhandled two or three times a day. Yesterday, as a controlled experiment of sorts, I went out to do a few errands in the neighborhood. In an hour and ten minutes I was asked for money twenty-eight times. At my usual quarter-per-request rate, that's nearly seven dollars an hour. Actually, I was surprised it wasn't more.

The homeless population is currently estimated to be between sixty and eighty thousand in New York. For the busy urbanite, figures like these require tactics. For a long time, in the interests of triage, I gave money to the guys who had the best come-ons. That meant I gave a quarter to the black guy who rushed up, mock angry, shouting, "I do not, under any circumstances, give change for one-hundred-dollar bills!" Ditto for the fat white guy who sang opera, at the top of his lungs, interrupting himself only to do station breaks for "W-I-N-O, on your radio dial."

Gradually, I recognized the inequity of such a policy. It meant that the guys who were well off enough to think up these little hustles got my quarters, while the more far gone ones did not. Not giving money to some poor soul who could offer no more entertainment than standing there drooling seemed antithetical to the point. It can be difficult. One snowy night last winter I was walking home when from the gloom and mist emerged a giant man, a hulk with tattered blankets strewn over his head, hiding his face. He was emitting guttural, muffled sounds. He staggered forward, with his hand out. I could do nothing but watch him lurch along, into the night. It was like being back in Benares, overwhelmed into inaction. Yet I overcame it, pulled out a quarter. The man didn't even notice. The quarter dropped into the fresh snow, making an inch-deep hole for itself. I dug it out, put it back in my pocket, and went home.

Recently we've gotten a little tight with a street guy named David. David started standing in front of my apartment building about a year ago. We'd walk by and he'd ask for change. It was all automatic with him, he hardly ever looked up, you could walk by three times in ten minutes and he'd ask you for money every time. This got sort of tedious. Once my wife was coming down the street with our two kids. She had bags in both hands. When David asked her for money yet again, she turned to him, explaining that this was the fourth time that morning he'd panhandled her, that she gave him money when she felt she could, but with kids and an erratic income, that was all she could do. During this our older kid stuck her hands into my wife's pocket, got hold of a dollar, and gave it to David.

It was an odd, ritual-shattering moment. Holding the bill with a mixture of joy and terror, David tried to return it. My wife said no, he should keep it. Right then, something changed. To David, we stopped being just another pair of marks, and to us, David ceased to be another obstacle on the path from the subway. We began to say hello. On my wife's birthday, because of a mixup, she got two chocolate cakes. We gave one to David. He couldn't believe it. Almost immediately he started weeping. How could we possibly know that the very next day was his birthday? He was going to be twenty-five and never once had he ever had a cake. They didn't give cakes in the foster homes in which he'd grown up. Sometimes cupcakes, but never a real cake. The next day, when we passed by, David handed my wife a handwritten "thank you" card. He said the cake we gave him really changed his luck. He'd been waiting for a call from a construction foreman he used to work for. When he got back to the shelter, the guy called. Now he'd have work, and wouldn't have to stand outside our house anymore, begging.

It would have been nice if that was it, if David kept the gig, got his own apartment and was able to provide for his son, now living with his crack-head mother in Brooklyn. But that's not how it went. A week later, David was back. The construction project fell through. Mostly they were using union guys, anyway. So David was back on the streets. Sometime we invite him up to our apartment for a cup of coffee.

Now, I have no illusions. I recognize how paltry this small relationship I maintain with David is when compared with what I think I should be doing. What a real do-gooder would do. I think of friends of mine, people who work in soup kitchens, man the phones on all-night hot lines. Also, I notice that David hasn't been looking all that great recently, how most days he barely gets it together to beg. I ask him if he wants to come upstairs, take it easy. He smiles and says no. "Someday," he says, "if I really need it, I know you'll take me in."

"Sure," I reply, dreading that day. I mean, I don't want to turn him away, especially now that he expects me to be good to him. But our apartment is small. We've got two kids, another on the way. Certainly he'll understand that. Won't he? It's hard to know how to play it, when you're learning how to help.

18
Terence McKenna, Far Out

Originally entitled "Is Terence McKenna the Brave Prophet of the Next Psychedelic Revolution, or Is His Cosmic Egg Just a Little Bit Cracked?" Didn't care for that since I never considered that Terence had a crack in his egg. His brain on drugs always seemed sunny-side up, never scrambled. This was a difficult article to report. Travel pieces, especially this kind, really take it out of you. Unfortunately for all thinking beings, Terence passed away a few years ago. I miss him all the time, especially when orbiting somewhere out by Jupiter. From Esquire, *1992.*

So then I was under the ground, diving through dirt, past the roots of trees, the bottoms of boulders, the tissues and sinews of the planet. A swooping mole I was, twitch-nosed, incisors chompy, plumbing all geology, fur around my face. The pounding got louder (was it the pulse inside my chest, or was it more? The beat . . . a *beating, boundless Heart!*). Then: I felt the rush of air, inhaling, exhaling, an incredible bellows, rising, falling. (Could it be? *Terra breathing!*)

That's when I saw them, up ahead, insect faces poked through the thicket, a green-and-black-eyed swarm. Life inside. A world within the world. The center of the living earth.

Except then, just when I felt I could reach out and touch what had always been withheld, the central processes of everything I sought, the image blurred, pulled away. The heart and lungs of the planet were gone. I wasn't underground anymore. I was lying on a mattress in an indifferently furnished room in Occidental, California, the wan morning light clamping down my irises.

"It's something about the earth," I said after a while.

"Right . . . something about the earth," Terence echoed, putting aside his bedside copy of *Chaldaean Oracles and Theurgy*, his voice that intoxicating, ever-inclusive nasal lope that says: Yes, we share the same dream, so let's dream some more.

There was no doubt that the DMT (N,N-dimethyltryptamine) experience was "about the earth" Terence allowed with the stoic patience of shamanic empiricist patting a neophyte on his willing, if seriously addled, head. If I was seeking the full informational font of the drug, however, I'd gone very little beyond the edge of things. DMT used to be called "businessman's acid" owing to its ultra-intense yet short-acting hallucinogenic properties, but such street nomenclature was a reductionist misnomer, Terence said. This was because DMT was no dumb drug that some idiot Hell's Angel might whip up on a hot plate in the back of doublewide trailer. Coming as it did from wholly natural sources (primarily the Amazonian chacruna plant, *Psychotria viridis*, but also extant in such humble grasses like Illinois Bundleweed, which grows alongside many interstate highways), DMT was, Terence said, "a premeditatedly positioned transdimensional doorway to the vegetable mind of the planet." The secrets DMT was capable of revealing could not be glimpsed in a single session, or ten. The fact that I hadn't pierced "the chrysanthemum," which is what Terence calls the subterranean curtain beyond which true knowledge begins, was far from unusual.

Terence McKenna, of course, has been beyond the chrysanthemum. Way, way beyond it.

Terence has had long-term transit with "the meme-trading, self-transforming machine elves" who live on the other side of the membrane, a race of impish alien tykes who have been known to greet the weary psychonaut effusively, smothering him with wet, gooey leprechaun kisses. Then again, Terence has also found himself lying paralyzed on a beach while a crab crawled across the sand and used its pincers to clean all ten of his fingernails. Terence has also felt himself suddenly flying in the company of silvery disks, moving over Soviet Siberia, ahead of him the Great Plain of Shang and red-yellow waste of India. During his commerce with the naturally occurring plant psychedelics put on the earth by either God or simple natural selection, Terence has lain naked with a manifestation of the frightening yet sexy Hindu goddess Kali Leucothea, whom he describes as "pure anima . . . erotic but not human, a presence addressed to the species and not the individual, glittering with the possibility of cannibalism, madness, space, and extinction."

Like Dr. Seuss, these are the places Terence McKenna goes, on beyond zebra. Where he feels "more real." Over the past decade or so Terence has been talking about these places to people who also get their kicks out of traveling on what McKenna calls the "gleaming, alchemical abyss of hyperspace" where the initiated speak in "the special tongues of translinguistical places and things." Phraseology such as this, delivered in his wholly indelible flat, hypnotic cadences, most often heard on bootlegged ninety-minute cassette tapes with titles like *The Ineffable Tremendum,* is how Terence makes a living. He is, for better or worse, the more or less universally accepted Timothy Leary of the 1990s, (the always canny Leary says so himself), the reigning spokesman of what has been called "the psychedelic position."

"I've always gravitated to the patently strange," McKenna says, recalling his voracious intake of *Weird Tales*, the *Book of Knowledge*, and Roger Corman interpretations of Edgar Allen Poe during his 1950s upbringing as "the kind of odd kid" in a remote Colorado mining town. Likely it is safe to conclude that few other six-foot-two fourteen-year-olds in the Rocky Mountain state busied themselves reading Jung's *Psychology and Alchemy* on their walk to school, not to mention committing to memory whole swatches of Stephen Dedalus's well-documented day. But McKenna felt these readings necessary because "in our school if you were not interested in the vicissitudes of the pulling left guard, you learned nothing." In retrospect, Terence assumes the obsessive autodidacticism of his youth would have led to "a life sentence in the staid precincts of academia."

Except then, like magic, it wasn't the fifties anymore and McKenna was in Berkeley, California, regarding a tiny pink pellet of LSD-25, an encounter that Terence says "would set my course." Indeed. Now when interviewers ask him, "How many times have you taken LSD?" Terence replies, "Oh, maybe 150 times when I was young. Not a lot." After which Terence will go on to define the "heroic dose" of psilocybin mushrooms. "Five dried grams. Five dried grams in silent darkness will flatten the most resistant ego."

As some hippie burnout must have said some time or other: so old it's new. With the seemingly endless Reagan-Bush "war on drugs" staggering under the weight of its own contradictions (as we used to say), Terence McKenna may have caught a tiny but unmistakable culture wrinkle—just recently the *New York Times* ran a full-page, decidedly unjudgmental article denoting LSD "a drug of allure." Within the next year, no less than five books by McKenna, not one of them self-published on a mimeograph machine and held together with plastic rings (as his earlier works were), will be on bookstore shelves. One of these, *The Archaic Revival,* a compendium subtitled *Speculations on Psychedelic Mushrooms, the Amazon, Virtual Reality, UFOs, Evolution, Shamanism, the Rebirth of the Goddess, and the End of History* and blurbed by Tom Robbins as "a cyclone of unorthodox ideas capable of lifting almost any brain out of its cognitive Kansas," basically circumscribes the shortform of Terence's message.

One week earlier, as I arrived in San Francisco en route to attend the workshop Terence was teaching at Esalen Institute in Big Sur (Esalen! Forget memory lane, this was the Major Deegan!), I had little inkling that I would find myself under the ground, corkscrewing, like Jules Vernesville toward the center of the earth. I was more concerned with the air, how it had turned black, at least on the eastern side of the plane. It had been nearly fifteen years since I'd set foot in the Bay area, and now half of Berkeley—where I'd gone to college and been chased by the police for throwing a brick at Edward Teller's house—was on fire. It was the worst wildfire in United States history. The "perimeter" of the blaze, someone said, had been established as ranging from Grizzly Peak Boulevard on down to the area behind the Claremont Hotel. From the plane, it might have been the end of the world, the way the fire came rushing in broken lines down the Oakland Hills.

Was it a sign? How can you tell about such things? Berkeley, after all, was where I'd taken most of the acid I took, where I'd eaten peyote, consumed many mushrooms. I'd walked down Dwight Way as the Sun King, whimpered for my mommy in Blake Street bathtubs. It seemed no great coincidence that Terence McKenna also had lived in Berkeley, in a house behind the Park and Shop on Telegraph Avenue. We were, at least intermittently, contemporaries on the scene. Who knew how many times we'd passed each other on the Ave, stood shoulder-to-shoulder skimming books in Moe's, hitchhiked to the city, thumbs out on University, attended the same Antonioni movie in Wheeler Auditorium?

Who knew if we would have gotten along back then, in what was called The Day. Somehow I doubted it. Me and my crowd, mostly from the east, more political, into spending most of the day taking in the life's work of Nicholas Ray and Samuel Fuller at the Telegraph Repertory Theatre, had little time for what we assumed to be the rambling inarticulateness of acidhead detachment. They were a different tribe. Sure, we took a lot of drugs, but did it mostly for fun. I mean, if you didn't believe in God, what was the point of seeing Him?

I was thinking of that odd dichotomy—the rationalist pols against spiritualistas—which always seemed to break up communes back in the Berkeley days, as I made my way down the California coast in my rent-a-car. Whizzing past Garlic World and fields full of stooping artichoke pickers, I stopped at a Safeway to get a piece of sprayed fruit and was immediately confronted by a gauntlet of evangelicals brandishing their Bibles, demanding I take Jesus into my heart.

Oh, yeah, the rest of California . . . it all comes back now.

I probably would have gotten away unscathed if it weren't for this Mexican teenager planting his thin body upon the rubber mat of the automatic doorway. Such a sweet-looking kid he was, nicely turned out in an over-laundered white shirt and Kiwi-larded boots. "I lost my brother to drugs, he had no idea what he was doing to himself. Drugs are the work of Satan," he said to me, holding out a tract highlighting the Book of Daniel. "That is why I carry the message of Jesus, so the nightmare of my brother's final days does not overtake us all. He is coming you know, any day now, and we want to be clean for Him . . . drugs are demons. Jesus is the only protection."

I was about to lurch into my rap, how it is insane to lump all drugs together, pot and smack, blah, blah, blah, when this kid started crying. It was his brother, dead in the street in East L.A., that needle in his arm. Didn't I want to prevent more horrors like that? "You are a gentleman, I know you understand what I'm talking about." He reached over and felt my cuff. It was only then I remembered that I had a suit jacket on. Tie too. Somehow, I'd managed to forget, yet again, that I was forty-four years old, not twenty-one, a freak no more but rather a father of three who, much to his surprise and chagrin had found himself occasionally worrying about "drugs" in a manner not completely unlike that professed by the most brimstone-laden Falwellian.

So, with that sweet-faced Mexican kid moving closer, donation cup in hand, crying about his dead brother, knowing in his heart that Jesus Christ was the only salvation from certain eternal hellfire, what was I supposed to tell him, "Maybe next time, dude, I'm already late to talk to a guy whose whole bottom line it is to *just say yes*." I just turned and split.

Rattled, I fled back into the car and slapped a Terence McKenna tape into the deck. The man's soothing planetarium-style elocutions filled the rented Plymouth. "Without a symbiotic relationship to the biodynamic, God-laden constituency in the exterior natural environment, the unaided human mind is almost certain to fail in its effort to assimilate the mystery of being," he said. "It is so counterintuitive, so unexpected, but if ships from Zeta-Reticule were to arrive tomorrow and land on the South Lawn of the White House, it would not change the fact that the DMT flash is the weirdest thing that you can experience this side of the yawning grave."

Soon enough I was feeling a whole lot better. Oh, that Terence! He's such a tonic; he really knows how to talk you down from a deficient reality trip.

The tape I was listening to, *Psychedelics Before and After History*, contains a relatively succinct rendition of McKenna's current Ur theory, a flamboyant construct detailing how psilocybin, the psychoactive component present in the *stropharia cubensis* mushroom, is the missing link in the development of human consciousness. Doggedly comprehensive, it goes like this, give or take a nuance: About one hundred thousand years ago, due to the increasing desertification of the African continent, man's forerunners, the advanced, arboreal primates of the increasingly withering tropical canopy, were pushed southward. Abandoning vegetarianism in favor of a more diversified omnivorous diet, they developed a taste for the beetles and other insects that can be found on the underside of ungulates' excretion mounds. It was during this process that the primates encountered the *cubensis*, a coprophilic, or dung-loving, mushroom that is often found growing out of cowpies. They ingested small-to-middling amounts of the psilocybin-containing fungus, which has been proven to increase visual acuity and stimulate sexual desire, two traits that would likely be valuable assets to a baboonlike tribe looking to establish a foothold as hunters and gatherers in a foreign land.

McKenna's mushroom-as-monolith idea hurtles on from there, an overheated chain of free association. He posits psilocybin's "pivotal" role in the development of language. Then, getting only slightly more expansive, suggests that mushroom "spore fall" has created an intricately connected matrix spreading across time and space, "a divinely spun cobweb of planetary information that has been the catalyst for everything about us that distinguishes us from other higher primates, for all the mental functions that we associate with humanness."

This particular spiel was not unknown to me. Much of it is contained in "Having Archaic and Eating It Too," one of McKenna's semiprepared talks I happened to catch a few months earlier. The lecture was delivered inside the Great Hall of Cooper Union where Abraham Lincoln, Ralph Waldo Emerson, and William James once spoke. And right then, if you were stoned and giddy enough, you could choose to throw Terence McKenna in the mix with those decidedly American visionaries. So what did it matter that there was no proof in the fossil record (and no chance of there ever being any) that some red-assed monkeys got smashed on mushrooms and that's how come, as McKenna seemed to be inferring, hepcats throughout recent history have been able to walk the set, digging Monk and Miles.

It sounded good. It sounded real good, especially since Terence is a rapper who would never think of using the word *causality* when *causzooistry* would do. Outside the homeless were freezing, the crack dealers stalked, and the bubble-gum lights of cop cars went round. We lived in a grim, tyrannizing world of uncertain authorship and even less distinct destination, but in here was this living contact high, like hearing a deejay playing all those old records you forgot you liked, but doing it with a new spin.

"The psychedelic position is the antidrug position," Terence proclaims, calling for an etymological reevaluation of the word *drug* itself. The "repetitive, obsessional, unexamined" behavior of the dope fiend is not only dumb but it plays directly into the hands of the power structure, which, as "we" (Terence is big on the conspiratorial, collective first-person plural) all know, is behind the coke-and-smack trafficking to begin with. To combat this manipulation, synthetic drugs of all types must be banished from the pharmacopoeia. Underground designer substances without proper laboratory testing, from the export of the Medellín cartels to dime bags of Blue Magic horse, are to be avoided. Terence's attitude toward the hallowed LSD-25 and its derivatives proves fulcrumatic. While acknowledging acid's seminal (and sentimental) role in unhinging sixties perceptional doors, McKenna lambastes the "better living through chemistry" ethic as the fundamentally wrongheaded last gasp of what he calls "the science cult." An expansively conceived green politics of intoxication is the basis for renewal. The plant hallucinogens—primarily the tryptamine-containing psilocybin mushrooms, DMT, and the South American brew ayahuasca—are paramount. These naturally occurring representatives of the biosphere function, according to Terence, as "Gaian information centers" capable of imparting the most necessary of global news.

This, of course, is no bulletin to the supposedly primitive elements of humanity. As thousands of years of shamanistic practice reveals, human interaction with plant hallucinogens is often central to the very core of religious expression, or, as Terence puts it, it is "an alchemical pheromone for infusing the devalued profanity of everyday life into a *prima materia* of the sacred."

That's it: The psychedelic is not only nothing to be taken casually, an anonymous pill popped into the mouth at a mall or on the street corner, but it is the very opposite of a recreational drug. Ideally one should have to quest for the psychedelic, go to the ends of the earth, suffer through the black jungle night and raging tropical sun before you're allowed to lay your hands on it. Because it's important. Essential. The key to our continued existence on this spinning rock. The planet knows the mess we're in! It's trying to tell us how to save ourselves!

"Whether the object waiting for us at the end of our historical adventure is the mushroom of Teller, Fermi, and Oppenheimer or the one that grants us entry to the revisioned archaic paradise of the shaman remains to be determined," Terence says with the same engulfing tenor he says everything else. Prohibition of hallucinogens (almost all are listed as Schedule One substances, indicating "no currently accepted medical use"), McKenna maintains, is just one more instance of negative backscatter in the long line of soul-alienating acts perpetrated by the patriarchal "beer and wool" hordes that swept down from the northlands in the late Neolithic. Allying himself with feminist myth-revisionists, Terence asserts that the vanquishing of the earth-based Great Goddess-worshiping societies by male "dominator" tribes has resulted in the adversarial relation to Nature that has lockstepped humanity into a ruinous, fifteen-thousand-year "death march of history" culminating in the Bomb, Auschwitz, eco-disaster, et cetera, et cetera.

For an old pothead, it is a vicarious kick, hearing a guy say it's your sacred birthright—*your duty!*—to get wasted, and if you don't, you are not pulling your weight in the fight against global moral calcification. Terence can be quite the stemwinder when he gets going. An impressive polymath of the off angle, an ever-diligent honer of his own personalized cosmology, one moment he's blizzarding you with left-field references from Meister Eckhart, Teilhard de Chardin, and the great Blake, giving chapter and verse on sci-fi masters like Philip K. Dick (of course) and Alfred Bester, then backtracking to impart how people used to come from miles around just to watch St. Augustine read a book in silence because they'd never seen anyone do it without moving their lips.

Paul Herbert, who's been recording (and marketing) tapes of workshops and lectures at Esalen and has been around for more than thirty years and seen them all, says, "Oh, Terence is a special one. He's more entertaining than Aldous Huxley. Why, he's *twice* as entertaining as Aldous Huxley."

"What I'm offering here is really a very-low-demand program," Terence likes to say. "No one's asking you to give them all your money, or telling you to sweep up around the ashram for ten years and then, maybe, they'll lay a bit of the good on you." No, Terence said, it was the mushroom, psilocybin, and the DMT plant that really were the Way, the democratic, low-cost, 100-percent-natural hope for the future. Right then, it seemed the most marvelous dream. I mean, where could we sign up?

At Esalen, framed by a picture window affording a spectacular view of the sun over the ocean, Terence sat on the floor of a thickly carpeted room wearing an oversized purple sweater and dhoti pants, his bandy legs wrapped into the lotus position. With his thick, rumpled skin loose over a lantern jaw and rowdy helmet of graying hair, he looked to be a very weary harbinger of the next psychedelic revolution. He'd just returned from a two-week tour of Europe, flogging his message across the Continent. He'd arrive in a strange town and never have a problem picking out the individual sent to meet him. "I'd just look for the most insane person. I knew they were waiting for me."

Being the new Timothy Leary can string you out. Everywhere you go, in the supermarket or coffee shoppe, there is always some swirl-eyed skulker pulling on your oversized Irish seaman sweater desperate to discuss their most mind-blowing interface with gelatinous hyperspace amorphs. You come home and the answering machine is clogged with missives from unseen legions pledging undying fealty to "the cause we fight for: enlightenment from the dark." And, of course, everyone wants to turn you on to what they're sure is the greatest single stash in the history of hydroponics, which, of course has its downside. It all starts to run together after a while.

Especially since, to hear Terence tell it, he never asked to be the leader of anything, much less some latter-day psychedelic revival. Leary, after all, was a Harvard professor with gilt-edged connections to various elites. He was a bosom buddy with heiress Peggy Guggenheim, his father was Eisenhower's dentist. Psychedelic stalwarts like Richard Alpert (Ram Dass) and John Lilly (the dolphin-communicating author of *Center of the Cyclone*, also top dog/faker Carlos Castaneda, carry serious academic credentials. Ginsberg and Burroughs were celebrities. McKenna, on the other hand, was a foot soldier in the hippie movement, a small-town doper kid who showed up in Berkeley because he'd heard that was where it was happening, went *wow* when he saw a book of Escher engravings, just like everyone else. It was a decidedly heartland/Beat life pitched against the grand backdrop of the last liberal American era of good feeling. Terence says one of the reasons for the rise of fundamentalism is a reflex for a drowning society to grasp backward to "the last perceived moment of collective sanity." That would also apply to the last moment of collective idealism. Maybe that's the secret to Terence's appeal, the way he emerges from the Reaganist dark ages as a forward-looking redeemer of the treasured, maligned past, the keeper of a certain kind of faith. A freak then, he's a freak now. *Ogga-booga, one of us.*

Plus, for someone who spends most of his time high enough to hunt ducks with a rake, he's surprisingly down to earth. Out of Berkeley, he was living with his wife Kat (whom he met during his "opium-and-cabalist phase" in Jerusalem) and two children in Occidental, a formerly-rural-now-edging-toward-Mercedes-ghetto small town north of San Francisco, their lives "an oasis of happiness" amid the trappings of a Doctor John the Night Tripper–scored sitcom: things like living on a road called the Bohemian Highway (really), driving a 1975 Ford Granada with the license plate NN DMT, which his kids were embarrassed to be seen in, Hindu gurus stopping in unannounced for dinner. Can't you hear it? Disgruntled preteen: "No, I *can't* play, Dad's got me watering the damn *Psychotria viridis*."

This was fine, especially since Terence and Kat had secured a parcel of land on the big island of Hawaii, where they'd established Botanical Dimensions, a garden/farm dedicated to collecting tropical medicinal plants, most particularly those endangered by habitat destruction. But there wasn't any money. "I needed a job and the mushroom gave it to me," Terence explains. Or at least it was all that psilocybin that "turbocharged" his "innate Irish ability to rave" and turned him into "a mouthpiece for the incarnate Logos."

He made his first foray into what Ram Dass calls "the holy man circuit" in the late seventies. Tapes were circulated along with spores guaranteed to grow magic mushrooms. He appeared on underground radio stations, joining such seasoned practitioners of the form as Robert Anton Wilson, Budd Hopkins, and various paganists. Eventually Terence, who refers to his mouth as his "ax," made it to the New Age equivalent of a Catskill comic's big room, joints like Esalen, where he pocketed "about two grand" for his weeklong workshop.

"You go where they'll have you," says Terence with the unfeigned desperation of the freelance wage-earner, flinching at the prospect of running his spiel past still another gaggle of low-end crystal hoarders and past-life analyzers. I mean, he does wear Birkenstocks, but the look on his face as he lines up in the Esalen cafeteria with his bowl, singsonging under his breath, "Oh, tonight we're having veggie stew," tells you that for Terence, the job description "New Age guru" is not a perfect fit. Immediately upon leaving Esalen, he drove like a maniac to a gas station where he bought three Hershey bars and a bag of Doritos.

But as he lurches from the underground, Terence will leave the realm where he can count on running his spiel to rooms of wall-eyed acceptors. Now, he says, "My shit is going to come under *scrutiny*." It is a process that Terence, who has always had a lot of ideas, cracked and not, is familiar with. There was the time McKenna imagined himself on the verge of articulating a theory that would partially refute Newton's work on gravitational force. He brought his findings to Dr. Gunther Stent, a famous molecular biologist at Berkeley's Laboratory of Virology and Bacteriology. The austere Scandinavian professor sat in his leather chair as Terence, holder of only a humble

B.S., and that in a fluky "distributed major" encompassing "ecology, resource conservation, and shamanism," attempted to propound his thesis. After a few moments the professor started fidgeting. "Dr. Stent," McKenna asked, "do you feel this work has any validity or is it simply fallacious?" The professor rose from his chair, walked to the window, and peered through the blinds to the light settling on the Berkeley Hills.

"My dear young friend," the professor sighed in his thick accent, "these ideas are not *even* fallacious."

It's something to consider, this "notion of rejection," Terence says, now sitting in his barely furnished apartment with nothing but a jar of pickles in the refrigerator, a place that smacks much more of the divorced than the monkish. After nearly sixteen years, his marriage is busted up; next week his thirteen-year-old son, Finn, whom he warns off hard drugs but buys Butthole Surfers records for, will move in with him. Even though he obviously is upset about all this and loves his children very much, it's clear that Terence regards much of this unpleasantness as an ingress of the hated commonplace. After all, this is a man who, when his car is rear-ended, starts screaming, "The mundane! Oh, the mundane!"

"We were hippies," Terence shouts, reagitated about his split-up. "Why did we get married in the first place? Hippies weren't supposed to get married! We used to think how wonderful it would be to have two houses, one for each of us. Now we have two houses and it's a catastrophe." Then he says that probably it was "being away from home and on the road" that doomed his relationship. "You know, my missionary zeal."

Beyond invocations of supralinguistical predilections of octopi and reverence for Siberian shamans who drink reindeer pee to get inspired (the animals eat the Amanita mushroom; it only gets stronger in the excrement), Terence finds it "ironic that my current situation is best expressed in a *Peanuts* cartoon . . . Charlie Brown is talking to Lucy or Linus, I can't remember . . . Charlie Brown says, 'When I grow up I want to be a burning-eyed fanatic.'"

Then Terence turns, in that demented zoom-lens way he has, as if he's asking you to finish the unspoken punch line along with him: "And now I am."

To get a sense of the mania at hand, it is instructive to look at *True Hallucinations*, Terence's epic account of the journey he and his younger brother Dennis undertook with three companions to the Amazon in 1971, ostensibly in search of the mythical shamanistic drug of the Witoto, *oo-koo-he*. Many prefer the acoustical McKenna to the typeset version (the sixty-minute lecture is his most arresting form), but as drug narratives go, this one reads like a tortured Tom-and-Huck-on-the-Great-Mother-river saga of brother-bonding. Terence tells how he and Dennis found themselves embroiled in a rising wave of psilocybin and DMT exhilaration that culminated in the Experiment at La Chorrera, so named after a small settlement in the Putumayo jungle. During this time, Terence writes, Dennis became obsessed with the notion that the mushroom offered entry to "the bonded complex of superconductive harmine-psilocybin-DNA" of the planet. Eventually entering "the turbulent maw of the vortex," where he sees "titanic archetypal forms unimagined . . . gibbering abysses touched with the cold of interstellar space," Dennis assumed "the embodiment of all the members of our vast and peculiar Irish family."

It is in this state that the younger McKenna came to believe that he was capable of "electronic-impulse time travel" that gave him the power to make any telephone (in the history of telephones) ring, simply by concentrating on a specific, "undisclosed" image. According to Terence's account, Dennis demonstrated this ability by "mind-dialing" the McKenna brothers' recently deceased mother back in the fall of 1953. "He caught her in the act of listening to Dizzy Dean announcing a World Series game," Terence writes. "She refused to believe he was on the phone as she could see his three-year-old form asleep in the bassinet in front of her."

Dennis (now a respected ethnopharmacologist with a Ph.D. in botany who says he remembers little of these events and "prefers to keep it that way") remained in what normative medical practitioners would likely refer to as a schizophrenic state for nearly two weeks. Terence suggests that his brother was actually undergoing a transformation not unlike the classical mental/spiritual death and rebirth of the shaman. "Because," Terence says now, "that's how I regard my brother, as a modern-day shaman."

Terence's experience at La Chorrera was less antic but equally telling in its own way. He found himself walking through what he imagined to be ground fog only to see the sky begin to "swirl inward like a tornado or waterspout. It was a saucer-shaped machine rotating slowly. It was making the *whee, whee* sound of science-fiction flying saucers."

Despairingly calling his saucer vision hopelessly stereotyped and "already debunked" (how galling it was to come all this way just to see the same stupid spaceships dairy farmers in Tennessee see every other night, especially in comparison to the sublimely original hallucinations cooked up by Dennis's unfettered mind), Terence nevertheless maintains that the thing was there. He writes that "by appearing in a form that casts doubt on what it seemed to be, it achieved a more complete cognitive dissonance than if its seeming alienness were completely convincing." From this he concludes that the experience was "an ecstasy, an *ecstasis* that lasted hours and placed the seal of completion upon all my previous life."

Needless to say, it is somewhat difficult to thumb through *True Hallucinations* as an adventure tale-loving child might devour a gothic hollow earth novel (a favorite genre of the young McKenna). Seven or eight pages at a shot is pretty much the max. Nonetheless, I found McKenna's description of the La Chorrera experiment to be strangely moving. The idea of seeing something all rationality tells you is nothing but an illusion of the pop culture, some preconditioned, prepackaged vision (a goofy B-movie flying saucer: like, *really*) yet being unable to shake the feeling that it is absolutely real—this seemed an eloquent and melancholy assessment of the predicament of modern man in an increasingly technological world. It was as if a twenty-four-year-old Berkeley doper had looked up into the sky, felt a horrible distance between what he hoped for and what was, and then, in an epiphanic instant, sought to draw down this burning, dying thing and hold it to his breast, a knight-errant act aimed at redeeming not only the ridiculousness of the object, but the devalued perceptions of an entire brain-addled species.

It's a funny thing about Terence McKenna, how when you hang around with him, he way manages to touch so many macro-emotional bases. One minute you're laughing because (you think) he's just said the most hilarious thing you've ever heard. The next you're thrown into this kind of blackish Thomas Hardy novel despair over seemingly nothing. In other words, being with Terence McKenna is not unlike the act of dropping some orangish pill handed to you in a club, or even ingesting what the avatar himself calls "the heroic dose" of whatever plant life The Creator in his infinite wisdom and/or sadism has chosen to put on the planet.

In this way, I've come to believe that McKenna, who thinks 150 acid trips are "not that much," has merged with the psychedelic itself. He gets into your head. Not so long after we first met, I had the misfortune to have eaten far too much of a pot-laced brownie, a condition I did not realize until I was already on the rush-hour downtown N train in New York. Claustrophobia was rapidly ingressing. At Twenty-third Street, I was about to jump out of my skin. It took a serious raising of the level of the game to stablize my mentality by the Fourteenth Street station.

It was then I heard Terence's unmistakable drawl broadcasting from somewhere within my neocortex. "Some uneasy moments, huh?" he said.

Fuck yes, some uneasy moments. Spoken like a true trickster, an impish Cheshire cat/ghost in the machine. For, as much as I truly love him, there's a lot about Terence, a lot about "the heroic dose," that makes me nervous. It always has, just as the moment of committing a psychedelic to your gullet is similar to the slow inching of the Cyclone roller coaster up that suicidal first hill. It is a seductive promise, all this enlightenment via the vegetable mind of the planet. But it is a reckless one, too. Talk of some uneasy moments—watching Terence fill up these auditoriums with latter-day would-be psychonauts is enough to make you think about calling up Nancy Reagan and her "your brain on drugs" crew for a little equal time. No one who was around back in the day when guys named STP hawked wares on Telegraph Avenue doesn't have their share of bad memories of those who never quite came back from wherever they went that afternoon in the park. The immutable truth was: This shit wasn't for everybody. When asked about the risks involved in an across-the-board psychedelic program of world-healing, Terence said "Well, of course, there has to be a quotient of self-policing," didn't really calm fears.

These trepidations did not, however, dissuade me from undertaking what would come to be known, at least in our household, as The Experiment on East Seventh Street. This occurred a few weeks after my return from Esalen, at a friend's apartment around the corner from the site of the former Electric Circus. The idea was, in the interests of self-knowledge and journalistic inquiry, to follow one of Terence's regimens and see what happened. To raise the degree of difficulty bar, we eschewed the relatively gentle balm of magic mushrooms and headed straight for the harder stuff. In McKenna's pharmacopoeia, nothing is harder than ayahuasca, a.k.a *yage*, the legendary South American stew once ardently sought by William Burroughs throughout the Amazon. After finally succeeding in ingesting the viscous liquid form of the drug, Burroughs more or less summed up the experience in a poem he sent Allen Ginsberg called "I Am Dying, Meester?"

You see, that's the thing about ayahuasca, it's not like the mushroom, you don't pick it out of the cowpie, thereby entering into direct commerce with the vegetable mind. It is a product of human hands, which opens up any number of tricky possibilities. Down along the malarial banks of the Rio Putumayo in the upper Amazon, the *ayahuasqueros* hack large strips of bark from the *Banisteriopsis caapi*, the massive, harmine-containing woody climber that can extend to one hundred meters, and then beat it with a club until it's soft. The mash is then set in an enameled pot with chacruna (DMT) and a variety of other plants—a millennial muck of the forest itself—and boiled together to render just the right bubbling crude. Richard Evans Schultes, the pioneering Harvard ethnobotanist, says of ayahuasca: "One wonders how people in primitive society, with no knowledge of chemistry or physiology, ever hit upon a solution to the activation of an alkaloid by a monoamine oxidase inhibitor." Clever fuckers, those Putumayan magicians. Bet they knew someday a would-be hepcat like me would come trying to tap into the Gaian info net, then they'd lick their cracked lips and think: Oh, you want something weird? Here's something *really weird*.

So, this time, in between the de rigeur throwing up and toilet bouts, I wasn't under the earth, seeking to pierce the chrysanthemum, hoping to break bread with lovable machine elves. I was in the jungle, my feet cold and clammy, and if I had any concern about the lack of social reality in psychedelic experience, those Indians were about to give me a peek of what it was like to be them. E.g.: how it was to sit by a riverbank, under the impenetrable canopy of the forest, and know it had rained yesterday, it was raining today, that it was going to rain tomorrow morning, and that there was nothing, nothing whatsoever, you could do about it. It is said that one of the psychotropic effects of yage is to create the illusion of a breakdown of the barriers between life and death. It is common for large numbers of interrelated people to take the drug communally, enabling a wholescale reunion with tribal ancestors that enables a sense of cultural continuum between generations. But I was not part of any tribal collective. I was some rootless cosmopolitan in an apartment on the Lower East Side, alone except for my friend who kept playing records I didn't like. In this psychic configuration I had no desire to have the barriers between life and death broken down. Quite the contrary. I was hanging on for dear life to the accoutrements of modern existence, things like my ego, for instance. For sure I wished I hadn't messed with time. Because there I was, as a rain-sodden Indian, on the banks of a river, except now it wasn't a river at all. Now it was the endless stretch of existence, an inexorable continuum that promised nothing beyond the horizon but an eternally indifferent, ever-ticking clock that would go whether I was there to hear it or not.

Also, I knew: *This is it*. That's what I learned from being a jungle-bound Indian, the utter finality of: *This is it*. There isn't anything else. Trying to keep notes during my trip, I wrote "this is it" on a piece of paper several times, although my handwriting is not what you'd call legible. I keep this paper in my wallet as a souvenir. If you would care to see it, I have it right here.

The whole time my fellow traveler kept asking me if I was okay. Apparently I'd been groaning a lot. "It's not as bad as it looks," I told him. That was so. Because my experiment—the nature of which I didn't realize at the time—was a success. I wanted to see if, at forty-four, father of three, I still could weave the psychedelic into my "normal life." Early exit polls were tending in the negative, although I suppose I could have picked a better day, one on which my four-year-old daughter didn't wake up with a 104 temperature and my two-year-old son didn't fall down the steps and bust up his lip.

I was thinking about these matters as I managed to stumble out of my friend's apartment on East Seventh Street after the ayahuasca let up a bit. Along the Putumayo, the shamans dole out the dusky liquid after nightfall, so that's how we did it, according to Terence's prescription. Now it was dawn. My sweatshirt had a brown splotch on it where I'd spilled some of the foul-tasting drug. I held my hand over the stain as if it were some Hawthornian letter. Not that any of the creeps in my neighborhood might notice or care. Anyway, as I got closer to my apartment, I began to get happier. Maybe it was a little like how Dorothy, gone from fabulous Oz and returned to flat, awful, Republican Kansas, was happy. Because I was home, no place else, and this was it. I went around hugging the somewhat nonplussed kids, like Jimmy Stewart at the end of *It's a Wonderful Life*. It was good to be back from the dead.

Then my wife told me this strange thing. Seems that my son had crawled out of his crib in the middle of the night, which he'd never done before, and come into our room. Seeing I wasn't there, he said, "Where Daddy . . . *jungle?*" He'd never said that word before, ever.

How amazing was it that this primeval drug whipped up by South American sorcerers could extend its telepathic range to the Lower East Side of New York, where the brainwaves of a whacked-out Dad could navigate through brick and steel into the tender head of his two-year-old son? Of course I had to call up Terence and tell him about this interesting hyperlinguistical detail of my ayahuasca experience. His response was properly eloquent, befitting the mouthpiece of the incarnate logos.

"Far out," he said.

THE BIG CITY

19

Night Shifting for the Hip Fleet

This story served as the basis for the long-running TV show, Taxi. *I didn't get rich, but Danny DeVito once bought me a sandwich while we talked about his character. Plus I didn't have to go back to cab driving, which is way harder than writing. As predicted, "leasing" did spell the end of the artist/writer cabby. You'll never find someone like me driving an NY taxi now. They're all from Lahore. From* New York *magazine, 1975.*

It has been a year since I last drove a cab, but the old garage still looks the same. The generator is still clanging in the corner. The crashed cars, bent and windshieldless, still lie in the shop like harbingers of a really bad night. The weirdo maintenance guys continue to whistle Tony Bennett songs as they sweep the cigarette butts off the cement floor. The friendly old YOU ARE RESPONSIBLE FOR ALL FRONT-END ACCIDENTS is as comforting as ever. Danny the dispatcher hasn't lost any weight. And all the working stiffs are still standing around, grimy and gummy, sweating and regretting, waiting for a cab at shape-up.

Shape-up time at Dover Taxi Garage #2 still happens every afternoon, rain or shine, winter or summer, from two to six. That's when the nightline drivers stumble into the red-brick garage on Hudson Street in Greenwich Village and wait for the day-liners, old-timers with backsides contoured to the crease in the seat of a Checker cab, to bring in the taxis. The day guys are supposed to have the cabs in by four, but if the streets are hopping they cheat a little bit, maybe by two hours. That gives the nightliners plenty of time to stand around in the puddles on the floor, inhale the carbon monoxide, and listen to the cab stories.

Cab stories are tales of survived disasters. They are the major source of conversation during shape-up. The flat-tire-with-no-spare-on-Eighth-Avenue-and-135th-Street is a good cab story. The no-brakes-on-the-park-transverse-at-fifty-miles-an-hour is a good cab story. The stopped-for-a-red-light-with-teenagers-crawling-on-the-windshield is not too bad. They're all good cab stories if you live to tell about them. A year later the cab stories at Dover sound a little bit more foreboding, not so funny. Sometimes they don't even have happy endings. A year later the mood at shape-up is just a little bit more desperate. The gray faces and burnt-out eyes look just a little bit more worried. And the most popular cab story at Dover these days is the what-the-hell-am-I-doing-here story.

Dover has been called the "hippie garage" ever since the New York freaks who couldn't get it together to split for the Coast decided that barreling through the boogie-woogie on the East River Drive was the closest thing to riding the range. The word got around that the people at Dover weren't as mean or stodgy as at Ann Service, so Dover became "the place" to drive. Now, most of the hippies have either ridden into the sunset or gotten hepatitis, but Dover still attracts a specialized personnel. Hanging around at shape-up today are a college professor, a couple of Ph.D. candidates, a former priest, a calligrapher, a guy who drives to pay his family's land taxes in Vermont, a Romanian discotheque DJ, plenty of M.A.s, a slew of social workers, trombone players, a guy who makes three-hundred-pound sculptures out of solid rock, the inventor of the electric harp, professional photographers, and the usual gang of starving artists, actors, and writers.

It's Hooverville, honey, and there isn't much money around for elephant-sized sculptures, so anyone outside the military-industrial complex is likely to turn up on Dover's night line. Especially those who believed their mother when she said to get a good education so you won't have to shlep around in a taxicab all your life like your Uncle Moe. A college education is not required to drive for Dover—all you have to do is pass a test on which the hardest question is "Where is Yankee Stadium?"—but almost everyone on the night line has at least a B.A.

Shape-up lasts forever. The day-liners trickle in, hand over their crumpled dollars, and talk about the great U-turns they made on Fifty-seventh Street. There are about fifty people waiting to go out. Everyone is hoping for good car karma. It can be a real drag to wait three hours (cabs are first-come, first-served) and get stuck with #99 or some other dog in the Dover fleet. Over by the generator, a guy with long hair who used to be the lead singer in a band called Leon and the Buicks is hollering about the state the city's in.

"The National Guard," he says, "that's what's gonna happen. The National Guard is gonna be in the streets, then the screws will come down." No one even looks up. The guy who says that his family owns half of Vermont is diagnosing the world situation. "Food and oil," he says, "they're the two trump cards in global economics today . . . we have the food, they have the oil, but Iran's money is useless without food; you can't eat money." He is running his finger down the columns of the *Wall Street Journal*, explaining to a couple of chess-playing method actors what to buy and what to sell. A lot of Dover drivers read the *Wall Street Journal*. The rest read the *Times*. Only the mechanics, who make considerably more money, read the *Daily News*.

Leaning up against the pay telephone, a guy wearing a baseball hat and an American-flag pin is talking about the Pelagian Heresies and complaining about St. Thomas Aquinas's bad press. His cronies are laughing as if they know what the Pelagian Heresies are. A skinny guy with glasses who has driven the past fourteen nights in a row is interviewing a chubby day-liner for *Think Slim*, a dieters' magazine he tries to publish in his spare time. The Romanian discotheque DJ is telling people how he plans to import movies of soccer games and sell them for a thousand dollars apiece. He had already counted a half million in profits and gotten himself set up in a Swiss villa by the time Danny calls his number and he piles into #99 to hit the streets for twelve hours.

Some of the old favorites are missing. I don't see the guy with the ski tours. He was an actor who couldn't pay his Lee Strasberg bills and was always trying to sign up the drivers for fun-filled weekends in Stowe. Someone says he hasn't seen the guy for a few months. Maybe he "liberated" himself and finally got to the mountains after all. Maybe he's in a chalet by a brook right now waiting for the first snowfall instead of sweating and regretting at shape-up. Dover won't miss him. Plenty of people have come to take his place.

"I don't look like a cabdriver, do I?" Suzanne Gagne says with a hopeful smile. Not yet. Her eyes still gleam—they aren't fried from too many confrontations with the oncoming brights on the Queensboro Bridge. Suzanne, a tall woman of twenty-nine with patched blue jeans, is a country girl from the rural part of Connecticut. Her father gave her a car every time she graduated from somewhere, so she has three different art degrees. When school got tiresome, she came to New York to sell her "assemblages" ("I don't care for the word collage") in the SoHo galleries. There weren't many immediate takers, rent was high, Dad and his bankbook had split for Europe with his mistress, so now Suzanne drives for Dover several nights a week.

A year ago or so, any woman hanging out at shape-up was either waiting to report a driver for stealing her pocketbook, a Dover stiff's girlfriend, or some sort of crazy cabdriver groupie. In those days the two or three women who were driving were banned from the night line, which is notably unfair because you can make a lot more money with a lot less traffic driving at night. Claire, a longtime Dover driver, challenged the rule and won; now fifteen women drive for Dover, most on the night line. There are a lot of reasons why. "I'm not pushing papers anymore," says Sharon, a calligrapher and former social worker who drove for Dover until recently. "I can't hack advertising."

Sharon says many more women will be driving soon because women artists need the same kind of loose schedule that has always attracted their male counterparts to cabdriving. At Dover you can show up whenever you want and work as many days as you can stand. Besides, she says, receptionist and typist positions, the traditional women's subsistence jobs, are drying up along with the rest of the economy. The women at Dover try not to think about the horrors of the New York Night. "You just have to be as tough as everyone else," Sharon says. But since Suzanne started driving, the artwork she used to do in two or three days is taking weeks.

"I'm tired a lot," she says, "but I guess I'm driving a cab because I just can't think of anything else to do."

Neither can Don Goodwin. Until a while ago he was president of the Mattachine Society, one of the oldest and most respected of the gay-liberationist groups. He went around the country making speeches at places like Rikers Island. But now he twirls the ends of his handlebar moustache and says, "There's not too much money for movements, movements are *ga-stunk*."

Don sometimes daydreams in his cab. He thinks about how he used to dress windows for Ohrbach's and how he loved that job. But his salary got too high and now he can't get another window-dresser's job. Don offered to take a cut in pay but "in the window-dressing business they don't like you to get paid less than you got paid before, even if you ask for it. Isn't that odd?" Now Don's driving seven days a week because "after window-dressing and movements, I'm really not skilled to do anything else."

A driver I know named David is worried. David and I used to moan cab stories to each other when I was on the night line. Now he keeps asking me when I'm coming to work. After four years of driving a cab, he can't believe interviewing people is work. David is only a dissertation away from a Ph.D. in philosophy, which makes him intelligent enough to figure out that job openings for philosophers are zilch this year. The only position his prodigious education has been able to land him was a twenty-five-dollar-a-night, one-night-a-week gig teaching ethics to rookie cops. David worked his way through college driving a cab. It was a good job for that, easy to arrange around things that were important. Now he has quit school in disgust and arranges the rest of his life around cabdriving. He has been offered a job in a warehouse for which he'd make $225 a week and never have to pick up another person who has a crowbar stuffed into his pants, but he's not going to take it. When you're zooming around the city, there's an illusion of mobility.

The turnover at the garage (Dover has over 500 employees for the 105 taxis; it hires between five and ten new people a week) makes it easy to convince yourself this is only temporary. Working in a factory is like surrender, like defeat, like death; drudging nine to five doesn't fit in with a self-conception molded on marches to Washington. Now David's been at Dover for the past two years and he's beginning to think cab freedom is just another myth.

"I'll tell you when I really started to get scared," David says. "I'm driving down Flatbush and I see a lady hailing, so I did what I normally do, cut across three lanes of traffic and slam on the brakes right in front of her. I wait for her to get in, and she looks at me like I'm crazy. It was only then I realized I was driving my own car, not the cab."

David has the Big Fear. It doesn't take a cabdriver too long to realize that once you leave the joy of shape-up and start uptown on Hudson Street, you're fair game. You're at the mercy of the Fear Variables, which are (not necessarily in order): the traffic, which will be in your way; the other cabdrivers, who want to take your business; the police, who want to give you tickets; the people in your cab, lunatics who will peck you with nudges and dent you with knives; and your car, which is capable of killing you at any time. Throw in your bosses and the hack inspectors and you begin to realize that a good night is not when you make a living wage. That's a great night. A good night is when you survive to tell your stories at tomorrow's shape-up.

But all the Fear Variables pall before the Big Fear.

The Big Fear is that times will get so hard that you'll have to drive five or six nights a week instead of three. The Big Fear is that your play, the one that's only one draft away from a possible showcase, will stay in your drawer. The Big Fear is thinking about all the poor stiff civil servants who have been sorting letters at the post office ever since the last Depression and all the great plays they could have produced. The Big Fear is that, after twenty years of schooling, they'll put you on the day shift. The Big Fear is, you're becoming a cabdriver.

The typical Big Fear cabdriver is not to be confused with the archetypal Cabby. At least in the movies, The Cabby is a genuine New York City romantic hero. He's what every out-of-towner who's never been to New York thinks every Big Apple driver is like. The Cabby "owns his own," which means the car he drives is his, not owned by some garage boss

(58 percent of New York's 11,787 taxis are owned by "fleets" like Dover, which employ the stiffs and the slobs of the industry; the rest are operated by "owner-drivers"). The Cabby hated Lindsay even before the snowfalls, has dreams about blowing up gypsy cabs, knows where all the hookers are (even in Brooklyn), slurps coffee and downs Danish at the Bellmore Cafeteria, tells his life story to everyone who gets into the cab, and makes a ferocious amount of money. Sometimes he might even, accidentally on purpose, take an unsuspecting passenger to the Bronx by way of Staten Island (leading one such driver to say, "One day they'll put my picture on TV and every little old lady in New York will shout: *That's him!*) But for the most part, The Cabby is the genuine article, a Big City staple. As much as he complains, he really loves his work.

The Dover driver just doesn't fit this mold. He probably would have voted for Lindsay twice if he had had the chance. He doesn't care about gypsies; if they want the Bronx, let them have it. He knows only about the hookers on Lexington Avenue. He has been to the Bellmore maybe once and had a stomachache the rest of the night. He speaks as little as possible and barely makes enough to get by. He also hates his work.

The first fare I ever had was an old bum who threw up in the backseat. I had to drive around for hours in miserable weather with the windows open trying to get the smell out. That started my career of cabbing and crabbing. In the beginning, before I became acquainted with the Big Fear and all its attendant anxieties, the idea was to drive three days a week, write three, and party one. That began to change when I realized I was only clearing about twenty-seven dollars a ten-hour shift.

There are remedies. The nine-hour shift stretches to twelve and fourteen hours. You start ignoring red lights and stop signs to get fares, risking collisions. You jump into cab lines when you think the other cabbies aren't looking, risking a punch in the nose. You're amazed at what you'll do for a dollar. But mostly you steal.

If you don't look like H. R. Haldeman and take taxis often, you've probably been asked by a cabdriver if it's "okay to make it for myself." The passenger says yes, the driver sets a fee, doesn't turn on the meter, gets the whole fare for himself, and that's stealing. Stealing ups your Fear

Variables immeasurably. You imagine hack inspectors and company-hired "rats" all around you. Every Chevy with blackwall tires becomes terror on wheels. The fine for being caught is $25, but that's nothing—most likely you will be fired from your garage and no one will hire you except those places in Brooklyn with cars that have fenders held on with hangers and brake pedals that flap. But you know that if you can steal, say $12 a night, you'll have to drive only three nights this week instead of four and maybe you'll be able to finish that play, which some producer will love to death and this will lead to that, and you'll be hobnobbing at the Public Theatre in no time.

Well, you can dream, as long as you don't start dreaming in the middle of traffic on the BQE. What you want to avoid are the premonitions. Nothing is as bad as a cabdriver premonition. Sometimes a driver would not show up at Dover shape-up for a couple of days and when he came in he'd say, "I didn't drive because I had a premonition." A premonition is knowing that the Manhattan Bridge is going to fall in the next time you drive over it and thinking about whether it would be better to hit the river with the windows rolled up or down.

On a job where there are so many different ways to die, premonitions are not to be discounted. Of course, a smile would lighten everything, but since the installation of the partition that's supposed to protect you and your money from a nuclear attack, cabdriving has become a morose job. The partition locks you in the front seat with all the Fears. You know the only reason the thing is there is because you have to be suspicious of everyone on the other side of it. It also makes it hard to hear what people are saying to you, so it cuts down on the wisecracking. The partition has killed the lippy cabby. Then again, you can always talk to yourself, and most Dover drivers do.

When I first started driving, cabbies who wanted to put a little kink into their evening would line up at a juice bar where they gave Seconals along with the Tropicana. The hope was that some Queens cutie would be just messed up enough to make "the trade." But the girl usually wound up passing out somewhere around Francis Lewis Boulevard, and the driver would have to wake her parents up to get the fare. Right now the hot line is at the Eagle's Nest underneath the West Side Highway. The Nest and other nearby bars like Spike's and the Nine Plus Club are the hub of New York's flourishing leather scene. On a good night, dozens of men dressed from hat to boots in black leather and rivets walk up and down the two-block strip and come tumbling out of the "Tunnels," holes in the highway embankment, with their belts off. Cabdrivers with M.A.s in history will note a resemblance to the Weimar Republic, another well-known Depression society.

Dover drivers meet in the Eagle's Nest line after 2 A.M. almost every night. The Nest gives free coffee, and many of the leather boys live on the Upper East Side or in Jersey, both good fares, so why not? After the South Bronx, this stuff seems tame. Besides, it's fun to meet the other stiffs. Who else can you explain the insanity of the past nine hours of your life to? It cuts away some of the layers of alienation that have been accumulating all night.

Big Fear cabdrivers try to treat each other tenderly. It's a rare moment of cab compassion when you're deadheading it back from Avenue R and you hear someone from the garage shouting "Do-ver! Do-ver!" as he limps out to Coney Island. It's nice, because you know he's probably another out-of-work actor-writer stiff like you, lost in the dregs.

So it figures that there is a strong feeling of "solidarity forever" in the air at Dover. The Taxi Rank and File Coalition, the "alternative" cab union in town (alternative to Harry Van Arsdale's all-powerful and generally despised Local 3036), has been trying to organize the Dover drivers. Ever since I started cabbing, Rank and Filers have been snickered at by most drivers as Commies, crazy radical hippies, and worse. A lot of this was brought on by the Rank and File people themselves, who used to go around accusing old-timers of being part of the capitalist plot to starve babies in Vietnam. This type of talk does not go over too big at the Bellmore.

Now Rank and File has toned down its shill and is talking about more tangible things like the plight of drivers in the face of the coming Depression, and members are picking up some scattered support in the industry.

Dover, naturally, is their stronghold; Van Arsdale's people have just about given the garage up for lost. Suzanne Gagnes wears a Rank and File button. Suzanne says, "It's not that I'm a left-wing radical or anything. I just think it's good that we stick together in a situation like this."

Last winter a bitter dispute arose over an incident in which a Dover driver returned a lost camera and the garage allegedly pocketed the forthcoming reward money. The Rank and File leaders put pressure on the company to admit thievery. The garage replied by firing the shop chairman, Tom Robbins, and threatening the rest of the committee. Tempers grew very hot; petitions to "Save the Dover 6" were circulated. Robbins appealed to the National Labor Relations Board, but no action was taken. There was much talk of a general strike, but Rank and File, surveying the strength of their hardcore membership, decided against it. Now they have another NLRB suit against Dover and the Van Arsdale union for what they claim is a blacklist against Robbins, who has been turned down in attempts to get a job at twenty different garages in the city.

Gerry Cunningham, who is the boss at Dover, says Rank and File doesn't bother him. "You'd figure there would be a lot of those types here, the way I see it. Big unions represent the median sort of guy, so you'd figure that with the general type of driver we have here, there would be a lot of Rank and File. Look, though, I'm not particularly interested in someone's religion as long as he produces a day's work. If the drivers feel a little togetherness, that's fine with me."

Gerry, a well-groomed guy with a big Irish face, is sifting through a pile of accident reports and insurance claims in his trailer-office facing Hudson Street. It seems like all cab offices are in trailers or temporary buildings; it's a transient business. This is the first time, after a year of driving for Dover, that I've ever seen Gerry Cunningham. I used to cash the checks too fast to notice that he signed them. Cunningham smiles when he hears the term "hippie garage."

"Oh, I don't mind that," he says. "We have very conscientious drivers here. We have more college graduates here than any other group. . . . I assume they're having trouble finding other work." Gerry is used to all the actors and writers pushing around Dover hacks and thinks some of them make good drivers and some don't. "But I'll tell you," he says, "of all the actors we've ever had here, I really can't think of one who ever made it."

Well, thanks for the support, Gerry, baby! Not that Cunningham should care. He says he's got his own problems. "Owning taxis used to be a great business," he says. "But now we're getting devoured. In January of 1973, I was paying 31 cents for gas, now I'm paying 60. *Sixty cents!* I'm barely breaking even here. It costs me $12.50 just to keep a car on the streets for twenty-four hours. Gas is costing almost as much as it costs to pay the drivers.

Fleets like Dover are in trouble. They were the ones who pressed for the 17.5 percent fare rise and still say it's not enough to offset spiraling gas costs, car depreciation, and corporate taxes. Some big fleets like Scull's Angels and Ike-Stan, which employ hundreds of drivers, are selling out; many more are expected to follow. There is a lot of pressure for change. The *New York Times* has run editorials advocating a major reshaping of the industry, possibly with all cabs being individually owned.

According to Cunningham, president of the M.T.B.O.T (the Metropolitan Taxicab Board of Trade, which represents the fleets), the future is "leasing," a practice the gypsy cab companies have always used. "Leasing means," Cunningham says, "I lease my cars out to drivers for about two hundred dollars a week. That way only one man drives the car instead of the six or seven, the car lasts much longer, and you cut away a good deal of the maintenance and things like that."

One thing that Cunningham does not mention is while "leasing" will be great for the owners, who will be pocketing their $200 up front (and leaving all the financial risk to the drivers), it will spell disaster for the bohemian cabdriver. Cunningham says the "part-time driver" can always "sublet" taxis if they can't come up with the $200.

Every driver who ever had the Big Fear knows the lie in that. The Dover-style driver, people who don't work when the painting is going well or a premonition sets in, are not going to sublet. Subletting an apartment is commitment enough. The whole idea of driving for places like Dover, driving a cab at all, is the flex, the shiftlessness option. The topic is much in the air, and a couple days later some drivers who are really actors and musicians are talking about leasing while waiting in line at the La Guardia lot.

"What a drag leasing would be," says an actor who has only twelve dollars on the meter after four hours out of the garage. "If that happens, I don't know, I'll try to get a waiter's job, I guess."

"Yeah man, that'll be a bitch all right," says the musician. "I hate this goddamn job. Hey, I'd rather be playing, but right now I'm making a living in this cab. I won't dig it if they take it away from me. Damn, if the city had any jobs I'd be taking the civil service test." He sits there a moment amid the garage clatter and shouts, "Then I can be a sanitation guy like my dad. And how great will that be?"

20
Ghost Shadows on the Chinatown Streets

The compelling saga of Nicky Louie, leader of the Ghost Shadows youth gang, which for a brief and bloody time in the 1970s ruled about two hundred yards of sidewalk in New York City's Chinatown. A thousand years of history crushed into an immigrant story. A personal favorite. From the Village Voice, *1977.*

Midnight in Chinatown, everyone seems nervous. The old waiters look both ways before going into the gambling joint on Pell Street. Ladies bleary from a ten-hour day working over sewing machines in the sweatshops are hurrying home, and restaurants, usually open until four in the morning, are closing early. At the Sun Sing Theatre on East Broadway, underneath a hand-painted poster of a bleeding kung fu hero, a security guard is fumbling with a padlock. Ask him how business is and he shakes his head, "No good." Ask him why and he points his finger right between your eyes and says, "Bang!"

"Low Tow," which is what the Cantonese call New York's Chinatown, is on edge. A couple of blocks away, in front of the coffee shop at 56 Mott Street, Nicky Louie, the twenty-two-year-old leader of the Ghost Shadows street gang, and personification of much of the neighborhood's recent anxiety, looks no less relaxed. Pacing up and down the ruddy sidewalk in his customary green army fatigue jacket, Nicky has good reason to be watchful. It is only Wednesday, and according to the cops, there have already been two separate assassination attempts on Louie's life this week. Facing such heat, most gang leaders would stay inside and play a few hands of Chinese thirteen-card poker. Or maybe leave town altogether, go up to Toronto or out to Chicago. But not Nicky. When you are the leader of the Shadows, with so much money and turf at risk, it is a matter of face to show your face. You've got to let them know—all those other twenty-two-year-old killers—that Mott Street is yours. Yours and yours alone.

Born Hin Pui Lui in the slums of Hong Kong's Kowloon district, Nicky came to Low Tow in the late 1960s. The old Chinatown people called America "Gum Shan," which means Gold Mountain. But Nicky arrived on a 747 rather than a boat and is a different kind of immigrant. Older neighborhood residents might be content to work out their tiny sliver of the so-called American Dream serving up bowls of *yat kaw mein* to Queens tourists, but Nicky had different ideas. No way he would end up a faceless waiter headed for the TB ward. He was born for greater things. When he first got into the gangs half a dozen years ago, first as a foot soldier in the penny-ante protection rings, selling firecrackers to the undershirt-clad Italians on the other side of Canal Street, people say Nicky already had the biggest set of balls in Chinatown. He was the gun-wielding wild man, always up for action, willing to do anything to get attention. His big break came in the winter of 1973, when the Shadows' first chief, twenty-four-year-old Nei Wong, got caught with a Hong Kong cop's girlfriend. The cop, in New York for a surprise visit, ran across Wong and his betrothed in the Chinese Quarter Nightclub beneath the approach ramp to the Manhattan Bridge and blew off both their heads with his police revolver.

Since then Nicky's rise in the Chinatown youth gang world has been startling. He has piloted the once ragtag Shadows from the bleak days when they were extorting a few free meals and dollars from the greasy spoons over on East Broadway to their current haunt, Mott Street, Low Tow's main drag, in other words, the big time.

Controlling Mott Street means that the Shadows get to affiliate themselves with the On Leong tong, the richest and most influential organization ("tong" means association or organization) in Chinatown. In addition to securing the protection racket on Mott, the gang also gets to guard the gambling houses the On Leong operates in the musty lofts and basements along Mott and Bayard Streets, some of them taking in as much as seventy-five thousand dollars a week. The Shadows also act as runners in the Chinatown Connection heroin trade, bringing the stuff across the Canadian border and spreading it throughout New York. The money filters down to Nicky and his lieutenants; they filter the spoils down to the younger Shadows.

For Nicky this adds up to a weekly check that ranges from $200 to $2,000 depending on who you talk to. In any event, it's enough to buy a swift $7,000 Peugeot to tool down Canal Street in.

But tongs are fickle. If another group of Hong Kong teenagers—say their archenemy the White Eagles or the hard-charging Flying Dragons, who bide their time taking target practice on the pigeons down by the East River—should show the On Leong that they're smarter or tougher than the Shadows, Nicky's boys could be gone tomorrow.

No one knows this better than Nicky Louie. Two years ago Nicky and the Shadows pushed the surly Eagles off the street. In September, after licking their wounds over in Brooklyn and down in Florida, the Eagles with their leader Paul Ma—Nicky's main rival—returned. And they were not going to be satisfied with crummy Elizabeth Street. Soon the Eagles started appearing on Bayard Street, part of Shadowland. Paul Ma set up his own gambling house on the block; a direct affront to Nicky.

Several weeks ago the Shadows struck back, shooting a bunch of Eagles, including Paul Ma and a gang member's wife, in front of Yuen Yuen Snack Shop on Bayard Street. This set off the most hair-raising month of streetfighting in Chinatown history; no weekend went by without a major incident. The infamous Wong Kee chop-chop was the highlight of the war. According to cops, the Shadows, including Nicky himself, crashed through the door of the Wong Kee Rice Shop on the Italian end of Mott and carved up one Eagle with chef's kitchen cleavers and stabbed another with a fork.

Everyone figures the Eagles will try some kind of revenge, which is the major reason, people say, Nicky has spent the past two weeks pacing up and down in front of 56 Mott. His presence keeps things cool. In the long history of Chinese crime, a saga which goes back at least to the founding of the thousand year triad 14K, Nicky Louie is the newest legend. He is, as they say, no one to fuck with.

Fifty years ago, chances are Nicky might have been lying around the "joss houses" and streetfighting alongside the hatchetmen and gunmen of Chinatown's "tong wars." In those days, the two big tongs, the On Leong and the Hip Sing of Pell Street, battled on the sidewalks over the few available women and the opium trade, out of sheer boredom. Back then there were legendary *boo hoy dow* (warriors): like Mock Dock, the great gambler known as "the Philosophical Killer," and Yee Toy, "the Girl-Faced Killer." Most famous of all, however, was the plain-faced Sing Dock, "the Scientific Killer." Once, after hearing of an outbreak of war in New York, he rode in the baggage compartment of a train (Chinese weren't allowed to ride up front) for six weeks from San Francisco. That was when Pell Street was called "Red Street" and the crook on Doyers Street was known as "the Bloody Angle."

Today the Chinatown warrior has changed. The young gangs are not respected tong members, as Sing Dock was. Like most late-twentieth-century gangs, they're in for the bucks and the fact that none of them can figure out what else to do with their lives, especially considering the dismal choices confronting those entering the fiscal crisis job market with little or no English-language skills. There is also the whole style thing. Nicky and the Shadows have eschewed tong warrior black overcoats in favor of pegged pants and puffy hairdos. (Asked if their hair is a Hong Kong fashion, one gang member said, "No, man, it's cause we dig Rod the Mod, man." Meaning Rod Stewart.) In this world everyone must have a good nickname, a *nom de street guerre*. Hanging with Nicky tonight are old-time Shadows "Mongo," the wild-man enforcer who got his name from *Blazing Saddles*, and "Japanese," who shaved his head after he heard that things might go easier for him in jail if he looked like a "Muslim." There are some guys with grade-B movie monickers like Lefty and Four-Eyes, but most of the kids go for names like "Stinkybug," "White-Faced Tiger," "Pointy Lips," "Porkupine," and "Nigger Choy." There must be twenty kids called "Apple Head" running around Chinatown.

Strangely enough, the Ghost Shadows themselves got their unbeatable name from that bastion of street culture, the *New York Times*. It happened about four years ago when the Shadows were functioning as the "junior auxiliary" of the now-defunct Kwon Ying gang of Pell Street. A *Times* reporter was in Chinatown to cover an incident in which some of the young Kwon Ying were involved. The reporter wanted to know what "Kwon Ying" meant. (It means "not the Eagles," a reference to the rival gang, the White Eagles.) One wiseguy—likely an Eagle—said, "It means ghost shadow." This, unbeknownst to the *Times* reporter or just about any white person, was a terrible insult. Proceeding from the metaphor that a bamboo stalk is empty in the middle, Chinatown residents have long called white people *bak guey*, meaning a white piece of empty bamboo, or, more derogatorily, a "white ghost." Blacks are called *hak guey*, meaning "black ghost." The gist is that these people are incomplete—not all there. Being a "ghost shadow" went double. The *Times* reporter dutifully filed "ghost shadow" with his copy. The next morning, after reading about themselves in the paper, Nicky Louie and the rest of the Ghost Shadows decided they liked their new name. It was so born to lose.

Yet through all this posturing nomenclature, Nicky has no nickname. He remains, simply, Nicky.

Some say Nicky has nine lives. The estimates of how many slugs he carries around inside his chest vary. According to an ex-gang member, "When he turns over at night, he can hear them bullets clank together."

Last May teenage hitmen from the San Francisco–based Wah Ching gang flew across the country just to kill Nicky. Some say it was an Eagle contract. For whatever reason they pumped a dozen bullets into the middle of a Saturday afternoon shopping crowd on Mott Street while Nicky disappeared across Canal Street. The Chings missed everyone and wound up getting pinched by two drug cops who just happened to be eating won ton in the nearby Joy Luck Restaurant.

The *ging cha* (police) have arrested Nicky for everything from robbery to extortion to murder to rape, but he's never been convicted.

Detective Neal Mauriello, who is assigned full-time to the Fifth Precinct's Chinese gang section, is a smart cop. He realizes he's got a crazy and hopelessly complicated job. Chinatown gangs aren't like the bruisers fighting over street corners and ghetto reps up in the Bronx. There's piles of money, history, and politics behind what Nicky and his guys are doing. And since it's Chinatown, they'd rather do it quietly—which is why the Shadows don't wear dungaree coats with hard-on things like SAVAGE SKULLS emblazoned on the back.

Neal makes it his business to memorize all the faces on Mott Street. He also writes down the names and birthdays of the gang members so he can walk down Mott Street and say, "Hey, happy birthday Pipenose; seen Dice around?" This blows the gang members' minds, Mauriello says. "Because, the world they live in, a Chinese guy is supposed to be invisible. They're supposed to all look alike. That's what we think, right? Well, they know that and that gives them a feeling of safety, like the whities have no idea who we are. I try to break through that curtain. It freaks them out."

About Nicky Louie, Neal, with typical cop insouciance, says, "That kid is okay really. But I've been chasing him for five years and I'll nail him. He knows it, too. We talk about it all the time." Neal remembers the time he came upon Nicky lying facedown in a pool of blood near the Bowery. He said, "Nicky, come on, you're gonna die, tell me who shot you." Nicky looked up at Neal, his eyes blazing arrogance, and said, "Fuck you."

"That's Nicky," said Mauriello, shaking his head with a smile, because what else can you say or do when confronted with someone who lives his ethic to the end like that? (Of course, Louie would survive his wounds and be back on the streets within weeks.) It is more than that, because, as Mauriello, from an immigrant culture himself, says, "That's not just Nicky Louie, some kid gangster telling me to fuck myself. There's a lot of history behind that 'fuck you.'"

Toy Shan is a village in the mountainous region of Canton from which the great majority of those who settled New York's Chinatown came in the mid-1800s. It's possible that this Toy Shan settlement in New York was as closed a community as has ever existed in urban America. Much of this is bounded in mutual racism, including the horrendous series of "exclusion acts" that severely limited Chinese immigration to the United States for the better part of a century.

Probably the most draconian of these "yellow peril" fear laws prohibited immigration of Chinese women to the U.S. Males were allowed, in small numbers, to enter the country to maintain existing businesses. But they could not raise families or live anything approaching a normal life. Chinatowns became essentially male-only gulags of indentured restaurant workers and the like. By the 1940s, when the laws finally began to ease, the ratio of men to women in Chinatown ranged as high as ten to one. The havoc these laws wreaked on the Toy Shan consciouness is difficult to overestimate. Drinking and gambling, both venerable Chinese passions, became endemic. Apart from the neighborhood gambling dens where one could lose a month's pay in an hour of fan tan playing, Chinese faces became familiar at the city's racetracks—probably the only place they were, outside restaurants and laundries—which prompted wags to dub the Belmont subway special "the Shanghai Express." Prostitutes from uptown were frequent visitors to Toy Shan back then. Chatham Square was one of the best nonhotel beats in the city. "The money's always been good down there," said one current lady of the night. "They come in, say nothing because they can't speak English, shoot their load, and go."

It was a society within a society, not that most of the Toy Shans were complaining. They were not eager to mingle with the people they called *lo fan* (foreign devils) in any event. Determined to survive, they built an extralegal society based on furtive alliances, police bribes, creative bookkeeping, and immigration scams. The aim was to remain invisible and separate. To this day, few people in Chinatown are known by their real names; most received new identities—such as the Lees, Chins, and Wongs—from the family associations, who declared them "cousins" in order to get them into the country.

In place of the "Western government," they substituted the Chinese Consolidated Benevolent Association (CCBA), an organization to which the neighborhood's sixty-five-odd family and merchant associations belong. To this day every other president of the CCBA has to be a Toy Shan descendant.

In reality, it was the tongs, Hip Sing and On Leong, Chinatown's so-called "night mayors," who dominated much of the economic and social power in the neighborhood. They controlled the illegal activities in a community where everyone felt outside the law. Their spokesmen, with hatchetmen behind them, grew in power at the CCBA. Between themselves, they struck a parity that still holds. On Leong has always had more money and connections, mostly owing to their ongoing relationship with Chiang Kai-shek's Kuomintang Party, which has ruled Taiwan since its expulsion from the mainland by Mao's victorious communist army in 1949. The more proletarian-minded Hip Sing, which is known as "the friend of the seaman" for its ability to sneak Chinese off boats and into waiter jobs, has more members and branches throughout the U.S.

But in 1965 the Toy Shan traditions were seriously threatened. Federal laws were altered to allow open Chinese immigration to this country. Since then more than two hundred thousand Hong Kong residents have emigrated to America, with more coming all the time. Half settled in the New York area.

Chinatown is in the midst of a gut-wrenching change. The population is edging toward seventy-five thousand, a fivefold increase since the law change. It's one of the fastest-growing neighborhoods in New York and without a doubt the most densely populated. Once confined to the familiar pentagon bounded by Canal Street, Worth, and the Bowery, Chinatown is now sprawling all over the Lower East Side. Already Mott Street—above Canal up to Grand, once solidly Italian—is 70 percent Chinese. To the east, Division Street and East Broadway, formerly Jewish and Puerto Rican, have become centers of Chinese business and residence. Smaller Chinatowns have begun to appear in Flushing, Queens, and parts of Brooklyn.

Transition is underway. On one hand a good deal of the old Toy Shan separatism remains. Most Chinatown residents do not vote; currently there are fewer than three thousand registered voters in the area. In marked contrast to the Asian community in California, no Oriental has ever held major office in New York. The Chinatown Democratic Club has been repeatedly busted as a gambling house. Chinatown activists say this neglect is responsible for the compromised stand in the zoning fight with the Little Italy Restoration Association, which is seeking to ward off the Chinese influx and zone large portions of the area for the dwindling Italian population.

Yet changes are everywhere. Chinatown now functions for Chinese; it looks like Hong Kong. Investigate the brand-new Silver Palace Restaurant on the Bowery—it breaks the mold of the cramped, no-atmosphere Chinatown restaurant. An escalator whisks you up to a dining room as big as a football field. Almost all the thousand or so people eating there will be Chinese, many middle-class couples who've motored in from Queens to try a more adventurous version of Cantonese food than this city is accustomed to. (Many Chinese will tell you that the "exotic" Szechuan and Hunan food is "American" fare.)

The mass migration has transformed Chinatown into an odd amalgam of boomtown and ghetto. Suddenly half the businesses here are no longer in the hands of the old *lo fa kew*, the Cantonese Toy Shans. In their place have come Hong Kong entrepreneurs and Taiwanese investors, who are fearful about the future of their island. A Taiwanese combine, the Summit Import Corporation, has already done much to change shopping habits in Chinatown by opening two big supermarkets, Kam Wah on Baxter Street and Kam Kuo on Mott.

The Taiwanese money is an indication that even though the Nationalists appear on the verge of international political eclipse, their influence in American Chinatowns, especially New York, is on the rise. A Taiwan concern is also behind the proposed block-long Golden Pacific National Bank on Canal Street. It's one of the several new banks opening in this neighborhood of compulsive savers. The gold rush, prodded by extraordinary greed, has pushed real estate values here to fabled heights as Taiwanese businessmen seek to hide capital in the U.S. The defeat of South Vietnam, where Chinese interests controlled much of the economy, has brought untold millions into the local market. According to Mott Street scuttlebutt, the day Saigon fell, three Chinese restaurants were supposedly purchased in Chinatown. Tumbledown warehouses on East Broadway are going for Upper East Side prices.

All this has the Toy Shan powers hanging on for dear life. The newcomers, filtered through Hong Kong, come from all over China. The old Toy Shan loyalties don't apply. These people got here without the help of the associations and owe them little. The tongs and the CCBA are beginning to feel the crunch. They've begun to see more and more store owners break away. Suddenly there are publicly funded social service agencies, most prominently the Chinatown Planning Council, to challenge CCBA rulings. And the younger Chinese, sons and daughters of the *lo fa kew,* have been openly critical.

But one hundred years of power isn't something you give up without a fight. Recently the CCBA held a meeting to discuss what to do about Nicky Louie and his Ghost Shadow buddies shooting up the neighborhood. Chinatown has traditionally been one of the safest areas in the city. Crime figures are remarkably low here for a place with so many new immigrants. That's what made the recent violence all the more shocking. Especially in a neighborhood so dependent on tourism. Although the battles were being waged among the various Shadows, Dragons, and Eagles around, merchants were reporting a 30 percent drop in business. Places that stayed open late were doing even worse.

The streetfighting is "disfiguring" Chinatown, said one merchant, referring to the April shootout at the Co-Luck Restaurant on the Bowery. That night, according to the cops, a couple of Shadows roared up in a late-model blue Ford, smashed through the glass door, and started spraying .32 automatic slugs in the general direction of some Dragons who were *yum cha* (drinking tea and talking) in the corner. One of the Dragons, who may not have been a Dragon at all, got clipped in the leg. For the rest of the people in the restaurant, it was grimmer. By the time the Shadows were through, they had managed to hit three New York University law students, a waiter, and a lady from Queens who later died on the floor, her daughter crying over her body. The cops said, "The place looked like a slaughterhouse; there was blood all over the linoleum."

Since then Co-Luck has been considered bad luck for prospective buyers. It remains vacant, rare in a neighborhood where no storefront is empty for long. On the door is a sign: CLOSED FOR ALTERATIONS.

"Perhaps we keep it that way," said a merchant, "as a scar to remind us of our shame."

Restaurant owners say there won't be so many wedding banquets this summer because of an incident in the Hung Gung Restaurant a few months ago. Gang members crashed the banquet hall, stationing sentries outside to make sure no one came or went, and instructed a hundred celebrants to drop their valuables into shopping bags. "It was just like the Wild West," says someone close to the wedding guests.

The police don't see things looking up. In October they made sixty gang-related arrests, the most ever in a single month. They say there are more guns on the street than ever before and estimate gang membership—before the recent crackdown—at about two hundred, an all-time high. The gang kids are younger, too—fourteen-year-olds from Junior High School 65 are common these days.

Pressured by editorials in the Chinese press, the CCBA swung into action. It called a public gathering at which the community would be free to explain its plight to Manhattan district attorney Robert M. Morganthau.

This was quite a change in tactics for the CCBA. Until quite recently one of its major functions had been to keep the lid on Chinatown's considerable and growing urban problems. The fact that Chinese women sew garments for twelve cents apiece, that more than one-third of the area's males work as waiters (toiling as much as sixteen hours a day, seven days a week), that Chinatown has the highest rate of TB and mental illness among city neighborhoods—all that was dirty linen better kept under wraps. But Nicky and the Shadows, they make noise. They get picked up for killing people and get their sullen pictures in what the Chinese still call "the Western press." Keeping that quiet can make you look awfully silly, such as when Joseph Mei, the CCBA vice president, told the *New York Times*, "We have no problem at all about youth gangs in Chinatown," the day after Nicky's people allegedly shot five White Eagles in front of the Yuen Yuen Snack Shop.

The meeting was held in the CCBA's dank auditorium (underneath an alternating string of American and Nationalist Chinese flags.) Yut Yee, the seventy-year-old CCBA president, who reportedly has been known to fall asleep during meetings, was unusually awake that night. He said, "Chinatown will become a dead city" if the violence continues. He urged residents to come forward and "report cases of crimes: We must be witnesses." This seemed unlikely, for in a culture where the character for "revenge" means literally "report a crime," the act of informing tends to be a complicated business. It confuses and angers the *lo fan* cops, who say that even though just about every restaurant in Chinatown has been robbed or extorted from in the past few years, the incidence of reporting the crimes is almost nil. Despite the fact that gang members have been arrested for more than a dozen murders in Manhattan, there has been only one conviction: that of Yut Wai Tom, an Eagle who made the mistake of putting a bullet through the throat of a Shadow in front of a couple of Puerto Rican witnesses.

Morganthau sighed during the debate of Chinese businessmen, looked at his watch, said he'd "help," and left. By this time, however, many people were openly restive. "My God, when will this bullshit stop?" asked a younger merchant.

No one talked about the tongs and their relationship to the gangs. How could they? Of the seven permanent members of the CCBA inner voting circle, one is the On Leong, another the Hip Sing. No wonder people tend to get cynical whenever the CCBA calls a meeting at which the tong interests are at stake. Perhaps that's why, when a Chinese reporter asked what the D.A. was planning to do to help the community, one of Morganthau's people said, "What do you want? We showed up, didn't we?"

But, if you wanted to see changing Chinatown in action, really all you had to do was watch Benny Eng. Benny is director of the Hip Sing Credit Fund (which drug cops figure is a laundry room for dirty money). He is also an officer of the Chinese-American Restaurant Association, an organization that deserves blame for keeping waiter wages in Chinatown at about fifty dollars a week for the past twenty years.

As people entered the CCBA hall, Little Benny—as he is called, in deference to Big Benny Ong, the old Hip Sing bossman recently arrested while sneaking out of the tong's venerable gambling house at 9 Pell Street—greeted everyone with a grave face. "So happy you are interested in the security of Chinatown," Little Benny said. But later, after the meeting, Benny, now attired in a natty hat and overcoat, could be seen nodding respectfully to the skinny-legged honcho pacing in front of 56 Mott Street.

Part Two

A pockmark-faced guy who nowadays spends ten hours a day laying bowls of congee in front of customers at a Mott Street rice shop remembers the day the White Eagles, the original Chinatown youth gang, ripped off their first *cha shu baos* (pork buns).

"It was maybe ten years ago. We were hanging out in Columbus Park, you know, by the courthouse, feeling real stupid. Most of us had just got to Chinatown. We couldn't speak English worth a shit. The *juk sing* (American-born Chinese, a.k.a ABCs, or American Born Chinese) were playing basketball, but they wouldn't let us play. We didn't know how to anyway. I remember one of our guys said, 'Shit, in Hong Kong my old man was a civil servant—he made some bread. Then he listened to my goddamned uncle and came over here. Now he's working as a waiter all day. The guy's got TB, I can hear him coughing. And I ain't got enough money for a goddamned *cha shu baos*.'"

Even then the *juk tuk* (Hong Kong–born Chinese) were sharp to the short end of the stick; they looked around the Toy Shan ghetto and sized up the possibilities for a sixteen-year-old immigrant. The chances had a familiar ring—what the tourists call "a Chinaman's chance," which, of course, is no chance at all. There might be moments of revenge, like lacing a *lo fan*'s sweet-and-sour with enormous hunks of ginger to watch his white lips pucker. But you knew you'd wind up frustrated, throwing quarters into the "Dancing Chicken" machine at the Chinatown Arcade. You'd watch that stupid Pavlovian-conditioned chicken come out of its feeder to dance and you'd know you were watching yourself.

So the eight or nine kids who would become the nucleus of the White Eagles walked up the narrow street past the Italian funeral parlor and into the pastry shop, where they stole dozens of *cha shu baos*, which they ate—and got so sick they threw up all over the sidewalk.

Within the next week the Eagles got hold of their first pieces—a pair of automatics—and began to terrorize Toy Shan. They beat the daylights out of the snooty ABCs, who were just a bunch of pussies anyway. They ripped off restaurants. They got tough with the old men's gambling houses.

It seemed so easy. In Hong Kong, try anything shifty and the cops would bust up your ass. They would search an entire block, throwing pregnant women down the hillsteps if they got in the way, just to find a guy they suspected of boosting a pocketbook from the lobby of the Hyatt Regency. Here the cops were all roundeyes—they don't know or care about Chinese. Besides, the old guys kept them paid off. The fringe benefits included street status, fast cars to cruise uptown and watch the *lo-fan* freaks, days to work on your "tans" at Coney listening to the new Hong Kong–Filipino platters, plenty of time to go bowling, and the pick of the girls—in general, the old equation of living quick, dying young, and leaving a beautiful corpse.

It took the Toy Shans a while to comprehend what was happening in their village. By the late sixties, several *juk sing* "clubs" began to appear. Foremost was the Continentals, a bunch who spent a good deal of time looking in the mirror, practicing complex handshakes, and running around ripping the insignias off Lincoln Continentals. In the beginning the family associations did their best. They marshaled the new kids into New Year's dragon-dancing. For the older, more sullen ones, they established martial arts clubs. But these kids didn't seem interested in discipline; besides, they smoked too many cigarettes. That's when the tongs intervened. Within weeks of the first extortion report, several White Eagles and representatives of the On Leong tong were sitting in a Mott Street restaurant talking it over. When they were done, a pact was sealed that would establish the youth gang as a permanent fixture of "New Chinatown."

It was agreed that the Eagles would stop random mayhem around the community and begin to work for the On Leong. They would "guard" the tong-sponsored gambling houses and make sure that no one ripped off restaurants that paid regular "dues." In return, the Eagles' leaders would receive a kind of salary, free meals in various noodle houses, and no-rent apartments in the Chinatown area.

It seemed a brilliant arrangement, especially for the tongs. The On Leongs and Hip Sings no longer struck fear in the heart of Chinatown. With warriors like Sing Dock barely a misty reminiscence, the tongs had become paunchy, middle-aged businessmen who spent most of their time competing for black-mushroom contracts. The Eagles brought them the muscle they felt they would need in changing times. It was like having your own private army, just like the good old days.

But the tongs weren't used to this kind of warrior. The kids mounted a six-foot-tall statue of a white eagle on top of their tenement at Mott and Pell. One night ten of them piled into a taxicab and went uptown to see *Superfly*; afterward they shot up Pell Street with tiny .22s for the sheer exhilaration of it. They went into tailor shops, scowled, and came away with two-hundred-dollar suits. Once Paul Ma—Eagle supreme commander—showed up for an arraignment wearing a silk shirt open down the front so everyone could see his bullet holes.

During eight or so years on top in Chinatown, the Eagles set the style for the Chinese youth gang. Part was savagery. Eagle recruiting practices were brutal—coercion was often used to replenish their street army. They kidnapped merchants' daughters and held them for ransom. They also set the example of using expensive and high-powered guns. No Saturday-night specials in Chinatown. The gangs used Mausers, Lugers, and an occasional M-14. One cop says, "You know, I've been on the force for twenty-two years, and I never saw nothing that gave me nightmares like watching a fifteen-year-old kid run down Bayard Street carrying a Thompson submachine gun."

But there was another side to this. A new style was emerging in Chinatown. Chinese kids have had a tough time of it in schools like Seward Park. Blacks and Puerto Ricans as well as meanies from Little Italy would vamp Chinese students for sport. Groups like the Eagles were intent on changing this. It was a question of cool. In the beginning they copied the swagger and lingo of the blacks—it is remarkable how closely a Chinese teenager can imitate black speech. From the Puerto Ricans they borrowed souped-up car styling as well as the nonfashion of wearing army fatigues, which they added to their already zooty Hong Kong–cut shirts.

But it was Bruce Lee, the Hong Kong sex-symbol kung fu star who did the most for the Chinese street presence. Gang kids ran around Chinatown carrying *nunchahas*—kung fu fighting sticks—which few of them knew how to use, and postured like deadly white cranes. When "Kung-Fu Fighting" became a number one hit on WWRL, being Chinese was in. They became people not to mess with (although the police report there has never been a gang incident in which martial arts were used). "It was like magic," says one ex-Continental. "I used to walk by the Smith projects where the blacks live, and those brothers would throw dirty diapers out the window at me and call me Chinaman. Now they call me *Mr. Chinaman*."

The image of the Chinese schoolgirl was changing, too. Overnight they entered the style show on the subway. A lot of the fashion—airblown hairstyles, mucho makeup, and tiny "Apple jacket" tops—came from the Puerto Ricans. Classy tweezed Oriental eyebrows produced a new "dragon lady" look. Openly sexual, some of the Hong Kong girls formed auxiliary groups. Streaking their hair blonde or red to show that their boyfriends were gangsters, they were "ol' ladies" expected to dab their men's wounds with elixirs swiped from Chinese apothecaries. Who can blame them? More than half of Chinatown's women work in the three-hundred-odd garment factories in the area, buzzing through the polyester twelve hours a day, trying to crack a hundred dollars a week. Hanging with the bad kids risked an occasional gang bang, but it was a better risk than dying in a sweatshop.

It seemed only a matter of time before the youth gangs would get into dope, especially since drug peddling has been the key staple of the Chinese underworld for centuries. The present-day version of the Chinatown connection dates back to the end of the Chinese civil war in 1949. Several Nationalist units were cut off in the poppy-rich area known as the Golden Triangle near the Burmese/Thai/Laotian border as the rest of Chiang Kai-shek's army fled to Taiwan. A large smuggling route was then established, with the Nationalist government reaping the benefits. This was not unprecedented, as many historians cite Chiang's involvement with the notorious dope-peddling Shanghai-based Green Gang during the 1920s.

According to the federal Drug Enforcement Agency, with Mao's takeover on the mainland, several KMT officials with drug-selling connections soon found their way to New York, where they eased into the On Leong power structure. It wasn't long after that, the DEA says, that the On Leong people went across Canal Street to strike a bargain with Italian organized crime. Soon a new adage was added to Mafia parlance: "If you want the stuff, get yourself a good gook."

The connection—which is believed to be kept running by a manager of an On Leong restaurant who is also believed to be the only Chinese ever admitted to the Carlo Gambino crime family—works well. While most of the country is flooded with Mexican smack, in New York the percentage of Golden Triangle poppy runs high. The dope money is the lucrative tip of Chinatown's pyramid crime structure. DEA people say the gangs are used as runners to pick up dope in the Chinese community in Toronto and then body-carry it across the border. But they may play a greater role. Chinese dope hustlers have always felt on uneasy ground when dealing with flashy uptown pushers. Now, however, street sources say the gutterwise gangs are dealing directly with black and Puerto Rican dealers.

Then again, junk has always been an issue in Chinatown. Even now you can walk by the senior citizen home on East Broadway and see eighty-year-old Chinese men and women who still suffer from the effects of long-ago opium addiction and live out their lives on methadone. They're probably the oldest addicts in America. The specter of the opium days is still horrifying down here, where landlords continue to find lamps and pipes in basements.

That's why the sight of fourteen-year-old Eagles nodding on Mott Street during the smack influx of the early '70s was so galling to the old men. It was a final indiscretion, a final lack of discipline. Actually, the Eagles had been tempting fate for some time. They insulted tong elders in public. They extorted from restaurants they were supposed to be protecting. They mugged big winners outside of the gambling houses. It was playing havoc with the tong's business as usual. Often the old men threatened to bring in sharpshooting hitmen from Taiwan to calm the kids down.

So in 1974, when Quat Kay Kee, an aging street hustler looking for a handle in the tong hierarchy, told the On Leong of a new and remarkable gang leader, the old men were ready to listen. Nicky Louie and his Ghost

Shadows were not only tougher than the Eagles, but they knew how to do business. To show their style, Nicky and his top gun, Philip Han (known as Halfbreed), supposedly put on masks and pulled off a ballsy submachine-gun holdup at the Eagle-guarded gambling house in the local VFW post, knocking off a pair of sentries to boot.

Soon after, in another gambling house, a drunken Eagle poured a water glass of tea down the brocade jacket of an On Leong elder. The word came down: The tong was formally withdrawing its support of the Eagles; the Shadows could make their move. A few nights later, the 4:00 A.M. quiet on Mott Street was broken by Shadows honking the horns of their hopped-up cars. They rode around the block, screeching their tires. The Eagles tumbled out of bed clutching their pieces. The shooting woke up half the neighborhood. Amazingly, no one was injured. But the change had come. The Eagles fled to Brooklyn. And Nicky Louie was pacing back and forth on Mott Street.

A relationship was forged. For the most part, Nicky's Shadows have been model rulers during their stay on Mott Street. "I'm a businessman, and I know how to stay in business," Nicky once told Neal Mauriello. The gang takes its cut and protects the status quo. Would-be neighborhood reformers have learned to be fearful of visits from gun-wielding gang members; one lawyer who spoke out against the Chinatown establishment woke up the next morning to find Mott Street plastered with wall posters telling him to get out of town.

It is a strange reign of terror that could flourish only in a limbo-land like Chinatown. One hundred years of neglect have distorted the links to the *lo fan* power. The cops and tongs have maintained a nonaggression pact well oiled with palm grease. One On Leong insider says, "Those guys are crooks. I was pit boss at a gambling house and gave two hundred a week to the same sergeant for two years." It goes on. Fifth Precinct cops are not allowed to make gambling arrests unless they actually see money on the table. But since the chance of a *lo fan* getting into a Chinese gambling house unnoticed is akin to a snowcone in hell, they might as well not bother. "When you do raid the houses, it's almost like they've been tipped," says one detective. "By the time you get through all the trick doors, there's no one there but a couple of one-hundred-year-old men smoking cigarettes."

For years there was only one Chinese cop, the fabulous Johnny Kai. Kai walked a thin line between American and Chinese law and did a good job for both. Today, however, with the Chinese making up the majority of the Fifth's constituency and youth crime skyrocketing, there is still only one Chinese cop on the beat, Barry Eng, who once said with a straight face, "Of course, everyone knows the associations disowned the youth gangs a long time ago."

One thing that Nicky Louie makes fairly clear is that he is not interested in talking to reporters, especially this reporter. No, he says, when approached in front of 56 Mott Street, he is not up for a little *yum cha* to discuss his life and times. Avoiding eye contact, he claims to speak "no English!" For sure he doesn't want his picture in the paper. In fact, he says, he doesn't even know who the fuck this Nicky Louie is and, in any event, he is not him. So maybe you should get the fuck away, like now.

Not that you could blame the Ghost Shadow for wanting to keep a low profile. The past several months have been a kind of hell for the gang leader. It was only a few Saturdays ago that he reportedly saw an old Eagle enemy gesturing in his direction from across the street. It was a finger. Nicky was being fingered. He stood like a freeze frame, looking at the two strangers drawing down on him. One had a Mauser, the other a Colt .38. The first gunshot whistled by his ear and broke him out of his trance. He ran down Mott, pushing aside the tourists and the old ladies, turning down Canal until he was safe, panting against a wall.

That afternoon haunted Nicky. Battling Paul Ma made sense. But these unknown hitmen had no reason to shoot except money.

It was scary; things were getting out of control. Eagle Yut Wai Tom had been convicted—the first gang kid to be sent up for murder. Word was around that Tom had cracked up when he got to Rikers Island. The cops were doing a suicide watch on him. Quat Kay Kee, Nicky's old sponsor at On Leong, had been flipping out, too. Shot at in the Wiseman Bar on Bayard Street by a group of Eagles wearing ratty wigs they had bought from a hasidic shop on East Broadway, Quat railed that he'd tell all. He managed to compose himself just before the drug cops got there with their tape recorders.

Being a Chinatown warlord was a tough gig. To keep up their street army, the Shadows had been forced to recruit younger and younger kids. But what exactly do you say to a fourteen-year-old when you're a twenty-two-year-old legend? The young Shadows were griping about their wages. In the early part of the year some of the kids had broken away from Nicky to ally themselves with the scuzzy Wah Chings. For a couple of nights in January, they had actually succeeded in pushing Nicky off the street. It took all of his negotiating prowess to fix things again.

For months he'd let it be known that he was tired of being a youth-gang leader, but the tong gave little indication that they'd allow him to move up in the organization. Quitting was out of the question. First of all, he knew too much and had far too many enemies. It wouldn't be enough to leave Chinatown, or even New York City. Anyplace there was On Leong—like Toronto or Chicago—or Hip Sing, which is just about everywhere, he'd be known and fair game. Anyway, if he did get out, what was waiting? He knew lots of ex-gang guys who'd "retired" and now broke their humps for their families in the old restaurant grind.

Ironically, it was the old men who provided Nicky and the other gang kids with an escape from street-fighting. Despite Chinatown's traditional reluctance to look for outside help, poverty money is beginning to find its way down here. Funding scams may not be as venerable as gambling houses, but in a modern world, there must be modern hustles. People had been telling the old men about a Harlem incident in which the *hak guey* youth gangs had given up their arms. The federal government had laid a sizable chunk of cash on groups promising to reform the kids. The old men saw an opening; if they could get the gangs to call "peace," they could get the uptight merchants off their backs as well as pick up a large grant.

The plan was laid out to Nicky. He liked it and promised to set it up. He contacted Eagle Paul Ma and Dragon Mike Chen—who hated each other more than they both hated Nicky—and got them to say "Cool."

Next step was to make it respectable. The gangs contacted one of the old Continentals, now a well-known Chinatown social worker, and told him they wanted to give up their evil ways. The worker, eager to be known as the man who stopped Chinatown gang warfare, went for it. Everything was set.

But somewhere along the line, Nicky began to forget that it was all a scam. Suddenly he liked the idea of "reforming," learning English for real and getting a decent job. And he wasn't the only one. Around *lo tow*, guys were still packing rods, but they also were talking about what they'd do when they went "legit."

The first "peace" meeting was at the Kuo Wah Restaurant on Mott Street. Kids embraced each other, saying it was crazy for Chinese guys to kill other Chinese guys. Nicky sat down with Paul Ma. They'd been trying to wipe each other out for years; but now they spent hours reminiscing about their favorite extortion spots on Mott Street.

The old men were flabbergasted. What a double cross! If these kids were on the level, then the whole vice structure could go down the tubes. Then again, it could be a trick. The gangs might be pulling a power play to cut Chinatown up for themselves. Either was disaster. After that the tongs did everything they could to sabotage the peace. They spread mistrust among the merchants; they tried to bribe the gang leaders. The old men unsuccessfully tried to cancel the press conference formally announcing the "peace." But, on August 12, Nicky and the other gang leaders read their joint statement. They didn't expect to be forgiven, but then again they weren't apologizing. They had become wiser; being a gangster wasn't so great. Other kids shouldn't get into it. It was moving; several of the old family association leaders wept. Even Nicky looked a little misty.

But time had run out on Nicky's peace: The old Toy Shan forces of secrecy and mistrust were working overtime. The merchants, brutalized so often, never believed the gangs were sincere and offered no support. The social service agencies failed to come up with concrete programs. The cops offered a ten-day amnesty period for the gang kids to turn in their guns, nothing else. "Oh yeah," said one Shadow. "I'm gonna turn in my gun so they can do a ballistic and fingerprint check on it? Sure." No weapons were turned in.

Of course, it is not possible to know if Nicky was ever truly sincere about declaring peace in Chinatown. The cops, cynics that they are, said, "They might have called it peace, but they spelled it 'p-i-e-c-e.'" Still, no one disputes the fact that three weeks went by without anyone getting shot at around Mott and Bayard. Nicky must have known it was over the night the Eagles ripped off a restaurant at the other end of Mott Street. He ran over to find Paul Ma and see what was up. An Eagle told him that Paul was "out" and laughed. After that, Nicky kicked chairs in a Mott Street rice shop. Gang members say the sear was back in his eye. By then it was just a matter of time. Within the next week the Shadows, Eagles, and Dragons were shooting at each other; the two-month-long war would prove to be the bloodiest in Chinatown history.

The tongs, fearing total loss of control, responded to the madness by calling in some old friends from across Canal Street. According to the Chinese newspapers, a couple of Shadows walked into the wrong restaurant at the wrong time. Five smashnoses imported from Mulberry Street were waiting for them. Reportedly the kids wound up in a meat grinder, their remains dumped into a plastic bag and driven to Newark.

This got the gangs' attention. Except for a few gun violations, the cops say Chinatown's been quiet for the past few weeks. However, reports of gang extortions in local Massapequa and northern New Jersey Chinese restaurants have begun to come in.

But in fanning out of Chinatown, the gangs broke a New York City rule: Don't mess with the rich white people. Someone goofed when they rubbed out the young couple who run the Szechuan D'or on East Fortieth Street. It mobilized whole armies of uptown cops. Determined to strike Chinese crime at its root, the police have shut down the gambling and extortion rackets in Chinatown. This has caused widespread panic. Word is, big gamblers walk around in a daze at the OTB, trying to latch on to private *pi gow* games uptown. Nicky and the Shadows, seeing no percentage in hanging around for the onslaught, split for greener fields in the On Leong–run towns of Toronto and Chicago.

No one, of course, expects this to last. Balances of power are constantly shifting downtown. Just the other day the cops busted Flying Dragon Mike Chen with a 12-gauge shotgun and 150 rounds of ammunition hidden in the ceiling of his apartment. Paul Ma, Philip Han, and Big Benny Ong are on their way to the slammer. And some even say that the good people at Hip Sing could stage a takeover in Benny's absence.

But much more remains the same. Go tonight to a restaurant on Mott Street and look out the window. Across the street you're likely to see a good-looking skinny guy in a green fatigue jacket pacing back and forth. Nicky Louie is back in town, vigilant as ever. Look into his eyes and wonder what he's thinking. But, then, remember . . . it's Chinatown.

21

From the Annals of Pre-Gentrification:

Sleaze-Out on East Fourteenth Street

A case study from before the invention of the two-thousand-dollar studio apartment. Back in 1977, the so-called Summer of Sam, soon after the near-bankruptcy of the city, there were many contenders for the title of "sleaziest street corner in New York." Fourteenth Street and Third Avenue was closest to my home, and I like to walk to work. Now East Fourteenth Street is "redeveloped." Jullian's, once the most picturesque pool hall in the city, is now an NYU dorm. Ditto the Academy of Music. The Gramercy Gym, where fighters good and bad trained, is long gone. So is the studio where Bettie Page took her famous bondage pics. This is called progress. Even if it is a perverted nostalgia to long for the bad old days when the city's major thoroughfares were lined with nodding junkies, it is hard to dismiss the lingering (loitering?) feeling that something has been lost. From the Village Voice, *1977.*

All the popcorn pimps, penny-ante pross, nickel-and-dime pill-pushers, methadone junkies, and doorway-living winos felt the hawk wind as it blew down East Fourteenth Street. It's late October, the time of the year when one night, all of a sudden, you know you better break out the warmer coat. Except that on East Fourteenth Street, who has a warmer coat? One creep—a downer-selling vermin—knows the raw of it all.

He stands in front of the pizza joint on Fourteenth and Third Avenue, begging for eye contact. "Robitussin, man, Robitussin." Robitussin? "Robitussin," he croaks. He's selling cough syrup. Over-the-counter cough syrup.

It is enough to stop you in your tracks. "Robitussin, man? Don't you got no Luden's or Vicks VapoRub?" I mean: Two-dollar Placidyl is low enough. But Robitussin? "You have got to be kidding."

The creep's voice squeaks up a couple of octaves, his scarred-up head sags. He says, "Just trying to get over. This gonna be a rough winter."

It's always a rough winter at Fourteenth Street and Third Avenue. Rough for the blond junkie and his girlfriend. They told the people at the methadone center on Second Avenue and Twelfth Street that they were going out of town. Back to Ohio to visit the chick's parents. The methadone people gave them a week's supply of bottles. It sounded like a good plan since the blond guy and his girlfriend weren't going nowhere except to Fourteenth Street to sell the extra shit. But they got into a pushing match with some of the Spanish guys drinking Night Train Express on the subway stairs. The methadone bottles fell down the stairs. A scuffle broke out, then the cops were there. One thing led to another, and soon the blond junkie and his girlfriend were back at the drug center trying to explain why they weren't in Ohio. Now they're on "permanent release," which means no more state-issue methadone. You can see the two of them out on the street, scratching and begging, looking for a taste, any taste.

A rough, cold winter. Some of the usual skells have taken off. Nobody in the Durkin, the creep joint with the tilted bar, has seen Joey the Eye for weeks. Joey the Eye was messed up—too fucked up to cop pills, never had a girl out on the street. But he could—and would—take his bloodshot eyeball out of his head and hold it in the palm of his hand. He said if you didn't give him a cigarette, he'd tighten the grip, crushing his own eyeball, which would make it all your fault: him having nothing but a dark pit where his eye should be. The Hung Man is also missing. He spent some of the summer leaning on a parking meter, stark naked. Valium pushers came over, slapped five, and said. "Man, you hung."

Beat Shit Green is gone, too. But no one in the pill-pusher ginmills on Second Avenue figures Beat Shit is soaking up rays in Miami Beach. Beat Shit is one of the worst scumbags ever to stand at Fourteenth Street and Third Avenue hustling "Ts and Vs" (Tuinals and Valium). He used to claim that he was the one who sold the white boy that fatal bunch of beat shit in Washington Square Park last year. Bragged about it. What did he care, he made his $2.50. Beat Shit has been known to sell methadone that was really Kool-Aid and aspirin. He'd suck the juice out of a Placidyl and sell the shell. But, they say, that kind of beat shit comes back on you. They say Beat Shit's not going to make the winter because he got thrown off a roof on East Thirteenth Street.

Rough. Cold. In one of the bars next to the cuchifrito stand, Willie ("call me Big W") is wondering if he'll see April. For a downer salesman, Willie is a pretty sweet dude. Sometimes if one of the barmaids in the Durkin is smooching it up with an off-duty cop, Willie will take a bar stool next to the chick and wait. Soon she'll curl her hand around her back and make a little cup. Willie will slip her a couple of Valiums. The barmaid will put her other hand in the cop's crotch and pull her face away—pretending to cough or something. While the cop is dealing with the barmaid's squeeze, she'll swallow the pills and go back to tonguing before the guy knows anything. Willie digs that kind of move. He says, "She's slick, huh?"

Recently, though, things haven't been going too good for Big W. Mostly he gets over selling pills to kids from Jersey. But, like they say, Willie is his own best customer. Talking to him gets you seasick; he's always listing from side to side. Tonight Big W is wearing his skullcap funny. It's not pulled down over his head; he's got it done up in a little crown. Willie says he don't want it skintight, it puts too much pressure on his stitches. Seems as Willie was in the Durkin a couple of weeks ago and got into an argument with a pimp. Willie thought the guy was just bullshitting until the iron rod came out. He forgets what happened next. Except that he woke up in Bellevue with a head that looks like a roadmap.

The stitches have made Willie mad. Mad enough to "get violent." The other night he decided he was "just gonna go mug myself somebody." He went around to the stage door of the Academy of Music. Aerosmith was playing. Willie picked out a kid who was completely destroyed on Tuinals. The kid was waiting for an autograph, but Willie figured anyone jive enough a wait for a fucking autograph has to be an asshole. It got better when the rock star came out the door, "got into his fucking limo, and didn't even give the sucker an autograph." So Willie made his move. The Jersey kid beat Willie into the sidewalk and "stole my Placidyls." At this rate, Willie figures he'll be lucky to live till spring.

I have always wanted to write a story called "The 10 Sleaziest Street Corners in New York." I mean, why did certain street corners—excluding obvious "ghetto"-area ones—become hangouts for pill-pushers, prostitutes, winos, bums, creeps, cripples, mental patients, mumblers, flimflam men, plastic-flower sellers, peepshow operators, head cases, panhandlers, and other socially unacceptable netherworld types. How did these corners get this way? How long had they been this way? What was their future? Which ones have McDonald's? Which ones have Burger King? Did this matter?

I compiled a fairly comprehensive list off the top of my head: Ninety-sixth Street and Broadway—the first subway stop down from Harlem; Seventy-second Street and Broadway—good old needle park; Fifty-third and Third—the Ramones sang about chicken hawking there; Twenty-eighth and Park Avenue South—the Bellmore Cafeteria cabdrivers brings the pross; Second Avenue and St. Mark's—the dregs of the burned-out hippies; Bowery and Houston—the cabbies will run over a bum before they let him wash their windshield; Sixth Avenue and Eighth Street—the aggressively plastic up-and-comer; Ninetieth Street and Roosevelt in Queens—home of the low-level Colombian coke dealer; and, of course, the granddaddy of them all: Forty-second Street and Eighth Avenue, the whole of Forty-Deuce Street actually.

Soon, however, it became apparent that it was crazy to "do" all the corners of crud in New York. How many burgers can one be called on to eat for the sake of journalism? It would be better to hone in on one singular slice of sleaze.

Fourteenth Street and Third Avenue was the natural choice. I live around there; it's my neighborhood sleazy street corner. The pross have seen me enough to know I don't wanna go out. But, also, Fourteenth Street and Third Avenue is a classic, time-honored choice. Fourteenth Street—the longest crosstown Street in Manhattan—has been on the skids, for the past 120 years.

Once, long ago, blue blood coursed through this stem. An 1853 edition of the *New York Herald* said of East Fourteenth Street, "Here, there are no stores—nothing but dwelling houses, which are substantial, highly finished, and first class." When stores did come, they were Tiffany's and FAO Schwarz. When the Academy of Music was built, in 1854, it was hailed as the city's center of classical music and opera. Europeans sang there. The Metropolitan Opera House was built uptown by smarmy nouveaux riches, like the Vanderbilts, who couldn't get boxes at the Academy.

It didn't last long. East Fourteenth Street did one of the quickest and earliest "there goes the neighborhoods" in New York history. By 1865, the *New York Times* was reporting that "all of the once-splendid row houses of the 14th Street-Union Square sector are now boarding houses." In 1868, Charles Dickens saw Fourteenth Street as a precursor of Levittown. He said: "There are 300 boarding houses exactly alike, with 300 young men exactly alike, sleeping in 300 hall bedrooms exactly alike, with 300 dress suits exactly alike. . . ."

Prostitution was firmly rooted on East Fourteenth Street by the turn of the century (a *Gentleman's Companion* of the time lists fifteen whorehouses in the area), and it aided some unlikely causes. Emma Goldman writes of doing a little flat-backing on Fourteenth Street to pick up revolutionary pocket money. Those days, there were plenty of Reds around. Socialists stood on soapboxes in Union Square Park. During the Sacco-Vanzetti trials, the cops mounted machine guns on top of the Guardian Life building. John Reed and Trotsky discussed eventualities in the Fourteenth Street cafeteria, which had a sign on the wall: A TRAYFUL FOR A TRIFLE.

Today the only vestige of leftist activity on Fourteenth Street is the sign from the sixties underground newspaper *Rat,* which had its offices next to the Metropolitan porno theater. It reads, HOT RATS WHILE YOU WAIT. Once-flourishing capitalists have also fallen on hard times. Macy's, Hearn's, Ohrbach's, and Klein's all were here. Now only Klein's on the Square remains as a massive, empty three-hundred-thousand-square-foot hulk. The square-rule logo makes the place look like a decrepit Masonic temple; except there's no "all-seeing eye."

The *East Village Other*, in one of its last issues, published a secret report predicting a deadly and monumental earthquake about to flatten half the city. The scientists (all Hitlerians, said *EVO*) were keeping the news from the public. The report said all the major fault lines ran right underneath Fourteenth Street. It was a totally believable story.

East Fourteenth Street should have settled into a typical cycle of urban decline and upshift. But the street has resisted, plotting instead a flat-line course. Down and down. Most around here say it hasn't bottomed out yet.

Fourteenth Street at Third Avenue is more than a sleazy street corner, it's the epicenter of a mini-sleazopolis. In the blocks around the hub, several different creep scenes operate side by side, and almost independently. Occasionally a pimp hanging out in the Rio Piedras bodega, on Third Avenue near Eleventh Street, will go up to Fourteenth Street to sell some pills, but not often. The girls stay fucked up most of the time but don't sell. Pill-pushers don't even go to the same bars as the pross. It's a real division of labor. The thing that holds it all together is that it's all so low. *Low!* Ask anyone stumbling past the old Jefferson Theatre—they'll tell you: After Fourteenth Street, there ain't no more down.

Sure the pimps sit in the chairs of the barber college at Twelfth and Third pretending to get a swell $1.50 haircut like they're New Orleans patroons. But it is all front. Fakery and lies. These pimps have never gotten to check out the scene with a gangster lean from the front seat of an El D and they never will. They don't even have a fur hat to slouch about in. They're lucky to have one girl working, and you know she's going to be desperate. A working girl freezing skinny legs waiting for cars with Jersey plates turns two hundred dollars a week down here, when it's good. No chance of them taking their act to Lexington or even Eighth Avenue, either. They're on Fourteenth Street because the big pimps think the place is so funky they don't even care to organize it. The heartless say that

Fourteenth Street is one step from the glue factory. A few weeks ago the cops picked up a fifty-seven-year-old pross outside the Contempora Apartments. It was believed to be some kind of record, age-wise.

Pill-pushers are no better. Most of them started turning up on Fourteenth Street back in the late sixties after two doctors, Vincent Dole and Marie Nyswarder—the father and mother of methadone maintenance—shook up the dope-fiend world by setting up a clinic at the Morris J. Bernstein Institute of Beth Israel Hospital. Methadone was touted as a wonder drug. Everyone said it would be the end of the heroin problem in the city. Junkies from all over the city were sent over to Bernstein (on Second Avenue and Seventeenth Street) and other nearby "model" clinics to drink little clear bottles and kick.

Some kicked. But most just got a short course in how to manipulate the Medicaid programs politicians loved to pour money into. Drugs led to drugs. It was easy to take your little methadone card and Medicaid slip over to a "scrip" doctor who would be willing to write you an Rx for a hundred Valiums if you told him you were "anxious, very anxious." This led to the famous junkie refrain: "I'd go to Doctor Zhivago if he'd write." Otherwise, you could write your own. The forms were usually lying around the program offices. A scribbled "X" might be good enough to get a pharmacist to fill the scrips. What you didn't use to get fucked up on, you could sell. Same thing with extra methadone.

Fourteenth Street and Third became the flea market. It was an Eco-101 example of supply and demand. The drug of choice among the dumbo suburban kids these days is downers: the Fourteenth Street stock and trade. Throughout Long Island and Jersey, blond-haired types driving their papas' Le Sabres know that Fourteenth Street is the place to go. Any night a useless boogie band is playing the Palladium (what they call the Academy of Music now), you can see the most mediocre minds of the next generation drag themselves through negro streets into the most desultory madness.

It is a game anyone can play. Go over to the emergency room at one of the hospitals in the area, tell them you're dying from a headache and want some Percodan. The intern there will be surprised and ask you, "Sure you don't want Valium?" Insist on Percodan and the intern will tell you, "Take the Valium. If you don't use them, sell them on Fourteenth Street. None of them have heard of Percodan."

There's no night (except for Sunday, when the Street is eerie and dead) when you can't walk from Fourth Avenue to Second Avenue on Fourteenth Street without at least half a dozen ballcap-wearing, pinpoint-eyed junkies asking you if you want downers. The price list fluctuates with supply: Placidyl usually go for $2.50; Valium, 75 cents; Tuinal, $3; Elavil, $2 on Fourteenth Street, with a 25 percent markup for rock show nights.

You'd figure that would add up. Especially with no overhead and Medicaid usually picking up the initial tab. But these guys ain't got no money. They're too spaced out. That's why they're on Fourteenth to begin with. They couldn't get over selling smack on 123rd Street. They couldn't even get over selling smack on Avenue B and Sixth Street. They don't got the concentration. Pusher wars don't happen. No one can remember where their turf is, or was. They are in trouble if you ask them for more than three Valiums. They pour the pills out into their hands and start counting. Then they recount. Order more than eight or nine and it can take an hour.

If you want to draw a map of the Fourteenth-and-Third sleazopolis, give the pill-pushers Fourteenth Street between Second and Fourth. That's the south side of the street; for some reason they're never on the north side. No one knows why, they sure aren't working on their tans. Scoring spots include the doorway of the Larry Richardson Dance Company at the corner of Fourth Avenue. Most of the guys up there are in business for themselves but there are also "steerers," creeps who will tell Jersey kids to come around the corner to Thirteenth Street. This is usually for "quantity" and sometimes for rip-off.

The rest of the scene, working from the west and down, goes like this: Union Square Park is bonkers these days, the sight of curving benches packed with leathery, saliva-streaked faces is truly impressive. The park isn't a major retail center for the pill-pusher, but many will come over for a little rural R and R. After a tough day of Placidyl pushing, you can lose your profits back playing craps or three-card monte. On the other side of the George Washington statue there are also several "loose joints" guys who got off the wrong subway stop on the way down to Washington Square.

The pross take Third Avenue. Their spiritual home is near Thirteenth Street, where there are two miserable excuses for peepshow joints as well as three porno theaters (that includes the Variety when it's not showing devil movies). The 'toots will also graze down to Fifth Street. The Regina Hotel on Third and Thirteenth (a featured backdrop in Scorsese's *Taxi Driver*) is no longer a big pross hole. The cops broke the manager's balls so now he's on the up-and-up, although you wonder why anyone would stay there if they weren't getting laid. The Bowery flops are the Ritz-Carlton compared to the Regina. Now most of the hotel tricking goes on at the Sahara, a little oasis on Fourteenth. The Sahara has a sign saying LOW WEEKLY RATES even though most guests spend less than a half hour at the Sahara. Seven dollars is the room tariff. A lot of the action, though, goes on in the parking lots along Third. The West Indian guy who used to work there charged two dollar a pop to get in the backseat of the car. Hope they didn't use yours.

The "he-shes" (also called "shims" or "he-haws") hang near Second Avenue and Twelfth Street and also congregate at Little Peters, a swish bar by St. Marks Place. This is one of the biggest t.v. scenes in the city. Of the fourteen hundred pross arrests the cops made in the area during the past year or so, nearly half were men dressed up as women. Ask why he-shes are usually Puerto Rican, a working "girl" says, "Our people are so mean to us . . . besides, haven't you ever heard that Latins were made to love?" The he-shes are much classier looking than the straight pross. Johns claim you can't even tell until you get real close. And, even then . . . you can't. But, then again, most of the johns who cruise Fourteenth Street just don't care.

With this kind of scene it makes sense that many of the "legitimate" businesses that have stayed on East Fourteenth Street during the downtimes fall into the seedy category in most Upper East Siders' book. Up the stairs at the Gramercy Gym, where Cus D'Amato trained Patterson and Jose Torres, the fighters don't think too much about the sleazos below. Fighters figure they're on the fringe of the law themselves. They don't point fingers. But they keep distance. They know that Placidyls make it tough to run six miles in the morning.

At Jullian's Billiards, one of the great film-noir light-over-the-faded-green-cloth-Luther-Lassiter-played-here pool halls in New York, hardly anyone makes mention of the scene either. The old men who sit on the wood benches, watching the nine-ball games, don't have time to think about creeps. Nine-ball's got a big element of luck, true. But it's the money game up there, and anytime money's on the table you've got to concentrate. So just shoot pool, Fast Eddie. Who cares who pisses in the hallway?

Down the street, Paula Klaw has her private thoughts. She's been on East Fourteenth Street for better than thirty years. She remembers when the cuchifrito stand was a Rikers Coffee Shoppe. And when there were two Hungarian restaurants on this block. She is not, however, complaining. "Who am I to complain?" says Paula Klaw. Paula Klaw runs Movie Star News, a film-still and "nostalgia" store stuffed into the second floor of the building next to the Jefferson Theatre. It's the best place in the city to buy photos of Clive Brook and Irene Dunn. As Paula says, the street has a "strong movie pedigree." D. W. Griffith's original Biograph Studio, where Lilly and Dolly Gish made one-reelers, was on Fourteenth Street near Second Avenue. Buster Keaton became a star here.

But most film shot here never played a Saturday afternoon matinee. As attested to by the half-soot-covered sign painted on the window, this used to be the studio of IRVING KLAW, THE PINUP KING. Irving, Paula's late brother, shot thousands of bondage pictures up here during the 1940s and 50s. Most of those pictures were of Bettie Page, the most famous bondage model of them all. Irving used his 8x10 camera to shoot Bettie for a variety of rags that had names like *Eyeful*, *Wink*, and *Black Nylons*. Most of the pics were distributed by mail order, which would lead to Irving running afoul of the bluenose Kefauver Hearings on "juvenile delinquency."

"They harassed my brother," Paula says now, adding that Irving always maintained "a tasteful relationship" with his famous model. When Howard Hughes once asked to meet Bettie Page after seeing some of the shots Irving took, Paula's brother advised Bettie to see the billionaire, but "only if he promises to be a total gentleman."

Paula was in charge of posing the pictures. She personally tied up Bettie Page "at least a hundred times," to various chairs, gagged her on beds, and manacled her with leather. Bettie was always sweet about it, Paula said, never complained, except when the ropes were too tight. Paula sometimes helped Irving title the pictures, items like "Bettie Comes to New York and Gets in a Bind."

"It was wonderful those days," Paula says now, "we had politicians, judges, prime ministers coming here to buy our photos. They would park their limos right outside on Fourteenth Street." After a while, however, the court cases weighed everything down. Fighting back a tear, Paula says, "It was all that that killed Irving, I think. They said we sold porno. We did not sell porno." Today Paula sells a book called *The Irving Klaw Years, 1948–1963*, containing "more than 200 out-of-print bondage photos." Paula calls it a "fitting remembrance to my brother." Paula, who has white hair, blue makeup, and wears Capri pants, doesn't have to come to Fourteenth Street every day. She lives in Sheepshead Bay and has "plenty of money." But she "just likes it . . . you know, this used to be quite a glamorous street." She says she hasn't washed the IRVING KLAW, PINUP KING window in twenty years. She does not intend to.

If Paula, Jullian's, and the fighters add aged seed to the surroundings, it's the cynical "businessmen" who give Fourteenth Street and Third Avenue its shiny veneer of plastic sleaze. Who could have been surprised when Burger King opened in the old Automat where John Reed, currently buried near Lenin in the Kremlin, once ate club rolls? Burger King knows its customers when it sees them. The burger boys probably have whole demographic departments to psyche out every sleaze scene in the galaxy. No doubt they felt they had to keep pace after McDonald's sewed up Ninety-sixth and Broadway.

Then there are the donuts. There are at least five donut joints in the immediate area of Fourteenth Street and Third Avenue. One even replaced Sam's Pizza, a lowlife landmark for years. Donuts are definitely the carbo-junkie wave of the future. In fact, if some doctor would publish a weight-losing diet of Placidyls and donuts, airline stewardesses would make Fourteenth Street another Club Med.

But, of course, the real merchants of Fourteenth Street and Third Avenue are the sleazos. They control the economy. And why not? No one else wanted to sell stuff on East Fourteenth Street. You have to figure that more

Placidyls and pussy gets sold at Fourteenth and Third than the pizza joint sells pizza or the cuchifrito place sells pork rinds.

No wonder the sleazos were pissed the other day. The Third Avenue Merchants Association was having a fair. They closed off the avenue. Ladies in print dresses sold pottery. Bug-eyed kids stood by tables of brownies. A nice day in the sun for the well adjusted. But the fair halted abruptly at Fourteenth Street, even though Third Avenue continues downtown for several streets before it turns into the Bowery. The implication was clear, and the sleazos weren't missing it. A whole slew of the local losers stood on "their" side of Fourteenth Street, gaping at the fat-armed zeppoli men pulling dough and the little kids whizzing around in go-karts.

One Valium pusher looked up at the sign hung across the avenue and read it aloud. "T . . . A . . . M . . . A . . . ," he said. "What the fuck is a T.A.M.A.?"

The Third Avenue Merchants Association, he was informed. "Shit," he said, looking very put out. "Motherfucker, I'm a goddamned Third Avenue merchant."

So what if Fourteenth Street is low? Does every block have to look like SoHo or one of those tree-lined numbers in Queens? The other night I was helping my friend move. He had been living on Fifteenth Street and Third Avenue in a high-rise, but the money got tight. So he took a place on Twelfth between Second and Third. As we were carrying an enormous filing cabinet into the lobby of his new building, he said, "Well, this place is dumpy, but at least I won't have to pass the prostitutes every day on the way to work." A couple of seconds later we heard a noise on the staircase. A 'toot was slapping a solid on a guy who we swore had a turned-around collar. A *priest!* We almost dropped the cabinet, laughing.

Besides, where else but on East Fourteenth Street can you hear a blasted Spanish downer freak abusing a little Polish guy, saying, "*Que pasa? Que pasa? Que pasa?*" To which the Polish guy says, questioning, "Kielbasa? Kielbasa?"

Of course, there are those who do not ascribe to this type of thinking. Like Carvel Moore. Explaining why sleaze is essential to the big-city experience to her is like explaining it to Clay Felker. Except that Carvel Moore takes it more personally. She is the "project coordinator" of Sweet 14, an organization dedicated to making Fourteenth Street "The Livingest Street in Town."

They are a cleanup group. The list of names who attended their kickoff meeting reads like a who's who among New York powermongers. Con Edison head Charles (Black-out) Luce, David Yunich, Mayor Beame, Percy Sutton, representatives of Citibank, the phone company, and Helmsley-Spear. They issued a joint statement saying that Fourteenth Street wasn't dead, it could "be turned around," and it was up to the businessmen and government to do it. Luce, chairman of the group, offered $50,000 of Con Edison money each year for three years to this end.

Carvel Moore, a prim lady who once headed a local planning board, said it was "dead wrong" to assume that Sweet 14 was a front group for Charles Luce, the phone company, or anyone else. Sweet 14 was an independent organization looking out for everyone's interests on East Fourteenth Street. She said that Luce's $50,000 was "just a small portion of the money" the group had to work with. Then she brought out a bunch of art-student line drawings showing me how "incredibly inefficient" the Fourteenth Street–Union Square subway station is. It is one of Sweet 14's major tasks to "help remodel the station," said Ms. Moore, pointing out how the station's "awkwardness" made it difficult for employees to get to work. The project will cost $800,000.

She also was very high on "Sweet Sounds in Union Square Park," a concert series sponsored by Sweet 14. Ms. Moore detailed how these musical events brought "working people on their lunch hour back into the park . . . and made the drunks and junkies feel uncomfortable." Drunks and junkies always feel uncomfortable when "normal" people are around, Ms. Moore said.

The most important task of Sweet 14, however, continued Ms. Moore, was "to break up the vicious drug trade and prostitution on Fourteenth Street near Third Avenue." What kind of business, Ms. Moore wanted to know, would want to move to this area with things the way they are now?

Sweet 14, said Ms. Moore, was now working closely with the cops to take "special action" in the area. One of the main problems with local law enforcement, Ms. Moore said, is that the yellow line down Fourteenth Street separates the jurisdictions of the Ninth and Thirteenth Precincts. Some of the more nimble-footed degenerates in the area know this and escape the cops, who are loath to chase bad guys into another precinct. Sweet 14, however, has been "instrumental" in getting Captain Precioso of the Ninth Precinct to set up a "Fourteenth Street Task Force" to deal with this situation. The organization has also "been active" in monitoring the OTB office at the corner of Second Avenue and Fourteenth Street. According to Ms. Moore, people have been known to *loiter* at the OTB, making it a "potential trouble spot."

I wanted to tell Ms. Moore that I often make bets at the Fourteenth Street OTB and then hang out there (admittedly not inhaling deeply), waiting to see how my nag ran. But I held it in. Instead, I wanted to know what, after Sweet 14 succeeded in making East Fourteenth Street safe for businessmen, she suggested doing with the several thousand nether-creatures now populating the street? She indicated that this was a "social problem" and not part of her job. All in all it was a somewhat depressing conversation. And I walked out feeling I would rather buy electricity from Beat Shit Green than a cleanup from Charles Luce.

More troubling was a talk I had with George and Susan Leelike. They are the coheads of "East Thirteenth Street Concerned Citizens Committee." The very name of the group brings up images of whistle-blowing at the sight of a black person and badgering tenants to get up money to plant a tree. But George and Susan Leelike are a little tough to high-hat. After all, they are from the block. They've lived on East Thirteenth Street for fifteen years. Raised a son there. And they came for cool reasons: Back in the late fifties and early sixties, the East Village was hip. Charlie Mingus and Slugs made it hip. The Leelikes related to that.

So, when these people tell you they don't think a pross and a priest in a hallway is funny, you've got to take them seriously. They do have a compelling case. George explains it all: He says the Lower East Side gets reamed because the neighborhood's major industry is "social service." Anytime a neighborhood is poor, "social service" expands. The Lower East Side is both poor and liberal. So, says George Leelike, it has a higher percentage of social work agencies than any other neighborhood in the city. He questions the validity of some of these projects, pointing out that one place, Project Contact, started in the sixties as a teenage runaway home, then went to alcohol treatment, then to drug rehab, and now is back to runaways. This is "grant-chasing," says Leelike. For the social workers to keep their jobs, the projects have to stay open. To stay open, they have to get grants. To get grants, they have to show they understand the "current" problems (read: whatever tabloid papers are screaming about this week) of the community and attract "clients." George Leelike says there are more "clients" on the Lower East Side than any other place in the world.

"Clients," the Leelikes say, are not the most stable neighbors. The worst are the methadone junkies. Beth Israel, says Leelike, has made "millions" from its methadone-maintenance programs that bring thousands of "clients" to the Lower East Side. So have the individual private doctors who run their own methadone clinics in the neighborhood. The Leelikes were a major force in a community drive that shut down one Dr. Triebel's clinic on Second Avenue and Thirteenth Street. Triebel pulled in more than seven hundred thousand dollars in one year, much of it in Medicaid payments.

This kind of activity brought still more sleazos to the neighborhood, the Leelikes said. They pulled out Xeroxed arrest reports from the Ninth and Thirteenth precincts, showing that the majority of the pill-pushers pinched on Fourteenth Street said they were on some kind of methadone program. They said it was a vicious cycle, that many of the people on methadone had no desire or intention of kicking. Most of the local meth freaks were here on "force" programs. The city told them, sign up with a methadone clinic or no welfare.

These were frightening charges, not just because they were indisputably well thought out and apparently true. But because they went to the very core of the two most important issues in the city—race and class. Talking to George Leelike, you had to admire his rational approach to subjects that usually inspire mad, inflammatory outbursts. You also got a closer look at why Ed Koch will be the next mayor of New York City. Koch is the coming wave of politician in New York. His major policy thrust is to appeal to the get-the-creeps-out-of-my-neighborhood constituency. He takes the side of the harried, postliberal middle class against the nether class. It is, after all, a tremendously winning point of view. Even in New York we have to admit that we're so mad we're not going to take it anymore. I even feel like that myself. I'd be crazy not to.

It is chilling and inescapable. Tolerance levels have gone down. The Leelikes said the thing they hated most about the sleazos was that they're so snotty. In the old days, when Susan Leelike went to Cooper Union, junkies hung out in the Sagamore Cafeteria, near Astor Place. Dope fiends those days knew they were outcasts and acted accordingly. The Leelikes remembered these Burroughsian types with a touch of romanticism. Now, they said, methadone makes being a junkie legal. And the creeps have come out into the daylight, where it quickly becomes apparent that junkies aren't the nicest people you'd ever want to meet.

This hit home. A few weeks ago I was walking by Cooper Square. A guy in his mid-twenties was stretched out on the ground, twitching. He didn't look like a lowlife; he had French jeans on. A small crowd gathered around him. A cabbie stopped and put on his emergency blinker. The guy seemed to be having a seizure. Maybe he's an epileptic, said the cabby, pull his tongue out of his mouth. Two people went for the cops, another to call an ambulance. Finally an older man rolled up the guy's sleeve. The dude's arm looked like a Penn Central yard. The older guy threw the arm back on the sidewalk in disgust. "He's just a fucking junkie," the cabby said. "A fucking junkie." Half the people in crowd said, "Shit . . ." And everyone just split. Me, too. I split. When the guy's an epileptic he's human; when he's a junkie, fuck him.

So I knew the Leelikes had the trend on their side. Also, it was clear—they are determined. They are willing to run the risk of being called redneck—Susan Leelike says, "I hate it when they call me the white lady"—to get rid of sleazos. And they don't flinch when you ask them where they propose the sleazos go. "It's just not our problem," they say.

* * *

Patrolmen Bob Woerner and Dennis Harrington are in an empty office above Glancy's Bar on East Fourteenth Street and Irving Place, hiding. Harrington and Woerner have been partners for six years. They used to work the smack detail on Avenues A, B, C, and D (called avenues X, Y, and Z in cop parlance). But pressure from Sweet 14 and local politicians on the department to "do something" about Fourteenth Street brought them here eleven months ago. Since then Woerner and Harrington, tough and smart cops, have been the most effective (in terms of arrests) of the twenty men on the Ninth Precinct's "Fourteenth Street Task Force."

Sometimes Woerner and Harrington walk down Fourteenth Street and ask buzz-brained cats, "Hey, man. What you doing?" It's a torture technique; they know that the toughest question in the world for a sleazo is "What are you doing?" Creeps' knees buckle under the weight of that one; they say, "I dunno, what *am* I doing?"

But what Woerner and Harrington really like to do is make busts. Which is why they are hiding in the empty room above Glancy's Bar with their binoculars trained on the action beneath the Palladium marquee.

Making busts on Fourteenth Street isn't tough. Sometimes guys will be so loaded they come right up and say, "Placidyl . . . Placidyl . . . oh, shee-it" before they realize they're talking to a uniformed policeman. It is tricky, however. First of all, the captain doesn't like cops to make too many arrests. He says busts take police off the street and put them in court. But cops say the department doesn't give enough of a shit about what's in the street to pay overtime. Primarily though, when you're making "observation" busts on Fourteenth Street, you've got to see them good. Most of the sellers get their stuff from scrip doctors, which means their own name is on the bottle. It is not a crime to carry "controlled substances"—if the (not-forged) scrip is made out to you. Selling the stuff, however, is illegal. So, instead of just grabbing a single party, like a smack bust, cops have to get both the buyer and the seller as well as recover the stuff. They also have to see the deal go down perfectly—that is, if they're not into fudging evidence in court.

Woerner and Harrington say, why fudge, on Fourteenth Street if you miss one sale, they'll soon be another. But still, it hurts when you've been freezing behind the Con Edison fence at Fourteenth and Third, waiting for just the right view. And then, right at the big moment, a bus goes by.

Tonight, however, it ain't gonna be no prob-lem. Aerosmith is back in town at the Palladium and a dozen suburban kids are milling around in front of the theater, looking to get stupid. Woerner and Harrington are licking their lips. All they need is a seller. And from down the street, trudging slowly up from Third Avenue by the poolroom, here he comes. In unison the cops shout, "*all right, Ernest James . . . come on, Ernest James.*"

Ernest James, a gangly guy with a face and beard like Sonny Rollins, came on.

He walked into a crowd of leather-jacketed white kids. Got into a conversation with one. Took him off to the doorway of the fight gym. Then it couldn't have been clearer if Otto Preminger were directing. Out came the bottle. There went the pill. Across came the three dollars. And down the stairs went Woerner and Harrington.

Like nothing, Harrington was reading Ernest James his rights. Woerner had the buyer, a blond boy from Pelham Bay, up against the wall. Ernest James, the perfect degenerate, pulled out a slew of false IDs, a pack of Kools, and looked impassively at the sky. Against the wall another kid was screaming to the spread-eagled buyer, "Jeff, Jeff . . . give me your ticket for the show."

Ernest James was in big trouble. He had a goddamned drugstore on him. Ten bottles of pills in all: 26 big white tabs thought to be Quaaludes, 21 Tuinals, 15 Seconals, 40 unknown peach-colored pills, 34 unknown white pills, 23 ampicillins, 29 unknown yellow pills, and several dozen Placidyls. Most of the bottles were made out to Ernest James. Some to Ernest Jones. Others to A. Ramos. One was just to "Ernest," which prompted Woerner to wonder if Ernest James was on a first-name basis with his pharmacist. Also found were two Garcia y Vega humidors full of 5- and 10-mg. Valium. Almost all the scrips were supposedly written by one Doctor Jacob Handler of West 103rd Street. Doctor Handler is a Fourteenth-Street favorite. Harrington keeps a little scorecard of doctors' names that appear on bottles. Doctor Handler is way up near the top of the list. But the cops say nothing will happen to him because "it's tough to bust a doctor."

Apparently to maximize his pill-gathering ability, Ernest James also had half a dozen different medical identification cards. Some were made out to the name William Summersall, others to A. Ramos and Ernest Jones. He also had a little notebook in which he has apparently been practicing different signatures. Most are Ernest Jones. But there is also a page on which Texas Slim is written a dozen times.

Under the fifteen-watt glare in the Ninth's arrest room, Harrington books Ernest James. This is nothing new—Harrington has arrested Ernest James before. In fact, Ernest has six busts for pills this year already. Too bad, figures Dennis Harrington: Ernest James is not a bad guy. In fact, Dennis thinks, most of the guys he busts aren't real bad. Just a bunch of losers. Ernest James had $84 on him, but that had to be his life savings. Most guys have about $30. "Sometimes it is that 'there but for fortune thing,'" says Dennis, who is haunted by the memory of his brother, who was "into junk." He also thinks about that same picture they always show of Karen Quinlan. Dennis wonders if she got her downs on Fourteenth Street.

Asked where he got all the pills, Ernest James is cool. "I'm qualified to have as many pills as I want," he says. Asked about all the different IDs, Ernest says, "I'm qualified to have as many names as I want."

While the cops count up the rest of Ernest's stash, I ask him if he thinks the businessmen and cops can clean up Fourteenth Street. He says, "I dunno 'bout no cleanup. All I know is I wanna get to St. Louis. I can do security over there. I can't sell these pills no more. But if I don't, I got bread and water. My philosophy is that if the city put the clean in the street, they put the dirt in the street, too. Goes both ways. There is one thing that's sure. Ain't no way to clean up this. Cops come fuck up with Fourteenth Street, people just gonna go somewheres else. If they want to get rid of the dirt, they gonna have to shoot those motherfuckers. Line up those motherfuckers and kill them. All of them. Dead."

Woe is Ernest James. He got caught in the cleanup. Usually Ernest winds up with one of those mumbo-jumbo raps like time-served or adjournment contemplating dismissal. In other words, he gets off. Not bad, considering pill-pushing is a class-D felony worth up to seven years. This time, however, Ernest James is taking the fall. The D.A. is making an example of him. A special grand jury on soft drugs is indicting him. Instead of the usual weekend at Rikers, they're offering Ernest a year. And that's if he pleads.

Tough shit, Ernest James. Add insult to injury: When Ernest got picked up on September 30, he claimed it was his birthday. No one believed him. But it was true. *Happy birthday, Ernest James*.

Another thing Ernest James was right about: If you move a sleazo, he'll just go somewhere else. You got to kill the motherfuckers . . . dead. Down in Chinatown, they say that's what Mao did with the opium addicts. Hopheads can't drive tractors, so Mao's guys just put them up against the wall and blew their brains out. Bet there ain't no sleazy corners in Peking.

For a society stuck with half a million sleazoids (conservative metropolitan-area estimate) this could be an eminently modest proposal. Discussing this alternative with liberal city councilman Henry Stern, he says, "Of course, I'm not in favor of killing these people."

But Stern admits that he can't figure out what to do with them. "It's a dilemma," he says, "maybe it's one of the biggest dilemmas in the city today." Miriam Friedlander, another liberal councilperson who has been working closely with Sweet 14, also does not favor wholesale annihilation. She takes a more conventional tack, saying. "It's my primary function to break up that situation and get them out of the neighborhood."

In place of execution, the politicians offer "redevelopment." "Redevelopment" is a coming concept in the city-planning business. A modification of the pave-it-all-over-and-start-from-scratch school of urban studies, "redevelopment" essentially means taking over "depressed" areas and transforming them into middle-class shopping and residential areas. The best-known example of "redevelopment" is on Forty-second Street between Ninth and Tenth Avenues. A civic group came into possession of several "tax-arrears" buildings and redid them into boutiques. Henry Stern, Miriam Friedlander, Koch, and the rest feel that "redevelopment" is at least worth trying on Fourteenth Street and Third Avenue. And with economic biggies like Charlie Luce, Helmsley-Spear, Citibank, and Restaurant Associates around, you know the job will get done right. Oh, boy, will it.

Of course, "redevelopment" stops short of final solutions. So Ernest James's philosophy holds up. Due to the hard-nose police work by the "Fourteenth Street Task Force," the sleazos have begun a minor migration. Routed from parts of Fourteenth Street, they camped in Stuyvesant Park on Second Avenue and Fifteenth Street. According to the locals, who say they pay extra rent to live near the park, the situation is becoming disgusting. Methadone addicts are leaving their bottles all over the place. Pill-pushers are dealing. The other day two of the he-shes got into a little mutual around-the-world.

The neighborhood forces rallied, led by one Jeanne Pryor, a right-minded lady who loves a firm grip on the bullhorn (who last week opened a cleanup storefront at Fourteenth and Third). They decided that the Thirteenth Precinct was not providing adequate protection from the sleazos. They demanded police guards in the park.

One night last month a protest march was organized. About 150 people showed up to carry signs saying things like OUR CHILDREN ONCE PLAYED FRISBEE IN THIS PARK. Others carried shopping bags full of empty scrip bottles they said were collected in the park. These were a present for Capt. Joseph Neylan of the Thirteenth, who, Ms. Pryor kept shouting, "has been out to lunch for the past six months."

The march, accompanied by a man in a kilt playing a bagpipe, began at Fifteenth Street and headed up Third Avenue toward the precinct house on Twenty-first Street. Ms. Pryor had planted stories in the *Daily News*, so the local television stations sent out crews to cover. Arc lights flooded the streets as Ms. Pryor led the chant of "junkies out of the park."

As the march reached Seventeenth Street, it started to get interesting. A messed-up black guy bounded in front of the marchers and held up his hands like he was stopping a runaway team of horses.

"Stop!" he said, the TV lights glaring in his buzzed eyes. Stunned, Ms. Pryor halted in her tracks. The whole march bumped to a stop. There was a silence. Then the guy started chanting, "Junkies out of the park. Junkies out of the park." The marchers stepped back. They guy kept screaming, "Junkies out of the park. Junkies out of the park." Then he stopped and looked the bagpipe player right in the eye and said, "I'm a fucking junkie . . . I'm a fucking junkie . . . I'm a fucking junkie . . . Get me out of the park . . . Get me out of the park . . . Get me out of the park . . ."

The mock has turned to a plea.

It was then that Jeanne Pryor should have acted. She should have taken out a 12-gauge shotgun and blown the creep's head off.

22
In Old Times Square

An annal of post-gentrification, to be read as a bookend/addenda to the previous Fourteenth Street piece. A short take on the cleaned up Forty-second Street. From New York *magazine, 2001.*

Back in the 1970s Day, it was considered an excellent chemistry project to walk down Forty-second Street between Seventh and Eighth Avenue, a.k.a. The Deuce, the heart of Times Square, and buy every drug offered. This might include, in the contemporary vernacular of the local denizens, "snow" (cocaine), "bush" (pot), "t's and v's" (Tuinals and Valiums), "dust" (PCP), "ludes" (Quaaludes), and of course "skag" (heroin). The experiment entailed testing the acquired stuff in the lab to determine what percentage, if any, of the alleged drug existed amid the baby powder, mannite, battery acid shavings, and oregano. From a forensic point of view, it made you wonder: If a dope-pusher pushed dope with no dope in it and got busted, what was the charge, beyond fraud?

It was on Forty-second Street that I saw my first bare breast, outside of my mother's, that is. It was a Saturday afternoon. Likely some lie was told about going bowling at the seventy-two-lane emporium back in our Queens homeland, when actually we were on the 7 train, heading toward The Deuce. So many Saturdays were spent surreptitiously there, pawing through the backdate magazine stores, whiling away hours in the grand cornucopia of belly-run cinemas—the Harris, the Selwyn, the Anco, the Apollo,

the Lyric, etc. We knew them all—"legitimate" theaters back in another Times Square Day but by then gone to sticky-floor seed and triple bills of horror movies like William Castle's *Mr. Sardonicus*. If you were lucky, as we were one memorable afternoon, you might hear an immortal shout from the balcony: "*Sorry?* You piss on my date and you say you're *SORRY?*"

We would invariably wind up at Hubert's Museum and Flea Circus. On the ground floor, Hubert's was the usual Forty-second Street mélange of pinball machines and presses to print up fake newspaper headlines, like MR. HAINES, DICKHEAD ALGEBRA TEACHER DEFENESTRATES SELF, CROWD GOES WILD.

But it was the lower level, down the wide flight of linoleum-covered stairs, that was the true lure. Down there, the famous fleas pulled tiny covered wagons and toy taxis. Down there was the Atomic Man. Radiation from the fallout of Cold War nuclear testing had sprouted a crêpe papier nose on the back of his head. Here, also, were the ancient flip card machines. You put a nickel in a slot, pressed your eyes to a rubber cup, and turned the crank. Inside was a woman by the seashore. She smiled and took off her blouse. Turn the handle backward, she put the blouse back on, reverse and you got to see her take it off again.

Hubert's disappeared into the mists of time, and I didn't think much about the place until the early 1980s, in the realm of Koch, when Times Square, The Deuce in particular, was at its cruddiest, full of wall-to-wall porno and crack sellers who sold real crack. One day I was riding uptown on the train that used to be called "the double R." Across from me sat an attractive Latin-looking woman in jeans and a tight white top under a thin leather jacket. She had a book on her lap. She looked tired, every once in a while her eyes would close. It was a moment of urban intimacy, an instant of unguardedness: As she dozed off I could really stare. Then her book fell out of her hand, onto the subway floor, landing at my feet. It was a self-help book with what appeared to be an astrological spin, *Make the Future Your Friend.*

I tapped the shoulder of her leather jacket, handed the book back. She smiled sleepily, said thanks. Slayed me, that smile, sweet, unassuming, a little ravaged but touching. That seemed to be that, except that we both got off at Times Square, and there she was again, walking west on Forty-second Street. Halfway down the block she turned and went into Peepland.

Now, I knew Peepland. Some of it I learned from my cousin Irv, the family smutmeister who happened to run Super Sound Peeps XXX down the street. Onetime confederate of the legendary Martin Hodas, reputed inventor of the twenty-five-cent film loop booth, Irv bragged that his arm had once been personally broken by Matty (The Horse) Ianello, the primero Times Square mobster magnate.

Cousin Irv once explained to me what I've always taken to be the essence of pornography. To wit: When he first opened, like many of The Deuce smut shops, Irv offered "Live Girls." He had a flashing neon sign that blinked GIRLS . . . LIVE . . . LIVE . . . LIVE . . . which seemed a little redundant, but likely warded off the stray necrophiliacs. The customer entered a small booth, put a quarter into a slot and a metal window would rise, offering a peek of a woman. Oftentimes they were standing there buck naked completely stoned, teetering about on five-inch heels. Others could be seen fast asleep in a chair. One day, however, cousin Irv decided to get rid of his "live girls." They were one hassle after another, he said. They took drugs, got in catfights. Their cheap mugger boyfriends were always hanging around.

Irv replaced the "live girl" booths with more film stalls. It was much better that way, Irv said memorably. "If there's one thing I've learned in this business, it is that you don't need actual women."

Not all the Forty-Deuce porno places followed Irv's edict, however. Peepland always had "live girls." Upstairs were the film and video booths, and downstairs, as the barkers so pungently put it, were the "live girls." Obviously the woman who'd ridden with me on the train was a "live girl." It was a strange opportunity to indulge an idle subway fantasy. You see a woman and you wonder. Now, for a quarter I could look through a window and see this particular woman naked. For a dollar I could touch her breasts.

As I headed for the staircase, it dawned on me: I'd been here before. This was the same linoleum staircase down which I'd once strode with my horny junior high school buddies. Peepland was Hubert's Museum, former home of the Atomic Man, where I'd spent a nickel to see my first ever so genteel naked breast. The realization stopped me in my tracks. Here, in Hubert's old basement, I couldn't feature myself pushing a sweaty dollar bill through a metal slot to touch the breast of a woman who was reading a self-help book about making the future your friend.

Now, of course, The Deuce is a different place. As a form of full circle, Easy Everything, which claims to be the "world's largest Internet cafe," where tourists stop to send e-mails back to Iowa and Australia, occupies the space formerly occupied by Hubert's and Peepland. For a dollar you get an hour of surfing, but the firewalls block out the porn, an irony which is in keeping with the Times Square we have now.

First conceived in the decrepit seventies, stalled in the flatline eighties, built in the go-go nineties, and now, in the gone-gone 2000s, Times Square is host to an indoor ferris wheel (at Toys "R" Us), a million new billboards, a dozen "theme" restaurants (the WWF restaurant and the Frank Gehry–designed cafeteria at the Conde Nast building are only two of these heavily branded offerings), plus *The Lion King*. Instead of PCP/Drano salesmen, blowout videos, *Scream Blacula Scream* in the grind houses, and the skells bumming Kools in front of Al Shark's bodega, there's Ernst and Young, the Yankee store, and the Hilton, where unlike the hot, dirty sheets of the National Hotel, they'll put a mint on pillow in your seven-hundred-dollar suite. Just the other day, instead of flipping through backdate numbers of *Jugs*, *Cavalier*, and *Leg Show*, I went into the Universal Magazine store (at the same address as cousin Irv's joint) to pick up the new issue of *Parabola*, the journal of "Myth, Tradition, and the Search For Meaning." Even if those reprints of Krishnamurti Q and As don't really have the same pith of a *Dude* pictorial, at least now I can buy a four-dollar cup of coffee and thumb through the wisdom in a Ranch One food court.

Really, it doesn't pay to get upset about this. They couldn't really leave it the way it was: Times Square, the most famous intersection in the world, a totally feral sleazolopolis. All that money off the books. Who can say it isn't nice to sit on the lawn at Bryant Park without some zombie hurling on you. But progress—why does it always have to look like this: one big shiny and stupid product placement canvas. The big bitch is that only tourists go to the Disney Deuce now. Sounds right, I'm a tourist here myself. Every time I'm up here, they've got some brand-new building, another giant ad. You stand there and gawk, like all the rest of the Iowans.

The Deuce used to be an escape from parents. But now, like all good tourists, we bring the kids. We eat at the ESPN Zone where they've got little TVs in the bathrooms, so you don't miss a moment of a really crucial Georgia Tech–Clemson game while taking a piss. Then we go over to Madame Tussaud's, to see the dummies. It costs only about $125 for a family of five to walk around and get their picture taken with Castro, Hitler, Ru Paul, Lou Reed, and the rest. But there are compensations. They just put in this really fabulous likeness of Giuliani, smiling like the courageous, selfless hero that he is. Someone had already taped a "kick me" sign to the back of his waxy blue suit. A blowtorch would have been better but it was good to see the spirit of the Street isn't totally dead.

23
Under the Boardwalk

Of Sunken Barges, Oil Spills, and the Fight for a Cleaner New York. From the Village Voice, *1978.*

It could have been still one more urban horror story in a season already chock full of municipal duress. On Monday the steam dredge *Pennsylvania*, under contract to the Army Corps of Engineers, was working in the Rockaway Canal. The seas grew rough. The dredge sought safe harbor off Breezy Point. Visibility, however, was limited, and the vessel touched ground in the shallow waters. It sank. A Coast Guard cutter rescued the crew members. But nothing could be done about the oil—30,000 gallons of thick, viscous number 6 and 7,000 more of lighter number 2—that began to leak from the ship's storage tanks.

On Tuesday, driven by high winds, traces of the tarlike number 6 began to wash up on Rockaway beaches. On Wednesday the oil was pushed eastward toward the shoreline of Manhattan, Brighton, and Coney Island. That's was then that tensions began to mount. No one was sure how much of the sticky petroleum might discharge from the submerged barge. The National Weather Service added some grim news. Heavy seas were predicted—heavy enough to completely break the dredge up. Environmentalists feared the spread of the oil slick into the bird sanctuaries of Jamaica Bay. By Thursday morning the newspapers carried a much more frightening story. Some experts felt the oil could be washed out toward the huge sewage deposits in the Atlantic. Then, health officials said, the sewage and all its attendant diseases could spew out onto the city's beaches. At 2:30, after careful consideration of the facts, city parks commissioner Gordon Davis ordered Brighton, Manhattan, and Coney Island beaches closed.

That set the stage for Friday, Saturday, and Sunday. The weekend. Just two weekends earlier, nearly 2 million people, seeking relief from one of the hottest summers on record, flocked to these now-closed beaches. Weathermen were predicting more of the same, ninety degrees or more.

The upcoming scenario wasn't hard to imagine. By 10:00 A.M. Saturday, disc jockeys were barking from radios everywhere that it was already 89 degrees and going to get "a whole lot hotter." A scorcher!

And they'd come. The multitudes traveling the graffiti-painted, unair-conditioned Sea Beach trains, irritable from standing through forty minutes of fits and starts, their flowered shirts stuck to the damp contours of their armpits. From everywhere they'd come. From Brooklyn, from the Bronx. Families of eight jammed into blue Impalas slung so low the muffler spit sparks as it scraped the baked pavement of Mermaid Avenue. By the tens of thousands they'd come—orange towels draped across their sweaty necks like a uniform, plastic woven beach chairs in their hands—desperate to cool the frustration of a week in the life of the mailroom.

The Parks Department WATER POLLUTED signs would not deter them. Nothing would. Certainly not the thin blue line of cops telling them the beaches were closed. At first there'd be some minor pushing and shoving. Then, in the shadow of the Coney Island parachute jump, the Homicides, pork-pie-hatted pint-sized gangsters, would slit their eyes and sneer, "What you mean, we can't go swimming?" It would only be a matter of time before a local was run through with the business end of a beach umbrella. The Trampps' "Disco Inferno" would play, loud as a massive surf, black as night with oil, crashed onto the strand.

The Oil Slick of 1978 could have rivaled the Blackout of 1977. But it came up rainy on Friday, Saturday, and Sunday, too. So there was no great lemming chase to the unctuous Coney ocean. There were only the paint-chipped STAUCH BATHS signs against the gray sky, the even-spaced rusted mesh garbage cans on the mottled sand, and the distant screams of the self-destructive taking the first drop on the Cyclone. The cops were in no fighting mood. Standing on the boardwalk in groups of three, they said, "If they want to go in the water, hey, fuck 'em. It's a free country, free to be an idiot." Actually, only one person was swimming at Coney. He was a middle-aged man in a white bathing cap who went out fifty feet and started yelling, "I'm a Polar Bear, a Puerto Rican Polar Bear, I don't taste no oil. You can taste oil."

Still, the oil spill was up front on every newscast. The *Post* ran page-one headlines detailing the FIGHT TO SAVE CITY BEACHES. Gordon Davis got more TV face time than the last four parks commissioners put together.

The swimmers and surfers might be few and far between, but the oil was supposed to still be coming. The Parks Department informed us that they were concentrating their "major effort" Friday at Brighton Beach. The city had several workers out there constructing "berms," a kind of sand ridge. The idea is: the "oil-impacted" water spills over the "berm" at high tide and, hopefully, the sludge stays on the rise so it cannot be swept out to sea again or soil the beach sand. Then the trapped oil is put into plastic bags and carted away to landfill projects.

As we arrived at Brighton, one crew of New York City's frontline environmental soldiers was breaking for lunch after two hard hours of battling the oncoming oil slick. A thin and haggard foreman with eyeglasses as thick as his wrist was leading the shovel-carrying detail. He was also screaming—to no one in particular—"What's the story here? Do we eat, or don't we eat? Nobody tells me nothing." His men were not listening. Some were running down the boardwalk to Hirsch's Knishes Stand. "We're not eating whatever shit they got for us back at the office," they offered.

Soon a dump truck pulled up on the boardwalk. The guys threw their shovels in the back and jumped aboard. The truck was crowded with workers. Somewhat overcrowded, as it would turn out. After everyone posed for a photograph, the truck pulled away and began to rumble down the boardwalk. As it got further away, I began to think—shit, we're sure not going to get much of a story about heroic civil servants risking all to battle a potential ecological disaster. Instead of casting themselves into the breach, the Parks Department guys seemed on permanent lunch hour. The seaside calm, however, was quickly shattered by the sound of splintering wood. The truck carrying the would-be oil slick fighters had fallen through the boardwalk.

It took less than a minute to run down to the scene, but things were already shaping up quite definitively. There was a fifteen-foot gash in the boardwalk where the truck was wedged, its chassis bent out of alignment. All around, in differing states of supposed disrepair and suffering, were Parks Department employees.

Each worker had at least one pant leg or shirt sleeve rolled up. To a blind person, the boardwalk could have passed for the Wailing Wall. But a closer look could have made it a sensory class at the Actor's Studio. Everyone was moaning. "I'm dying, I'm a fucking dead man," cried one guy. "I'm a CETA worker four years, got no title, almost got killed right here in Brighton!" yelled another. The next claimed to have been "shot with ack ack in his spinal cord in 'Nam . . . but nothing ever hurt like this." He claimed two of his ribs were about to break through the skin. Another guy, clutching his leg, said, "Shit, I live in the Bronx, had to come down here to get fucked up. Shoveling oil, can you believe that. Fucking Koch." Another was holding his back and yelling, "I need a massage, I need a massage."

As soon as I got my pad out one of the heroes said, "You a lawyer? They better get a lawyer down here." "Yeah," said another man holding his knee, "one who can count."

Meanwhile, the apartment terraces over the boardwalk were filling with curious Brighton old people. A crowd gathered around the truck. One lady with blue hair looked at the gaping hole in the boardwalk and said, "I don't know what's with them today, can't they see there's a hole here? They got to drive right into it?" Also on the scent was a young man in green overalls that said FRANKLIN TYPOGRAPHERS on the back. He looked at the truck and shook his head. "You know," he said, "I was just on my way down here to put a sign up telling you guys not to ride on the carriage lane, it's weak, you know." And over by the railing a black transvestite in a blue dress and a face full of Nixonian stubble taunted one of the fallen workers. "Bet I make more money than you." The worker made an amazing recovery. He knocked a bag of Cheez Doodles out of the t.v.'s hand and said, "Least I don't got to take no dick in my ass."

"You are really a BITCH," answered the transvestite, sheer rayon shirt snug against her bottom as she sought to pick up the scattered Cheese Doodles. "A faking, stupid bitch. You're not hurt, you stupid bully."

The whining grew more intense as two truckloads of "white shirts" (bosses) pulled up. One enormously fat and blasé supervisor, who'd obviously seen this drama before, said, "Okay, okay, all men claiming injury go over to the railing." Those who said they could walk moved in unison. At least ten workers said they couldn't move. "Okay," the supervisor intoned, "those claiming injury AND lack of mobility, just lie there, but stop screaming, all right?" Then, with a look of resignation, he took out a clipboard and said, "Just gimme your name, your title, and the extent of your injury."

Meanwhile, the blame was being shifted around. One white shirt called over the skinny supervisor. The supervisor muttered something about how he'd been "with the Parks thirty-one years, through Hoving, Heckscher, through them all . . . I could have told them they needed hay to get rid of oil, hay. They needed hay."

"Hay? Like horse hay?" asked another supervisor. "What's that gonna do?"

"Like a sponge . . . soaks the shit right up." Meanwhile two more Parks Department cars pulled up.

"How many guys on the truck, Arch?" asked the newly arrived white shirt. "Six, I think," answered the foreman.

"Six? You got at least ten guys here moaning. And what about the others?"

"Maybe we were a little packed," the foreman allowed.

"This is a problem: two dozen accident reports on a six-man truck."

They spent the next few moments getting their story straight. "Let's figure out what happened here," the white shirt said. "You had to swerve to avoid a pedestrian, that's right, right?"

"Right," the foreman said.

"You just hit a weak spot, right?"

"Right." With that the foreman looked at the ocean and said, "I knew I should have walked."

By now several ambulances had pulled up. A ruthlessly efficient man with a walkie-talkie was conducting the wounded. "Which ones can walk?" he bellowed. "Those go down to those ambulances in the street." Three workers headed toward a pair of ambulances and started to get into one of them. Seeing this, the walkie-talkie yelled, "Hey, yo, yo, not that one, the other one." Then he said, "Stay in there. You're last."

The workers groaned. "Now we got to wait," one of them said, as if he was wondering if all this was worth it. Another added, "Why don't they just gimme my check and a Band-Aid?" Up on the boardwalk, a chubby nurse was moving one of the supposedly more seriously hurt oil-slick fighters onto a stretcher. He grimaced magnificently, like a trench battler stunned by mustard gas. As they carried him away, the transvestite singsonged, "That's a phony, that's a phony. Oh, he is a phony."

It was more than an hour after the truck went through the boardwalk before the cops arrived. Immediately they told the remaining spectators to "get back, get back." In return, the cops were beseeched by a slew of Brighton matrons yelling, "No benches, no benches, they steal our benches." Seeing a camera, the ladies pointed to a barren stretch of boardwalk, again chanting, "No benches, take a picture, no benches. Tell Congressman Solarz he lied. He said benches but there are no benches. None at all." When the last of the ambulances had gone, a giant bulldozer pulled up. It was supposed to pull the truck out of the hole. The bulldozer driver was wearing sunglasses, shorts, and sandals. As soon as he got out of the cab, a cop dropped the heavy link-chain from the winch on the driver's unprotected foot.

"Hey," the trucker said, "that's my goddamn toe."

We felt we could do no more in this aspect of our oil-slick coverage. So we went over to the Coast Guard station, where we were informed that the slick had just about dissipated. The Guard, working with a company called Queen Venture—an independent contractor that makes millions out of cleaning up oil spills—had pumped the last of the gunk out of the sunken dredge and no more of the stuff was turning up on beaches. Then Paul Elliot, an official with the Environmental Protection Agency, said that the water around Coney Island was "really bad, but no worse than usual." In fact, the oil slick had pretty much been overblown to begin with. Very little oil had escaped the barge. This was a relief for swimmers, who plunged back into the mucky water. Still, it was kind of sad: all those Park Department heroes putting their lives on the line for nothing.

24
Terror on the N Train

A strange adventure of youth, recalled. From the Village Voice, *1977.*

I spied my old fat friend Bart the other day. Like old times, he was sitting in a snot-green foreign car eating a brownie and swigging milk from the quart container in front of Cakemasters on Thirty-fourth Street. For eight years of no see, Big Bart could have looked worse. The car was an improvement. Big Bart used to drive a Corvair that had holes in the floorboards. He heard that Ralph Nader said Corvairs were killer machines, moving time bombs, that they could go off the road, up the embankment, with a single nudge of the wheel. So Big Bart went out and got one with no front alignment. He was that kind of guy.

Still, he looked relatively the same. Big Bart was one of those bald-spot-in-the-middle/long-greasy-hair-on-the-sides type of hippies. Now the bald spot has grown like a spreading Rorschach blot, but the grease remains the same. So did the chub. We had some info that Big Bart was married to a woman who had a snake tattoo on her tummy who put him on a yoga diet. You'd never be able to tell.

Back then, in 1969, when we shared a seventy-dollar-a-month pad on Hillside Avenue and Sutphin Boulevard in Queens, there was a saying that Big Bart either had the lowest-cut pants or the highest-cut ass in town. The crack was always visible. Big Bart used to come out of his room naked.

(The room was painted orange and black: Mr. Rotherstein, our landlord, railed, "You painted this wall psychodeckic. Psychodeckic is not in your lease." But we were the only whites in the building, so we got over.) He'd lay that hairy ass on me and my former wife. Moon over Miami, Big Bart called it. We hid under the covers hoping it would go away. But every time we peeked out it would still be there, shining on.

I was with Big Bart the last time I took acid.

Those days Big Bart played drums in bar bands on Long Island. If the joint was past Exit 51, Big Bart played it. For a sweating slob in a flannel shirt, Bart was immortal, in that Island rocker kind of way. He twirled his sticks better than Sal Mineo in the *Gene Krupa Story*. He knew the Young Rascals greatest hits better than Dino Danelli. When Big Bart beat out "Can't Turn You Loose" on his meaty thighs, it could be magic.

On this particular night Big Bart was moving uptown. He had a gig in a church basement on Lexington Avenue and Twenty-second Street, borough of Manhattan. *The City!* Man, this was the big-time. But the show wasn't until ten o'clock. We had eleven hours to kill and Big Bart had two yellow pills shaped like pumpkin seeds he said would do the trick. I had my doubts. I had just returned from California and was skeptical of what the potent combo of pumpkin seed acid and the Big Apple might foment in my highly impressionable mind. Up in Tilden Park in Berkeley you could look at a tree for six hours, say "Oh, wow," and incur minimal permanent damage. New York was another story.

But after Bart dropped, there wasn't much choice. What was I gonna do, spend eleven hours watching him take acid? Everything was cool as long as the sun stayed up: we made faces at the gorilla in the park zoo, acted unruly on Park Avenue, stared at the guy blowing smoke on the Times Square Camel ad, watched the buildings weave like in a Stan Van Der Beek underground movie. For a kick, we bought some Gypsy Rose, the cheapest rotgut available, and went looking for our buddy, George Washington Goldberg.

G.W.G., as he called himself, spent the majority of his time in Washington Square Park, where he had achieved a modicum of fame for once making his way up into an NYU biology lecture room. Pushing his way by the professor, George erased the diagrams on the blackboard and told the hundred students, "Okay, now G.W.G. is gonna tell you what biology is really all about." The Wackenhuts carried him out. A star, G.W.G. He'd see you from a distance, stand up, bow, and say, "Oh, finally, a better class of people . . . would you guys like a job, Sonny Liston is looking for sparring partners." This time, though, we blew G.W.G's mind, pulling out our bottle of Gypsy Rose from the brown paper bag and handing it to him, as a present. "Unopened," George said, tears welling up in his eyes. "The seal not even cracked. No tooth marks. I'm overcome."

Later Big Bart and I went to Hong Fat on Mott Street to giggle over the bacon-wrapped shrimp with the rest of the hippies. Bart ordered his usual: curry beef, super hot extra sauce, five Seven-Ups. He ate the slop in sweaty spasms, banging his chest like a doctor gunning a pacemaker. And said, "Good!"

What a day we were having! Big Bart said there was only one hassle. For Big Bart, any time you had to do *anything,* it was a hassle. The hassle was that Bart had to call Ben the bassist to tell him where the gig was.

Bart went off to find a working phone booth while I sat on the curb of Elizabeth Street staring at the street lamp. It could have been the moon. Bart returned with a look of horror on his face. He was pasty white. Ben the bassist couldn't make it. He was sick. The only other bass player Bart knew was Lou, the crazed 650-Triumph freak who lived in Bensonhurst. There was something wrong with Lou's phone. We'd have to go out there.

Oh shit.

The N train, what the fuck do we know from the N train? We're from Queens. Brooklyn is a scary dark thing. The subway map. Fuck. Some Puerto Rican wrote on it. In, like, *Spanish*.

Journey to the end of the Nightsville. Drunk on the subway, okay. Glue on the subway, ride it out. But acid on the subway, *yaaahhh*. Big Bart and I held on to each other. All we knew was: Bay Ridge Parkway, get off. The train is packed. Across the way a pizza-faced white guy in a pea coat is playing 45s on a portable turntable. Like life or death, Big Bart dives at the guy's leg and asks, "Do you have any Chuck Berry?" The kid pulls "No Particular Place to Go" out of his pocket. Saved. Thank you, Lord! Saved again. The people on the train are going nuts. Half of them want the kid to turn it up, the rest want to kill him.

Somehow we found Lou, a husky weight-lifting type, communing with the television in his mother's living room. The mother, a Jewish-Italian widow lady, came to the door, took one look at our faces, and almost broke out crying. It was easy to see why. *Lou was taking acid too!* He was nearly catatonic. Big Bart and I breathed relief: Here, at last, was someone we could talk to.

Lou indicated, sure, he could play the gig. Only problem was he worked for Grand Union on Eighty-sixth Street and had to make his deliveries first. He said it would go faster if we came along. Eighty-sixth Street has an elevated train running over it. Lou shot that Dodge Tradesman between the subway pilings like a downtown slalom skier. Big Bart broke into a box of Oreos as we rolled around in the back of the van trying not to barf into the bags of groceries. How Lou had a nice smile for all those Italian ladies when he brought them their Ronzoni is an unsolved mystery. How we got to the gig is another event lost in the mists.

Talking in front of Cakemasters on Thirty-fourth Street, Big Bart and I agree that we can't remember much more of that day—except that the priest at the church smoked pot to show he was hip. Outside of that and a couple of questions about how our respective parents were, there wasn't all that much more to talk about, even if Bart did play "Can't Turn You Loose" on his leg for old times' sake. Bart has been in half a dozen bands since those days. Once he was supposed to go out on the road with Don Covay, author of *Chain of Fools*. But it fell through. Now playing in bands is just a job. Big Bart works in an auto parts store during the day. I remember when Big Bart slept all day. But what are you going to do when you're married and have three kids? Bart hasn't taken acid since that night either.

25
Signs of the Times

Meditation on the ad-scape. Not all billboards are created equal. From New York *magazine, 2001.*

One more bad Kafka dream in the Big City: you get up one morning and the view, such as it was, outside the window of your hideously overpriced sixth-floor studio is gone. Once you could see as far as the loft conversion across the street. A sliver of sky. Wide open spaces. But now there is nothing but dim murk. You are under water. In fact, you are inside a fifty-foot-tall bottle of Evian, three bucks a quart. Then you realize: Your cosmopolitan dream pad has been "wrapped," encased like a ham sandwich within the ad industry's newest (semi) see-through Mylar miracle fiber. You now live inside a gargantuan billboard. Today it is Evian, but "wrapping" allows admen to change messages quickly. Next week you might be seeing the world from inside the massive breast of an H & M model.

Like in *Blade Runner*, Ur-blueprint for the current-day ultragraphic selling-scape, now we're all "little people." It's only the forty-foot-tall guys in the Calvin Klein underwear ads who are big. All around town the corporate graffiti is thicker than the glyphs covering the inside of a 1978 IRT car. There ought to be a law, and with the thicket of faux-Vegas wrap jobs around buildings and buses maybe there will be one. Late last year, citing "advances in lighting and illumination technologies," the City Planning Commission had "a comprehensive plan to address the recent proliferation of large, out-of-scale advertising signs."

Which has its downside, since, as anyone who has ever attempted to sate interstate driving boredom by counting billboards while on the way to Wall Drug, South Dakota, knows, there's something un-American about not loving a giant sign.

At least that's what I was thinking the other day as I watched the first double rainbow I've ever seen in Brooklyn arch above the HOME OF EAGLE CLOTHES sign, which, more than a half century after it was first constructed, still towers like an Easter Island effigy over the low-slung factory zone along the Gowanus Canal.

Huge faded letters set with industrial elegance upon a fifty-foot-square metal frame topped by a reddish globe, the Eagle sign speaks of a more primal, less fleeting capital era. It was a time when unconglomerated sewing machine makers, staple manufacturers, coffin coopers, and a thousand other small-time merchants, Santini Brothers movers or Saltzman druggists, proud of their stake in the New World, felt the need to proclaim themselves—to carve their names upon the skyline in both paint and blinking neon so everyone knew: *Here we are!*

The sign that Stanley and Fred Goldman built on top of their menswear factory at Third Avenue and Sixth Street, in what used to be called South Brooklyn, was bigger than most. It has also lasted longer, nearly three decades beyond the day the Goldmans' plant, which once employed 750 people, closed up for good in 1976. Chances are, the sign, constructed of three-and-three-quarter-inch metal pipes, will also outlive the U-Haul storage facility that has occupied the bunkerlike building for the past twenty years.

To many, objects like the Eagle sign, which can be seen from half a mile around if you have the right angle, are invisible. When I walked into the U-Haul place and asked the people working there, some for ten years or more, "What do you know about that sign on the roof?" everyone said the same thing: "What sign?" Brought outside to look at the looming insignia, they squinted and said, "Oh, that."

People do notice it, however. Karl Szari, late of Belarus, who runs the transmission shop at the corner of Third Avenue, says he once saw an eagle perch on the Eagle sign.

"Right there, on the "g." *An eagle!* An eagle on the eagle sign! Maybe it could have been a hawk. I dunno. It looked like an eagle to me." An amateur sculptor who likes to weld together old pieces of engine parts, Karl thinks the Eagle sign is "beautiful . . . you know, sometime those old neon tubes will fall off like arrows and are gonna kill someone someday, but when the sun's going down the silhouette is great. I got a lot of pictures."

Dominic Lanzi, who owned an ironworks shop near Seventh Street for forty years, sees the sign as a piece of "history."

"I looked at that sign every day, through the window of my shop," says Dominic, now employed as a "senior welder" at Greenwood Cemetery. "It used to cast its shadow on the street so sharp that you could read the letters. EAGLE . . . It was owned by Jewish people, but Italians worked there. A lot of Italians. They were tailors, did cut goods. Hot weather, cold, in the morning I'd watch them come to work, walking from the subway. I'd look at the door, say hello. But I never bought an Eagle suit. Sometimes, if they had a inventory clearance sale, I'd go look. But I never bought."

My father, though, he was an Eagle man, at least when he wasn't venturing to moderately upscale Witty Brothers on Division Street, another defunct clothier. This is no surprise to Dennis Brenner, a genial, energetic man whose résumé (topped with the rubric 30 YEARS OF MANAGEMENT RETAIL AND APPAREL *I've been there, done that!*) is the only item that turns up when running an Internet search for "Eagle Clothes."

"Back then, quality-wise there were what we called 2 makers, 4 makers, and 6 makers. Eagle was a 4 maker. Right in the middle. It was the suit of the workingman. If your father was a teacher, "Eagle would be right for him," says Dennis, a former vice president at the firm, who was pleased to find out that my mother purchased my bar mitzvah suit at B and B Lorry's, one of Eagle's main outlets.

"You see, back in the fifties and sixties there were dozens of chains like Lorry's," remarked Dennis, who now lives in Jersey and says he "never gets tired" of talking about the menswear business. "Or at least what *used* to be the menswear business . . . There was Wallach's, Bond's, Hickey-Freeman,

Ripley's, Robert Hall, Howard's, Weber and Heilbroner, Field Brothers, plenty more. A lot of people don't understand this, but the fashion world was more dynamic then. Back then, when styles changed, they changed across the board, not just in some subculture. If side vents came in, everyone got side vents. Continental pants, that was through the roof. There were fifteen kinds of underwear . . . places like Eagle were conservative but they had to keep up, like everyone else. . . .

"In the end, Eagle was killed by its own customers. They pulled the rug out. The leisure suit, those kind of fabrics, that was the kiss of death. The cost of making stuff here compared to overseas, that was a problem, too. But mostly—like everything else—the middle got squeezed. These days you've got the top, the runway stuff on TV that no one wears, and the low end, the sneakers and jeans that everyone wears. A place like Eagle, they got strangled from both sides.

"For me, it was a disaster, because I grew up selling menswear. I really loved it. I could tell you the location of every Weber and Heilbroner branch in Manhattan. Hart, Shaffner and Marx, too. I had it all in my head, like some people remember stocks or baseball averages. Now that it is all gone, it's like it was a giant joke, played on me and others who believed in it.

"That's why I don't like to drive by that Eagle sign. For me it is this giant tombstone. The end of the world I knew."

Then, again, the South Brooklyn skyline is filled with many such semiological fossils. Few motorists who have plied the ever-snarled byways of the Gowanus Expressway are unfamiliar with the Kentile Floors sign, a billboard even more Goliathan, if somewhat less aesthetic, than Eagle. Its pale purple neon no longer flickering, the eight-story monolith was erected sometime in the 1940s by the Kentile company, which billed itself as "America's largest manufacturer of super resilient floor tile." Founded by Arthur Kennedy (hence Ken-tile) in 1898, the Kentile factory shut down in 1988 following a series of strikes, high-cost lawsuits concerning asbestos content in the tiles, and creeping plant obsolescence. But their towering, iron-framed sign, too costly to remove, lives on.

"That sign . . . it is like a mountain on the desert, a ziggurat on the horizon," says Jack Marmurston, a boisterously roughhewn man in a yarmulke who owns the New York Airport Service, which parks its many buses and minivans on the oil-slicked grounds where Second Avenue meets the Gowanus Canal.

"When I first came out here, it was just me and Kentile. That sign was my beacon. I could set my watch to it, depending on where the light hit," says Marmurston, surveying his bus fleet, which he describes as having three kinds of vehicles, "Running, not running, and monument."

Asked if he thought the Kentile sign should be landmarked (no commercial sign ever has been, not even the Pepsi logo on the East River, although the now-dismantled Swingline Stapler sign near Broadway Junction was once nominated), Marmurston, no sentimentalist, said, "What for? It's a sign, selling something they don't sell anymore. A relic. It is idiotic, the crap people will try to collect these days just to make themselves feel better about the past, which wasn't so hot to begin with."

Still, there are mysteries, untold histories, in the dead ads of Brooklyn. Foremost is the R. Set up on a steel grid, the R lords enigmatically over the Gowanus, visible from the IND train and the Battery Tunnel approach: a single, iconic twenty-foot-high R over Red Hook. The R was always a favorite in our house, since both my daughters have names starting with the letter. We used to call it "our sign."

"That's good, your kids made up their own meaning for it because a lot of others think it has something to do with some secret code, like R marks the spot," said Frank Turano, of the Turano company, the Italian furniture import firm that owns the building on the corner of Richards and Verona. "People come by and say, What's this R? What's it stand for? I say, I'm not at liberty to give out that information."

With a little prodding, however, Frank Turano tumbled to the "top secret" origin of the R.

"We bought this building in 1978 from E. J. Trum, which was an old-time paper goods manufacturer," Mr. Turano revealed. "He had his sign up there: E.J. TRUM. We wanted to take it down and put up our own. TURANO. We went on the roof and started pulling on these giant letters. They were big, three times the size of a human. The E, the J, the T came off. But the R wouldn't. We couldn't move it. My brothers and I, we started pulling, but it wouldn't budge. We decided to give it one more pull. Except my brother's hand slipped and he fell backward, almost off the building. He would have been dead, for the sake of that R. It put a scare into us. It seemed better to leave it up there. It's been like that for twenty-two years. Recently a lot of people, they want to rent the space. Put up their own sign. But we always turn them down. So it stays: just R.

Frank Turano says it is better that way because South Brooklyn needed a mystery or two.

26
9–11

The attack on the World Trade Center—with its attendant political and moral fallout—is without a doubt the biggest story I ever covered. It doesn't stop. It is a rare day that goes by that I don't think of the events of that nightmarish time. Along with most every journalist in the city, I've written several pieces on the WTC and its aftermath. Here are two articles, one from the days immediately following the attack, the other shortly before the Republican National Convention that nominated George W. Bush for a second term. If they reveal anything, it is that my feelings remain consistent: I experience as a New Yorker first, a citizen of the city. My allegiance to the Nation, at least as defined by fractious post–September 11 politics, is secondary.

This said, I must add that almost two years after I met Aaron Austin (described below in The Talking Cure*), I received a large package from him, completely out of the blue. Inside was a framed American flag that Aaron wrote had once flown over the USS* Arizona *at Pearl Harbor. His father gave him the flag many years ago and he'd always treasured it. But now he wanted me to have it, a "thank you" for "the camaraderie of a fellow American . . . as our nation came to terms with September 11, 2001." I have tried to reach Aaron through the navy, but have been unsuccessful. So let me take this opportunity to say that the flag will always have a safe harbor in my home. From* New York *magazine, 2001, 2004.*

The Talking Cure

At the corner of Madison and Forty-third Street, a businessman stops in his tracks and beseeches the sky, "What do you want?" More supplication than inquiry, was this cry addressed to the hijackers or to God? In either case, there is no response.

Of course, back on the box, cameras forever trained on the war room, the dialogue was more self-assured, full of short, clipped sentences. Artless talk of crusades, declarations of Dodge City–style dead-or-alive *fatwas* smoothed to steely resolve. People could think what they wanted, but Bush was the president, and the way he saw it, a president's job was to be deadly certain, unconditional, and to know, in his heart, that in a war between freedom and terror "God is not neutral."

Out here, though, on the streets, things are not so clear. Even the peace ticket is teetering. On the Brooklyn Promenade, a lady carries a sign saying REVENGE IS NOT THE ANSWER! Oh, yeah? What is the answer, then? "To work for peace and eliminate poverty." Sure, but what about bin Laden and his flight-school zombie crew? "Put him on trial. The rule of law must be maintained." Right, but what about when he's convicted—can we put his head on a plate then? "I'm against the death penalty." Yeah, but . . . Look across the river, why don't you? The smoke is still rising; it is a vast crematorium.

Then come the tears, because we are all shocked, jolted beyond preconceptions, past the standard raps. "I would hope," the peace lady says, "I would hope our justice system was evolved enough, that we were civilized enough . . . oh . . . I don't know. It is *so big*."

Walking around the big city these fateful days, numbly staring at the missing posters (stuck on a hundred street lamps, some faces are familiar by now: Davis G. Sevna, a.k.a. "Deeg"; Kimberly Bowers, with the yin-yang tattoo on her lower back; Angel "Chic" Pabon, from the 104th floor), one gets the feeling that the planes did more than shatter Sheetrock and steel. They punched a hole in rationality, punctured consensus realities.

Everyone talks about politics and economics, yet these temporalities have been transcended. A zone has opened, shadowy, inchoate. Wily old Pat Robertson knew Falwell would get whacked for saying the ACLU and the gays were responsible for tempting God's wrath, but tonally, Jerry caught the spirit.

Suddenly we are a city of seekers. It is an apocalyptic grope, a gigantic self-psychoanalysis project. For now, sound-byte TV punditry has become obsolete, replaced by three-by-five cards stuck to plate-glass windows.

PEOPLE SAY GOD HATES US. WHAT WILL YOU DO? it says down at Canal and Varick. Beside that, in succession, cards read: BE HUMAN, HEY MOHAMMAD FUCK YOU, TROUBLE IS BIN LADEN AIN'T BIN LAID LATELY, MY REAL HERO STRANGLED HITLER IN HIS CRADLE BUT THE FIREMEN WILL DO FOR NOW, THEY HATE THE MODERN WORLD SO DO I—LET'S KILL THEM ANYWAY.

At Washington Square Park, a commentary-crammed canvas encircles the arch. Pinned to it is a kid's drawing of the Twin Towers and the oncoming plane. "Turn around and go back," it says in crayon, "go back to the airport and let those people out. A nice lady is waiting for you at the airport and she will give you a kiss."

By the Forty-second Street library is one of the many impromptu folk-art shrines that have popped up around the city—candles, flowers, missing posters, poems pleading for peace and understanding. Someone has left, like a giant turd, a four-foot-high sign with a swastika and a screed about "the angel of death."

"This is disgusting," a woman complains to a cop. "Take it down."

"No," replies another woman. "Everyone expresses themselves about the WTC in the way they need." The cop, Officer Torcone, not taking sides, says he'll ask his supervisor what to do about "this Nazi thing."

A new normality unfolds. The stock market loses money, the Mets win in their NYPD hats. All day long people pour into Union Square; where the anarchists once made speeches and pushers once sold Valium, candle wax covers the sidewalks, spreading since Tuesday. Nothing has been seen like this since the hippie days. A woman dressed like the Statue of Liberty, her hair and face dyed green, declares tearfully, "I feel I've been waiting my entire life for this moment."

Through the throng of Christers, 911-fixated numerologists, Hare Krishnas, and Scientologists comes a Rasta man with a video camera: *What are your revenge fantasies?* he wants to know. At midnight, a giant roll of paper is unfurled like a hundred-foot-long runner. It is immediately set upon by people with Magic Markers, who write their most recent inner feelings. In a half hour, the paper is almost filled. Off by Seventeenth Street a man sits under a streetlight folding a five-dollar bill so the pillars of the Lincoln Monument come out looking like the vanished towers.

The new Dylan record, typically enough, was released on September 11, and the song "High Water" defines the mood music as one walks south. It is the second day of Rosh Hashanah. The East Sixth Street congregation reads from Genesis 22:1–24, the story of how, on God's command, Abraham took Isaac to Moriah, to sacrifice him. Things being as they are, the blind faith that Yahweh demands offers little solace.

A note taped to a fence says come to an apartment on Thirteenth Street to share your thoughts and feelings about the tragedy. The room is filled with people who ordinarily would have little to do with each other short of crushing into a subway car. "This planet isn't big enough to live on along with medieval, feudalistic religious fanatics," says a businessman who spends a lot of time in Italy. "What bothered me most," says a teacher from the South Bronx, "was the kids in the school said it was no big deal because all that got killed were bad white people."

Mostly, we are guilty, everyone agrees, guilty about doing anything normal. A flight attendant says she went to the movies, "to see some stupid picture called *Rock Star*. Usually this is fine, because I like stupid movies. This time I left before the middle. I was escaping. I *knew* I was escaping. And I don't want to escape. It feels wrong. Right now, very wrong." Everyone agreed when the Vietnam veteran said he was "just exhilarated" about how everyone had come together in the city, and "how beautiful that was in its way." The way people are dealing with it, how they're treating each other. "This is kind of great," the vet found himself thing. "You want to have it go on forever . . . but then you start thinking about the dead, always the dead . . . all around you."

The dead, in the air, everywhere. Last week I was down at ground zero, within an hour of the collapse of the second tower. No one stopped me, I walked right into Ground Zero. I've got one pair of fancy shoes, and I happened to be wearing them that day. Now those shoes sit in the shed behind my house, still covered with that dried gray mud. Ashes and dust. I don't plan on wearing them again, nor will I throw them out.

Since the eleventh I go down there almost every night. I can't stay away. It is as if I am imprinted on the ghost shadow of the towers, the vapor-lit smoke rising into the sky. It is like Richard Dreyfuss fixating on Devil's Tower in *Close Encounters of the Third Kind*. It has an involuntariness to it, a compulsion, either external or internal, I don't know. The Twin Towers might have been unloved while they lived, but dead they lure like a Jungian power vector, phantom tuning forks playing a siren song, drawing you like a magnet.

I was sitting on a wall watching the silhouettes of the giant cranes when this guy asked me if I knew what time "the public transportation" stopped running.

"Never," I said without turning to look at my questioner. "That's why they call it New York."

It felt good, coming out, that. Hackneyed or not, I liked the sound of my own civic defiance. Bush was on TV talking about how America was under attack. Maybe he's right. Take cover North Dakota. But the real truth was, I didn't give that much of a shit about the rest of the country. I knew where my true loyalties lay. This is home. The fuckers had come to my home. New York, where the trains always ran, even now.

Turned out he was a navy guy, Aaron Austin, a graduate of Annapolis who had flown up that day from the base in Jacksonville, Florida. Formerly a boat pilot doing drug interdiction off the coast of Mississippi, he was learning to fly a P-3 Charlie spy plane and decided right on the spot to get on a Greyhound bus to come up to see if he could help in the rescue and/or cleanup. Whatever, he was here, in the city, where he'd never been before. He'd arrived only three hours ago, found his way down to the WTC site. Like me, he said he *had* to be here.

But it was too late to do anything now, and he was wondering how to get to a hostel on 103rd Street he'd seen mentioned in his *Lonely Planet* guide. If that place was full, he had a bedroll of sorts and figured maybe he could crash in a park for a couple of hours. What was the name of the place? Central Park?

Well, if that was the case, I told him, he might as well try Union Square. A lot of people were bedding down there. Rudy was too busy being heroic to roust everyone.

"They aren't going to be singing 'Give Peace a Chance,' are they?" Aaron asked. Military all the way, son of an air force officer, veteran of Desert Storm, he said he wasn't "super gung ho" but thought he'd ask.

Didn't know about that, I told him. The way a lot of people were feeling, maybe they'd be singing "give war a chance." But if he wanted to go look, I'd walk with him. It is a thing with me. Someone comes to New York, I always want to be the one to show them around. Everyone has their own version of the city, but how I see it, mine is the best version. Provincial as the next slob, my ego is tied up in the place.

On the way up, Aaron said if war came, he'd certainly be called to fight in it. He wasn't fond of the saber-rattling rhetoric on TV. But he was a soldier, and he would do what he was called upon to do. If we were going to hit the Taliban, most of that would be done by F-15s and F-16s refueled in midair by KC-135 and KC-10 tankers, Aaron said. He knew those planes. More likely he'd be stationed in the Persian Gulf, doing surveillance. But it was hard to tell. If the war was going to turn into a full-scale assault against world terror, like Bush said, you never knew what might happen to you.

It was after midnight, but Union Square was still hopping. A man was standing by a sign that said FREE HUGS, but the free-hug people had gone home. COME BACK TOMORROW, the sign said. It was a zoo, so I called my wife and asked if there was any problem with Aaron's sleeping at our house.

"He's a sailor who came up here on his own money to volunteer to help New York? You have to invite him," she said, adding, "as long as he's not a nut." I asked Aaron if he was a nut. No, he was not a nut, Aaron said, pulling out his U.S. Navy ID, as if to attest to his sanity. We went home in a cab, because even if I always take the subway, he was a guest, an honored guest, and guests shouldn't have to wait for the F train. We gave him the couch. I hope he slept well, because more than likely he's going to need it, dodging those bullets. That much was for sure.

27

9–11:

Travels in the Red, White, and Blue Divided States

This was about as close to being a NASCAR dad as I was ever going to get, I knew, as the van rolled into the 30-degree bank of Turn No. 2 on the track at the Daytona International Speedway.

Four months earlier, in February, two hundred thousand race fans, dads and otherwise, filled this place to watch the famous 500 and cheer the guest starter: W., in "the kickoff" of his 2004 presidential bid, consolidating his downscale base in a slick black jacket, shouting, "Gentlemen, start your engines!" Today, however, the track, once home to white-lightnin'-running grease monkeys like Junior Johnson and Fireball Roberts, but now as corporate as everything else, was empty except for me and Sheri Valera, who grew up a bit down the road in Ormond Beach and who, at age twenty-one, will be the youngest Florida delegate to attend the GOP convention in New York.

State chairwoman of the College Republicans of Florida, recipient of the Ronald Reagan Future Leaders Scholarship, Sheri was my first delegate, the initial Bushie on my list.

It was part of an outreach project. The idea was that just because the Republican delegates were soon to launch their sure-to-be-surreal assault on the ole hometown, filling Madison Square Garden, home to Clyde, Pearl, and Ali, with teeth-brite cheers aimed at giving the war president four more years—that was no reason to hold it against them. Personally, I mean.

"Approach them as a missionary," my wife said. Not all the delegates were Enron crooks, oil sluts, Armageddon lusters, and their Limbaugh-Hannity-programmed enablers. No, my wife said ecumenically, it wasn't possible that every single one of the approaching delegates reflexively hated and feared the city of my birth, the city I grew up in and loved.

"Probably a lot of them have never even been to New York," my wife said. That's how it started, the notion to go to the heartland hometowns of the incoming Bush nominators. To arrive on their turf as a one-man big-city pre-Welcome Wagon. It made sense, since here I was, a living piece of New York, *a real New Yorker*, a former cabdriver to boot. An icon I was, less kinky than Woody Allen, not as obnoxious as Donald Trump, friendlier than Jimmy Breslin, and nowhere near as full of crap as Ed Koch with his typically sickening, no doubt paid, "make nice" spiel.

So what if I was from an Albert Shanker-worshiping union family that hadn't had a Republican voter since they stepped off the boat from Romania? A uniter, not a divider, I would attempt to set GOP minds at ease, make them understand there was no need to bivouac on huge ships in the harbor as once suggested by the Neanderthal Tom DeLay. I would convince them there was more to do in New York than simply shop and scurry back to the hotel, congratulating themselves that it took Giuliani, hero of 9/11—a Republican like them—to save the city from itself.

That was the mission, to present myself relatively unvarnished and *tawking* like this—and to make clear that even if several hundred thousand New Yorkers would soon be gathering in the streets to tell their faux-cowboy candidate exactly what they thought of him, we were human beings here. People, just like them.

I got a list of delegates who had never been to New York from the Republican National Committee, and when Sheri Valera met me at the airport, I figured I'd been snookered. The RNC people said, "Oh, you'll love her, she's a star." That much was manifest as she stood there in her jean shorts and stretchy top.

"Hi! I'm Sheri!" she said, kind of bubbly.

"Er . . . hi," I replied. Sheri seemed like a real go-getter, but this was not quite what I was expecting. With that long dark hair, those beachy tanned legs and grand green eyes, and that fabulous smile, Sheri Valera looked better than Ann Coulter's fondest dream of herself. What manner of Karl Rovean skullduggery was this?

"From the beginning, most everyone knew Sheri was special, not in any envious way—everyone loves her—but different," says Sheri's friend Kelly Hahne. It was Kelly's dad, Dick, facility manager at the Daytona Speedway, who'd set up our ride around the track. On the day of the 500, Sheri, Kelly, and many of their friends went over to see W.'s campaign-kickoff event.

"We got right up front," Sheri said. "That's how I am. A lot of people sit around waiting for something to happen. It's up to the zealous ones to make up for that. I'm one of the zealous ones." The kickoff was exciting, Sheri said. But today, as we went into the backstretch not far from where Dale Earnhardt Sr.'s car hit the wall one last time, she was talking about the separation of church and state.

The issue had come up the night before, at Wednesday-night Bible study at Riverbend Community Reformed Baptist Church. Wednesday Bible class was a must, Sheri had said. And so it was that night, as Associate Pastor Tommy Clayton read from Acts 4:3–5, relating how the apostles Peter and John spoke the Gospel outside the Temple in Jerusalem. This was a bold move on the apostles' part, said Pastor Tommy, a twentyish man in baggy jeans with punkishly close-cropped hair. "Them coming to talk about Jesus at the Temple would be like a Jew coming to preach to Hitler," he said. This was the essence of Acts 4, Pastor Tommy said: Christians will always be persecuted for their religious—"and political"—beliefs.

What about this? I asked Sheri. What about the rehearsal we watched for the church's "Celebrate America" Fourth of July pageant, in which congregation members, dressed up like Li'l Abner and Daisy Mae, mixed gospel tunes with songs like "This Land Is Your Land" (I didn't have the heart to tell them it was written by a communist)? What about churches running voter-registration drives that often seemed like Bush pep rallies? Wasn't it in the Constitution, the separation of church and state?

"It is not in the Constitution," Sheri said sharply. A tenacious arguer who "takes pleasure" in crushing overconfident college Democrats in debates over affirmative action, Sheri has this church-and-state rap down cold. "The First Amendment says 'that Congress shall make no law respecting an establishment of religion' . . . The term 'building a wall of separation between church and state' comes from a letter written by Thomas Jefferson, plus later in the letter Jefferson says the nation should adhere to our Christian principles."

Actually, Jefferson's 1802 letter extends only salutary "kind prayers for the protection and blessing of the common Father and creator of man," but Sheri had proved her point. Sheri says she got "the political bug" as a little girl when her father had her accompany him into the voting booth on Election Day, an experience she calls "almost mystical."

Citing morality in government and low taxes as her "core issues," Sheri takes inspiration from "strong women" like her idols; Condi Rice, Laura Bush, and Katherine Harris, who "stood up to a lot of heat" during the 2000 Florida recount fight. On a first-name basis with presidential brother Jeb, Sheri discounts stories of blacks allegedly being disenfranchised in Jacksonville, but adds, "We probably haven't heard the last of that" because "Kerry will probably bring it up."

But this election is about the future, not the past, says Sheri, a finalist in the MTV-GOP "Stand Up and Holla" competition, in which Republicans aged eighteen to twenty-four were asked to videotape themselves speaking on issues that "best answered President George W. Bush's Call to Service." Sheri's tape detailed how the Riverbend community came together during the 1998 Volusia County forest fires. "Our great American values are preserved through volunteers who have selflessly given their time," Sheri says, a white flower pinned to her demure dark top. "President Bush understands the value of time and volunteering."

Posted on the RNC and MTV Web sites, Sheri's video gained a good deal of notice, some of it owing to an article from the University of Florida *Blue and Orange* titled "Liplocked," in which Sheri explains why she is not only planning on saving herself for her husband but has decided not to even kiss a man until she gets married.

"What's up with the no-kissing policy?" the reporter asks.

"To guard my heart. It protects me emotionally and spiritually," Sheri answers.

"But if a guy would kiss you, how would you feel?"

"I'd slap him because that shows he is only thinking of himself." Sheri says she doesn't even like it in the movies. "In most movies, the girl is too good for the guy. I'm like, '*Nooo!* Get your hands off!! R-E-S-P-E-C-T!' and I want to sing like Aretha Franklin."

This engendered some snide Internet commentary, including on the July 29 edition of the right-leaning blog Whizbang, where a poster with the potentially subversive handle of "Allah" opines, "Hot though she may be, do we really want a chick who refuses to *kiss* to be the voice of young conservative America at the convention?"

"I don't have to tell you that Sheri is a beautiful young woman," said Roy Hargrove, senior pastor at Riverbend Community Church, whom Sheri describes as "one of the people whose ideas mean the most to me." Pastor Roy, a casually impressive man from Rector, Arkansas (Sheri says, "That's why he knows so much about the Clintons"), who has built Riverbend Community into an ecclesiastical presence that has an annual operating budget of $2.6 million, said, "Someone with that sort of outward beauty might allow themselves to be seduced by it. But Sheri retains her inward life, her drive. That can be a powerful force. I can see Sheri becoming the first woman president of the United States."

Told this, Sheri blushed. "Pastor Roy said that? That's very flattering. Well, he might be right."

But outside of working on beating out the hated Hillary, what did Sheri plan to do when she came to New York? We were talking about it over steak-and-portobello fajitas at Chili's in Ormond with Sheri's mom, Reatha, who will accompany her daughter to the convention. A friendly, charming woman in her forties who bakes a heck of a banana bread, Reatha hasn't been to New York, either. "The closest we got was driving by. We were going sixty miles an hour but still locked the doors and windows." This time, Sheri and Reatha agreed, would probably be more fun.

This opinion was shared by several of Sheri's friends who joined us for dinner after Bible class. Proud that Sheri would represent them at the convention, several noted how instructive it was to hear Pastor Tommy talk about Christian persecution in light of the massive protests likely to greet President Bush in New York. "He'll be the underdog, that's for sure," one said. Beyond that, there were a lot of suggestions about what Sheri and Reatha should do in the Big Apple. While the Empire State Building and the Statue of Liberty were pretty cool, everyone agreed the city's number No. 1 attraction was ground zero.

"Right," Sheri said. "That place belongs to all Americans."

This was the commentary that tried the resolve of even the most committed New York City missionaries. Because I didn't feel like ground zero belonged to "all Americans," certainly not the sort of "all-Americans" who took it as a moral imperative to keep George Bush in the White House. Ground zero belonged to New York, to the people who died there and their families, to those who rode the F train every morning and never once looked at the skyline without noting the absence of those not particularly beloved buildings looming over the Brooklyn Bridge.

It was a question everyone asked out here: Where were you *that day?* I had a compelling answer, or at least one that people usually find compelling. Because I was *there*. Not when the planes hit, or when the buildings fell, but a couple hours later, when, in the horror and confusion, no one kept me from walking through the twisted rubble, right to the pile of dust that would come to be called ground zero. "Where are the buildings? Where are the people?" I asked a weary firefighter. "Under your shoe," was the answer.

I told my WTC story to the delegates because—more than what restaurant to eat in or what play to see—this seemed to be what they really wanted to know about New York. Reliving that day is always emotional for me, and hearing about it was emotional for the delegates. If there was any real bond between us, it started there, as legitimate as it was *that day*.

Yet I begrudged them their emotion, their sense of outrage that 9/11 had been an attack on them, too, a thousand miles from the half-empty firehouse of Squad One. Perhaps it was provincial—should only Hawaiians have been pissed about Pearl Harbor?—but it bothered me that 9/11 had redefined the city in the minds of those who hitherto would have agreed with John Rocker's assessment of the 7 train.

It has been declared sacred ground, a place of pilgrimage, separate from the real city. For many, Republican delegates certainly included, ground zero has acquired the patina of a Revelation-style Valley of Decision, with the steel girder "cross" found in the wreckage taken as proof of where God's allegiance lies in the War on Terror. Don't they know that cross is a fireman's cross, a cop's cross, an ironworker's cross—*a Democratic cross*, if it's any kind of cross at all?

Thinking about it was enough to make you shake your head, yet again, at the audacity of Bush's bringing his convention here, so close to the anniversary of that day. Like he imagined he was really invited.

On the other hand, wasn't it sheer bad manners to do anything but say "thanks" when someone like Wes Rice asserted, "I think everyone in the country became a New Yorker that day"?

Then again, Wes Rice, a delegate from Zephyr Cove, Nevada, on the shore of Lake Tahoe, and his wife, Eileen, also a delegate, are another kind of Republican.

"I'm a Republican because my father would roll over in his grave if I wasn't," says Eileen, who works as a nurse in the local emergency room and has never had a problem making herself heard even if she is only five feet tall. It was her orphaned dad, a man who pressed his pants underneath flophouse mattresses so he could keep looking for work even while hoboing around the country (later becoming an electrical engineer) who taught her the value of self-sufficiency, Eileen said. This was what the Republican Party was really about, Eileen declared.

True political conviction came not from handed-down ideology or some loudmouth rant on the radio, but from life experience, Eileen said. Back when she was working at the Arcadia Methodist Hospital east of L.A., "They brought in two victims of Richard Ramirez, the Night Stalker. These were elderly ladies, dismembered. One had a pentagram carved into her leg. I didn't know how I felt about the death penalty, but then I knew: Richard Ramirez had to die. Even now, thinking of him living a fat life in prison with new teeth paid for by tax dollars sets me off."

Politics was about "trying to stay in the real world," agreed Wes Rice, a large, wry-humored man of sixty-one, who spent twenty-eight years in the Pasadena, California, Police Department, many as chief of detectives, and who now pilots a patrol boat on the lake for the Douglas County Sheriff's Department. To this end, Wes's most difficult task as chairman of the Douglas County (population: 44,000) Republican Party is "beating back the single-issuers . . . mostly the anti-abortion people."

With five grown daughters and ten grandchildren between them, he and Eileen "maintain a strong sense of spirituality," says Wes. "I just don't think you have to go around telling everyone about it." Religious beliefs were simply not a political issue, said Eileen, a strong supporter of stem-cell research ("Nancy Reagan, you go, girl"). It was in the middle of this conversation that Eileen, who has been known to enjoy an episode of *South Park,* announced she was about to use "the dreaded M-word."

"Not the dreaded M-word," Wes exclaimed in mock horror. "Rush says there's no such thing as a *moderate* Republican."

"Oh yeah?" replied Eileen. "Just try me."

What it came down to, said Wes, was "We may be Republicans, but we're not nuts."

"Going to New York is kind of like a nightmare that became a dream," said Wes, who once thought of the city as "this place where people closed their windows while women called for help in the alleyway." Now Wes, an admirer of Giuliani-style policing, ran his finger with gleeful expectation along the orange path of the D train on the subway map I'd brought to Zephyr Cove. Just that morning the UPS man had arrived with the "official welcoming packet" from the RNC. Several letters beginning with "Dear Delegate" offered entertainment choices including Broadway plays. Mostly, though, aside from eating "some really good corned-beef sandwiches," the Rices were most looking forward to taking part in the nomination of George Bush.

"You want to know why I like George Bush?" Wes Rice asked me as we puffed on sweet Jamaican cigars in the crisp, piney air outside his house.

"Last month, he was in Reno. We got onstage. It was such a thrill to be twenty-five feet from a sitting president. I was able to make eye contact with him. He seemed very genuine. I felt he would never knowingly lie to me. Maybe it is a cop thing. On the street, you've got to trust your assessments of people or you could be in serious trouble. I trust myself on George W. Bush."

Like a moron, I'd left the lights on in my rental car. We were charging the battery, using Wes's Cherokee. Cigars and jumper cables, these were "*man* things," said Eileen. She was going to bed. It had been a big day, driving around the lake, checking out Emerald Bay, stopping by the Coast Guard station where the chief officer reported how they'd picked up "a man of Middle Eastern descent behind our HAZMAT shack." It turned out to be a false alarm, but you couldn't be too careful, even six thousand feet up, in such beautiful country.

"No need to go to heaven," said Wes, expressing his fealty to the great lake. "We're already in paradise." But it was a paradise with a dark side, said Wes, relating how Ed Callahan, his patrol-boat partner, fell overboard in a storm and drowned on Memorial Day weekend in 1998.

"The water was 44 degrees," Wes recalled. "You can't last long; the hypothermia shuts you down. I tried to save him, but it was impossible. I was passed out when they dragged me back into the boat."

It was a sad, rueful tale, how Ed Callahan, who made it through several tours of duty in Vietnam, came to die in the seductively blue waters of Lake Tahoe, where college students came on weekends to shatter the silence in their Ski-doos. It was the sort of story men sometimes tell when they're trying to get through to each other, nodding at the ineffableness of it all. In another time and place, Wes and I, similar in age, laughing at some of the same things, could have been friends.

Too bad we had to talk about politics. Wes had warned against it. "I'm not going to change your mind, and you're not going to change mine." But I'd come twenty-eight hundred miles because he and Eileen were Republican delegates, so what else were we supposed to talk about? I couldn't figure how Wes, who seemed like such a smart, soulful guy, could look into the eyes of George W. Bush, orbs I found beady and vacant, and decide this was a man he could trust.

A lot of things Wes said didn't make sense to me. He said, "I know those weapons of mass destruction are there. They are there, or in Syria, and they will be found." He said, "John Kerry represents everything I hate. Who knows how many American lives people like him and Jane Fonda cost us protesting the Vietnam war?" He said whatever happened in the 2000 Florida vote count was worth it, because, as he said his Democratic friends agreed, "Heaven help us if Al Gore was the president on September 11, 2001."

Then again, Sheri Valera nodded when one of her friends from Riverbend said, "Kerry's war record is a lie. Bush was training to go over there, and if they called him, you can bet he would have been a better soldier than Kerry." Even Eileen Rice, so flinty under fire, said, "You've got to have faith that the government knows more than we do and is doing the right thing."

These were the views of the very nice people I had set out to welcome to New York. Wes Rice was correct. It would have been better if we didn't talk about politics.

It was a matter of what version of America you believed in, I thought, driving along the banks of the Ohio, great heartland river of flatboats, murder ballads, and shuttered Appalachian factories. I like my America big, a sea-to-shining-sea big, a boiling regionalized stewpot, freaky off-angles seeping between the corporate cracks. I deplored the idea that New York should secede from the country. My America is not complete without both Joey Ramone and George Jones, to say nothing of Dr. Dre, Emerson, and Randy Weaver. How could New York be its own nation? It didn't even have one truck stop. My America *needed* America.

When the RNC gave me its list of delegates, they kept referring to my final interviewee, the auditor and tax assessor of Lawrence County, Ohio, as "Moose."

"What's his real name?" I inquired. I didn't want to call up and just ask for Moose.

"Ray," they said. "Ray Dutey. But everyone calls him Moose."

"His name is Moose Dutey?"

"That's his name."

And there it was, RAY T. DUTEY, AUDITOR, on three different wooden signs outside his second-floor office in the Gothic Lawrence County courthouse in downtown Ironton, once the center of the southern Ohio pig-iron empire but now one more mining town hanging on by the skin of its teeth. Resplendent in a beige suit with boldly matching gold tie, Moose bounded out of his oversize chair to greet me. No way he's more than five-foot-four. Smiling, Moose said, "I guess now you know why they call me Moose."

If all politics is local, then Moose Dutey, who grew up playing on the river sandbars, was politics itself. Recently turned seventy-four, one of ten siblings, Moose has been in Lawrence County public life for fifty-five years, starting as a councilman in his native Coal Grove, about three miles east on U.S. 52. In 1960 he was elected mayor of Coal Grove ("won by 146 votes," Moose recalls), and was reelected in 1962, during which time he managed to raise enough money to replace the fire truck the town had been using since 1936. In 1964 he was elected county recorder and moved to the courthouse in Ironton, where he's worked ever since.

Never beaten in an election, Moose is chairman of the Lawrence Country Republican Party. On his fiftieth year of public service, the county threw him a parade. They renamed his street, so now he lives at 200 Dutey Drive. He could run for another term in 2006, but he figures he's done. "I'm going to retire," Moose said.

Of course, Moose Dutey has never been to New York. Outside of when he was sent overseas in the Korean War and stopped in San Francisco, Moose said, "I haven't been around the country that much." He hardly even goes to Kentucky, though the state, right across the river, is visible from his office window. When he does cross the bridge, it's usually to eat at Applebee's or Ruby Tuesday's. Ironton, a shrinking town of twelve thousand, where a quarter in the parking meter buys you five hours, and the sign in the pool hall window says FIGHTERS WILL BE PROSECUTED, doesn't have "a single decent restaurant that you'd want to eat in."

Fondly recalling several New Yorkers in his infantry unit in Korea, "guys with lots of colorful expressions," Moose said he'd wanted to visit the city since he first watched the ball drop on New Year's Eve in Times Square on TV. "All those people in one place. That always amazed me." Happy to hear that his hotel, the hulking Marriott Marquis, is in the middle of the Crossroads of the World, and looking forward to visiting Yankee Stadium (the Indians are in town), Moose still couldn't believe he'd been chosen to be a delegate. "I'm small-town. I didn't even know I was under consideration," Moose said in his reedy, relentlessly modest drawl.

"You know, we've been Republicans here a long time, back before Robert Taft. We're not rabid. But I like President Bush. I like that he takes a position and sticks to it," said Moose. No policy wonk, Moose reeled off the names of failed or failing local businesses ("Dayton Iron Company . . . out of business . . . Allied Chemical . . . out of business . . . the Ammonia plant, used to employ two thousand, out of business") and then concluded, apparently without irony, that "They say the economy is picking up." As for Iraq, Moose said, "That's slackened up . . . you don't hear much about American casualties now." I handed Moose a newspaper listing the names of twelve U.S. soldiers killed in recent days. Moose looked at the article grimly. "I hadn't seen that. I've been real busy this week, over at the fair."

By this Moose meant the Lawrence County Fair in Proctorville, which was where we went next, walking across the muddy tractor-pull patch to check out grand-champion hogs and steers. In election years, local politicians bid up the prices on the winners of the livestock contests. The Republicans had gone "sky-high" for the 4-H's grand-champion hog. The champ steer was way outside the budget.

Moose was not averse to munching a funnel cake or two, but he went to the fair in his capacity as county party chairman, to keep tabs on his candidates. Most of them were there, seated at the pin-neat Republican booth, beside giant pictures of Bush and Cheney. There was Cheryl Jenkins, secretary of the local Republican club, Rod DePriest, candidate for county treasurer, and Richard Holt, a fresh-faced twenty-four-year-old African-American Republican who was running for the legislature even though

Lawrence County has a black population of less than 2 percent. Holt said he was running "for the experience."

As soon as Moose arrived, every candidate, many of whom had known him for decades, emerged from behind the booth to shake his hand. "He'd never let on, but Moose is the littlest big man around here," said Sharon Hager, running for Dutey's old recorder job. Moose had taken her "under his wing," said Sharon, towering over her benefactor. "In Lawrence County, Moose Dutey means something."

That much was clear as we picked our way through the cow pies toward the Democratic booth. The Democrats, sitting around like a bowling team, had a picture of Kerry, but it was on the floor, upside down.

"Moose!" called out George Patterson, an imposing man in his fifties. The Democratic county commissioner, Patterson, a Lawrence County version of Philip Roth's Swede Levov, was remembered, Moose said, as "one heck of a football player, maybe the best we ever had." Still in Coal Grove, still best friends with Moose's younger brother, Patterson said it wasn't easy being a Democrat here. "Even my wife voted for Reagan."

But this time it would be different. "I'm getting six this time, Moose." By this Patterson meant that the Democrats would win half of the countywide offices. "Don't be silly," Moose said with grinning dismissal. "You'll be lucky to get two, George, you know that."

"Three?" Patterson asked, bluster diminishing.

"Two's all I can give you. Not another stitch."

The fact is, Moose said later, the Democrats might win only one, Patterson's own race, for county commissioner. The Republicans were running Kenneth Ater, son of a well-known Lawrence County judge. Ater was putting up billboards, getting his name on pens and T-shirts. But he wasn't going to beat George Patterson. "He'll get beat real bad," Moose said. Asked if he is ever wrong about such things, Moose winked and said, "Hardly never."

Moose Dutey was a kick. I liked his self-effacing manner, and that he was secretly a killer of a local pol. I liked that he pronounced Bush's name "Booo-ish." So what if he didn't believe in evolution? There is a place in my America for Moose Dutey. I hoped there was a place in his for me.

That night, Moose had been invited to hear Laura Bush call the upscale, hilltop Chesapeake, Ohio, home of Rick and Kathie Gue. "'Goo,' they pronounce it 'goo,'" Moose said as we went up the long driveway, passing a sign saying THE GUES WELCOME YOU TO BUSH COUNTRY.

Kathie Gue, a thin, perky blond woman in what looked to be her forties, was "real gung-ho for Bush," Moose said. This seemed true as she greeted us by jumping up onto a chair and shouting "W!" This was the cue for the twenty-five or so people, both young and old, many wearing elephant-shaped jewelry, to jump from lawn chairs arrayed in the Gues' driveway and yell "Four more years!" This call-and-response was repeated as Mrs. Gue passed out slices of red-white-and-blue cake. Chowing down, Moose and I chatted with the head of the Lawrence County Chamber of Commerce, Bill Dingus.

Dingus, Dutey, and Gue: They didn't have this back in Brooklyn.

In the pleasant twilight air, even Laura Bush saying, "All of you know what makes George such a great president . . . It is his heart. I know his heart," sounded faintly bearable.

It was only when the Gue family began speaking that things began to unravel. One of the Gues' four strapping sons made reference to "thousands of babies murdered" since *Roe v. Wade* and called for everyone to "Hannitize the vote," by making sure everyone they knew registered. This was seconded by Kathie Gue, who said how upset she was that "only 22.5 percent of Christians" voted in 2000 and how that "had to change."

Then came Rick Gue, a salt-and-pepper-haired man dressed in a dark blue suit, who, after thanking "the Lord" that he'd been able to raise "four Christian, conservative sons," said, "If there is anything that really turns my stomach, it is a liberal man. The idea of raising children without Jesus Christ and conservative values as the centerpiece of family life is unthinkable to me."

Earlier in the evening, as a visitor from a far-off metropolis, I'd been asked to speak and said how happy I was to be here, in the Ohio River Valley. Now I looked up to see if Rick Gue was staring at me or not. But by this time, he'd slapped a plastic George Bush mask onto his face as everyone jumped out of their lawn chair to shout "Four more years" yet again.

We rode back to Ironton, passing the rusting factories along the river, saying little. Finally, Moose, attempting to lighten the mood, offered that he sure was looking forward to visiting New York, to see my hometown, just as I'd seen his.

"I'll be happy to see *you*," I said. "But I won't be happy to see Bush, or a lot of these people." It just slipped out, what I thought, what most people in New York thought: that the Republicans were coming only because of 9/11, and how creepy it was that Bush would use this supreme heartbreak for his own personal gain. I told Moose that and immediately regretted it, because that wasn't what I'd come to Ohio to say.

I could feel my heart, which I'd imagined to be an infinitely expanding canvas—like New York itself—close down. I had my America, and, sad to say, lots of Americans, people I liked, appeared not to fit inside it. Not now. Not in 2004.

Moose, noting my dismay, said, "It is true that I feel more comfortable over at the Fair, with people like that. Those are the people I grew up with. I've known them all my life. But the Gues are good people, good Republicans. I respect and like them. They're doing what they believe in. Everyone is entitled to their own opinion. That's what the country's all about."

Couldn't argue with that, I supposed, a few days later, back in the city. I'd done what I could, tried my best. Made nice. Now I can go to Central Park and scream for Bush to go home, like everyone else.

THE HOME FRONT

28

How Summer Camp Saved My Life

A tender memoir of selfhood in and around puberty.
From Rolling Stone, *1984.*

"Come on, it's not like somebody died," my dad said from the other side of the hedge when he heard me crying on the flagstone porch that late-summer day.

I didn't answer.

Then, doing his best to display a burst of sympathy, my dad came closer, his gleaming garden shears in his hands, inches from my chest, and said, "Well, what will you miss most?"

"I dunno," I said after mulling over that one for a while. "Everything."

"You can't miss everything."

I thought it over again, trying to be more specific. Would I miss softball more than canoeing? Down at the end of our block, New York's Parks Department was ripping out my beloved vacant lots, the scene of much fort-building and immortal dirt-bomb fights. Soon we'd have nice, neat baseball diamonds, as if playing on the concrete with balls covered with electrician's tape was no longer good enough. Still, if you compared that with the canoeing possibilities in north Queens—there's Newtown Creek but the paddle disintegrates once it hits the water—I guess you'd have to say I'd miss canoeing more than softball.

It was a stupid comparison, though. There wasn't any way to separate the experience into components. The sense of loss was too complete.

The horrible drowning feeling, like a bottomless Sunday afternoon, had been enveloping me since mid-August, snowballing until the camp bus entered the Lincoln Tunnel. Until then, there was a maniacal hope that somehow the calendar would confess its lie. It would be July 1st again, not August 28th, and instead of the parents waving hello in front of the columns of old Penn Station, they'd be saying good-bye. They'd become smaller and smaller out the window, as the bus roared off, until a right turn, and they'd be gone.

But it wasn't to be. On that hated day, the parents were in their accustomed spot with the same WELCOME HOME banner they used the year before, and the thud of my trunk into the back of the station wagon was like a spike being driven through the heart. Even the egg rolls at the Chinese restaurant that was supposed to be my favorite tasted rancid.

"I just miss everything," I said again to my dad.

"You'll recover," my dad said, and he smiled because even then we were a pair of reticent guys, around each other at least. Then my dad went down to the basement where his power tools were, and the band saw began to rip through wood, *wah-wah-wah*, until my mother's voice pierced the drone to say the pot roast was ready, and I cried the whole time because I truly did miss everything and it was like somebody died.

Now that I think back on it, the summer camps I was sent to were almost inevitable in character. The parents thought it undignified to send me to one of the YMHA two-week sessions where half the time was spent cleaning out the latrines. On the other hand, for sure I wasn't going to some swell rich red-diaper place like Buck's Rock, where Pete Seeger was the music counselor or something and the eight-week tariff exceeded half my father's annual salary. Even my nine-year-old mind understood the economics of the situation. We were middle class, the lower of the middle, but middle nonetheless. When my mom became an Industrial Arts teacher like my dad, that's when we moved from that cramped two-family house we shared with my aunt and uncle over to the new pad, a palatial corner job in the "fresh air" district of Flushing, Queens.

It was a break from the past. My parents grew up in Brooklyn's ethnic ghetto neighborhoods of Williamsburg and Sheepshead Bay. Now we were one of the few Jewish families on the street, pioneers in a vast goyishaflecked sea. It was another step in our inexorable march toward assimilation, to the realm where Jews like Kissinger rated highly enough to help Nixon wipe out whole countries, just like any other hyphenated American. That's what summer camp was about, from my parents' point of view—another increment in the great saga of fitting in. No one in the history of my family had ever gone to summer camp.

So, there was nothing radical about the camps where I was sent, nothing, on the surface at least, to clash with my resolutely beige home life. No, my camps were just eight Jewboys to a wood box on the hillside, plenty of bug juice and mystery meat, morning and afternoon "general swims," and the chicks across the lake.

At the prospect of first entering this new and verdant landscape, I was in my usual mode. Whatever downers they gave my mom during my birth had gained a solid foothold up in my gray matter and had a hell of a half-life. According to sketchy memory, I spent large portions of my early youth as if shrink-wrapped in plastic like a box of Good & Plenty. That's the sort of deck I was playing with when I set out to Pine Grove Camp that first time. Back home, my place was known. I was one of the few Jews who couldn't do math. Ghettoized again. Cut off from social mobility. It wasn't as if I was going to get to hang around with Italians, or even the Irish, just because I had no clue when it came to common denominators.

But this new thing, this camp thing—where was the handle in this? For the entire journey, as the oil tanks of Secaucus gave way to the low brick buildings of New Brunswick and finally to the rolling hills of Middlesex County, I sat in my seat near the back of the bus, numb. Later, assigned to bunk seven, I sat on my cot, still numb.

"First time away from home?" a crew-cut guy who sat down next to me asked.

"Yeah," I nodded.

"First time away from your parents?"

"Yeah."

"Biggest break of your life."

Uncle Phil Kogan, who was counselor of bunk seven, Pine Grove Camp, 1958: my first unalloyed good influence.

"What do they call you?" Uncle Phil asked.

"Well, in school they call me Mark J., because there are three other Marks in the class."

"That what you want to be called?"

"I'd rather be called Jake."

"What position you play, Jake?" Uncle Phil asked, because it was pretty important what position you played.

I had to be cagey on this. The truth of the matter was I'd envisioned myself as Gil Hodges often enough to make my father buy me a first baseman's mitt, a Ted Kluszewski model, despite his warnings that such a specialized glove was "impractical."

"Sometimes I play outfield, but I'd rather play first," I said.

Then Uncle Phil was up off my cot and screaming to the other kids: "Hey, Jake here, he's a fabulous first baseman, and he can hit, too." It worked out that none of the other guys in the bunk especially saw themselves as first basemen, and they also proved to be a little more spasticated than the usual kids around my house, so I looked good at the bag, and I hit, too. That clinched it. My name was Jake, and I played first.

Bingo! With Uncle's Phil guidance, I exercised the rights of every American to totally reinvent themselves.

Those first couple of summers were spectacular bliss. We had the regulation fun, we threw the Welsh rabbit, frenched the beds, gave the pink bellies. There were moral lessons, too: We weren't supposed to play hardball on the main campus, so, of course, the first time we did, the ball hit me in the face and broke my nose. The blood of guilt and retribution streamed over the webbing of my mitt. Stuff happened I didn't get till later. Like that strange drama counselor who decided to put on an "all guys" show and kept us up to midnight rehearsing for a week. I mean, really, eleven-year-old boys in drag doing a Pirandello play; someone should have guessed.

Then there was the time Uncle Phil told me to go over to Uncle Bernie and say "how."

Uncle Bernie, the tightly strung son of Uncle Bob, the camp owner, was exceedingly into Indians, especially those of the Eastern woodlands. He'd wear feathers and greasepaint his Yeshiva face like some aboriginal

Chagall figure and spend hours boring everyone with solemn lore about nicks in trees and campfires. Instead of "color wars" we had "tribes." For "tribal sing," we had to make up odes to the Mohawk Nation to the tune of "Ebb Tide."

"Just go over, hold up your hand, and say 'how,' nothing else," Uncle Phil instructed me.

So, like the complicit moron I was, I went through the cavernous dining hall to the "Chief's Table," where the nervous Uncle Bernie sat eating chicken à la king with his steel-eyed father. Hand up, palm forward, "How!" I said.

"What?" Uncle Bernie asked.

"How!" I repeated.

That did it. Uncle Bernie screamed that I was the last little creep to make fun of him and docked me from canteen for a month. Uncle Phil told me not to worry. He would sneak me all the Hershey bars I could eat. Even if I didn't quite catch on to the actual nature of the joke, I knew I'd been in on a howl, a top howl, and that was more than all right.

It was during my second year at camp that Uncle Phil invented the chevrons. Phil's chevrons were based on the camp's chevrons, little color-coded *v*'s of cloth a lady sewed onto your jacket. Each one symbolized some arcane amalgam of a Hebraic-Algonquin virtue, like the ability to make a hospital corner. If you got four chevrons, you made honor society and got your name engraved on the dining-room wall, which was pretty impressive since they had lists on that wall that went all the way back to the thirties. At age eleven, it seemed like a stab at immortality.

Uncle Phil's chevrons had different meanings. You got a purple one if you danced close at a social, a purple one with a white border if a girl wrote you a letter and left it at your dining room setting, and a purple one with a red border if the letter was doused in perfume. There were successive degrees for first kiss and beyond.

Clearly, Uncle Phil, his cunning fratboy mind churning, figured that we were ready to enter a new realm and he wanted to prepare us like the failed Boy Scouts we were. I can't say the shift from batting averages to babes made me comfortable. One of the few insufficiently repressed memories of my pathetic grammar school days involves one Emily Weinstein turning around during a math test and giggling. "He's picking his nose," Emily said to her friend. "Ick!" was the rejoinder. I looked around, hoping they weren't talking about me. I made it a point not to pick my nose in class to avoid this very situation. But no: it was me. Fear replaced obliviousness in my relations with the opposite sex.

Three weeks into the season, Uncle Phil caught me behind the backstop and asked me if everything was all right.

"I'm okay," I replied with conviction.

"Sure, you're okay," Phil said, with a pitying tone. "The Wolfeman's already got his pink with orange border, you know."

"Great for the Wolfeman."

"Don't want to see you fall behind, that's all, not make honor roll. I think you should ask Annabella to dance at the social tomorrow night."

Annabella. Nobody wanted to go out with Annabella. If anybody's dad really wanted a boy, it must have been hers. She was a tremendous jock and could play ball better than most guys. The year before, she'd almost won "tribal" for the Arapaho Nation single-handedly. Although she seemed completely all right to me, this athletic prowess had gotten her ostracized by some of her junior-league JAP bunkmates.

"No one wants to go out with Annabella," I said. At eleven, you can smell an outsider a mile away.

"Hey, tell me the truth. Uncle Phil ever give you a bad steer?"

"Well, no."

"Ask Annabella to the dance. It'll be good. Believe me, I know about these things."

So I asked Annabella to dance, and we danced close, right then and there, with "Venus" and "Sealed with a Kiss" on the hi-fi. Uncle Phil was right, of course. Annabella was a total Jewish Artemis and a natural shot-putter to boot. She was a natural at many things. While Alan Dworkin and Harry Wolfeman sat petrified with their unspeaking girls—who were supposed to be so great-looking and have dads who made fortunes in the garment center—Annabella struck up a nice conversation about who was better, Mickey Mantle or Willie Mays. Being young liberals, we of course, agreed Mays was better, for what reasons we were not exactly sure. Wow, it was like you could talk to her. That was the opening, a bunch of jokes went through it, and soon we both were laughing. Then came the moment when my cheek entered the realm of alien softness.

A little bit of heaven just in time for puberty. It seems more marvelous with every passing year.

Too bad none of this summery bloom slopped over to the forlorn rooms of gloom that encased the other ten months of my year. There was "me" and "other me." Camp me and the so-called real me. Rushed along, like an empty bag of Fritos on a cold and windy night, I approached the wretched precipice of junior high school. Suddenly it wasn't enough to be Jewish to assure being in the top half of the class. There were subjects like Spanish, and algebra, and terror took hold. All through the deadly winter months, I longed for that evening when my mother would make the final double-check for name tapes. When the camp bus was thrown into gear that July 1st, I felt a desperate hope rise in my chest.

Almost immediately, however, it was clear that a disaster was in the making. Many of my bunch were back, but on the counselor cot, where Uncle Phil's Playboy key chain and Al Kaline model glove were supposed to be was a clipboard filled with graph paper. The top leaf was divided into three vertical columns. At the top of the first column was written "Camper," the second, "Strengths," and the last, "To Be Improved." Uncle Phil, he was gone, off to dental school or wherever, and we had a new counselor, Uncle Nat Fleischman. Even today, if you ask me to make a list of the ten worst people ever to live, Uncle Nat Fleischman would be on it, rubbing elbows with Hitler, Stalin, and Walter O'Malley.

For the life of me, I can't remember if I did anything to set him off, but Uncle Nat was on my butt from day one. Truth is, I'm kind of a slob; I don't fold my underwear—not that Uncle Phil cared. No one really did. We'd have bunk inspection and usually get a 9, or even a 9.5, no sweat. Uncle Nat though, he said that from now on there were going to be two inspections, the official one and his. Guess which one was the bigger ball-breaker? Man, that jerk made me make and remake my bed a hundred times before he was satisfied with the way the quarter he bounced off my stretched army blanket twirled in the air. With Uncle Nat around, the life Uncle

Phil had so carefully helped me construct for myself was laid to ruin. The first day we were scheduled for softball, I trotted out to my usual spot at first, and Uncle Nat said we were going to have practice at least twice a day if we were going to show Uncle Mort and the crybabies from bunk two who was really boss around here. To this end, no one's position was safe. Some changes would very definitely be made.

"We might as well start at first," Nat said, fungoing these hard choppers into the hole that somehow I was supposed corral. Then he'd shoot these liners over the bag, those slice shots that curve away from you and that Vic Power couldn't have grabbed on a good day.

"Mark, you can't play with that mitt you've got," Nat shouted after I missed about ten in a row. "You better get another one." This, about my Ted Kluszewski model! Soon enough, I was out in right field gulag where you get a ball every Shavuoth, and by the time you do, you're daydreaming so hard there's no chance to make the head's-up play. My hitting suffered, too.

Everything turned rotten. Pine Grove was located in a small town in New Jersey, and like every town that ever had a summer camp in it, it was said to have a home for criminally insane boys who were continually escaping. Uncle Phil really milked the scenario during lights-out. At any moment some junior Norman Bates might jump out from under your bed with a bloody hatchet. This was good stuff. With Nat at the helm, however, all we heard about was the extreme heroism of the Israeli freedom fighters during the 1948 war, how some spies pinned Stars of David to the inside of their cheeks, or even shoved them up their butts, so the Arabs wouldn't find them out. Nat's life ambition was to work for the Mossad. He said places like Pine Grove were responsible for making Jewish youth soft, setting up another Holocaust. If the place was run as a kibbutz, with self-sacrificing discipline instilled, then it might be worth the money our parents paid. Cries that "but this is camp" were met with hard-nosed indifference.

Worse was the time we had a "mixed period" with our corresponding girl group, sort of a daytime social. The camp had just shelled out bucks for a trampoline, and we all took turns bouncing on it. When it was my turn, Nat, all smarmy with the counselor of the girls' bunk, said, "Watch this kid, you won't believe it." The sarcasm in his voice burned through me. I fucked up, of course, bouncing right off the mat. Right in front of Annabella, too. To top that off, old Nat, Joe Religious that he was, probably wormed an extra C-note from tightfisted Uncle Bob to run Friday-evening services, so right in between "Tzena, Tzena" and "Dayeinu," I had to watch his slitty features go all righteous and listen to him talk about "fair play and the value of unconditional love."

I had no notion of the depth and breadth of the feelings that bubbled up from within me because of Uncle Nat. In the world from whence I came, rebellion was for the guys named Vinnie. No matter how bogus, how arbitrary a teacher was, their authority was to be endured. Best thing you could do was tune them out. But Nat, this asshole, he was a wrecker. He trod on my idyll, stomped on my dream of alternative selfhood. He had to be resisted, at all costs. I entered into a new and wholly different phase of selfhood. Where once had been the mellow, get along, go along me now stood this raged-fueled refusnik. I talked back, declined to participate in dumb activities, I appealed to the rowdier tendencies of my bunkmates, leading them in hunger strikes and noisemaking binges.

"What's gotten into you? You used to be such a quiet camper," Uncle Chris, the head counselor, asked me.

I became more recalcitrant. Once I pretended to be asleep on the bench when Nat tried to send me up to pinch hit in a crucial moment in a game against Uncle Mort's bunk two. Nat retaliated. He docked me from the prom social, a big deal where no one even wore white socks. I wrote Annabella a tearful letter, telling her my fate. And the night of the prom, I sat on my cot watching my friends, a total cloud of Canoe, stride up the hill, the evening sun crowning their Ban Lon shirts.

Not willing to submit to Nat's idiot decree, I decided, along with Doug Steinberg, a fellow dockee, that we would make the arduous journey through the poison-ivy fields and across the lake to the girls' side. We'd be with our babies on the big night, after all. It was the greatest dare, the worst possible offense. Just a few days before, we'd seen what that sort of audaciousness had cost Benny Feinstein, a good infielder from Center

Cabin. He'd made his break towards the girls' campus and run right into a line of rusty barbed wire. Fifty tetanus shots they said he had, some of them right in the eyeball. He showed up to mealtime with bandages on his face like the Invisible Man. But big deal, risks are risks.

Our plan was to be waiting around the girls' bunk when they got back from the social, that way we could get them to peel off from the rest. We split around eight. The woods were easy. It was the lake where we ran into trouble. We slipped a canoe off the rack and started to paddle out. Halfway across, we started hearing screaming on the shore. Freaked, we forgot all about across-bow rudders and J-stroke stern control. Doug lost his paddle. Then, that flashlight beam sheared through the thick humidity. It was Nat, all right, doing his Mossad thing. Someone must have tipped him; to this day, I often wonder which one of my "pals" would stoop that low. Anyway, he caught us and towed us back to shore, so I never did get to see Annabella, though a lot she probably cared since she'd gone obsessive about making the gymnastics team for the junior Maccabiah Games and hadn't given me more than half a glance for a month.

Nat fixed the next day for punishment. He got all the guys to make a circle in back of the nature center and pulled out a paddleball racket. It's half-inch-thick wood with holes, if you don't know. He made me lean over a bench and started in. Around the third swat, I remembered a movie I'd seen, a World War II picture, where the Germans are torturing Jimmy Cagney, trying to get him to tell where the air strike is coming. The air strike is really coming right where they all are, but Cagney won't tell, and then the planes are overhead and Cagney has this incredible smile on his face.

"What are you smiling about?" Nat demanded in midswing.

"That's for me to know and you to find out," I shot back.

Of course, that didn't do much for the state of my rear, since Nat really wound up on the next swat. He was trying to make me cry. But I would not cry. My ass was still killing me on the bus ride back to Penn Station a couple days later, but it was way worth it. I never told my parents what happened, because even when it involves a scum like Uncle Nat, what went on at camp was none of their business. I did, however, say there was no way I was going back to Pine Grove Camp. Asked why, I said the food had really gone downhill, especially the size of the portions, something my mother instinctively related to.

When it was time for camp to open the next summer, I wasn't in front of Penn Station, I was in the parking lot of Alexander's department store, at the corner of Queens Boulevard and the Long Island Expressway. I was going to a new camp, a joint named Skybird, which was pretty much the same sort of setup as Pine Grove except that it was in Vermont and was smaller and probably cheaper since it was run by a gym teacher from the junior high where my mom taught, and she likely got a deal.

So, once again I boarded a bus filled with unknown, potentially hostile faces, bound once again for an undoubtedly verdant but certainly alien world. From the tinted window of the Green Mountain Special, I watched my parents until they got so small they just blended into the crowd of other faceless wavers. Then, as the *thrum* of the New York Thruway gave way to the twisty upstate two-laners, a nice-enough-looking guy in his early twenties came over and sat down next to me.

"This'll be your first year at Skybird?" the guy asked.

"Yeah," I nodded.

"My name's Uncle Warren, I'm your counselor. Who are you?"

"My name is Jake, and I play first," I said.

29
The Visiting Nurse Leaves the Lower East Side

This really is a family piece, since the Visiting Nurse is my sister. We share the same DNA, give or take a few wacky little chromosomes, so this is a pretty personal story. And truly, it was the end of an era—when she moved out of the Lower East Side. Eventually she'd move out of New York altogether, to Alaska (if you can believe that), where she's been for the past twenty years. Of course I've always missed her, but I understand. There's something about seeing one too many guys come into the Bellevue ER with a machete stuck in their forehead that kind of makes you want to get away. From the Village Voice, *1979.*

The Visiting Nurse peeled off a dozen ten-spots and stuck them in the hand of the Mother Trucker moving man. A hundred twenty dollars—for moving cross-town? Once it seemed you could go around the world for $120. Still, the Visiting Nurse thought, she was more than getting her money's worth. Some might calculate a move from East Sixth Street near Avenue B to West Fifteenth Street at about a mile. But the Visiting Nurse knew better. She knew East Sixth and West Fifteenth are light-years apart.

Sure, she mulled, it's still a walk-up, Spanish is still spoken in the hallway, and you still had to step over creeps on the stoop to get to work. But as the Visiting Nurse looked at the white brick Helmsley-Spear apartment house across the street, she was comforted. The building would likely mess up her TV reception, but at least the thing would be there tomorrow morning.

Back when she was living on Suffolk Street, south of East Sixth, such solidity was not assured. Every morning the Visiting Nurse would roll out of bed and see the tenement across the street out her window. It would always be there, full of aluminum-shuttered windows and breeding rats. Except once. She was awoken by an excess of sunlight shining into her room. That was when she realized that the tenement had crumbled into rubble while she snoozed.

It was that kind of impermanence, the Visiting Nurse mused, that made living on the Lower East Side so . . . er . . . existential.

She remembered when she'd first come to the old neighborhood. It was nine years ago, right after giving up her classics major at Buffalo State University. She was a member of the Buffalo Venceremos Brigade. All sons and daughters of garment-center big shots and schoolteachers, they were going to Cuba to wear sidearms and spout poetry in the cane field. Her platoon, however, got lost on the march south. They wound up bivouacked on Suffolk Street above Delancey, a block famous for having more murders per square inch than any other in New York. The Visiting Nurse scanned all the open hydrants, mange-ridden dogs, vicious gunmen. Suddenly there was no need to go to Cuba. She was already on the front lines of the war.

If it hadn't been for Chino, the Visiting Nurse concluded, as she unpacked her Nero Wolfe books and looked for the proper place to put the full-length mirror, the Lower East Side might have been just a rapidly passing phase, not the decade-long obsession it became. But there Chino was, that fateful night ten years ago, crouching in the corner of the unfurnished, unheated apartment the Visiting Nurse shared with the militant dyke: one hunk of rumpled, triple Scorpio Latin Lover.

The Visiting Nurse thought it was the most compelling thing she'd ever seen, Chino crouching there, his paisley shirt stretching across his barrel chest, sweat rising beneath his leather headband. He spoke, finger jabbing, about how the Puerto Ricans of the Lower East Side were blind. They would never see what they needed to see without Art. Art would give them the ounce of human dignity they needed to lead them through this cold, brutal, hostile, racist world. Without a fleck of modesty, Chino said that he was the Artist to do the leading. He wrote poems about the landlords who shut off heat in pregnant women's apartments, plays about the future liberators of the Island, essays about the sad street stars who thought they had it cool in Caddies and minks when really they were just more miserable victims of the stacked deck. He played flute and made plans to translate Marx into Nuyorican slang. Then he ripped off a twenty-minute free verse about the attempted assassination of the Puerto Rican nemesis Harry Truman as easy as Do Re Mi.

The Visiting Nurse always had a profound weakness for Lorca, Neruda, Marx, and Jesus Christ. She threw her ass-length dirty-blond hair over her shoulder and shifted in her chair. She knew she could look absolutely ravishing or completely plain, depending on the pose and lighting. This was an emergency situation, the right note had to hit. She couldn't take her eyes off Chino's pocked face. This was big, very big.

That very night the couple went on a revolutionary maneuver. Along with the junkie David Ramirez and Muhammad Ray, the brand-X Muslim who drank rat milk for protein, they piled into Chino's truck—the one with no windshield—and headed for East Tenth Street, where a Phoenix House drug rehab joint was being built. And stole a couple dozen two-by-fours Chino said he needed for his storefront theater on East Sixth Street.

Things were cool until a Ninth Precinct green-and-black stumbled on the scene and put everyone against the wall. Stealing from junkies was a federal offense, the cops said, inasmuch as Phoenix House got bread from Washington. David Ramirez screamed that this was totally a trumped-up charge, since he was a junkie himself, so why would he go to all this trouble to steal from himself? Chino yelled bilingual biblical insults. Spread-eagle, the Visiting Nurse was flying. Since growing up in Fresh Meadows, a less interesting section of the pretty-dull-to-begin-with Flushing, Queens, she had been desperate to remove the stain of middle classness her parents had broken their poor immigrant necks to acquire. Tonight, the blot of eighteen years of two-car garages and white blouses on assembly day were being washed clean in the scuzzy blood of the Lower East Side lamb. She'd already been carried across college greens by hick cops, but that was junior league. This was Night and the City.

The cops were too lazy to fill out arrest forms, so everyone went free. When Chino and the Visiting Nurse got back to Suffolk Street, the apartment door had been ripped off the hinges. Later, Chino found the door, one of those heavy police lock jobs, on the roof, three stories up. Obviously the neighborhood was being beset with some new race of superhuman strength junkies. It was the second time that week they'd been robbed. All that was missing was the Visiting Nurse's three-dollar Westclox alarm clock, the last thing left to steal.

Chino took out one of the little red spiral notebooks he always carried, to record the evening's events. His life was a living art project, he said. It all had to be set down, with all detail. The racism of the cops, the Frustration of the Artist, all of it would make great street theater, he declared on the tenement rooftop as the sun rose over the Williamsburg Bridge. To the Visiting Nurse it was all poetry; she was hopelessly in love.

The couple set up housekeeping in Chino's unfinished Cienfuegos Theatre on East Sixth Street. He said he wanted to live and work in a place made holy by the sweat of the People. The Cienfuegos was once a Chinese hand laundry, so it fit the bill, sort of. Next door were the mutant cats. The idiot potters who once lived there had spent their time collecting cats from the street. Deformed, six-toed, three-legged cats. They had had at least forty of these horrors. When they left town for upstate, they kept paying the rent on the place. They couldn't bear to have their cats go homeless. It became some feline *Lord of the Flies* deal in there. For months no one on the block had the nerve to look in the place.

After growing up with vinyl covering the living room couch, the Visiting Nurse got all her furniture from the street. She found a refrigerator on Avenue C, a little banged up, but working. When the Visiting Nurse tried to clean the fridge, however, about two hundred thousand roaches ran out of the fan mechanism. Immediately the thing stopped running. Chino, who worked for the Transit Department and had the house wired up to a streetlamp in the middle of the block, tried to fix the thing but it never ran again. Only on the Lower East Side would there be an icebox that didn't run unless the bugs were inside. None of this bothered the Visiting Nurse except for the water bugs, those two-inch jobs. The first time she saw a water bug crawling up a Tropicana container, she sat down and cried. Chino laughed at her and said she was soft. After that, if some baby roaches found their way into her Red Zinger, she thought nothing of it.

Those days, as now, the ethnic groups of the Lower East Side mixed only on special occasions. Like the time Gottlieb's Cheap Clothing had a fire. Gottlieb's put their half-burned panty hose and white socks in a huge dumpster on First Avenue. Moments later representatives of the Polish, Ukrainian, Rican, and hippie communities were scaling the six-foot steel dumpster walls, searching for salvage. People got carried away. One Polish lady, about seventy five, fell in the dumpster, dropping out of sight. Chino and the Visiting Nurse climbed to the top but there was no sign of the Polish lady except a tiny withered hand clutching an E. J. Kurowycky Pork Store shopping bag. The Visiting Nurse flashed to the time she read about the man who fell into the forty-foot high Flakee Krust Bakery's flour silo, never to be heard from again. That man probably got ground into doughnuts, she thought, as Chino pulled the old lady out from under the overcoats.

Chino and the Visiting Nurse were part of their own Lower East Side ethnic group, the interracial hips. The interracial hips have been on the Lower East Side since the Beats, at least since the Slavs, Ricans, and Jews learned enough English to bang on the pipes and scream, "Shut up with that way-out music up there!" Sociologists could call it a syndrome. White people, notably white women, from Shaker Heights, or Upper Darby, or Brooklyn, came to the Lower East Side looking for exotic black men wearing skullcaps or poets screaming defiance in the street. They found many men more than willing to take them up on it. "We're mongrelizing the races," the Visiting Nurse and Chino liked to proclaim. Then they'd argue which race was being mongrelized more.

The Lower East Side set the Visiting Nurse free. In high school people had said she was gawky and talked too loud. Being on the Lower East Side was like learning it was okay to blast one in bed with a lover—everything seemed easier.

Her friends—all suburban escapees—were real off-angles. Millie was a monster redhead. From Polish stock, she grew up in Greenpoint. In the their late sixties, her parents had never been to Manhattan, even though they could see the the Empire State Building from their kitchen window. There was an idea that Millie, a prodigy, would become a classical musician. But she only wanted to take jazz lessons from Roland Hanna. Once she bought a grand piano from a Chinese flimflam man on Oliver Street for fifty dollars. The thing weighed two tons. It took every junkie on Avenue B to get it up the stairs. That night Millie sat down to play "Perdido." The piano went right through the floor to the Ukrainian people's kitchen below.

Millie had a beautiful mulatto kid named Mikail. Almost all the Visiting Nurse's girlfriends had beautiful mulatto kids with Middle Eastern names and fathers who hadn't been seen since the one night, or month, long ago. Selma, from a rich Chicago family, was the queen of the scene. She'd been on Avenue B for fifteen years and said she'd never once gone out with a white guy. To listen to her, she'd slept with the entire New York contingent of the Black Panther Party, and half the young Lords.

In the day, the White Women brought their kids out to Tompkins Square Park, chasing the junkies off the see-saws. At night there were bars to hang out in: Dirty Stanley's on B and Twelfth, Peewee's, the Annex, and sometimes Slug's, where, if you hit the right night, you could see trumpeter Lee Morgan get his head shot off by his old lady. But most time was spent in Leshko's Coffee Shop, a Ukie joint on Seventh and A. The pierogis were better at Odessa, but over there you couldn't look out the window and gossip about everyone who passed by. The Visiting Nurse spent whole weeks with Selma, Millie, and the rest, talking of once and future lovers. Some men were passed around, especially Jack, the bassoonist from Sun Ra's Solar Arkestra, who never went anywhere without his special Egyptian power pyramids, and Thomas, the Indian, who claimed his grandfather had been the model for the Indian head nickel and had never been paid for his work. He was going to sue the government "for every nickel they got."

Going out with Chino made the Visiting Nurse a kind of royalty, a regular slum goddess. Their relationship was, for the most part, like any other Lower East Side relationship. Sometimes Chino would go out for a pack of cigarettes, disappear for two days, then stick his head in the door and ask, "Filters or not filters?" Once he didn't come home for a whole week. The Visiting Nurse had nightmares about him stepping on the third rail. Puerto Rican spiritual ladies told her to light candles. Turned out he'd gone to San Juan for a few days. But he always apologized with red roses. And when he turned on those eyes, they could pierce beams.

The Visiting Nurse had to admit it, she was crazy about Chino. She didn't care that she was five inches taller than him. To her, it didn't matter that their official song was Martha and the Vandellas' "Live Wire," in which the singer laments how it's her birthday and "he forgot again."

Art held them together. Chino loved to have the Visiting Nurse read Greek myths to him. She'd get those old college books and knock off Leda and the Swan or the Birth of Dionysus in an evening. Finally, there was a use for all those liberal arts. Chino especially liked the inter-species Zeus procreation stories. Also anything involving thousands of soldiers and peasants. He was attracted by the scope, since even if the Cienfuegos Theatre stage barely held three people at a time, his work longed for VistaVision and a cast of thousands. None of his plays spanned less than one hundred years of racist, imperialist history or failed to tackle themes based on at least six of the seven deadly sins.

He did true street theater in the sense that he built all his sets with things he found in the gutter. He was always bringing stuff home from the 207th train yards, where he worked. Hardly any evening went by that there weren't dozens of "live-in" actors at the Cienfuegos. The Visiting Nurse, a fiend for second-rate mystery writers, couldn't get through half a Stanley Ellin or a Dorothy Sayers without twenty juvenile delinquents rehearsing politico-salsa numbers beneath her loft bed. Chino said the soul of the Puerto Rican Artistic Consciousness must come from the young. And the Visiting Nurse didn't mind making rice and beans for a thousand wiseass kids. But when Chino wanted her to sew fifty-eight dashikis in the colors of the Puerto Rican flag, she drew the line.

It was worth it because Chino really could write up a storm when he got going. The play the Visiting Nurse always liked best was *The Landlady of The Lower East Side*. The protagonist of the play walked in the door one morning, in the form of a very pretty, very skinny black lady about thirty-five. She spoke with a West Indian lisp, dressed in a chiffon skirt and fringed hat, dragging a giant trunk behind her. She swept into the Cienfuegos, calling Chino and the Visiting Nurse her "little darlings." Then she got a pot and put up water for a "little morning tea."

It was 7:00 A.M., so she couldn't be sure, but the Visiting Nurse thought she had seen this lady before, but couldn't remember where. On this morning the lady's conversation was full of flighty Blanche Dubois cadence and ellipse. She said her parents once owned the land where the Panama Canal is today, so she was very rich. Then she said it was so nice to sit down for a cup of "morning tea" with her tenants, especially when they were such nice tenants.

Chino and the Visiting Nurse looked at each other. They knew their landlord was not this lady but rather Rifkin the Foul, the man who had single-handedly turned avenues A, B, and C into his own personal Rifkin's Field. Was the woman nuts?

When the black lady left with a flourish of feather boa, Chino and the Visiting Nurse decided to follow her. They tailed her to a miserable tenement over in "Little Vietnam," Eleventh Street between B and C. They watched as she opened up a huge trunk, pulled out a domestic outfit, and proceeded to sweep out the rotten stairwell, singing "out on the rolling sea and Jesus speaks to me." Strange, the Visiting Nurse thought.

It got stranger still a few days later when the Visiting Nurse and Chino saw the lady on Lafayette Street, trying to break the lock on a warehouse door. The lady smiled when she saw them, explaining that she'd left her keys home and had to move a bunch of "properties" she was storing.

Chino said he'd pick the lock, and did. The black lady kept talking about her nieces in Barbados as Chino and the Visiting Nurse moved some old radiators out to the sidewalk. Just then four Puerto Rican guys dressed in green coveralls came running down the street.

"Get away, crazy bitch," they yelled at the black lady, knocking her to the ground. Chino demanded to know what was going on. And when he stepped in, one of the Puerto Ricans hit him. "*Brothers!*" Chino shouted in Spanish. But these guys were not his brothers; they couldn't wait for him to get up so they could knock him down again. The Visiting Nurse started screaming and ran for a cop.

When she got back with two bored Ninth Precinct cops, Chino was taking a shot to the stomach. The black lady was out cold next to one of the radiators, her chiffon dress up over her head. Just then a fat man appeared in the warehouse door. He looked like a blimp in a gray pinstripe suit and chewed on a cigar as fat as a chair leg. He blew his nose into his hand and ripped off a wad of snot the Visiting Nurse thought would take out her eye. It was Rifkin the Foul.

"What's the trouble, officers?" Rifkin asked with the innocence of someone who says "That's showbiz" at funerals. The cops looked at each other and said, shit, sure beats them. Then Rifkin pointed to the black lady, whom, he said, was loony and had been trying to steal his property for some time. Chino started to say that was a lie when the cops crushed him against the wall and banged his thighs with their nightsticks. The black lady revived slightly, enough to start whimpering; what Rifkin said was not true, she said. She could prove it.

The black lady wobbled over to her trunk and started pulling out long pieces of white paper. On each was scrawled a florid, completely illegible signature.

"See," the lady said to the cops, "deeds, all deeds." Then she turned and looked Rifkin right in the chub face. "Little darling," she said with the sincerity of an abused seven-year-old, "How could you lie? How could you say it isn't so. You know you gave me these deeds."

Rifkin's pig eyes darted in his head. He chewed hard on his spit-wet cigar and began to stutter. "She's crazy," he said, "ask anyone. She's crazy." He turned to one of the green-suited guys, who were supers. They put their fingers to their temples and made circular motions—definitely wacko.

This gave Rifkin renewed virulence. "Let me see those deeds," he steamed, walking over to the piles of paper flying out of the black lady's trunk. He grabbed one piece and held it up. It was blank except for an indecipherable scrawl. "This look like a deed to you?" Rifkin questioned the cops. They shrugged no. Rifkin said he was the owner of the warehouse and didn't like people breaking his padlocks. The cops gave Chino another whack with their sticks and asked the landlord if he wanted to press charges. No, he said magnanimously. Just get them out of here.

The black lady kept screaming, tears streaming, as she tried to stuff her pieces of paper back into the trunk. The Visiting Nurse tried to help but the lady pushed her away. Then she dragged the trunk across Astor Place and went into the subway. It was the last time either the Visiting Nurse or Chino saw her.

Later that afternoon, a drunk super on Avenue B told her what really had happened. Rifkin the Foul had been banging the woman in his trailer office. But it was a transaction, or at least the lady thought it was. Every time Rifkin wanted it, she made him cough up a deed to one of his buildings. Unfortunately, she was crazy enough to believe the deeds were real. That was why she spent her time cleaning half the hallways on Avenue B. She thought she owned the buildings. She thought she was the Landlady of the Lower East Side.

Chino worked days for weeks on *The Landlady of the Lower East Side*. He called in sick, spending night after night up writing. The play had "all the tenderness, all the humor, all the racism" an Artist could ever hope for, Chino said. The Visiting Nurse quit telephone operator's school so she could be on hand to bring beer, correct spelling, and read inspirational myths. This was to be Chino's masterpiece.

That's what made it so tough when she came home that day and found the manuscript ripped to shreds; it was stuffed underneath her pillow. Chino didn't believe in Xerox, the play was dead. Chino was gone. The Visiting Nurse went howling into the Lower East Side, looking for her lover.

Felipe, the gypsy cabdriver, said he thought he'd seen Chino down in the East River projects with Luis, the revolutionary. Luis worried the Visiting Nurse. He was the only one of Chino's friends who wouldn't laugh at her raunchy jokes. In fact, she'd never even seen him smile.

This was insane, the Visiting Nurse thought, running down Avenue B, screaming "Chino" with panic in her voice. It was a familiar scream. The kind her mother used when she couldn't find her in the supermarket. The Visiting Nurse would always get found right away, anything to shut up those embarrassing screams. At Seventh and B the guys from the motorcycle club mocked her, yelling, "Chino, Chino." For the first time since she came to the Lower East Side, she felt like a chump, the enemy.

When she got back to the Cienfuegos, Chino was sitting at the telephone-company-drum-table with Luis and half a dozen would-be revolutionaries. They were chanting revolutionary slogans in Spanish. Chino must have said, "*Vaya. Vaya, Vaya*" twenty times without taking a breath. He looked totally remade. His hair was cut short and slicked back; he was wearing a green iridescent shirt and orange pants. The Visiting Nurse almost broke out laughing, ready to ask if he was dressed to skip some Rheingold bottles over the mucky surf at Orchard Beach.

"Why did you rip up the play?" she wanted to know.

Chino answered her in Spanish, *The Landlady of the Lower East Side* was a reactionary, sentimentalist play, he contended. Giving it up was a symbol of his abandonment of these bourgeoisie feelings. He was giving up the Visiting Nurse, too. Chino said living with a white woman was not in keeping with "the reassertion of my identity as a Puerto Rican."

The Visiting Nurse knew Chino had been under pressure to dump her. But she always figured the love he wet-whispered in her ear with the lights off was bigger than any self-image trip. Wrong. Chino narrowed his eyes and said his "true" *vida* was Maria, the chubby red-haired one who lived above the "flat fixed" place on Avenue B. Chino said Maria was in the Bellevue maternity ward. She had just given birth to a boychild, Chino Jr.

In the days that followed, The Visiting Nurse came back to this moment, thinking of what she could have, should have, said. She could have said, "Maria. What a laugh. You can see her stretch marks through her toreador pants." She could have said, "You no-good lying phony. You fuck. Snake-in-the-grass chauvinist phony . . ."

But the Visiting Nurse did not say any of this. She ran into the street again, hysterical. What had she done wrong? Didn't she dance good to

Willie Colón? Didn't she act cool when Chino's grandmother came up from the Puerto Rican hill country for the first time?

The word was already out that Maria's relatives were looking for the Visiting Nurse. She didn't like white girls messing with her man. The Visiting Nurse went underground, hid in her friends' houses.

The White Women of the Lower East Side treated the Visiting Nurse tenderly. They knew what she was going through: they'd all been there before. They told the Visiting Nurse things they would never admit to themselves. Living with guys like Chino, or Indians whose grandfather was on the nickel, or bassoonists in Sun Ra's band, was great. Totally fantastic. Sooner or later, the class thing would get you if the race thing didn't. You couldn't eat yellow rice forever. The gap was too big to straddle.

The Visiting Nurse said no. It's not so. Love and Idealism could get you across. But the White Women of the Lower East Side had all been to Medicaid shrinks. They knew that only self-hatred could keep you going in that kind of relationship. The question was, how much abuse could you take before you were satisfied?

The Visiting Nurse saw the lights go around the room and paint the faces of Millie, Selma, and the rest of the old and tortured. She felt a nagging melancholy when she saw her friends wait outside the Asher Levy School on First Avenue for their mulatto kids. These really were women alone, the Visiting Nurse thought. Once they played at bilking the welfare department and got a thrill out of living in arson target buildings. Now they were welfare mothers and the terror of living in those buildings showed in their eyes. These women could never go back to Upper Darby.

It had been a break, the Visiting Nurse knew, that Chino had never asked her to bear his (boy) child. Maybe he was too preoccupied being the greatest living P.R. playwright. But the Visiting Nurse felt as trapped on the Lower East Side as any of her friends. This was her home. To her there were only two choices—Avenue B or the suburbs. It was irrational, but that's the way she felt.

There were nights, after she moved to her own place on East Seventh Street, when a Lestoil gargle seemed the only solution. There were plenty more afternoons gossiping in Leshko's. And many more black bartenders, sons of jazz musicians, and freelance plumbers. Some were nice, some hit. The Visiting Nurse was half waiting for one of them to get her pregnant and put the final touches on her self-hatred.

Chino was around, getting famous. His plays were all over the loft and streetcorner circuit. Grants rolled in. Every time the local TV stations did their obligatory minority-culture features, Chino would be on the tube, reading his poem about the *Marin Tiger,* the boat that carried the first Ricans to America. The *Mayflower* of Oppression, Chino called it. Sometimes the Visiting Nurse saw Chino in the Pioneer Supermarket, but they never spoke. Until one day. Chino was building a new theater, up on Eleventh Street.

Eyes down, he called the Visiting Nurse over and asked her if she'd gotten her degree yet. When they lived together, Chino convinced the Visiting Nurse to go to nursing school. He talked about "getting a trade" with the obsession of the immigrant parent world the Visiting Nurse thought she'd escaped.

The Visiting Nurse said she was still going to Hunter-Bellevue, but looking through electron microscopes gave her headaches, so maybe she was going to quit. Chino got mad. Did she want to spend the rest of her life in Leshko's window? Then Chino looked at her with more love than he ever showed when they were fucking and said she had more compassion and sympathy than anyone he knew. It would be a crime against the People if she didn't become a nurse.

So the Visiting Nurse finished school, wondering if Chino was right or if this was just more jive. She put it to the test. She took a gig with the Visiting Nurse Service. When it came to plunging yourself into other people's misery, it was better than working in a hospital. Hospitals were sterile, neutral places. Only the patient's disease was visible there. As a visiting nurse, you got to go to TB sufferers' SRO hotel rooms that haven't been painted in an age and see that one unfaded spot where the crucifix hung for twenty-five years. Visiting nurses get to see the misery that people manage to surround themselves with. It was much more depressing, and the Visiting Nurse had always been a sucker for the depressing.

Two weeks on the job, the Visiting Nurse volunteered for the Central Harlem beat. No other nurse would take it. Accompanied by murderous-looking black "escorts," the Visiting Nurse climbed six-floor walk-ups to see old men whose feet were covered with swarms of maggots, senile ladies whose uteruses hung down out of their vaginas, and thirteen-year-old mothers who threw their babies in trash cans.

She saw Midge Kelly, too. The idea of Midge Kelly touches the Visiting Nurse's heart. She is the only white lady living on East 132nd Street. She's been there for sixty-seven years. Midge Kelly is blind, but her very insistence at staying alive has convinced muggers she has a secret power, so they don't mess with her. The Visiting Nurse, however, knows what this power is: Midge Kelly is too mean to die.

Three times a week the Visiting Nurse had to take Midge Kelly's blood pressure. Once a month she had to take her downtown to buy clothes. This was no fun. Once she had the salesman at Mays bring out one hundred different pairs of shoes. They were all too tight or loose. Finally she picked a pair and on the bus back uptown Midge Kelly turned to the Visiting Nurse.

"What do they look like?" Midge Kelly asked.

The Visiting Nurse got a lump in her throat. Midge Kelly, the battleaxe, was showing her the real tragedy of being blind. She couldn't see herself. Had no idea of what she looked like. That was why she was so mean; if she could see how she behaved, she'd be a better person altogether.

So, in her sweetest voice, the Visiting Nurse said, "Oh, they're beautiful. They have this cute little bow, and they're a wonderful *cream* color." To which Midge Kelly started heaving crazily. "*Cream*," she yelled, "I don't wear *cream*. We're taking this shit back, now!"

To which the Visiting Nurse, fighting the impulse to kill, said. "Shut up or I let you off at Forty-second Street and Eighth Avenue."

The Visiting Nurse started to get great at her job. Uptown they said that this white girl could sterile-wrap a knife wound the size of the Grand Canyon with a single Band-Aid. A regular Florence Nightingale, she was. For every Midge Kelly and Greek waiter with oozing sutures the Visiting

Nurse ministered to, she felt better about herself. Maybe blood coughers and basket cases are buying off my guilt, the Visiting Nurse wondered. It was a selfish feeling, but it was working.

Little by little, the change was coming. The gossip in Leshko's got staler, the dogs in Tompkins Square Park uglier, the raps of the Ricans on East Sixth Street—now a cultural Mecca—grew more tired. The Visiting Nurse felt herself breaking away. She even went out with white guys. Irish men who came over at four in the morning when they were supposed to show at ten. They smelled like beer and said things like, "Look, if we fall in love and get married for the next sixty years. Or if I never see you again after tonight. This stands: First comes the fellows, second comes the force, third comes the bar, and fourth comes you."

Oh boy, the Visiting Nurse thought, Irish women are no sicker than me.

One morning she phoned a number in the paper. The apartment on West Fifteenth Street was nice and she took it. The Mother Trucker guys said eight in the morning, so the Visiting Nurse got up early—real early—to get her weaving wool in boxes. At 5:00 A.M. she went for a walk. Some cops and Ukrainians walking small dogs were in the park skirting the bench-sleeping winos and leather-jacket guys walking shepherds. A Puerto Rican woman who hadn't been to sleep screamed at her boyfriend as they trudged past the "Temperance" arch toward B.

But the park didn't look bad. The 101 different varieties of leaf trees (planted by Olmstead himself) made a not-bad autumn scene under the rising sun, the Visiting Nurse thought. She went over to Leshko's to get a cup of sludge. They were just opening up. And, as she sat in the window, the saw Chino walk by. She hadn't seen him for months. He looked like the old days: black beret, beard, and low swagger. She tapped on the steamy window, but he didn't hear. The Visiting Nurse only wanted to tell him that she was leaving. And it had been all right.

30
Mom Sells the House

This story got more letters, good ones that is, than any other piece in this book. Struck a chord, I guess. Or maybe it was that picture of me standing by my mom looking sheepish in my cap and gown because I showed up to graduation in shorts, an obvious sign of disrepect that earned me "a good klop" on the head. From New York *magazine, 1998.*

In the end, all mom said was "Good-bye, house." She tossed the keys through the mail slot, got into her Subaru, drove down 190th Street to Underhill Avenue, turned the corner, and disappeared behind the Fensels' hedges. Forty-three years, and now the house on the corner of 190th Street and Fifty-third Avenue—*The House*—was officially sold. Gone, like that.

It reminded me of the night, two years earlier, when my father died in The House, the one I grew up in.

Years of kidney treatment, cardboard boxes full of dialysis equipment stacked in the hallway, and then one gloomy November evening he comes out of the shower and keels over from a heart attack. He managed to make it to my parents' room and lie down on the bed before dying. He looked so normal there, stretched out, seemingly ready to open one of the mystery books he took from the library a dozen at a time, skull and crossbones on the spine.

Except he was on the wrong side. The far side of the bed (the left) was his, but he hadn't made it there. He was lying on my mother's side. There were so many rituals in The House, and this was one of them: Mom slept on the right, Dad on the left.

The front doorbell rang, another breach. We always used the side door. Only the Jehovah's Witnesses came to the front. But the funeral parlor men didn't know that. Somber in their dark suits and peaked caps, they carried a stretcher and black leatherette zippered bag. Already late for what they called "another pickup," the men paced in the kitchen while my mother stayed in the bedroom staring at my father's body. She was sure she'd seen him move.

"Look," she said, pointing at his stomach. "He's breathing." I embraced her, trying to calm her down, be cool, be the man of the house. Then I saw him breathe.

Alive again, same as you or me. Soon he'd get up, open the drawer of his mahogany dresser, put on his Witty Bros. suit (the best Division Street had to offer), go off to teach NYC Bd. of Ed. shop class at Junior High 74 just as he had for the past twenty-five years. Then he'd be home again at about 3:20, put on paint-smeared dungarees and hat (a quiet eccentric, he favored woolen fezzes and Nepali skullcaps), and work in his basement on whatever moonlighting carpentry job he had lined up. At dinner he'd read the "school page" of the *World-Telegram & Sun* over a plate of pot roast or some other suitably overdone meat. This routine (in spring, add gardening) varied, but not much. There was something about The House, its resolute rectangularism and boxy rooms, that narrowed the behavioral palette.

But he was still dead, still lying on the wrong side of the bed. It was "pretty common to imagine you see the loved one move," one of the funeral parlor guys said as they zipped their bag over my father's face and carried his body out the front door, the only time I ever remember him passing through that portal. As it turned out, one of the undertakers had gone to high school with me, thirty years before. We were on the track team together.

"Hey," he said, his face brightening as he recognized me. It was as if we'd just run into each other at a high school reunion."How you *doing*, man?"

"Not so good right now," I replied.

"Oh, yeah . . . well, maybe we can get together sometime," he said, carrying the bag containing my father's body toward the hearse waiting outside. Then they drove him down 190th Street, turned the corner, disappeared behind the Fensels' hedges, and were gone. Like that.

After that, The House's fate was sealed. As Mom, the master of utilitarian understatement, said, the place no longer "served its purpose."

"It was a reliable place to raise you and your sister," she sums up. And reliable (reliability being a key Mom meme) it was: strong and sturdy, a veritable Flushing fortress in red brick and gray siding. When that out-of-control Oldsmobile came tearing across the lawn and smashed into The House back in '58, did it crumble and fall? Not even a quiver. A couple of days later, I found the car's rocket 88 insignia in the azalea bushes. My father nailed it to the basement wall. It was a Queens version of a moose head: an 88 bagged by The House.

I understand the existential positioning of this modest shingled dwelling in the vast sweep of the Jacobsonian immigrant saga. Built in 1949, purchased in 1954 from an acrimoniously divorcing couple for the then-staggering sum of $18,000, The House was the prize—compensation for the steerage, sweatshops, and years of dragging the coal bucket up five tenement flights. The House was what my father got for following General Patton into the Battle of the Bulge as a member of the Third Army. The House was what my parents and others like them had coming in this nation if they played by the rules, which for a fleeting, astounding moment were actually rigged in favor of people not very long out of the *shtetl*.

East of Gatsby's ash dumps, this part of Flushing was the "fresh-air zone," a municipal version of God's country ("G-d" to you). Once, when I was seven, a lady ran over a raccoon in the parking lot of the Bohack Supermarket on Forty-sixth Avenue; everyone crowded around the flattened animal, congratulating themselves for living in a place still touched by the wild.

"Still the country, in parts," someone marveled.

Here, on the frontier, we maintained the Queens version of a classless society. All of us—sons of Jews, Italians, Irish, and a couple of Poles—played million-inning thrillers with taped-up hardballs down in the vacant lots until the Parks Department built proper diamonds and wrecked everything. Our dads were firemen, cops, teachers. They all worked for the City, belonged to the appropriate union, made about the same amount of money. We didn't know anyone all that much richer than us. Back then .260 hitters made twenty thousand or less. It was another kind of playing field. We were little princes of the American Dream, snot-nosed scions of our parents' striving, piloting our bicycles through spacious, near-empty streets, scarfing pizza (extra mushrooms and hormones on mine, please) at fifteen cents a slice.

Like Babe Ruth built Yankee Stadium, my parents built The House for me. My suzerainty remained intact even after that night Dave Bell and I, blasted on Champale Malt Liquor (advertised on WWRL, it was a black man's drink), tried to sneak into The House at 3:00 A.M. "Ah-ha," my mother shouted, flipping on the kitchen light in ambush. Startled like cockroaches, we both immediately threw up, Dave Bell on my mother's fuzzy slippers. But no matter, you've got to grow up somewhere and The House was a better place than most. Indeed, that was the real social alchemy at work inside those ever-reliable walls—the fact that my parents, barely removed from the primordial precincts of the Lower East Side and Brooklyn, were able, in a single generation, to produce such a thoroughly self-referential, proto-hipster creature like myself.

I never believed she'd really sell the place. It was a story she often told: how, when she was a girl in the Depression, my grandparents moved almost every year. Back then, the Brighton Beach/Sheepshead Bay landlord class was so hard up they'd throw in a paint job with each new rental, so why do it yourself? Paint cost money; movers charged only ten dollars. Bargain or not, my mother hated this shiftlessness. She vowed her children would not be uprooted for the sake of free paint. The House would last forever, she thought. But now, with Dad gone, too many things evoked her outsized hebraic capacity for worry. The boiler, the rosebushes, water in the basement: in my parents' strict division of labor, there was so much *he* did. But it was more than that. The doughty democracy of the neighborhood had shifted to the next, inevitable notch: Now, more often than not, those little civil-servant-style houses on the block were occupied by widows, old ladies living alone.

Then again, this is a different Queens than the one where my mother and father chose to become Americans, a wholly Other place from the one where I grew up. In the early sixties, in the waning years of my sojourn as an increasingly disgruntled outer-borough high school student, I'd return on the 7 train from some beatnik-in-training night in Manhattan and stand at the corner of Main Street and Roosevelt Avenue in Flushing. There, waiting for the Q-17 bus, which would take me deeper into what I regarded as the hopelessly provincial hinterlands, I'd look through the misty window of the Main Street Bar and Grille. On the steam table was a huge turkey with a giant fork jammed into its heavily browned breast. Men were at the bar, men about my father's age—Irish, Italians, Jews, the usual. They drank whiskey and watched *The Late, Late Show*. Even then, to the impressionable sixteen-year-old mind, it seemed like death.

Now the corner of Roosevelt and Main is a good deal livelier, and way more exotic. The bar is gone, replaced by places like the Flushing Noodle House, where a featured dish is "intestine and pig blood cake soup." Other landmarks of my youth, Alexander's department store and the RKO Keith's where I saw movies like *Mr. Sardonicus* and *Frankenstein '70* have been succeeded by establishments such as the Golden Monkey Pawnbrokers and the Korean Full-Gospel Evangelical Church. Down every street is a telescopic crush of neon Chinese ideograms hawking Taiwanese restaurants and sexual remedies. Billboards exhort travelers to sail down the Yangtze River. On the venerable Long Island Railroad Bridge hangs a sign advertising Asiana Airways: "Fly the youngest fleet to the old country." Somehow I don't think Bucharest, or Minsk, is one of those destinations.

I've always secretly believed that it was no mere coincidence that 1965, the year I left home to go to college, was also when Congress passed the Immigration and Naturalization Act, which threw the doors wide open and changed Queens forever. Now more than 125,000 Chinese and Koreans call Flushing home. A quarter of the city's newly arrived Latin American population lives in Queens. Peruvians, Bolivians, Colombians,

Nicaraguans—almost every country in the Caribbean and South America has a sizable representation. East Indians fill Jackson Heights. Once Jimmy Breslin, Queens' own Charles Dickens disguised as Archie Bunker, articulated the perfect nasal pitch of the borough's blue-collar white man. These days Breslin lives in Manhattan; much of his cop/fireman constituency has moved to Long Island or Florida; and if you go over to Elmhurst's Newtown High (a sleepy, Irish-dominated school when we played them in basketball during the middle sixties), you'll hear a hip-hop Babel of upward of forty different languages.

Thirty-five years after freezing on the corner of Roosevelt and Main, I am an eager tourist in the land of my upbringing. I love to get into the car and cruise the diversity hot spots, places like the intersection of Ninety-first Place and Corona Avenue, where within the space of a single block stand the Chinese Seventh-Day Adventist Church, Centro Civico Colombiano, Santería Niño de Atocha Botánica, Malaysian Curry House, Perla Ecuatoriana Restaurant, the Korean Health Center, and Elarayan Restaurante Chileano. Smack in the middle of this is Ana's hairdresser, where old Italian ladies, as if commanded by some recondite memory chip, still beehive their hair under conehead dryers. The Elmhurst Hospital emergency room is also good, especially on a Saturday night after a big soccer game piped from Bogotá. A more far-flung array of stabbing victims would be hard to find. Harried nurses call out the names of the evening's victims: "Gonzalez! . . . Patel! . . . Chu! . . . where the hell is Romanov's chart?"

These are a different crew from the immigrants my parents and grandparents came in with. My people, once they got on the boat—they weren't going back. America was their grail; they were here for the long haul. Now the world's smaller, it's sixty-nine cents a minute to talk to wherever at the *larga distancia* parlors on Roosevelt Avenue, and the new people aren't even called immigrants but "transnationals." You walk to Main Street, where the Hasidim are, and see that assimilation—becoming American—no longer seems the sole purpose of living in Queens. Maybe there are enough Americans. Indeed, sometimes, in the grip of postmodernist ennui, it seems to me as if these new people, by their very apartness—their refusal to buy the American deal lock, stock, and barrel—are the only fully fleshed-out humans around, the only ones with a palpable past, present, and potentially heroic future. They have rolled the dice with their lives; now the epic of New York belongs to them.

As for my mother, no one could ever accuse her of lacking a sense of adventure. Recently she went to Istanbul and preferred the Asian side. But she knows when things have come to an end. For months she walked the still quiet, verdant blocks around The House and felt out of place. "I'm lonely here," she said.

One fall day I was sitting at her kitchen table and heard the pounding. The realtor was outside hammering a FOR SALE sign into my father's lawn like a stake through the heart. Then they started to come, the prospective buyers. Local canard said someone Chinese would buy the place: a non-English-speaking man from Xi'an with a bad haircut, two daughters at the top of their class at Stuyvesant, and a suitcase full of cash, all of it up-front. But in this Queens you can never tell who might buy the house you grew up in. In the space of a fortnight, Syrians, Koreans, Chileans, and people from Bokhara and Thailand walked through the rooms my father painted and where he put up shelves. They sat on the sofa so long forbidden to me and my sister. It was a stirring ecumenical procession, a testament to the city's ever fecund, eternally replenishing genetic alloy. Soon The House would be the repository of an entirely different history, ringing with another sort of accent, the smells in the kitchen sharper, spicier. Soon the place, ever reliable, would serve someone else's purpose, only this time with a lot more TV stations than my sister and I ever got to watch.

My mother, she just wanted to sell. She's not the sentimental type. What no longer served a purpose had to go. In the end, Dominicans got the place. Nice people with a couple of kids and a travel agency business downtown, Mom said. Maybe she could have held out for another five or ten grand, with the market shooting up every day. But still, a 1,500 percent profit isn't too shabby, especially when all you want to do is get out.

"My heart is not broken," my mother announced at the closing.

Forty-three years ago, on the very first night I spent in my twelve-by-twelve-foot square room, Mom told me to bang on the floor if I got scared. Back on 174th Street, where we'd previously lived with my aunt and uncle, my room had been right next to my parents'. Here I was upstairs, by myself. But I never got scared. From the start I recognized the value of vertical separation. They were *down there* and I was *up here*. Ah, my room, that little incubator of me. What do you say about a place where you jacked off for the first time? Where you listened to Ali beat Liston on the radio? So much happened in my room, I thought, spending one last night up here, the movers due at seven the next morning.

The House was in boxes; my mother, never one to wait to the last moment, had started packing months before. I'd taken some things—my sixth-grade autograph book from P.S. 177 ("drop dead" is listed as my "favorite motto"), my Ted Kluszewski mitt, an old vinyl of *The Platters Greatest Hits*, the chair I sat in to do my homework. Mementos, souvenirs, nothing more. This seemed appropriate, since I'd always told myself that even though I'd grown up here, The House had never truly been mine. I was just passing through, marking time until my life started for real.

By midnight I was in the basement. It was straight down, like a plumb line, from my attic kingdom to that murky chamber of unresolved issues. Down there was what remained of my father's workshop. When I was a boy, this was the land of hulking steel machines upon which imposing sheets of plywood were made to scream in pain while being torn asunder. Now it was quiet. My mother had managed to sell the giant bandsaw and the huge metal lathe. Most of my father's hundreds of hand tools—he had dozens of files arrayed in varying increments of size and grade, at least fifty hammers and screwdrivers—had long since been given to friends and relatives. Their customized, meticulously labeled racks and holders were now empty.

The basement had always been an awkward place for me and him, not that we spent much time talking about it. I'd always assumed it to have been a source of mutual regret—that I hadn't inherited his marvelous skills, his reverence for the joining of two pieces of wood in a perfect right angle. It seemed like something a father and a son might do together, a gift to pass from one generation to the next in the old way. Now, however, on the last night of The House, with the machines gone or shut down, it was easy to believe that my father was relieved I'd shown no aptitude, that I was just another slovenly, uninterested teenager like the ones he taught all day long. In the stillness, I could feel him close, working away like some Queens hermetist in his fez, surrounded by his wonderfully precise toys, his files, planes, and grinding machines. Being a father now myself (as well as my father's son), I understood how Dad felt down here, his sanctum. With the ingressing ooze of life raging forth upstairs, it must have seemed like heaven.

That's when I started to pull that cabinet off the wall. It was one of the many built-in storage bins my father had attached to the paneling, each with several drawers bearing his familiar calligraphy (BRADS, ¼ INCH; BRADS, 1/3 INCH; BRADS, ½ INCH, etc). This was really what I wanted from The House, this symbol of his manic precision, a little bit of the peace he found down here. Except the thing resisted; I couldn't get it off the wall. I couldn't even figure out how and where he'd stuck it up there—the fastenings were invisible. It was something he'd always tried to teach me, how things might stick together without the gory slather of Elmer's, without the splintered bash of a dozen nails. This was the art of it, he said, to make things seem as if they'd always been there, as if they belonged. But then, like now, that sort of craft was beyond me. Anyway, I must have been making a bunch of noise, because soon my mother was descending the basement stairs.

There was an amusing retroness to the scene: Mom in her housecoat, demanding to know what I was doing, why I was making all that noise. She'd told the Dominicans those cabinets were "staying," and stay they would. I began arguing, saying that this cabinet meant a lot more to me than it could to anyone from Santo Domingo.

"You had your chance," she said with cold finality. She'd been trying to get me to take things from the basement for months, but I'd always been too busy.

"But Mom . . ." Reversion to former behavior is always lurking, even on the eve of your fiftieth birthday.

"He built those things for this place," my mother said. "They're not supposed to go anywhere else. So leave them."

Mom had pulled rank. There was nothing left to do but go upstairs, brush my teeth, and put out the light.

Six hours later, four Hell's Angels-style clad representatives of Movin' On (slogan: "The Company with the Clean Trucks") began carrying boxes out the long-shunned front door. It was more convenient, they said. By early afternoon the deed was done. "That," my mother said, "was that."

Now I visit my mom in her new apartment over on Seventy-fifth Avenue, near Bell Boulevard. Wanting to not move "too far" (no Florida for her), Mom found the place in a week. A totally nifty two-bedroom with a giant living room in a really nice development filled with "people to talk to," and close to her long-favored Key Food, the apartment "makes sense," Mom says, a little drunk on the novelty of it all. For Mom, to *hondle* is to live, and even as she misses my father terribly, there are all these new items to ruthlessly search out the best price on. At seventy-eight, she is finally living in a building that has an elevator. The view from the sixth-floor windows is fantastic. You overlook the old Vanderbilt Parkway, built as a private auto road by the old robber baron in 1908 so he could drive to his estate in Massapequa Park. Back in high school, my friends and I hung out on the overgrown parkway. It's where I first smoked pot, but Mom doesn't need to know about that.

After leaving Mom's place, as usual, I meander through the unending ethnikquilt that the borough of my birth has become. Driving past the Albanians and Afghanis on Hillside Avenue, I turn off to stop in at a candy store on Union Turnpike. My friends and I used to go to the place because the old man mixed his own Cokes and had a heavy thumb on the syrup. Now—the fountain long gone—it's owned by Sikhs. An old Russian, crucifix dangling on a key chain, is in there trying to buy cigarettes with food stamps. The Sikh won't allow it. "Why no? I pay tax!" the Russian screams in protest. This cracks up some Chinese kids who've been sneak-reading the comic books.

"I pay tax," they mock after the Russian has stomped off. Wise-asses. Like I said, now the epic of New York belongs to them.

In the end, I go by The House. It's been a couple of months now, and even if the grass looks a little patchy and my father would have have pruned the rosebushes, the place looks pretty much the same. But that won't last. Changes will be made. Which is fine, I think, silently watching from across the street, as the new people, all dressed up, come out the front door—as if they didn't know that, in The House, you always use the side.

31
Teenage Frankensteins

The nightmare of mortality arrives differently for different generations. For parents and kids alike, the Columbine school shootings were a seminal event. I mean: How far down the road to societal madness are we? New York *magazine, 1999.*

It is not your typical late afternoon here in the living room of the Brooklyn homestead *con der kinder*. The usual parental bleating about going outside, getting some exercise, doing homework, walking the dog, etc., etc., has been temporarily suspended. The TV's on, sure, but this time tuned to CNN. My two daughters, one teenager and one near teen, are transfixed, watching the Columbine massacre. Again and again they see footage of the students running from the besieged school, hands on their heads, bolting across the well-kept lawn. Over and over the stories of the library shootings are told, how Eric Harris and Dylan Klebold, TEC-9 and shotguns in hand, canvassed their terrified classmates, demanding to know who believed in God and who did not.

"I do," answered one frightened student, cowering in a corner.

"There is no God," Eric Harris said, and fired, point-blank.

On it pours from the Hitachi, the soul-shredding thrum of crying students, grieving parents, congressmen calling for action and/or compassion, reporters filling time. But my daughters can't get enough. They eat dinner in front of the set, fearful they will miss a single recap. In a tangential, contained way, it's like when Kennedy was shot and another crop of teenagers listened to Chet Huntley and Walter Cronkite intone those same things about Oswald and Ruby a thousand times until they became ritual knowledge, mantras to be repeated and carried about for a lifetime.

All hell breaks loose in different ways, for different generations. Thirty-six years after the grassy knoll (twenty-one past Jonestown), my daughters walk seemingly endless high school hallways fraught with adolescent terrors real and imagined, and now the nightmare of Columbine belongs to them.

"I can't believe it," my older daughter says, black-shadowed eyes glued to the tube. As a goth partisan and ardent adherent to the Cobainian-Anne Rice necro-Goddesshead, her first reaction was to be pissed that the media creeps had assigned the Trench Coat Mafia to her chosen fashion bag. Soon, however, the repeated viewings of the dead and wounded reduced her to a numbed, stumped silence. Littleton, Colorado, might be some far-off suburb, malled off and a million psychic miles from hanging out in New York's East Village. But to the extent that youth cements a bond, these students, victims and killers both, were my daughter's People. Still, knowing all she knows about the horrors of high school personal politics, which is about everything to be known about the topic, the disaster remained a mystery, even to her.

The pundits were now into blame. Affixing root causes. Outside of the sick kids who did the shooting, what elements of society can be held responsible for this climate of violence that—after so many other numerous similar incidents in the past few years—reached critical mass out there in Colorado? The usual suspects have long since been rounded up. Littleton SWAT teams may have frozen in the sight of perceived danger, but bow-tie-wearing *millennialistas* have been on the scene like a ball of heat. Was it video games, one more Arnold movie, or SS-lionizing rockers that have polluted the minds of the youth?

It is grim amusement to listen to corporate purveyors of the scuzzy pop culture mount defenses similar to the usual NRA fallback position—just as guns don't pull their own triggers, it's not the foul TV shows and movies that kill but the people who watch them. Well, sure. Who are we to mess with the market, not to mention the First (and Second) Amendment. If Mortal Kombat proves fatally seductive to a segment of the overly suggestible demographic, isn't this just the chance we have to take to live in the Land of the Fee? Censorship is a slippery slope, a can of worms. Today they're bleeping the Notorious B.I.G. (already victim to his own self-prophesized climate of violent demise, *You're Nobody until Someone Kills You*), tomorrow *C.S.I.* Soon the whole entertainment business will be wiped out and then where will we be?

The fact is, no one knows what really went through the mind of Eric Harris as he rolled strikes in his 6:15 A.M. bowling class on the morning of the murders. Likewise it is impossible to know the true thought patterns of other school shooters—Barry Loukaitis, who killed two students and a teacher in Moses Lake, Washington, on February 2, 1996, or Luke Woodham, sixteen-year-old alleged Satan worshiper who killed two and wounded seven in Pearl, Mississippi, on October 1, 1997, or Colt Todd, fourteen, who killed two students in the school parking lot in Stamps, Arkansas, or Michael Johnson and Andrew Golden, only eleven, who killed five and wounded ten in Jonesboro, Arkansas, in March of 1998, or Kip Kinkel, who killed his parents as well as shot twenty-four students in the cafeteria of Thurston High in Springfield, Oregon, on May 21, 1998.

It is horror, a kind of plague, the sort of thing you hope will just go away by itself. But that won't stop us from obsessive hand-wringing over this particularly virulent outbreak of teen madness. Theories? I have plenty. Try this: In its war on parents, the culture has so heavily invested in the "empowerment" of youth (and youthful spending) that kids have actually come to believe that, yeah, just like on any grown-up-devoid WB show, they are firmly in control and call the shots. Seven-year-old characters are written as wise sages. People get stupider as they get older. This makes sense: the longer we commerce in this fallen world, the more we are devalued. It is only at birth, when we are as close to God as we'll ever be, unsullied, that we are perfect. It is all downhill from there.

The latent Humberts among us might like those budding hardbodies on the tube, but there seems to be a cost in ceding the cultural landscape to the wrinkle-free. It is enough to make you long for the stodgy Republican lies of *Father Knows Best*. Back when I was a zombie teen, watching probably at least as much TV as my kids do today, I liked the way Paladin, of *Have Gun Will Travel*, gunned his way through the West. Sure, he shot people for money. But at least Paladin was a grown-up, a gainfully employed bounty killer who had a world-weary, adult remorse at the fulfillment of the nasty but necessary commitments of his job.

In our clueless, blunted authority, my generational bunch is in panic mode. For us youth-fetishizing boomers, the shoe is now on the other foot, it's *Reefer Madness* all over again except the other way around. We rail at the Internet, as if it's one giant *Joy of Cooking* slagheap of bomb recipes. We chastise Clinton, one of us, who sets such a slack example. There's no respect in the nation, I tell you. Trouble right here in River City! Maybe discipline is beyond us in this day and age. But what ever happened to a bit of sensible repression? Is the "Just do it" ethic a tad out of control?

Rationalizations "R" us. The much-quoted reaction of Dylan Klebold's father, who called his son "pure normal," states the indictment most succinctly. "Our society feeds off our children," said the father of the killer. What else is left but to blame the world we've made? Rekindling the notion of the Bad Seed? The acceptance of palpable evil in our midst? More remakes of *Village of the Damned*? This is not to forget Hitler, ever the hardy perennial. One of the little-noticed items of the coverage of the Columbine shootings was how slow the media, the *New York Times* included, was to mention that the shooting occurred on Hitler's birthday, a date, it would turn out, of special significance for Harris and Klebold. Despite the codification of 4-20 as a street moniker for marijuana, April 20 has slipped as an infamous date in the public brainpan. If the killings had happened only a day earlier, on April 19, the anniversary of the Waco Massacre and the Oklahoma City bombings it inspired, the date would have made the opening graphs. If things keep on like this, the entire third week of April will be a no-go zone.

The mind of the parental unit reels. As my daughters were watching the Columbine coverage, my nine-year-old son sat at the dining room table with four of his friends. Game Boys linked, they were electronically transferring Pokémons, the Japanese animation characters (a.k.a. Pocket Monsters) that are all the rage with their bunch. On that very day, with Columbine dominating the news, the *Times* had a front-page piece about how Nintendo was making billions from Pokémon despite recent charges that watching the TV show may have induced epileptic fits among youthful Japanese viewers. This said, compared with some of the other body-count extravaganzas my son has run up on the screen, Pokémon is pretty benign. The idea is to be an honorable, nurturing *sensei* for your menagerie of weird little creatures—not just to teach them to fight like cybercocks but also to help them evolve onward to a more ennobled state.

Yet who really knows about these things? As any old pinball wizard who could never beat a single level of digital Asteroids can tell you, if there's a *Time*-mag-style generation gap fomenting, it is a disparity in hand-eye coordination as much as anything of the mind or heart. Clearly people, even people with very similar DNA, are hooked up differently these days. I have read my son's Pokémon manuals more than once and still can't grok the methodology by which Charmander, the baby "fire" Pokémon, mutates into Charizard, a two-hundred-pound monster whose breath can melt boulders.

I watch my son and his e-coven of friends conduct their cyber séance and wonder: Who knows what lurks in the heart of the Poké-matrix? If, as it is fashionable to say now, memes (what used to be called ideas) travel like viruses, contagious and fast-acting like Melissa or Ebola, could not Pokémon, shiny, bright, and preternaturally popular, be the perfect surreptitious vector for such an infection? Was this the transfer happening at my own kitchen table, a controlling *Manchurian Candidate* virus being downloaded into the wetwear of my own son and his buddies at this very moment? How long would it take for this murderous brainwashing to germinate? What kind of school-annihilating hardware might be available by the time this virus came full-blown?

Likely, by the time this next upgrade of teenage Frankensteins hatch out, their programming will be too well refined for them to exhibit such warning signs as watching *Natural Born Killers* twenty times in a row, or sharding up hundreds of Coke bottles for shrapnel like a personal Kristallnacht. Ever since teenagers were invented, some time before Elvis, they've been perceived as a kind of (self-propagating) Other. A separate adolescent species. Them of the dirty room, them of the smart mouth, them who cut classes. Them who once sat in your lap and now can't stand the sight of you.

Them.

Here in the city, we pride ourselves on at least partial immunity from these meme-loaded violence tropes. It might have been part of Eric Harris's master plan to hijack a jet plane and crash it into midtown Manhattan, but there is a sense that we New Yorkers are too practical, too hard-bitten, for Columbine-style psycho-killing. If someone stabs you for lunch money because they think you're rich and they're poor and criminal, if someone shoots you because you're black and they're a cop—well, what else is new? These large-scale post office freakout-style shootings, especially by children who should be running around in Shark and Jet jackets sticking shivs into each other, is not our style.

Yet the other day I found myself driving over to the William McKinley Intermediate School in Bay Ridge, where it was alleged that five Chinese eighth-graders, all of them in the top "E"-tracked classes, had plotted to blow up the building on graduation day. The five were also supposed to have compiled a "hit list," marking many of their classmates for death. The plans were overheard in the cafeteria, and police from the Sixty-eighth Precinct arrested the kids, which led to much bewildered hand-wringing in the nearby Chinese community, known more for producing quiet, Stuyvesant-bound achievers (as these kids were—the band teacher, clearly distressed, bemoaned, "This sticks and I'm out my two best trumpet players!") than mad bombers. In the wake of Columbine, the media descended on William McKinley, one of only two intermediate schools in Brooklyn named after an assassinated president. Before the 2:45 dismissal, as blue-haired ladies in large plastic glasses expressed shock as they looked up at the news trucks, the retractable cable towers thrust up into the midspring Bay Ridge sky.

The students, however, seemed to take the whole episode in stride. Well versed in the nuances of disaster coverage, they jostled for camera position and delivered their lines. The whole thing was "a big surprise," said one fourteen-year-old, because even if the supposed bombers were "outsiders and unpopular," they "weren't *that* unpopular . . . You know, they were hated, but they weren't *that* hated." For sure no one "ever thought they'd do anything like *this*."

Later, it was said, the so-called bomb might have been little more than a Gilbert-chemistry-set-style assemblage of vinegar and baking soda and—despite several kids running around screaming "I'm on the hit list!"—that the whole incident was likely a misunderstanding. Still, everyone was given the day off. "We need a rest," said one of the middle school teachers. "With this stuff, even the false alarms are traumatic."

So now "no more pencils, no more books, no more teachers' dirty looks" has gone ballistic. "Copycat" incidents multiply. The meme moves on. Standing on the steps of the William McKinley School as the media swarmed, Vincent Grippo, head of School District 20, said, "It's not the system; it's the society." It's comments like that that recall motorcyclist Marlon Brando's being asked what he was rebelling against and his answering, "What have you got?" Indeed, the horrific details of Harris and Klebold's rampage aside, there's been an undeniable current of sympathy for the murderers. As many times as the memorial crosses for Harris and Klebold in Jefferson County's Clement Park were ripped down by the grieving and angry, someone put them back up again. The gnawing fact is, like the people they killed, Harris and Klebold were only kids. Somewhere, somehow, along the line they should have been protected, or slapped—anything.

In the end, that's what it comes back to, kids and parents. Last week I was riding uptown on the No. 6 train and saw a woman reading a book called *Get Out of My Life, But First Could You Drive Me and Cheryl To the Mall*, by Dr. Anthony Wolf, which, as many parents of teens know, is one of the better manuals on how to live with the teenage Frankenstein in your midst. The woman's eyes and mine met; we acknowledged the presence of the book and sighed. Nothing needed to be said.

Whatever its virtues, I doubt Dr. Wolf's book would have been much help to Mr. Thomas Klebold of Littleton, Colorado. In all this, I think of him most. Geophysicist; arguer for gun control; married to the former Susan Yassenoff, whose grandfather endowed the biggest Jewish community center in Columbus, Ohio, Klebold named one son for Lord Byron and the other after Dylan Thomas. Yet his son turned out to be a Jewish Nazi mass murderer. To think of Mr. Klebold's grief is to swallow hard and walk shakily away.

The other night I told my daughter that since the Columbine massacre, the sale of columbine seeds has increased tenfold in some places around the country. Not that she cared much. We were in a cab, going to a club called the Bank, a hangout for her goth crew, and I was far from an invited party. She was too busy arranging her black tights, black coat, black shirt, and black eye makeup to care much about the sales of pink and purple flowers. Despite reporting the mordant graffiti found on her high school wall—"15 jocks got killed in Colorado and all i got was this lousy trench coat"—she was still mad that the media morons continued to associate Klebold and Harris with goths. "They said they got ideas from the lyrics of KMFDM," my daughter railed. "That's stupid. Half the stuff the band says is in German and no one can understand it anyhow, so you know that's not true." Then she said it was time for me to split, because there was no way she was going into the Bank with her dad.

And let me say: I didn't feel so good about it, watching my daughter standing there with her subculturist friends, all of whom seemed very nice even if made up like a brace of Morticias. No, it didn't feel good at all seeing my daughter waiting on line to enter a club on Houston Street, past eleven o'clock, in her black velvet coat, those homie boys checking her out. But I'd already said okay, and there wasn't any going back now, not without the most egregious of scenes. Then the bouncer, an obligatorily fearsome Mr. Five-by-Five, parted the rope and the line began to move. Industrial blare tumulted from the door. Already having waved good-bye, my daughter stood with her back to me, paused in the vestibule, awaiting entry.

An orange light shone down from the ceiling upon her hair. From the day she was born, she has always had very beautiful hair. People remarked on it, always. Through all these years, her hair has never been cut. She just lets it grow, and it is beautiful still, long and shiny, hanging down. When we're battling, as we are so often during these teenage times, I forget how beautiful her hair is, and how beautiful she is. But now, the orange light pouring down, the luminousness could not be missed. She just shone. And then the bouncer beckoned again, and my daughter entered the club, disappearing into darkness filled with noise. It was a moment to take a deep breath. Because you never know.

32

The Boy Buys the Wrong Hat

When it comes to baseball, hate is a wholly acceptable family value. Written on the occasion of the "Subway Series." New York *magazine, 2000.*

The Yankee hater in me, sometimes dormant but never dead, stirred last summer inside Modell's out by Caesar's Bay in Bensonhurst. I'd promised my ten-year-old son a new hat, and there on the wall was a veritable riot of sports merchandising. Logos as odd and alien as crop circles embellished snapbacks representing Devil Rays, Sharks, and Hokies. Through the glut, my son's eyes settled on a far more familiar emblem. There, a beacon amongst the ESPN trash jungle, stood the most famous trademark in all sports, maybe in all the world.

The n and the y, like lovers so entwined, haughty, perfect. It was a fearsome icon, one that had been branded in my soul, stamped like a hot iron on my forehead, seared like a forever damning pair of letters on my back. My son, blood of my blood, DNA of my DNA, was about to purchase a Yankee hat.

This was a problem. For sometimes fashion is not just fashion and symbols are too evocative to be worn casually, by punk-rockers or little boys. Still, I'd promised. I'd get him a hat, any hat he wanted. As I drove home, the sight of this Yankee thing on my son's lovely, unsullied head struck me as a possibly ominous first salvo in a long-running Oedipal struggle. My son, the Yankee fan. It struck dread into the heart.

"I don't see what the big deal is," my son said, feeling the tension as we rolled up the Gowanus Expressway. "It's just a hat."

Just a hat. How to explain? How to make it clear that in our family tradition, it was not considered proper to cry when Gary Cooper gives that claptrap "luckiest man" speech in *The Pride of the Yankees*? That one need not feel awe while walking past Mickey Mantle's restaurant on Central Park South because, even with all that corny violin music about his knees and being the son of a coal miner, Mantle, soul of stolen youth or not, was still a Yankee? Like Serbia, like Hatfields and McCoys, there are ancient hatreds that transcend conventional irrationality. Wherever I am, whatever I'm doing, news of a Yankee loss makes my day.

But what choice is there? It is bred in the bone. Shot through the DNA. We do, after all, live in Brooklyn. Not counting Romania, Brooklyn is our ancestral home. A tug on the wheel of the ole Camry, a dodge of a few trolley tracks seeping up from beneath the tattered asphalt, and we'd be on Empire Boulevard and Bedford Avenue. Even now, the place remains a power vector, drawing you closer, even though all that remains are projects and the Ebbets Field Donut Shop, corn muffins $1.25. Holy Happy Felton!—even now it is like yesterday: how on May 12, 1956, date of my eighth birthday and year of the last Subway Series, I strolled with my grandfather down Franklin Avenue, to the legendary ballpark where Carl Erskine pitched a no-hitter against the Giants. "Some game, no hits," my father would later say.

It was an experience no eight-year-old forgets, especially as seen with Grandpa, the first generation of Jacobson Yankee haters, who spent his youth hauling overcoats through the Lower East Side and told me, in no uncertain terms, that the Yankees were the team of the bankers, every last one of them against meaningful social change and the workingman, from Jacob Ruppert on through DiMaggio, that flattop-headed Marine Hank Bauer, and the batboys, too.

Since Walter O'Malley really might be the third-worst person of the twentieth century behind Adolf Hitler and Joseph Stalin, it seems unfair to hate the Yanks all the more because the Dodgers left town in 1957. But that's when it clicked in for me. There they were: the all-powerful inevitable, like the phone company, the only game in town.

The Yankees: Take it or leave it. I just couldn't do it, couldn't root for a team that won the pennant fourteen out of my first seventeen years of life. Rooting for the Yankees was like declaring yourself to be a front-running prick, a defender of the status quo. Beyond this there was the fact that they played in the American League, always so Gentile in comparison with the funky National. There was the phrase *Yankee co-owners* (meaning Dan Topping and Del Webb, forerunners of indicted Nixon/Watergate contributor Steinbrenner). There was the much rumored passing-over of first baseman Vic Power because he caught the ball with one hand, which was so (jive) un-Yankee, not to mention the tacit reluctance to hire black players in general outside of Elston Howard, who, as Casey Stengel pointed out, couldn't even run. Beyond this were the pinstripes themselves, which, like Grandpa said, were so much more Wall Street than River Avenue.

Then came the Mets, the anti-Yankees, a team for their times. Instead of lockstep victory, the Mets offered Marvelous Marv Throneberry failing to touch first and second while hitting a triple, and Everyman Roger Craig throwing down his mitt after picking off a runner on consecutive throw-overs only to have the first baseman, Ed Bouchee, drop the ball each time. The Mets were cosmic. What Yankee fan could possibly have found himself lying smashed on a kitchen floor in Berkeley, California, in 1969 as Ed Kranepool hit a homer to help beat the Orioles in the World Series, so giddy in the belief that it was all a fabulous hallucination?

This isn't to say that Yankee-hating has been a walk in the park. There have been moments of weakness, instances of doubt, dramas that cannot be denied. The Billy Martin story, from the Copa riot, to beating the crap out of the marshmallow salesman, to his lonely death on the highway, is epic. And who can discount Mike Kekich and Fritz Peterson swapping wives in the middle of the season? Mostly, though, you've got to hate them. Hate them even if Yogi and Phil ran a bowling alley off Route 3. Hate them even when they sucked and Horace Clarke led them in hitting with a .272 average.

Luckily, now there's Giuliani. In an era in which most Yanks (outside of Clemens—dig in, Rog, dig in) seem okay, the Yankee hater is thankful for Giuliani in his little shiny jacket, holding inane placards given him by the only adviser he actually trusts, Freddy the Fan. Even in his kinder, gentler mode, he's just so junior high. Still the prick hanging by the cyclone fence waiting to prey upon the weaknesses of the more sensitive, the less aggressive, the potential loser: hell's own perfect Yankee fan.

So that settles it. The Subway Series has finally returned to us after forty-four years, and the moral lines are firmly drawn—the Mets: good; the Yankees: bad.

Along with everyone else, my son Billy is psyched. Too bad B can't get his own Carl Erskine no-hit birthday party instead of the three-to-five slot at Funtime USA. But that's what happens when you're born on February 4 and mucky old baseball eats Latrell Sprewell's dust. Still, even if it will never be 1956 again, the current brace of games, waged by millionaires, dispassionate and not, offers a taste. Fodder for tales told too often twenty and thirty years hence. Also, it is an opportunity to do some yeoman Yankee-hating.

For Billy, the breakthrough came early this season. Someone gave us tickets, so I dutifully took him up to the so-called Big Ballpark. Bill couldn't figure why so many people were rooting for the Red Sox. At the Garden and Shea, no one cheered for the visitors. "They're not for the Red Sox; they're *against* the Yankees. It happens all the time," I told him, in all accuracy. He found something liberating in that, the idea that you didn't have to root, root, root for the home team, the subversive notion that you could be against the likely winner. Besides, the Yankees didn't need him. They always won anyhow. They were the champs, just like back in 1956.

"If you're going to hate a team, it might as well be the Yankees," my son sagely told me this morning on the way to school. Just last night we found ourselves, two generations of Yankee haters, forced into hoping the Bombers beat the Oaklands, since their victory would assure the grail-like Subway Series. When the Yanks pushed across the winner, my son frowned as if he'd swallowed some bad but necessary medicine and went to bed without a word. A hard-core but wholly appropriate reaction.

Now, Mets hat firmly on his head, he was ready to enter the schoolyard. It wasn't going to be easy the next week or so. There were a lot of fifth-grade Yankee fans in there, annoying, smug, and loud, leaning against the cyclone fence, ready to pounce when their inevitable juggernaut began to roll. The Yanks will win, they always do. But Billy can handle it, secure in his love, secure in his hate.

33
What I Have Learned about the Future

Some of it, anyway. This little entry comes from 12,000 Miles in the Nick of Time: A Semi-Dysfunctional Family Circumnavigates the World, *a recent book detailing the saga of our bunch's trip around the planet. The following item is from a section called "Night Train," which describes a twenty-seven-hour journey across northern India.* Atlantic Monthly Press, *2003.*

My children are my teachers. This is one more thing I learned on the Lower East Side, on Sixth Street, between First and Secind Avenue, home to one of the oldest Orthodox Jewish temples in New York as well as many Indian/Bangladeshi restaurants so similar in menu and quality that urban legend posited they were connected via pneumatic tubes to a single central kitchen. In the midst of this is a Buddhist meditation center where I'd signed up for a class. The leader of the group was a monk from Haiti. In the spirit of postmodern spiritualistic mix-and-match, he'd grown up believing in voodoo and zombies before discovering an Alan Watts book on Zen in the lobby of a tatty Port-au-Prince hotel where his mother worked as a washerwoman. Later he would escape his poverty-stricken homeland in a ten-foot boat.

"Think of your true teacher," the monk said, leading the meditation in his rollicking creole English. "Think of the teacher as small, then growing bigger. Bigger and bigger. Think of your teacher as bright light streaming from the center of your forehead. See the face of your teacher. Your teacher is smiling at you. Your teacher is pleased, delighted at your progress. . . . It is good to have made your teacher happy!"

This was followed by a moment of grand suspense. Because, as the monk always said, the character of the teacher was not fixed. Different situations, different meditations called for different teachers. As the world was fluid, so would be the identity of the teacher. "See your teacher," the monk said. "The face may surprise you."

Legs aching from my haphazardly configured lotus position, I waited for my teacher to make him or herself known. It was a moment to pay homage to all the real teachers I'd had, the ones who actually succeeded in teaching me something, anything. There was Mom and Dad, of course. There was Billy Raphan, who taught me how to look cool throwing a baseball, Linda Porinno, who taught me how to kiss, Mr. Frederick, my eleventh-grade English teacher, who taught me how to write, a little. There was my first wife, who taught me how to cheat, and get cheated on.

But really, there were only three, at least only three faces that ever projected from the center of my forehead like white light: Rae, Rosie, and Billy, in rough rotation—each of them, their faces as big as moonsized Cheshire cats, smiling down at me, so delighted at my progress.

Now, clattering through the Indian night on the Shatabdi Express, I paused to examine what my children, trio of glowing gurus, had tried to teach me over the years, and what of it I had actually learned. Much of their teachings involved time, I understood—the way it goes by, eternal in its crossing, each moment distinct. I could trace their flow through my life, how each stage was sown with the seed of its own dissolution, a built-in short fuse.

Sometimes, riding on a train or bus, I'll idly remove their photos, outdated and dog-eared, from my wallet. Rae blowing a soap bubble at age five, Rosie still small enough to take a bath in the sink, those wild curls on her smiling face, Bill, with his own long blond curls, now crew-cut straight. The knowledge that this was what they once were, and now they had grown to something altogether different—the simple idea of them *growing*—would be enough to set me off.

How long does it take to get used to being a baby? To familiarize oneself with the vicissitudes of simply being alive? So much information passes to obsolescence the moment an individual stands upright. It is like this throughout childhood, data gathered, then filed away or discarded. This is how it is: You get comfortable, they spring something else on you. The twelve-year-old kid is a most perfect master, a king among kids, worldly in their world. They get so confident they forget to duck when blindsided by adolescence.

A sense of urgency entered the subcontinental night. For an Indian train may go slow, it may stop. But sooner or later it gets to its destination, often quicker than the lulled, indifferent passenger might imagine. Time on the journey, seemingly unending, was actually fleeting.

They would not be children long. The three of them walked around with expiration dates on their heads. The girls were already, uh, women. I'm already looking at girls on the subway younger than Rae. Who knows, I'm probably looking at girls younger than Rosalie. Fashion has created an army of doggy Humberts. No doubt, the Dads of those girls I'm looking at are probably looking at my girls, not that any man will ever be as intimate with their skin as I once was.

Pressure, man. I can feel the tick of the clock. Soon the hair will sprout from under Billy's arms. Stubble will sully his smooth face. Who he is now will be found only on photographs and in addled memory. There is nothing to be done about it. When he complains, as he does, about not wanting to grow up, about wanting to stay his perfect twelve forever and ever, it is my job to tell him it is only in Never-Never Land that boys never get old, and the boys in Never-Never Land aren't boys at all, but middle-aged women with names like Mary Martin who pretend to fly but are really suspended by ropes that you can see if you look hard enough.

A man, that's what I want him to be—big, smart, and sweet like he is now. It won't be long either. Already he doesn't mind beating me one-on-one, employing that killer crossover dribble he practices every night, up in his room, until the house shakes.

Everything has its limit. Children are excellent teachers when it comes to limits. The limits of patience, the limits of forethought, the limits of empathy and ego. Perspective, they call it. Like tracing the border of a leaf fallen from a bodhi tree, like sailing on the flat earth, if there is one lesson my guru children have taught me it is that there is an edge, a boundary, to everything. Once it was impossible to imagine any of us without others, but those days have begun to fade. There is a place where I stop, a place where they begin.

It has become visible, the spaces between us.